D0180361

POETRY
CLASSICS

SPARK PUBLISHING

Copyright © 2006 by Spark Publishing

"Stopping by Woods on a Snowy Evening" from *The Poetry of Robert Frost* edited by
Edward Connery Lathem. Copyright 1923, 1969 by Henry Holt and Company. Copyright
1951 by Robert Frost. Reprinted by permission of Henry Holt and Company, LLC.

"Leda and the Swan" and "Sailing to Byzantium" were reprinted with the permission of
Scribner, an imprint of Simon & Schuster Adult Publishing Group, from *The Collected
Works of W.B. Yeats, Volume I: The Poems, Revised*, edited by Richard J. Finneran.
Copyright © 1928 by The Macmillan Company; copyright renewed © 1956 by
Georgie Yeats.

All rights reserved. No part of this book may be used or reproduced in any manner
whatsoever without the written permission of the publisher.

SPARKNOTES is a registered trademark of SparkNotes LLC

Spark Publishing
120 Fifth Avenue
New York, NY 10011
www.sparknotes.com

First edition.

Please submit all comments and questions or report errors to www.sparknotes.com/errors

ISBN-10: 1-4114-0432-7
ISBN-13: 978-1-4114-0432-8

Printed and bound in the United States.

Library of Congress Cataloging-in-Publication Data

Poetry classics.
    p. cm.
  ISBN-13: 978-1-4114-0432-8
  ISBN-10: 1-4114-0432-7
  1. English poetry—History and criticism.
  2. American poetry—History and criticism.
  PR502.P64 2006
  821.009—dc22

                2005032117

CONTENTS

How to Use This Book

Poetry Classics provides you with important tools to begin your study of English poetry. We cover sixteen of the most important poets in the English language, organized by their dates of birth. These are the poets whose poems are most frequently taught in high schools and colleges around the country. Here are some quick tips and explanations to help you get the most out of this book:

Chapters 1–16: Each chapter provides a complete overview of the poet's major works, as well as a concise overview of the poet's life and career. The main features of each chapter are:

- **Themes, Motifs & Symbols:** An explanation of the important concepts that run through each poet's work.
- **Summary & Analysis of Major Poems:** A concise overview of each poet's major works, followed by a discussion of each poem's significance. Our analysis sections give you examples of strong interpretations of the poems. We've also reprinted short poems and excerpts from long poems so that you can read the poems for yourself.

Glossary: We've included a glossary of key terms and poetic movements at the back of the book to help you interpret and discuss poetry. Key terms are in **bold** throughout the book.

We hope *Poetry Classics* helps you, comforts you, and makes you a better reader of poetry. Your input makes us better. Let us know what you think or how we can improve this book at: www.sparknotes.com/comments.

INTRODUCTION

INTRODUCTION

> *"If I read a book and it makes my whole body so cold no fire can*
> *ever warm me, I know that is poetry. If I feel physically as if*
> *the top of my head were taken off, I know that is poetry."*
> —*Emily Dickinson*

Emily Dickinson's quote perfectly captures the feelings of the many people who love poetry. Unfortunately, her thoughts also capture the feelings of the many people who hate poetry. Too often, reading poetry can be an exercise in painful boredom, and readers frequently slog through poetry in a daze, wondering what on earth it is that poets are trying to say. That's why we created *Poetry Classics*— to help you understand some of the greatest poets in the English language and to show you how to read their poetry with a deeper understanding and, we hope, a new appreciation.

WHY DO WE READ POETRY?

There are lots of reasons why people read poetry: for pleasure, out of a sense of duty, to impress potential boyfriends or girlfriends, to find quotations for graduation speeches and other significant life events. But there are two important reasons why we keep reading poetry today:

- *Poetry is a record of human experience.* Just like we study history even though we might never need to know when the Magna Carta was signed, we read poetry in order to understand what people have thought and felt in different times, places, and circumstances. Doing so helps us to better understand complex ideas, difficult emotions, and, perhaps most important, ourselves.
- *Reading poetry teaches us how to read critically.* Poetry is the hardest kind of writing there is to read and comprehend. Poetry can be dense, difficult, complicated, and ambiguous. But reading poetry challenges us as readers, and therefore poetry is an excellent way to sharpen our reading and critical-thinking skills.

How to Read a Poem

The most common complaint people have about poetry is that they just don't get it. Alas, there is no supersecret method that allows you to suddenly understand all poetry. Instead, you have to rely on close reading, which means paying attention to all of the features of a poem and understanding how these features work together. This is the same kind of reading you do when you read a novel or the newspaper—you try to understand what's being said, who's saying it, how it's being said, why it's being said, and what kind of interpretations you can draw from that novel or article.

But reading a poem is harder work. Even though reading a poem draws on the same sets of skills we use to read other written texts, reading a poem sometimes seems tougher or more complicated than reading a novel or newspaper article. Like we said before, poetry can be thorny, tricky, opaque stuff. Reading poems takes practice and patience. And with that practice and patience come great rewards: after all, we wouldn't read poems written centuries ago if the experience of reading poetry wasn't somehow worthwhile or relevant to contemporary life.

In addition to having practice and patience, reading poetry requires you to remember a few poetic conventions. As you'll see, some of these conventions apply to prose as well. We're repeating them here for emphasis. Keeping these tips in mind as you read will make you a stronger reader of poetry:

- *The speaker is not the poet.* Just as Hamlet and Shakespeare are not the same person, the speaker of a poem is different from the poet. The speaker is a character, just like in a novel or play. So when Robert Browning writes a poem in the first person about strangling someone, that doesn't mean he's confessing to something from beyond the grave.
- *Poems use structure to convey meaning.* The most remarkable feature of poems is that they are not written in prose. In poetry, sentences break off in the middle, single words take up whole lines, stanzas and lines are spaced strangely, and lines sometimes rhyme in different ways or not at all. Poets don't do this to be difficult. Rather, poets are trying to capture and convey feelings, thoughts, and ideas through these formal features. The way a poem is structured affects the poem and its meaning as a whole.

- *Poems are meant to be read aloud.* Unlike most prose writers, poets use sound as a critical part of their art, and you should pay careful attention to the sonic qualities of the poem. The easiest way to do this is simply to read the poem aloud and notice its sound patterns. When reading aloud won't work, like in a library or classroom, you need to make sure to read the poem slowly and carefully, listening to how it sounds in your head.

- *Poems need to be reread.* When ideas and feelings are simple and predictable, you don't need to spend more than a moment thinking about them. But poetry demands to be read several times before you can really begin to make sense of it. Fortunately, most poems are short enough that this isn't a chore, and even long poems are nearly always broken into sections that allow for such rereading.

- *Poems have multiple interpretations.* Reducing a poem to a thesis statement or one central idea that the poet is trying to express is tempting, but wrong. Avoid this temptation by remembering that poets are trying to explore multiple ideas and feelings. Be careful not to go too far the other way, though—poems are not entirely subjective, and they do not mean whatever you want them to. Instead, the meaning of a poem is what a reader is able to get from the evidence that the poem presents. This means that there are multiple strong interpretations, but also interpretations that are weak, because there is nothing in the poem to support these interpretations.

WILLIAM SHAKESPEARE

(1564–1616)

CONTEXT

William Shakespeare, the most influential writer in all of English literature, was born in 1564 to a successful middle-class glove maker, landowner, and moneylender in Stratford-on-Avon, England. The young Shakespeare's formal education did not progress beyond grammar school, which he finished at around age fifteen or sixteen. In 1582, at eighteen, he married an older woman, Anne Hathaway; their union produced three children. Around 1590, Shakespeare left his family behind and traveled to London to work as an actor and playwright. He quickly earned public and critical acclaim, eventually becoming the most popular playwright in England and part owner of the Globe Theatre. Shakespeare's career bridged the reigns of Elizabeth I (ruled 1558–1603) and James I (ruled 1603–1625), and he was a favorite of both monarchs. He retired to Stratford a wealthy and renowned man and died in 1616 at the age of fifty-two. At the time of Shakespeare's death, literary luminaries, such as Ben Jonson, had already hailed his works as timeless.

Following his death, Shakespeare's poems and plays were collected and printed in various editions. By the early eighteenth century, his reputation as the greatest poet ever to write in English was well established. The unprecedented regard in which Shakespeare's works were held led to a fierce curiosity about his life, but many details of Shakespeare's personal history are unknown or shrouded in mystery. Some people have concluded from this lack of information and from Shakespeare's modest education that someone else actually wrote Shakespeare's plays—Francis Bacon and the earl of Oxford are the two most popular candidates—but the support for this claim is overwhelmingly circumstantial, and many scholars do not take this theory seriously. Scholars generally consider Shakespeare to be the author of the thirty-eight plays (two of them possibly collaborations) and 154 sonnets that bear his name. The legacy of this body of work is immense. A number of Shakespeare's plays have transcended even the category of brilliance, influencing the very course of Western literature and culture.

Shakespeare invented a new **sonnet** form when he began writing his sequence in 1593. A *sonnet* is a fourteen-line lyric poem, traditionally written in **iambic pentameter**—that is, in lines ten syllables long, with accents falling on every second syllable, as in "Shall *I* compare thee to a summer's *day*?" from Sonnet 18. During the Italian Renaissance, the poet Petrarch published a series of love poems addressed to an idealized woman named Laura. Petrarch's sonnets, the Petrarchan form, consist of a contrasting **octet** (eight lines) and a **sestet** (six lines). In contrast, the so-called Shakespearean sonnet is divided into four parts: three quatrains (four-line stanzas or groups) and one couplet (a two-line stanza or group). A Shakespearean sonnet follows an *abab cdcd efef gg* rhyme scheme. A typical Shakespearean sonnet consists of the three quatrains that form three discrete units, with the closing couplet distorting or playing with the **metaphors** expressed in the previous lines. Today, the sonnet is considered to be the most important and influential verse form in the history of English poetry.

A series of alternately loving, chiding, dark, and humorous poems, Shakespeare's sonnets are unique. Unlike other sonnet sequences, such as those composed by Edmund Spenser and Sir Philip Sidney, Shakespeare's sonnets do not tell a specific story with a beginning, middle, and end. The sonnets first appeared in print in 1609, but it's possible that Shakespeare did not authorize either the printing or the order in which the poems appeared. Some critics argue that Shakespeare intended an order that has been lost to us, perhaps because the original printer rearranged the sonnets. Other critics suggest that the sonnets were never meant to tell a complete story. Another group of scholars argue that the sonnets do, in fact, tell a story: the speaker begins by urging a noble friend to marry. In time, the speaker falls in love with the young man, but the young man begins sleeping with a dark-haired woman, with whom the speaker eventually falls in love and begins a sexual relationship.

Three principal characters appear throughout the sonnets: the young man, the so-called dark lady, and the rival poet. Scholars have tried, unsuccessfully, to pin down the real-life identities of Shakespeare's fictional characters. Because the initials "W. H." appear throughout the sonnets, some scholars propose either William Herbert, earl of Pembroke, or Henry Wriothesly, earl of Southampton, as the young man. The dark lady was probably Emilia Lanier, the beautiful, brunette wife of a middle-class musician at the Globe and the mistress of Lord Hunsdon. As for the rival poet, Shakespeare, like all Elizabethan poets, largely relied on the patronage of wealthy noblemen; this system fostered intense competition between artists of the day and also led to the dedication of works to well-known members of the upper class. George Chapman, Christopher Marlowe, and Spenser, among others, were Shakespeare's real-life rivals and thus possible candidates for the fictional rival poet. Due to the scarcity of biographical information about Shakespeare, the true identities of these characters will probably never be known.

Sonnets 1–126 are addressed to the young man. The narrator of Sonnets 1–17 urges the young man to have babies and assures him that he will live on forever in these sonnets. In Sonnets 18–126, the poet scolds the young man for not procreating, for sleeping around, and for developing an ugly soul, which greatly contrasts with his beautiful face and body. These sonnets also show the speaker grappling with the aging process and wondering about the relationship between time and art; he concludes that his verses guarantee the immortality of the young man. Because many of the first 126 sonnets are romantic and have homosexual overtones, some critics cite them as evidence of Shakespeare's possible homosexuality or bisexuality. Readers must be careful about committing the **intentional fallacy,** or using a fictive work to try to make an argument about its author and his or her intentions toward the work—a particularly dangerous trap when reading Shakespeare, since so little reliable biographical information exists. Sonnets 127–152 address the dark lady with whom the speaker is in love but who betrays the speaker with the young man. In these sonnets, the speaker expresses his admiration for the lady, admits her faults, and speaks of his sadness when the lady betrays him. The last two sonnets, 153 and 154, are about Cupid. Shakespeare's poems contain examples of the most finely wrought and complex **conceits** (extended metaphors) in English.

THEMES, MOTIFS & SYMBOLS

THEMES

DIFFERENT TYPES OF ROMANTIC LOVE

Modern readers associate the sonnet form with romantic love and with good reason: the first sonnets written in thirteenth- and fourteenth-century Italy celebrated the poets' feelings for their beloveds and their patrons. These sonnets were addressed to stylized, lionized women and dedicated to wealthy noblemen, who supported poets with money and other gifts, usually in return for lofty praise in print. Shakespeare dedicated his sonnets to "Mr. W. H.," and the identity of this man remains unknown. He dedicated an earlier set of poems, *Venus and Adonis* and *Rape of Lucrece*, to Henry Wriothesly, earl of Southampton, but it's not known what Wriothesly gave him for this honor. In contrast to tradition, Shakespeare addressed most of his sonnets to an unnamed young man, possibly Wriothesly. Addressing sonnets to a young man was unique in Elizabethan England. Furthermore, Shakespeare used his sonnets to explore different types of love between the young man and the speaker, the young man and the dark lady, and the dark lady and the speaker. In his sequence, the speaker expresses passionate concern for the young man, praises his beauty, and articulates what we would now call homosexual desire. The woman of Shakespeare's sonnets, the so-called dark lady, is earthy, sexual, and faithless—characteristics in direct opposition to lovers described in other sonnet sequences, including *Astrophil and Stella*, by Sir Philip Sidney, a contemporary of Shakespeare, who were praised for their angelic demeanor, virginity, and steadfastness. Several sonnets also probe the nature of love, comparing the idealized love found in poems with the messy, complicated love found in real life.

THE DANGERS OF LUST AND LOVE

In Shakespeare's sonnets, falling in love can have painful emotional and physical consequences. Sonnets 127–152, addressed to the so-called dark lady, express a more overtly erotic and physical love than the sonnets addressed to the young man. But many sonnets warn readers about the dangers of lust and love. According to some poems, lust causes us to mistake sexual desire for true love, and love itself causes us to lose our powers of perception. Several sonnets warn about the dangers of lust, claiming that it turns humans "savage, extreme, rude, cruel" (4), as in Sonnet 129. The final two sonnets of Shakespeare's sequence obliquely imply that lust leads to venereal disease. According to the conventions of romance, the sexual act, or "making love," expresses the deep feeling between two people. In his sonnets, however, Shakespeare portrays making love not as a romantic expression of sentiment but as a base physical need with the potential for horrible consequences.

Several sonnets equate being in love with being in a pitiful state: as demonstrated by the poems, love causes fear, alienation, despair, and physical discomfort, not the pleasant emotions or euphoria we usually associate with romantic feelings. The speaker alternates between professing great love and professing great worry as he speculates about the young man's misbehavior and the dark lady's multiple sexual partners. As the young man and the dark lady begin an affair, the speaker imagines himself caught in a love triangle, mourning the loss of his friendship with the man and love with the woman, and he laments having fallen in love with the woman in the first place. In Sonnet 137, the speaker personifies love, calls him a simpleton, and criticizes him for removing his powers of perception. It was love that caused the speaker to make mistakes and poor judgments. Elsewhere the speaker calls love a disease as a way of demonstrating the physical pain of emotional wounds. Throughout his sonnets, Shakespeare clearly implies that love hurts. Yet despite the emotional and physical pain, like the speaker, we continue falling in love. Shakespeare shows that falling in love is an inescapable aspect of the human condition—indeed, expressing love is part of what makes us human.

REAL BEAUTY VS. CLICHÉD BEAUTY

To express the depth of their feelings, poets frequently employ hyperbolic terms to describe the objects of their affections. Traditionally, sonnets transform women into the most glorious creatures to walk the earth, whereas patrons become the noblest and bravest men the world has ever known. Shakespeare makes fun of the convention by contrasting an idealized woman with a real woman. In Sonnet 130, Shakespeare directly engages—and skewers—clichéd concepts of beauty. The speaker explains that his lover, the dark lady, has wires for hair, bad breath, dull cleavage, a heavy step, and pale lips. He concludes by saying that he loves her all the more precisely because he loves *her* and not some idealized, false version. Real love, the sonnet implies, begins when we accept our lovers for what they are as well as what they are not. Other sonnets explain that because anyone can use artful means to make himself or herself more attractive, no one is really beautiful anymore. Thus, since anyone can become beautiful, calling someone beautiful is no longer much of a compliment.

The Responsibilities of Being Beautiful

Shakespeare portrays beauty as conveying a great responsibility in the sonnets addressed to the young man, Sonnets 1–126. Here the speaker urges the young man to make his beauty immortal by having children, a theme that appears repeatedly throughout the poems: as an attractive person, the young man has a responsibility to procreate. Later sonnets demonstrate the speaker, angry at being cuckolded, lashing out at the young man and accusing him of using his beauty to hide immoral acts. Sonnet 95 compares the young man's behavior to a "canker in the fragrant rose" (2) or a rotten spot on an otherwise beautiful flower. In other words, the young man's beauty allows him to get away with bad behavior, but this bad behavior will eventually distort his beauty, much like a rotten spot eventually spreads. Nature gave the young man a beautiful face, but it is the young man's responsibility to make sure that his soul is worthy of such a visage.

Motifs

Art vs. Time

Shakespeare, like many sonneteers, portrays time as an enemy of love. Time destroys love because time causes beauty to fade, people to age, and life to end. One common convention of sonnets in general is to flatter either a beloved or a patron by promising immortality through verse. As long as readers read the poem, the object of the poem's love will remain alive. In Shakespeare's Sonnet 15, the speaker talks of being "in war with time" (13): time causes the young man's beauty to fade, but the speaker's verse shall entomb the young man and keep him beautiful. The speaker begins by pleading with time in another sonnet, yet he ends by taunting time, confidently asserting that his verse will counteract time's ravages. From our contemporary vantage point, the speaker was correct, and art

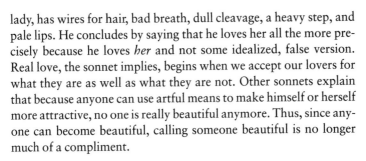

WILLIAM SHAKESPEARE

has beaten time: the young man remains young since we continue to read of his youth in Shakespeare's sonnets.

Through art, nature and beauty overcome time. Several sonnets use the seasons to symbolize the passage of time and to show that everything in nature—from plants to people—is mortal. But nature creates beauty, which poets capture and render immortal in their verse. Sonnet 106 portrays the speaker reading poems from the past and recognizing his beloved's beauty portrayed therein. The speaker then suggests that these earlier poets were prophesizing the future beauty of the young man by describing the beauty of their contemporaries. In other words, past poets described the beautiful people of their day and, like Shakespeare's speaker, perhaps urged these beautiful people to procreate and so on, through the poetic ages, until the birth of the young man portrayed in Shakespeare's sonnets. In this way—that is, as beautiful people of one generation produce more beautiful people in the subsequent generation and as all this beauty is written about by poets—nature, art, and beauty triumph over time.

STOPPING THE MARCH TOWARD DEATH

Growing older and dying are inescapable aspects of the human condition, but Shakespeare's sonnets give suggestions for halting the progress toward death. Shakespeare's speaker spends a lot of time trying to convince the young man to cheat death by having children. In Sonnets 1–17, the speaker argues that the young man is too beautiful to die without leaving behind his replica, and the idea that the young man has a duty to procreate becomes the dominant motif of the first several sonnets. In Sonnet 3, the speaker continues his urgent prodding and concludes, "Die single and thine image dies with thee" (14). The speaker's words aren't just the flirtatious ramblings of a smitten man: Elizabethan England was rife with disease, and early death was common. Producing children guaranteed the continuation of the species. Therefore, falling in love has a social benefit, a benefit indirectly stressed by Shakespeare's sonnets. We might die, but our children—and the human race—shall live on.

THE SIGNIFICANCE OF SIGHT

Shakespeare used images of eyes throughout the sonnets to emphasize other themes and motifs, including children as an antidote to death, art's struggle to overcome time, and the painfulness of love. For instance, in several poems, the speaker urges the young man to admire himself in the mirror. Noticing and admiring his own beauty, the speaker argues, will encourage the young man to father a child. Other sonnets link writing and painting with sight: in Sonnet 24, the speaker's eye becomes a pen or paintbrush that captures the young man's beauty and imprints it on the blank page of the speaker's heart. But our loving eyes can also distort our sight, causing us to misperceive reality. In the sonnets addressed to the dark lady, the speaker criticizes his eyes for causing him to fall in love with a beautiful but duplicitous woman. Ultimately, Shakespeare uses eyes to act as a warning: while our eyes allow us to perceive beauty, they sometimes get so captivated by beauty that they cause us to misjudge character and other attributes not visible to the naked eye.

Readers' eyes are as significant in the sonnets as the speaker's eyes. Shakespeare encourages his readers to see by providing vivid visual descriptions. One sonnet compares the young man's beauty to the glory of the rising sun, while another uses the image of clouds obscuring the sun as a metaphor for the young man's faithlessness and still another contrasts the beauty of a rose with one rotten spot to warn the young man to cease his sinning ways. Other poems describe bare trees to symbolize aging. The sonnets devoted to the dark lady emphasize her coloring, noting in particular her black eyes and hair, and Sonnet 130 describes her by noting all the colors she does not possess. Stressing the visual helps Shakespeare to heighten our experience of the poems by giving us the precise tools with which to imagine the metaphors, similes, and descriptions contained therein.

SYMBOLS

FLOWERS AND TREES

Flowers and trees appear throughout the sonnets to illustrate the passage of time, the transience of life, the aging process, and beauty. Rich, lush foliage symbolizes youth, whereas barren trees symbolize old age and death, often in the same poem, as in Sonnet 12. Traditionally, roses signify romantic love, a symbol Shakespeare employs in the sonnets, discussing their attractiveness and fragrance in relation to the young man. Sometimes Shakespeare compares flowers and weeds to contrast beauty and ugliness. In these comparisons, marred, rotten flowers are worse than weeds—that is, beauty that turns rotten from bad character is worse than initial ugliness. Giddy with love, elsewhere the speaker compares blooming flowers to the beauty of the young man, concluding in Sonnets 98 and 99 that flowers received their bloom and smell from him. The sheer ridiculousness of this statement—flowers smell sweet for chemical and biological reasons—underscores the hyperbole and exaggeration that plague typical sonnets.

STARS

Shakespeare uses stars to stand in for fate, a common poetic **trope**, but also to explore the nature of free will. Many sonneteers resort to employing fate, symbolized by the stars, to prove that their love is permanent and predestined. In contrast, Shakespeare's speaker claims that he relies on his eyes, rather than on the hands of fate, to make decisions. Using his eyes, the speaker "reads" that the young man's good fortune and beauty shall pass to his children, should he have them. During Shakespeare's time, people generally believed in astrology, even as scholars were making great gains in astronomy and cosmology, a metaphysical system for ordering the universe. According to Elizabethan astrology, a cosmic order determined the place of everything in the universe, from planets and stars to people. Although humans had some free will, the heavenly spheres, with the help of God, predetermined fate. In Shakespeare's Sonnet 25, the speaker acknowledges that he has been unlucky in the stars but lucky in love, thereby removing his happiness from the heavenly bodies and transposing it onto the human body of his beloved.

WEATHER AND THE SEASONS

Shakespeare employed the **pathetic fallacy**, or the attribution of human characteristics or emotions to elements in nature or inanimate objects, throughout his plays. In the sonnets, the speaker frequently employs the pathetic fallacy, associating his absence from the young man to the freezing days of December and the promise of their reunion to a pregnant spring. Weather and the seasons also stand in for human emotions: the speaker conveys his sense of foreboding about death by likening himself to autumn, a time in which nature's objects begin to decay and ready themselves for winter, or death. Similarly, despite the arrival of "proud-pied April" (2) in Sonnet 98, the speaker still feels as if it were winter because he and the young man are apart. The speaker in Sonnet 18, one of Shakespeare's most famous poems, begins by rhetorically asking the young man, "Shall I compare thee to a summer's day?" (1). He spends the remainder of the poem explaining the multiple ways in which the young man is superior to a summer day, ultimately concluding that while summer ends, the young man's beauty lives on in the permanence of poetry.

SUMMARY & ANALYSIS

SONNET 1

From fairest creatures we desire increase,
That thereby beauty's rose might never die,
But as the riper should by time decease
His tender heir might bear his memory.
But thou, contracted to thine own bright eyes,   5
Feed'st thy light's flame with self-substantial fuel,
Making a famine where abundance lies,
Thyself thy foe, to thy sweet self too cruel.
Thou that art now the world's fresh ornament
And only herald to the gaudy spring,   10
Within thine own bud buriest thy content,
And, tender churl, mak'st waste in niggarding.
   Pity the world, or else this glutton be,
   To eat the world's due, by the grave and thee.

SUMMARY

The speaker says that we want beautiful people to reproduce because then their beauty won't die with them but will live on in their children. When old people die, their children will keep their memories alive. Next the speaker addresses the young man directly, saying that the young man is in love with himself alone. Instead of coming together with another and reproducing his beauty, the young man subsists with himself alone. Like a fire, he feeds on himself, and he undercuts himself by failing to have children. The young man, who is now a carefree, youthful decoration in the world, will eventually die, and with him will die the children he did not have. The speaker calls the young man a miser for wasting his capacity to procreate. He entreats the young man to think of others by bestowing beautiful children upon the world. If he does not, the young man will be a "glutton" (13) who gobbles up his offspring, which should belong to the world.

ANALYSIS

Sonnet 1 introduces a theme that Shakespeare will develop over the subsequent sixteen sonnets: the urgent need for the young man to sustain his beauty by producing an heir. Shakespeare uses the image of a rose to suggest that human life is as beautiful and ephemeral as flowers, which bloom gloriously and wither quickly. The speaker urges the young man to imitate the flowers, who replace themselves with buds, and he chastises the young man for cutting off his own line. Without an heir, the young man consigns himself and the countless future generations that could spring from him to the grave. In Elizabethan England, nature represented the world as it should be: orderly and truthful. Poets took metaphors from nature to imagine a world unburdened by human error. Shakespeare uses images of roses and fire to illustrate the young man's crime: nature wants the young man to reproduce as roses do, but instead the young man consumes himself like fire. When a fire's "fuel" (6) is exhausted, the fire dies and cannot be revived, just as the young man will die forever if he does not have children. The rose represents cyclical life, or reproductive life, and the fire suggests the inevitability and irreversibility of death.

The preoccupation with immortality that characterizes Shakespeare's first seventeen sonnets reflects historical concerns. The bubonic plague (or "Black Death") had killed three-quarters of Europe's and Asia's populations in the 1300s. Shakespeare himself lived through several plague outbreaks in London. In Sonnet 1, the poet compares the young man to "glutton[ous]" (13) death, a serious charge that has echoes of the grossly overfed reaper of plague times. When death is not only inevitable but likely to happen soon and to overtake even young men, it becomes even more important to reproduce and thus gain some measure of immortality. What seems at first glance to be a frivolous, flirtatious poem addressed to an attractive young man actually contains a strong social imperative: reproduction is one's duty to the community. Shakespeare calls children "the world's due" (14), as if one's life were merely a loan from nature that must be repaid through the production of more life.

SONNET 12

When I do count the clock that tells the time,
And see the brave day sunk in hideous night;
When I behold the violet past prime,
And sable curls all silvered o'er with white;
When lofty trees I see barren of leaves,   5
Which erst from heat did canopy the herd,
And summer's green all girded up in sheaves
Borne on the bier with white and bristly beard;
Then of thy beauty do I question make,
That thou among the wastes of time must go,   10
Since sweets and beauties do themselves forsake
And die as fast as they see others grow,
    And nothing 'gainst Time's scythe can make defense
    Save breed to brave him when he takes thee hence.

WILLIAM SHAKESPEARE

SUMMARY

The speaker begins by noting myriad signs of aging in the world around him, which remind him that his beautiful young man too will inevitably age and die. Then he lists markers of the passage of time: the chiming of a clock, the sunset at the end of the day, a drooping violet, a head of curly black hair turning white. Tall trees, which create shade for sheep and cattle in the summer, lose their leaves in the fall. Wheat and barley, crops of the summer, are harvested, tied up, and carried away on a wagon like an old man carried away on a funeral cart. These images prompt the speaker to wonder about his young friend's beauty, which is also subject to the ravages of time. All sweet and beautiful things must die while new ones grow to take their place. The speaker concludes that children, who live on to bear their parents' likeness, are the only measure of defense against time and death.

ANALYSIS

The first seventeen sonnets revolve around a single goal: convincing the speaker's young friend to procreate, and soon. These sonnets employ a wide range of tactics and tones to make their argument, alternately flattering, wheedling, nagging, and rebuking. Time is the eternal enemy, an incessant threat to the young man's beauty: time causes trees to lose their leaves and people to lose youth's grace, vitality, and attractiveness. To counteract time's ravages, the speaker wants the young man to replicate himself through children. These children, as they grow, will resemble the young man as he is now, in the poems, even as he ages and eventually dies. In this sonnet, the speaker argues by example, giving evidence from nature of time's erosion. The mournful, elegiac tone matches the mournful, elegiac descriptions of death and decay.

Sonnet 12 differs significantly from the rest of the first seventeen sonnets in tone, content, and execution. This sonnet lacks sprawling conceits and fanciful rhetoric, and its metaphors are simple and linear, their purpose less puzzling wordplay than evocative imagery. Shakespeare draws his examples of decay from nature, choosing to portray the gentle rotting of flowers and the soft shift of hair changing color rather than focusing on gruesome or violent signs of decomposition. Instead of cajoling and harassing, Sonnet 12 creates an atmosphere of anxiety about aging, decay, and death. The speaker defers the main argument until the couplet and does not even mention the young man until line 9. Though thoughts of the young man drive the first eight lines, these lines primarily concern the speaker and his emotional life. Subtle metaphors, such as the harvested wheat traveling on the cart in line 7, reinforce this preoccupation with death. Clearly the speaker fears his own aging process and eventual death, and he unfavorably compares his older middle-age self to the young man in several other sonnets.

SONNET 18

Shall I compare thee to a summer's day?
Thou art more lovely and more temperate.
Rough winds do shake the darling buds of May,
And summer's lease hath all too short a date.
Sometime too hot the eye of heaven shines,   5
And often is his gold complexion dimmed;
And every fair from fair sometime declines,
By chance or nature's changing course untrimmed.
But thy eternal summer shall not fade,
Nor lose possession of that fair thou ow'st,   10
Nor shall death brag thou wand'rest in his shade,
When in eternal lines to time thou grow'st.
  So long as men can breathe or eyes can see,
  So long lives this, and this gives life to thee.

SUMMARY

This very famous poem opens with the speaker trying to find appropriate metaphors to describe the young man. He wonders if "a summer's day" might do (1), then goes on to portray the young man as more beautiful than a typical summer's day. During summer, breezes blow, and summer itself is too short. The sun shines too hot, and often clouds darken its golden face. Eventually everything beautiful stops being beautiful, either by accident or simply through the course of nature. Addressing the young man, the speaker tells him that his "eternal summer" will never fade (9), he will never lose possession of his beauty, and death will never come for him once he's been captured by the poet's verses. As long as men are alive and have eyes with which to see, this poem will live and keep him alive.

ANALYSIS

Sonnet 18 might be the most famous lyric poem in the English language. It continues the theme explored in the first seventeen sonnets—the necessity of preserving the young man's beauty through reproduction—and it is the last sonnet to push procreation so strongly. Whereas in previous sonnets the poet proposed having children as a way of ensuring immortality, here he shifts his rhetoric to introduce another theme, immortality through verse. This shift in emphasis—from procreation to poetry—of the solution to the ravages of time happens gradually through Sonnets 1–18. Sonnet 15 marks the beginning of the poet's assumption of personal responsibility for preserving the young man's beauty. Sonnet 16 recants that assumption and laments that the speaker's versified words cannot guard the young man from death. Sonnet 17 reasserts the transformative and youth-sustaining power of poetry. In the couplet at the end of Sonnet 18, the speaker finally swears that his poetry guarantees the youth immortality. As long as his poem has readers, the speaker claims, the young man shall stay beautiful.

Throughout this sonnet, Shakespeare performs a self-conscious literary exercise. The speaker, reenacting the writing process, wonders which metaphors to use from the very first line: "Shall I compare thee to a summer's day?" (1). Almost every line ends with punctuation, which transforms the lines into self-contained clauses and balances rhythm with completed thoughts. Imagery comes from the same source—summer: "darling buds" (3), "gold complexion" (6), "shade" (11). Summer becomes an apt metaphor for youth and beauty, both because summer is a season of full and fruitful bloom and because summer is always followed by fall and with-ering. At the same time, the cyclical nature of the seasons promises that summer will come again. Just as the seasons progress, new gen-erations of people, including the young man's future children, will enter their prime. Alternatively, through Shakespeare's verse, the youth lives on, as beautiful as he was in sixteenth-century England.

SONNET 20

A woman's face, with nature's own hand painted,
Hast thou, the master-mistress of my passion;
A woman's gentle heart, but not acquainted
With shifting change, as is false women's fashion;
An eye more bright than theirs, less false in rolling,   5
Gilding the object whereupon it gazeth;
A man in hue, all hues in his controlling,
Which steals men's eyes and women's souls amazeth.
And for a woman wert thou first created,
Till nature as she wrought thee fell a-doting,   10
And by addition me of thee defeated,
By adding one thing to my purpose nothing.
    But since she pricked thee out for women's pleasure,
    Mine be thy love, and thy love's use their treasure.

SUMMARY

In this sonnet, the speaker addresses the young man, telling him that he is as lovely as a woman but has none of women's bad qualities, such as deceitfulness and unfaithfulness. As nature was creating you, the speaker explains, she fell in love with you and gave you the body of a man so that she could have sex with you herself. Next the speaker says that the young man's additional organ (his penis) means that the speaker, as a man, cannot have sex with him. Women may enjoy the young man's physical love—sexual intercourse—but the young man's true, spiritual love is reserved for the speaker.

ANALYSIS

Sonnet 20 may contain certain clues to the young man's real-life identity. The frequency of the letters *H, E, W,* and *S* throughout the sonnet could be a semi-secret code, meant to point the curious reader to well-known figures in Shakespeare's circle. In fact, *HEWS* could be an anagram, combining Shakespeare's initials (W. S.) with the young man's (H. E.). Due to these initials, some scholars argue that the real-life young man was either William Herbert, earl of Pembroke, or Henry Wriothesly, earl of Southampton, to whom Shakespeare dedicated two earlier narrative poems. The scarcity of biographical details almost guarantees that these questions will go unanswered, but sonnets such as this provide interesting clues. Of course, we must also guard against reading the sonnets for evidence of Shakespeare the man: like all poets, Shakespeare employs a **speaker** to speak his work. Although this speaker might share characteristics with Shakespeare, ultimately the speaker is a fictional entity created by Shakespeare, and the poems are fictional works, not autobiography.

This sonnet establishes a clear opposition between physical, sexual love and a more authentic spiritual love. The speaker portrays the young man as so beautiful that he has a woman's face and attracts both men and women. Like women, the young man has a "gentle heart" (3), but unlike the hearts of women, the young man's heart is faithful. These compliments align with the praise found in traditional sonnets wherein the poet compares his beloved to others, only to find further evidence of the superiority of the object of his affections. Here, however, a homoerotic tone underlies the compliments, particularly in the final sestet. In these lines, the speaker explains that nature designed the young man to be sexually active with women by playing on the word *pricked* in line 13. In other words, the speaker's body is sexually incompatible with that of the young man, and thus the young man can simultaneously enjoy physical relations with women while experiencing a purer, spiritual love with the speaker.

SONNET 65

Since brass, nor stone, nor earth, nor boundless sea,
But sad mortality o'ersways their power,
How with this rage shall beauty hold a plea,
Whose action is no stronger than a flower?
O how shall summer's honey breath hold out   5
Against the wrackful siege of batt'ring days,
When rocks impregnable are not so stout,
Nor gates of steel so strong but time decays?
O fearful meditation! Where, alack,
Shall time's best jewel from time's chest lie hid?   10

> *Or what strong hand can hold his swift foot back?*
> *Or who his spoil or beauty can forbid?*
>   *O none, unless this miracle have might,*
>   *That in black ink my love may still shine bright.*

SUMMARY

The speaker points out that death destroys everything solid, including land and ocean. If this is so, he asks, how can beauty, which has no power, hold its own against death? How can gentle summer days resist the passage of time when even rocks and steel cannot? Calling this a frightening thought, the speaker wonders how youthful beauty can escape death and asks which person can prevent time from ruining youth and beauty. He concludes that only by living on in print can the young man retain his youth.

ANALYSIS

Sonnet 65 combines two of the sonnet sequence's main themes: the desperate need to resist all-powerful, destructive time and the importance of preserving and cultivating beauty. The speaker states that time erodes everything, including seemingly invulnerable elements of nature, such as rocks and oceans. Although several sonnets portray time as simultaneously destructive and necessary, awe-inspiring and natural, detrimental and balancing, Shakespeare concentrates on time's negative characteristics in Sonnet 65: time acts as a malevolent force, a power that means to attack, destroy, and obliterate the beautiful and the ugly alike. This sonnet imagines time as violent and unthinking in its "rage" (3). Despairing, the speaker concludes that only art can counteract time in the final couplet, but even that would be a "miracle" (13). He uses the word *may* rather than *will* in the last line to demonstrate his reluctance to believe that anything could overcome time. Desolation pervades the poem, including its last lines, and the poem demonstrates a sadness rarely seen throughout the sequence. The speaker questions his love, questions his purpose, even questions his life given the fate that awaits us all: if we're going to die in the end, the sonnet wonders, why preserve beauty in life and describe beauty in art? Why bother? We have only death to look forward to, the sonnet mourns.

SONNET 73

That time of year thou mayst in me behold
When yellow leaves, or none, or few, do hang
Upon those boughs which shake against the cold,
Bare ruined choirs, where late the sweet birds sang.
In me thou seest the twilight of such day   5
As after sunset fadeth in the west,
Which by and by black night doth take away,
Death's second self, that seals up all in rest.
In me thou seest the glowing of such fire
That on the ashes of his youth doth lie,   10
As the deathbed whereon it must expire
Consumed with that which it was nourished by.
    This thou perceiv'st, which makes thy love more strong,
    To love that well which thou must leave ere long.

WILLIAM SHAKESPEARE

SUMMARY

The speaker invokes a series of metaphors to describe what he perceives as his old age. In the first quatrain, he compares his age to autumn, a season of gentle, natural decline; creeping cold; and bare branches. In the second quatrain, the speaker compares his age to "twilight" (5), a time of dwindling light and gradual loss of focus. In the third quatrain, the speaker associates his stage of life with the last gasps of a fire as it smolders and is smothered under its ashes. In the couplet, the speaker addresses the young man and acknowledges the strength of his love: since the young man continues to love the speaker even though he knows that the speaker will soon die of old age, the young man must love the speaker a great deal indeed.

ANALYSIS

Sonnet 73, like many of the first 126 sonnets, expresses anxiety about the relentless passage of time and the proximity of death. To develop this theme, Shakespeare deploys a carefully constructed sequence of metaphors, all of which portray liminal (or threshold) states: autumn hovering on the treacherous cusp of winter, twilight dwindling into blackness, and embers snuffing out into lifeless ash. These images derive their emotional force from their transitiveness: their closeness to death lends them a sinister hue. Shakespeare orders the metaphors to reflect increasing urgency. The first metaphor—late middle age as autumn—depends on the cycle of seasons of the year. By the second metaphor—late middle age as twilight—the cycle is radically shorter, and a year has become a day. The final metaphor—late middle age as dying embers—not only shrinks the time scale even more but also breaks with the cyclical aspect of the other metaphors. A fire burns out forever, just as dying is forever. By the end of the sonnet, death arrives with an unapologetic finality.

Some critics dismiss Sonnet 73 as an exercise in metaphor. To these scholars, Sonnet 73 and others like it simply propose a number of metaphors for the same thing, and these metaphors essentially have the same meaning. But Shakespeare masks a psychological narrative within the sonnet's metaphors: in the three quatrains, the speaker slowly comes to terms with the finality of his age and his impermanence in time. The final couplet is thus a bittersweet, romantic recognition of the speaker's mortality and the depth of the young man's love. Shakespeare's use of **caesuras**, or pauses, within the lines adds to the elegiac tone: they slow the reader down, forcing us to literally cease reading for a beat or two. Thus, even the form reflects the subtle shades of connotation embedded in the sonnet's content.

SONNET 116

Let me not to the marriage of true minds
Admit impediments. Love is not love
Which alters when it alteration finds,
Or bends with the remover to remove.
O no, it is an ever-fixèd mark   5
That looks on tempests and is never shaken;
It is the star to every wand'ring bark,
Whose worth's unknown, although his height be taken.
Love's not time's fool, though rosy lips and cheeks
Within his bending sickle's compass come: 10
Love alters not with his brief hours and weeks,
But bears it out even to the edge of doom.
    If this be error and upon me proved,
    I never writ, nor no man ever loved.

SUMMARY

Sonnet 116 attempts to define love by distinguishing what it is from what it is not. Shakespeare opens by describing true love as a cerebral "marriage of true minds" (1), untainted by lust. True love admits no obstacles and will not change under any circumstance, not even if the beloved changes or leaves. Like a beacon in the tempest of life's problems, true love is dependable. And like the North Star (which sailors used to navigate), love is always visible and guides people through life. Moreover, true love is immortal. Though beauty may fade with time, love cannot be reached by death's grim, all-destroying "sickle" (10). True love endures past the end of time, until Judgment Day. The speaker ends with a vow: if he is mistaken, he is no poet, and no one in the world has ever loved.

ANALYSIS

Sonnet 116 is one of Shakespeare's most famous sonnets. Its opening definition of love is one of the most frequently quoted and anthologized in the poetic canon: "Let me not to the marriage of true minds admit impediments" (1). Essentially, Sonnet 116 presents a hyperbolic, unattainable ideal of true love as constant. In a fickle world subject to the destruction of time, love stays constant as people leave, change, or die. In other sonnets, the speaker prescribes procreation and poetry as antidotes to time, but here the speaker recommends true love as the ultimate cure. Though the sonnet seems to fall for its own fine language and sentiment, ultimately it critiques the idea that love will never change. Using earnestness and force of conviction, the sonnet pretends to support the argument that true love remains steadfast in a world of mutability. Even the speaker, in his grandiose couplet, falls for the hyperbolic, albeit romantic definition of love.

Immortal love struggles against time by generating a lifelong, devoted partnership—the "marriage" of the opening. In an era troubled by outbreaks of the plague and foreign invasions (such as the Spanish Armada of 1588), marriage provided personal stability. Shakespeare evokes the uncertainty of life in difficult times by describing humankind as a fleet of "wandering bark[s]" (7) for whom love provides the necessary "mark" (5) or beacon. Sea voyages were (and still are) a dangerous mode of transportation, made perilous by storms and confused by poor navigation technology. The English language has preserved some of these worries: someone "at sea" or "adrift" is uncertain or lost. As an allegorical space for life's journey, the sea fits well with Shakespeare's fixation on the passage of time: like time, the sea is vast and endlessly cyclical. In the sonnet, love does not conquer time, and there are no martial absolutes. Instead, as a beacon, love helps guide individuals on their passage through time. Love endures time's ravages rather than combating them. But like life, true love must change and grow over time, much as people do.

SONNET 129

Th' expense of spirit in a waste of shame
Is lust in action, and till action, lust
Is perjured, murd'rous, bloody, full of blame,
Savage, extreme, rude, cruel, not to trust,
Enjoyed no sooner but despisèd straight,   5
Past reason hunted, and no sooner had,
Past reason hated as a swallowed bait
On purpose laid to make the taker mad;
Mad in pursuit, and in possession so,
Had, having, and in quest to have, extreme;   10
A bliss in proof, and proved, a very woe;
Before, a joy proposed; behind, a dream.
   All this the world well knows, yet none knows well
   To shun the heaven that leads men to this hell.

SUMMARY
Sonnet 129 grapples with the idea of lust (sexual desire) in three stages: anticipation, consummation, and retrospection. The first quatrain discusses lust prior to consummation as violent and irrational in the extreme. The second quatrain describes the change of state once the threshold of consummation is crossed. Here, impulsive desire crumples to crippling disgust. Lust is like a piece of bait: tempting before one has entered the trap but cursed once the ruse is played out. The third quatrain debunks sexual desire as miserable in all three aspects: anticipation, consummation, and retrospection. The couplet concludes that although everyone knows that lust is a dangerous trap, no one is able to avoid it.

ANALYSIS
In this moralizing, indignant sonnet, the speaker rails against lust with carnality and fervor. The emotional, vicious rhetoric belies the distancing, third-person narration (a rarity in the sonnets), suggesting that the speaker has indeed experienced the disorienting dervish of lust personally, probably through his affair with the dark lady,

and now wants to rise above lust's effects. According to the sonnet's argument, lust is all-consuming and disorienting. The sonnet enacts this disorientation through the savagery of its verse and repetition of its language: invective follows invective, building toward a climactic couplet that aims to universalize the sonnet's argument. Everyone, the speaker implies, should heed these warnings. Rather than express emotion between two people, sex, as portrayed in this poem, causes people to go crazy, become murderous, and develop addictions. The sonnet's key metaphor of lust as "bait" (7) most cleanly symbolizes lust in its three stages. For its victim, bait first represents a treat; then, once consumed, there occurs a moment of horrible realization; and, finally, shame and regret set in as the victim realizes that the bait has been used as entrapment. Similarly, lust first appears like "bliss" (11) but, once achieved, proves to be "a very woe" (11). This unsettling poem attempts to be an evocative cautionary tale.

SONNET 130

> My mistress' eyes are nothing like the sun;
> Coral is far more red than her lips' red;
> If snow be white, why then her breasts are dun;
> If hairs be wires, black wires grow on her head;
> I have seen roses damasked, red and white,   5
> But no such roses see I in her cheeks;
> And in some pérfumes is there more delight
> Than in the breath that from my mistress reeks.
> I love to hear her speak, yet well I know
> That music hath a far more pleasing sound.   10
> I grant I never saw a goddess go;
> My mistress, when she walks, treads on the ground.
>   And yet, by heaven, I think my love as rare
>   As any she belied with false compare.

SUMMARY
In this sonnet, the speaker contrasts his beloved with exaggerated, clichéd descriptions of women. His lady's lips, breasts, hair, cheeks, and breath all fall short of traditional, grand, poetic metaphors. Her speech isn't nearly as lyrical as music, and her gait is ordinary. However, the speaker still finds her more extraordinary than any imaginary ideal.

ANALYSIS

Sonnet 130, another of Shakespeare's most famous poems, plays an elaborate joke on the conventions of Elizabethan love poetry, and readers are still laughing today. The sonnet mocks the traditional conceits of sonnets. These traditions have their root in the work of Petrarch, the Italian Renaissance poet whose sonnet sequence *Canzoniere* proved highly influential in the development of poetry. In his poetry, Petrarch described his beloved, Laura, by comparing her features to natural phenomena: lips red as rubies, skin white as snow, hair like spun flax, and so on. After Sir Philip Sidney popularized the sonnet form with his successful collection *Astrophil and Stella* in sixteenth-century England, these Petrarchan conceits evolved into the clichés they remain to this day.

Shakespeare's sonnets subvert their Petrarchan origins in many ways. First, Shakespeare created his own sonnet form: rather than employ Petrarch's octet and sestet structure, Shakespeare modified the fourteen lines into three quatrains and one couplet. Second, Shakespeare addresses most of his poems not to an idealized woman like Laura, but to a flawed, if beautiful, young man. When the poems do address a woman, the so-called dark lady, frequently they accuse her of faithlessness, not the steadfastness or chastity so often praised by other sonneteers. Here, the speaker punctures Petrarch's conceits by taking them too literally, then countering their dramatic hyperbole with refreshing authenticity. In contrast to an imagined ideal, the dark lady has "black wires" (4) for hair and breath that "reeks" (8). Poetic figuration, the sonnet suggests, creates standards that are guaranteed to disappoint, and these standards should be replaced by a more realistic human perspective on beauty. In Sonnet 130 beauty—and love—belong to the beholder.

JOHN DONNE

(1572–1631)

Context

John Donne was born into a religious Roman Catholic family in 1572 in London, England. Perhaps as a result of the bias against Catholics, Donne spent his youth as a bold social climber. He traveled in Europe, joined military raids against the Spanish, positioned himself to get noticed at court, and did all he could to show off his tremendous intellectual gifts. As a Catholic, however, Donne faced the fierce opposition and financial penalties that Protestant England imposed on Catholics during this time. At some point in the 1590s, Donne returned to London and, bowing to social pressure, renounced his Catholic faith. Much of Donne's erotic love poetry was probably composed during this time. After fighting Catholics in Spain with the English army, Donne became secretary to Sir Thomas Egerton, Lord Keeper of the Great Seal, in 1598.

Donne's prestigious position with Egerton should have guaranteed him a successful career in public service, but he inadvertently destroyed his professional prospects by secretly marrying Egerton's young niece Ann More. Immediately fired, Donne was also briefly imprisoned. He spent the next decade in constant financial distress, particularly as his family grew. By the time Ann died at age thirty-three in 1617, she had given birth to twelve children and had an untold number of miscarriages. Their marriage seemed happy, according to surviving accounts. Donne's writing from this period consists largely of poems written for patrons on special occasions. His defense of some anti-Catholic policies proposed by the English king James I won him favor in 1610–1611. In turn, King James I urged Donne toward a career in the Anglican Church, going so far as to more or less bar Donne from exploring other options.

In 1615, Donne was ordained as an Anglican priest in the Church of England. Donne probably wrote the *Holy Sonnets*, a series of dark **sonnets** addressed to God, during or around his ordination. Throughout Donne's lifetime, great conflicts between Catholics and Protestants occurred. From 1618 to 1648, Europe erupted in declared and undeclared wars, now grouped together under the umbrella term Thirty Years' War. These conflicts included wars fought by the Holy Roman Empire and Catholic Spain as well as a German civil war. England also experienced much turmoil after the formation of the Anglican Church, also known as the Church of

England. Anglicanism began in 1534, when King Henry VIII broke England's religious ties to the Roman Catholic Church after the pope refused to annul the king's marriage to Katharine of Aragon. Although Anglicanism shares several beliefs with Catholicism, Anglicans, unlike Catholics, believe that the English king is the earthly head of the church—not the pope. Donne reflected on these conflicts in his work, including Holy Sonnet 18 (1633) and "Satire 3" (1633). Around 1621, Donne was appointed dean of St. Paul's Cathedral in London. Donne was a brilliant speaker, and crowds would spill out into the street just to hear him preach. Roughly 160 of his sermons have survived.

As an adult, Donne separated his early life as an adventurous libertine from his adulthood as a serious priest. Indeed, he differentiated between the "Jack Donne" of his youth and the "Doctor Donne" of his mature years. Although Donne wrote two distinct types of poetry, his love poetry intermingles and shares characteristics with his religious poetry. He wrote religious verse during his wild youth, and he continued to write love poetry after his ordination. Only a few Donne poems were published during his lifetime, for two main reasons: first, the intellectuality of his verse precluded a wide readership, and second, the erotic nature of his earlier verse would have damaged his reputation as a priest. Donne died in London in 1631. Two years later, in 1633, a group of his poems, including both love verse and religious verse, was published as *Songs and Sonnets*.

The poems of *Songs and Sonnets* blend Donne's experiences as an individual with the collective experience of the changing modern European world. During the sixteenth and seventeenth centuries, European explorers and conquistadors brought home tremendous riches from the Americas, Africa, and Asia. In his youth, Donne sailed as far as the Azores, and his poetry demonstrates a fascination with the fortunes and discoveries being made overseas and employs nautical **imagery** and **metaphors**. Donne's work also sometimes relies on medieval science, including the Ptolemaic model of the heavens. According to this view, the earth sits fixed at the center of the universe, while the moon, the sun, the planets, and the stars all rest on spheres that rotate about the earth. A divine intelligence, or angel, governs and keeps each sphere in motion, while God resides outside of the outermost sphere. Another medieval notion sometimes found in Donne's work is the idea that the human body exists as a small world unto itself, with its various parts corresponding to various parts of the physical world.

Critics regarded Donne as the father of the **metaphysical poets**, a group of poets writing in a similar style during the sixteenth and seventeenth centuries. Other notable metaphysical poets include Andrew Marvell, George Herbert, Richard Crashaw, Henry Vaughan, and Abraham Cowley. Although these poets shared some characteristics, the metaphysical poets did not form a coherent or organized school in the same way that the romantic poets would a few centuries later. Metaphysical poets consistently employed the **conceit** in their work, an elaborate, intellectual parallel **simile** or metaphor between two seemingly dissimilar objects or ideas. Donne's most famous instance of a conceit occurs in the final three stanzas of "A Valediction: Forbidding Mourning" (1633), in which he draws out the metaphor of a compass. In addition to the conceit, most metaphysical poetry uses simple vocabulary, colloquial phrasing, and jagged rhythms. An intense intellectual energy drives metaphysical poetry, and ideas, rather than emotion, abound.

Around 1660, during the restoration of the English monarchy, Donne and metaphysical poetry fell out of favor. In the early twentieth century, T. S. Eliot led a re-examination of metaphysical poetry, praising it for emotional and intellectual energy and contrasting it with the stiff, torpid verse of the nineteenth-century Victorian period. Signaled out for the directness and singularity of poetic **voice**, Donne's poetry remains our most outstanding example of metaphysical verse.

THEMES, MOTIFS & SYMBOLS

THEMES

LOVERS AS MICROCOSMS

Donne incorporates the Renaissance notion of the human body as a microcosm into his love poetry. During the Renaissance, many people believed that the microcosmic human body mirrored the macrocosmic physical world. According to this belief, the intellect governs the body, much like a king or queen governs the land. Many of Donne's poems—most notably "The Sun Rising" (1633), "The Good-Morrow" (1633), and "A Valediction: Of Weeping" (1633)—envision a lover or pair of lovers as being entire worlds unto themselves. But rather than use the analogy to imply that the whole world can be compressed into a small space, Donne uses it to show how lovers become so enraptured with each other that they believe they are the only beings in existence. The lovers are so in love that nothing else matters. For example, in "The Sun Rising," the speaker concludes the poem by telling the sun to shine exclusively on himself and his beloved. By doing so, he says, the sun will be shining on the entire world.

THE NEOPLATONIC CONCEPTION OF LOVE

Donne draws on the Neoplatonic conception of physical love and religious love as being two manifestations of the same impulse. In the *Symposium* (ca. third or fourth century B.C.E.), Plato describes physical love as the lowest rung of a ladder. According to the Platonic formulation, we are attracted first to a single beautiful person, then to beautiful people generally, then to beautiful minds, then to beautiful ideas, and, ultimately, to beauty itself, the highest rung of the ladder. Centuries later, Christian Neoplatonists adapted this idea such that the progression of love culminates in a love of God, or spiritual beauty. Naturally, Donne used his religious poetry to idealize the Christian love for God, but the Neoplatonic conception of love also appears in his love poetry, albeit slightly tweaked. For instance, in the bawdy "Elegy 19. To His Mistress Going to Bed" (1669), the speaker claims that his love for a naked woman surpasses pictorial

representations of biblical scenes. Many love poems assert the superiority of the speakers' love to quotidian, ordinary love by presenting the speakers' love as a manifestation of purer, Neoplatonic
feeling, which resembles the sentiment felt for the divine.

RELIGIOUS ENLIGHTENMENT AS SEXUAL ECSTASY

Throughout his poetry, Donne imagines religious enlightenment as
a form of sexual ecstasy. He parallels the sense of fulfillment to be
derived from religious worship to the pleasure derived from sexual
activity—a shocking, revolutionary comparison, for his time. In
Holy Sonnet 14 (1633), for example, the speaker asks God to rape
him, thereby freeing the speaker from worldly concerns. Through
the act of rape, paradoxically, the speaker will be rendered chaste. In
Holy Sonnet 18 (1899), the speaker draws an analogy between
entering the one true church and entering a woman during intercourse. Here, the speaker explains that Christ will be pleased if the
speaker sleeps with Christ's wife, who is "embraced and open to
most men" (14). Although these poems seem profane, their religious fervor saves them from sacrilege or scandal. Filled with religious passion, people have the potential to be as pleasurably sated as
they are after sexual activity.

THE SEARCH FOR THE ONE TRUE RELIGION

Donne's speakers frequently wonder which religion to choose when
confronted with so many churches that claim to be the one true religion. In 1517, an Augustinian monk in Germany named Martin
Luther set off a number of debates that eventually led to the founding of Protestantism, which, at the time, was considered to be a
reformed version of Catholicism. England developed Anglicanism
in 1534, another reformed version of Catholicism. This period was
thus dubbed the Reformation. Because so many sects and churches
developed from these religions, theologians and laypeople began to
wonder which religion was true or right. Written while Donne was
abandoning Catholicism for Anglicanism, "Satire 3" reflects these
concerns. Here, the speaker wonders how one might discover the
right church when so many churches make the same claim. The
speaker of Holy Sonnet 18 asks Christ to explain which bride, or
church, belongs to Christ. Neither poem forthrightly proposes one
church as representing the true religion, but nor does either poem
reject outright the notion of one true church or religion.

MOTIFS

SPHERES

Donne's fascination with spheres rests partly on the perfection of these shapes and partly on the near-infinite associations that can be drawn from them. Like other metaphysical poets, Donne used conceits to extend analogies and to make thematic connections between otherwise dissimilar objects. For instance, in "The Good-Morrow," the speaker, through brilliant metaphorical leaps, uses the motif of spheres to move from a description of the world to a description of globes to a description of his beloved's eyes to a description of their perfect love. Rather than simply praise his beloved, the speaker compares her to a faultless shape, the sphere, which contains neither corners nor edges. The comparison to a sphere also emphasizes the way in which his beloved's face has become the world, as far as the speaker is concerned. In "A Valediction: Of Weeping," the speaker uses the spherical shape of tears to draw out associations with pregnancy, globes, the world, and the moon. As the speaker cries, each tear contains a miniature reflection of the beloved, yet another instance in which the sphere demonstrates the idealized personality and physicality of the person being addressed.

DISCOVERY AND CONQUEST

Particularly in Donne's love poetry, voyages of discovery and conquest illustrate the mystery and magnificence of the speakers' love affairs. European explorers began arriving in the Americas in the fifteenth century, returning to England and the Continent with previously unimagined treasures and stories. By Donne's lifetime, colonies had been established in North and South America, and the riches that flowed back to England dramatically transformed English society. In "The Good-Morrow" and "The Sun Rising," the speakers express indifference toward recent voyages of discovery and conquest, preferring to seek adventure in bed with their beloveds. This comparison demonstrates the way in which the beloved's body and personality prove endlessly fascinating to a person falling in love. The speaker of "Elegy 19. To His Mistress Going to Bed" calls his beloved's body "my America! my new-found land" (27), thereby linking the conquest of exploration to the conquest of seduction. To convince his beloved to make love, he compares the sexual act to a voyage of discovery. The comparison also serves as the speaker's attempt to convince his beloved of both the natural-ness and the inevitability of sex. Like the Americas, the speaker explains, she too will eventually be discovered and conquered.

REFLECTIONS

Throughout his love poetry, Donne makes reference to the reflec-tions that appear in eyes and tears. With this motif, Donne empha-sizes the way in which beloveds and their perfect love might contain one another, forming complete, whole worlds. "A Valediction: Of Weeping" portrays the process of leave-taking occurring between the two lovers. As the speaker cries, he knows that the image of his beloved is reflected in his tears. And as the tear falls away, so too will the speaker move farther away from his beloved until they are sepa-rated at last. The reflections in their eyes indicate the strong bond between the lovers in "The Good-Morrow" and "The Ecstasy" (1633). The lovers in these poems look into one another's eyes and see themselves contained there, whole and perfect and present. The act of staring into each other's eyes leads to a profound mingling of souls in "The Ecstasy," as if reflections alone provided the gateway into a person's innermost being.

SYMBOLS

ANGELS

Angels symbolize the almost-divine status attained by beloveds in Donne's love poetry. As divine messengers, angels mediate between God and humans, helping humans become closer to the divine. The speaker compares his beloved to an angel in "Elegy 19. To His Mis-tress Going to Bed." Here, the beloved, as well as his love for her, brings the speaker closer to God because with her, he attains para-dise on earth. According to Ptolemaic astronomy, angels governed the spheres, which rotated around the earth, or the center of the uni-verse. In "Air and Angels" (1633), the speaker draws on Ptolemaic concepts to compare his beloved to the aerial form assumed by angels when they appear to humans. Her love governs him, much as angels govern spheres. At the end of the poem, the speaker notes that a slight difference exists between the love a woman feels and the love a man feels, a difference comparable to that between ordinary air and the airy aerial form assumed by angels.

THE COMPASS

Perhaps the most famous conceit in all of metaphysical poetry, the compass symbolizes the relationship between lovers: two separate but joined bodies. The symbol of the compass is another instance of Donne's using the language of voyage and conquest to describe relationships between and feelings of those in love. Compasses help sailors navigate the sea, and, metaphorically, they help lovers stay linked across physical distances or absences. In "A Valediction: Forbidding Mourning," the speaker compares his soul and the soul of his beloved to a so-called twin compass. Also known as a draftsman's compass, a twin compass has two legs, one that stays fixed and one that moves. In the poem, the speaker becomes the movable leg, while his beloved becomes the fixed leg. According to the poem, the jointure between them, and the steadiness of the beloved, allows the speaker to trace a perfect circle while he is apart from her. Although the speaker can only trace this circle when the two legs of the compass are separated, the compass can eventually be closed up, and the two legs pressed together again, after the circle has been traced.

BLOOD

Generally blood symbolizes life, and Donne uses blood to symbolize different experiences in life, from erotic passion to religious devotion. In "The Flea" (1633), a flea crawls over a pair of would-be lovers, biting and drawing blood from both. As the speaker imagines it, the blood of the pair has become intermingled, and thus the two should become sexually involved, since they are already married in the body of the flea. Throughout the *Holy Sonnets*, blood symbolizes passionate dedication to God and Christ. According to Christian belief, Christ lost blood on the cross and died so that humankind might be pardoned and saved. Begging for guidance, the speaker in Holy Sonnet 7 (1633) asks Christ to teach him to be penitent, such that he will be made worthy of Christ's blood. Donne's religious poetry also underscores the Christian relationship between violence, or bloodshed, and purity. For instance, the speaker of Holy Sonnet 9 (1633) pleads that Christ's blood might wash away the memory of his sin and render him pure again.

JOHN DONNE

Summary & Analysis

"The Flea"

Mark but this flea, and mark in this,
How little that which thou deniest me is;
It suck'd me first, and now sucks thee,
And in this flea our two bloods mingled be;
Thou know'st that this cannot be said   5
A sin, nor shame, nor loss of maidenhead,
   Yet this enjoys before it woo,
    And pamper'd swells with one blood made of two,
   And this, alas, is more than we would do.

Oh stay, three lives in one flea spare,   10
Where we almost, yea, more than married are.
This flea is you and I, and this
Our marriage bed, and marriage temple is.
Though parents grudge, and you, we're met,
And cloister'd in these living walls of jet.   15
   Though use make you apt to kill me,
   Let not to that self-murder added be,
   And sacrilege, three sins in killing three.

Cruel and sudden, hast thou since
Purpled thy nail in blood of innocence?   20
Wherein could this flea guilty be,
Except in that drop which it suck'd from thee?
Yet thou triumph'st, and say'st that thou
Find'st not thyself nor me the weaker now.
   'Tis true; then learn how false fears be;   25
   Just so much honor, when thou yield'st to me,
   Will waste, as this flea's death took life from thee.

Summary

In the first stanza, the speaker asks his beloved to consider a flea that has sucked blood from him and now sucks blood from her. She withholds her physical love from him, and he hopes to convince her to

sleep with him by using the flea to create an analogy. Because the flea has sucked his blood and now sucks hers, their blood has become intermixed within the flea. Yet no one would call the intermixing of blood sinful or shameful, nor would anyone claim that the woman has been deflowered by the bite and subsequent intermingling of blood. According to medical theories in Donne's day, sex consisted of the mingling of blood between men and women, and this mingling caused pregnancy. Alluding to this belief, the speaker complains that his beloved denies him a simple pleasure that even the flea enjoys.

In the second stanza, the speaker urges his beloved not to kill the flea. By not killing the flea, he reasons, she would save not only the flea's life but also the life of the speaker and her life since their blood is also in the flea. And since the flea contains their blood, the two of them have already married. The flea's body has become both their marriage bed and the church in which they were married. However much she or her parents might object, the two of them are already married within the flea. Since the beloved is well accustomed to killing the speaker because she consistently rejects his advances, killing the flea as well would not be out of character for her. The speaker reminds her, though, that since a part of her is also in the flea, she would be committing suicide in addition to murder. Finally, the speaker urges her not to kill the flea by pointing out that she would be committing three sins: murder in killing him, suicide in killing herself, and sacrilege in destroying the flea, which is the church in which they were married.

In the third stanza, the speaker reacts in horror as his beloved crushes the flea. He compares her to the biblical king Herod, who, having been warned that the future king of the Jews had been born, had all the infants under the age of two in Israel massacred. Traditionally, Herod is associated with the color purple. Similarly, the speaker's beloved has a purple fingernail after murdering the innocent flea. The speaker protests that the flea is guilty of nothing more than taking a drop of her blood. Yet, the speaker notes, his beloved claims that she has been proven right since neither he nor she feels any weaker for her having killed the flea. Clearly, she reasons, the speaker's claim in the second stanza that a part of them lived in the flea has proved false. Granting that his beloved is right, the speaker also takes this as proof that she should not worry so much about sleeping with him. If the blood she shared with the speaker in the flea turns out to be unimportant, so should the blood she would share with him in sexual intercourse. If she sleeps with him, she will lose no more honor than she lost life in killing the flea.

ANALYSIS

A characteristic Donne love poem, "The Flea" uses wry humor to convince a woman to have sex. Many metaphysical poets wrote so-called carpe diem poems, in which eloquent speakers tried to convince women to "seize the day" and have sex. Like Donne's "The Flea" and Andrew Marvell's "To His Coy Mistress," carpe diem poems relied on wit, charm, and hyperbole. In "The Flea," the speaker's analogies become increasingly outrageous as the poem progresses. At first, the speaker uses the flea simply to point out what a small thing it would be for the two of them to sleep together. By the end of the second stanza, the flea has become a church and a marriage bed, and the lives of the speaker, the beloved, and the flea have become intermingled within the body of the flea. Fortunately, the speaker's beloved has a sense of humor too, as she crushes the flea and neatly observes that the speaker's analogy is flawed: neither she nor he has come to any harm in the death of the flea. But the speaker then reverses his argument, taking the unimportance of the flea's death as proof of the unimportance of their sleeping together. Since the beloved has an intelligence that matches that of the speaker, the poem ultimately becomes an extraordinarily apt manner of wooing: rather than whisper sweet nothings, "The Flea" craftily and humorously relies on logic and argument.

The form of "The Flea" mirrors its wit. Each stanza contains nine lines, and the first six lines consist of three rhyming couplets, in which the first line has four feet and the second line has five feet. The effect is much like a set and spike in volleyball: the shorter first line creates a sense of anticipation and sets up the rhyme for the second line, and the second line delivers a kind of punch line, completing the thought set up in the first line. Donne repeats this pattern in the concluding three lines of each stanza, with a slight tweak: the first line has four feet, but the final two lines each have five feet. Thus, ten feet, rather than five, deliver the stanza's concluding punch line, enabling the speaker to elaborate and articulate in greater detail. He makes particularly good use of this additional line in the final stanza since here he reconfigures his entire argument. The rhyme scheme itself also employs a teasing wit. Even though the poem is called "The Flea" and many of the lines end on a variation of the words *be* and *thee*, none of the lines end on *flea*. Indeed, the words prepare readers for a climax that never occurs, an unfulfilled sonic expectation that reflects the speaker's unfulfilled desire for sex.

"The Flea" revels in pure physical pleasure, rather than masking or denying desire. Similarly, the speaker emphasizes the idea that his beloved is made up of flesh and blood, with desires and needs, rather than idealizing her as ethereal or angelic. Many love poems feature women who neither speak nor reason and who do not exhibit any earthly or genuine characteristics whatsoever. The beloveds merely sit mute while the speakers compare their features to flowers and extol their virtuous personalities. Unlike these silent women, the beloved in "The Flea" takes dramatic action by killing the flea and attempting to silence the speaker's arguments. The speaker's excitement over the intermingling of their blood within the flea underscores his physical desire for her physical attributes. By choosing to elevate an insect to the subject of an entire poem, as well as to make the flea an embodiment of a marriage and a church, the speaker shows a great delight in the coarser, baser aspects of nature. In Donne's day, the idea of mingling blood meant sex, so neither the speaker's beloved nor readers could harbor any illusions about the poem's content. So strong is his desire that the speaker can bend any situation or fact to suit his carpe diem argument and to persuade his beloved of the normality and naturalness of the sexual act.

"THE GOOD-MORROW"

I wonder by my troth, what thou and I
Did, till we loved? were we not wean'd till then?
But suck'd on country pleasures, childishly?
Or snorted we in the seven sleepers' den?
'Twas so; but this, all pleasures fancies be;   5
If ever any beauty I did see,
Which I desired, and got, 'twas but a dream of thee.

And now good-morrow to our waking souls,
Which watch not one another out of fear;
For love all love of other sights controls,   10
And makes one little room an everywhere.
Let sea-discoverers to new worlds have gone;
Let maps to other, worlds on worlds have shown;
Let us possess one world; each hath one, and is one.

> My face in thine eye, thine in mine appears,   15
> And true plain hearts do in the faces rest;
> Where can we find two better hemispheres
> Without sharp north, without declining west?
> Whatever dies, was not mix'd equally;
> If our two loves be one, or thou and I   20
> Love so alike that none can slacken, none can die.

SUMMARY

In the first stanza, the speaker addresses his beloved, asking her what he and she did before they fell in love with each other. Then, in an effort to answer the first question, he asks two more questions. First, he asks if, before they fell in love, they were like children who still nursed at their mothers' breasts. Second, he wonders if they were instead asleep like the seven Christian youths of ancient legend. (These youths hid in a cave to escape from Roman persecution and fell asleep for 187 years. When they awoke, they discovered that the whole world had converted to Christianity.) Whatever the case may be, the speaker says, all his previous happiness was just idle fun compared to the love he now feels for his beloved. Likewise, anything magnificent that he has seen, desired, or gotten before they fell in love was really just a vision of his lover.

At the start of the second stanza, the speaker wishes a good morning to his soul and the soul of his lover as they awake. Their feelings of love dominate all other potential feelings such that their small room becomes "an everywhere" (11)—that is, no other place or feeling concerns them. Explorers may have made discoveries, and maps of the stars may display other worlds, but all that matters to the speaker is the world he occupies with his beloved. Both the speaker and his lover are all small worlds, and they share those worlds together.

In the third stanza, the speaker remarks that he sees his reflection in his lover's eye, as her reflection appears in his. He also claims that the frank and honest love they feel for each other is evident in their faces. Comparing their faces to two halves of a globe, the speaker remarks that their two halves make up a perfect world. The speaker goes on to invoke the then-popular philosophical view that material objects decay because the elements in them are not mixed with a proper balance. Properly mixed compounds will never decay. If the love the speaker feels for his lover and the love she feels for him are one love or if their loves are so similar that they are equally mixed, then their love for each other cannot ever die or decay.

ANALYSIS

"The Good-Morrow" demonstrates many typical characteristics of Donne's love poetry: it uses unusual imagery; dwells on ideas rather than descriptions; employs an extended metaphor; and relies on allusions to then-current philosophical, cultural, and political ideas. Instead of comparing his lover to a rose or the sun and instead of describing her beauty or personality, the speaker of this poem compares her to a hemisphere of a globe. This reference to a globe sets off an elaborate series of allusions to mapmaking and voyages of discovery, as well as to medieval notions about the human body as a microcosm and about the composition of the world. The poem also emphasizes the totalizing experience of being completely in love, as the speaker discovers all he needs in his beloved. Indeed, the room in which they lie together becomes the entire world. Like all enraptured lovers, the speaker believes that his love renders him complete and that his love will last forever. Without relying on hackneyed imagery, "The Good-Morrow" nevertheless conveys the sweetness and beauty of waking up next to one's lover.

As befits its title, the three stanzas of "The Good-Morrow" present a gradual stirring from sleep. In the first stanza, the speaker and his lover awaken after having spent the night together, and the seven lines contain several references to sleep. The speaker alludes to a legend about dreaming youths and tells his lover that all the wonderful, beautiful experiences of his past were "but a dream of thee" (7). In the second stanza, the speaker bids "good morrow" (8), then launches into an extended comparison of the room they share to the world outside. Still somewhat sleepy, he begins lines 12–14 in the same way, with the word *let*. In the third stanza, the speaker and his lover stare at each other with fully open eyes, and the poem ends with a complicated allusion to philosophy, which requires the attention of a mind completely awake. The first six lines of each stanza use the steady rhythm of **iambic pentameter**, the meter most similar to natural English speech. However, the seventh line of each stanza swells into **iambic hexameter**, as if the speaker feels a surge of wakefulness or enthusiasm that cannot be contained by his previous steady murmurs.

Overall the tone of the poem demonstrates a sense of casualness befitting the narrative scene. Despite its elaborate conceits and references to major discoveries and ideas, the poem opens with a simple question: what were we like before we fell in love? Donne's diction also contributes to the poem's relaxed feel. In line 3 and 4, for example, the speaker refers to the "sucking" of sexual activity and to the "snorting" of sleep, both of which illustrate the comfortableness that comes with love. Clearly, the speaker and his lover take great pleasure in each other, and clearly they have been doing so for quite some time. In the second stanza, the speaker alludes to the casual comfort between them by telling his lover that they can simply enjoy the sight of each other and that they know each other so well that neither need be afraid. The time for the formalities of wooing has passed, and now the speaker can revel in the fleshy pleasures of having won his love.

Donne uses imagery from recent scientific and social explorations to create a series of complex conceits. In stanzas 2 and 3, the speaker refers to maps, globes, hemispheres, direction, and alchemy. Just as a map in a room contains the whole world outside it, claims the speaker, he and his lover in their room contain everything in the world outside of them. By waking up together, the speaker and his lover effectively say "good morrow" to a whole new world. So in love are the pair that they willingly forgo the exciting discoveries of the day, including new landmasses and astrological bodies. The speaker demonstrates his indifference with his use of the word *let*, as in line 14: "Let us possess one world." The pair do not need any other world but the one they have created between them. In the poem's closing lines, the speaker returns to the real world with his use of the word *if*. He says that if—and only if—the pair are a perfect blend will their love live forever, relying on medieval notions of mixtures and elements. His use of the word *if* awakens himself to the possibility that their love might die or fade. The word *if* also reminds readers of the real world of inconstancy, trouble, and mutability that lies beyond the fantasy world of love poetry.

"A VALEDICTION: FORBIDDING MOURNING"

As virtuous men pass mildly away,
    And whisper to their souls to go,
Whilst some of their sad friends do say,
    "Now his breath goes," and some say, "No."

So let us melt, and make no noise,   5
    No tear-floods, nor sigh-tempests move;
'Twere profanation of our joys
    To tell the laity our love.

Moving of th' earth brings harms and fears;
    Men reckon what it did, and meant;   10
But trepidation of the spheres,
    Though greater far, is innocent.

Dull sublunary lovers' love
    — Whose soul is sense — cannot admit
Of absence, 'cause it doth remove   15
    The thing which elemented it.

But we by a love so much refined,
    That ourselves know not what it is,
Inter-assurèd of the mind,
    Care less, eyes, lips and hands to miss.   20

Our two souls therefore, which are one,
    Though I must go, endure not yet
A breach, but an expansion,
    Like gold to aery thinness beat.

If they be two, they are two so   25
    As stiff twin compasses are two;
Thy soul, the fix'd foot, makes no show
    To move, but doth, if th' other do.

And though it in the centre sit,
    Yet, when the other far doth roam,   30

> It leans, and hearkens after it,
>   And grows erect, as that comes home.
>
> Such wilt thou be to me, who must,
>   Like th' other foot, obliquely run;
> Thy firmness makes my circle just,   35
>   And makes me end where I begun.

SUMMARY

A valediction is a poem spoken at parting or leave-taking, which is why the person who gives the parting address at a school's graduation ceremony is called the "valedictorian." The speaker begins this poem by explaining that righteous, moral people die peacefully, willingly allowing their souls to leave their bodies. They die so peacefully, in fact, that some people cannot judge for certain the moment at which these righteous people breathe their last breath. As he says good-bye to his beloved, the speaker suggests that they should part from each other just as peacefully. They should not make any sounds, cry many tears, nor sigh forcefully because these gestures would let everyone nearby know how much the speaker and his beloved love each other. Their love for each other is sacred, so they would profane it by letting others witness it. Other people do not and would not understand such great love.

The speaker next refers to two metaphysical ideas current in Donne's time. First, earthquakes herald worse things to come. Second, the earth sits in the center of the universe, and the moon, sun, planets, and stars revolve around the earth in a series of concentric spheres. Drawing on these ideas, the speaker points out that earthquakes cause damage and portend great misfortune, but the movement of the spheres, which involves a movement far greater than the movement of the earth involved in earthquakes, isn't harmful. In the fourth stanza, the speaker compares the parting of ordinary lovers to the movement of the earth involved in earthquakes. These ordinary lovers should consider their separation to be a bad thing because their love cannot last while they are apart. Essentially, their love consists of the sensual pleasures they enjoy in each other's company.

But, the speaker explains in stanza 5, the parting of the speaker from his beloved is harmless, like the movement of the spheres. Their love for each other is so pure that they themselves hardly understand it. In fact, the connection between their minds is so powerful that the separation of their bodies will not be particularly traumatic. Their two souls actually make up one soul, so their physical separation from each other does not separate their souls. Instead, their separation enlarges the area covered by their one united soul, like a piece of gold hammered out until it expands and spreads over a wide area.

In stanzas 7 through 9, the speaker spins an elaborate metaphor of a twin compass. If, the speaker explains, he must consider himself and his beloved to be two souls rather than one soul, he shall think of their souls as the two feet of a compass used in drawing a circle. His beloved's soul will be like the fixed foot at the center of the circle, and his soul will be like the foot holding the pencil, which circles about the fixed foot at the center. The fixed foot at the center stays stationary although it rotates, leaning in the direction of the foot holding the pencil as if the fixed foot were always looking out for the foot with the pencil. When the compass closes, the fixed foot at the center stands up straight in welcome as the foot holding the pencil comes back into contact with it. Similarly, the speaker tells his beloved, she will always look out for him while he is away and will always welcome him when he returns home. While he is away from her, her firmness will keep him steady, just like the steadfastness of the fixed foot at the center of the circle ensures that the other foot draws a perfect circle and finishes the circle by coming back to where it started.

ANALYSIS

Some scholars speculate that Donne wrote this poem for his wife in 1611, before he left for an extended visit to Europe. Regardless of the actual circumstances of the poem's composition, the poem features a cool, rational speaker trying to convince his lover not to be sad as they say good-bye. We do not know anything about the speaker, the lover, or the situation other than the fact that the speaker maintains enough composure to enumerate the reasons why the two should be silent upon leaving each other. Unlike ordinary lovers, whose love is based solely on the physical, the speaker and his lover possess an extraordinary love, which will last throughout their physical separation because their souls come together to form one soul. While ordinary lovers part like earthquakes, full of tremors and noise, the speaker and his lover shall part quietly, like the movement of the spheres in Ptolemaic astronomy. Their love relies on spirituality and possesses an inner significance that exceeds outward displays. Even the structure of the poem demonstrates an inner quietness: the poem uses a steady, simple *abab* rhyme scheme in even, measured **quatrains**.

"A Valediction: Forbidding Mourning" contains the most famous example of a metaphysical conceit in all of English love poetry: the twin compass. In a conceit, the speaker draws an analogy between two unlike objects, and here the speaker makes the twin compass used in drafting analogous to two lovers about to be separated. The speaker stretches the simile over three stanzas, finding a number of unique ways to compare his relationship with his lover to a compass: they are joined but separate, she is steady in the center while he moves about, she keeps him steady by inclining toward him when he is away and welcoming him home when he returns, his journey will bring him back to where he started, and they construct something perfect between the two of them. The comparison to a drafting instrument heightens the relationship rather than cheapening it. The feet of the compass "roam" (30), "lean" (31), and "hearken" (31); these active verbs create a very human sense of wandering and yearning in the movements of the compass. Ultimately, the ingenuity with which the speaker reassures his beloved about their upcoming separation shows his ability to solve difficult problems. This display of verbal problem-solving skills should reassure his beloved that he will show similar ingenuity in finding his way back to her again.

To underscore the perfect relationship between the speaker and his beloved, the speaker consistently compares their relationship to a circle. In Donne's time, the circle, or sphere, was considered to be the most perfect and most divine shape. The speaker compares ordinary love to earthquakes, which produce jagged shapes, while he compares his love to the movement of spheres in the heavens, which produces a smooth arc. As the feet of the compass move apart, they too draw a smooth circle. Like the compass, the separation of the two lovers, far from being traumatic, makes it possible to trace a circle, and thus a perfect shape forms from the distance between them. Also, their bond is as extraordinary as the heavens and as never ending as a circle. Seen in this way, the separation should not cause either the speaker or his lover any consternation, as their love is too faultless and complete to be damaged by mere physical distance.

HOLY SONNET 14

> Batter my heart, three-person'd God; for you
> As yet but knock; breathe, shine, and seek to mend;
> That I may rise, and stand, o'erthrow me, and bend
> Your force, to break, blow, burn, and make me new.
> I, like an usurp'd town, to another due,   5
> Labour to admit you, but O, to no end.
> Reason, your viceroy in me, me should defend,
> But is captived, and proves weak or untrue.
> Yet dearly I love you, and would be loved fain,
> But am betroth'd unto your enemy;   10
> Divorce me, untie, or break that knot again,
> Take me to you, imprison me, for I,
> Except you enthrall me, never shall be free,
> Nor ever chaste, except you ravish me.

JOHN DONNE

SUMMARY

In this fourteen-line poem, the speaker addresses the Christian Holy Trinity of God—the father (God), the son (Christ), and the Holy Ghost. The speaker asks the Trinity to break down the door of his heart. So far, God has only tapped politely, whispered gently, and illuminated him, seeking to improve the speaker but without being too invasive. But in order for the speaker to be made worthy of becoming a good person and, eventually, of going to heaven, he needs God to knock him over forcefully, shatter him, and, essentially, destroy him so that he might be transformed and improved.

The speaker compares himself to a town that has been captured by enemy forces. He wishes to admit God in the way that a captured town would admit a friendly army that has come to liberate it, but the speaker cannot. God's representative within the speaker, his reason, should defend the speaker against his enemies and against sin, but reason has somehow failed: perhaps the speaker's reason isn't strong enough, or perhaps his reason has betrayed him. Nevertheless, the speaker asserts, he still loves God and wishes that God would love him in return. However, the speaker claims that he is engaged to be married to sin. The speaker begs God to divorce him from sin and to break their bonds of marriage. He asks God to incarcerate him because he cannot be liberated unless God captures him. Similarly, the speaker claims that he can never be virginal unless God takes sexual possession of him.

ANALYSIS

Donne probably began writing the nineteen poems that constitute the *Holy Sonnets* in 1609 as a formal exercise in meditation. Each fourteen-line poem employs a rhyme scheme and meter, much like a traditional sonnet. Unlike traditional sonnets, however, each poem explores an aspect of Christian faith rather than expressing undying, hyperbolic love for an idealized woman. Holy Sonnet 14 follows the pattern of a Shakespearean sonnet: three quatrains, which develop three separate metaphors and reinforce the "three-person'd God" (1) to whom the poem is addressed. In the first group of four lines, the speaker imagines himself as a town being attacked and God as a battering ram, which has come to conquer the town. In the next group, the speaker imagines himself as a besieged city and God as its liberator. In the third group, the speaker imagines himself as sin's fiancé or husband and God as his would-be lover. Donne's **diction** also encodes the Trinity, as in line 4: God the father breaks; God the spirit blows; and God the son, playing on the homophony between "son" and "sun," shines.

Both the form and content of this sonnet reflect its shocking brutality. The alliteration of "b" sounds in lines 3–4 echo the speaker's plea in the first line, when he asks God to become a battering ram and pummel him. Donne also deviates from the sonnet's rhythmic iambic pentameter in order to represent the violent battering, as in line 7. Here, the repetition of the word *me* creates a sonic effect similar to the repetitive banging made by a battering ram. The lists of verbs perform a related function since they occur in the same imperative, commanding case throughout the poem, creating another kind of recurring echo. As for the content, the speaker asks God to destroy him, to set him on fire, to incarcerate him, to enslave him, and to rape him. Rather than plead or whine, the speaker aggressively commands God to make him worthy through violence.

An undercurrent of eroticism runs throughout Holy Sonnet 14, not simply in the sexualized plea of the concluding **couplet**. In the first eight lines, the speaker emphasizes his own weaknesses and inability to come around to God's way on his own. The speaker exhibits sexual masochism in his desire to be broken and rebuilt. Donne uses several double entendres to reinforce the poem's sexuality. For instance, in Donne's day, the word *heart* was slang for "vagina," and the word *labor* meant "having sex." Also, the image of a besieged, walled-off city was then a familiar symbol of a woman's genitalia. Finally, although the speaker does not mention a battering ram directly, he most certainly asks God to act as a battering ram, itself a phallic and highly sexual symbol. In the final two lines, the speaker asks God to enslave and rape him, paradoxically, in order to liberate and cleanse him. All of these words and images point to the paradoxical but erotic concluding couplet.

Since his reappraisal in the early twentieth century, Donne has been particularly praised for his ability to juxtapose very different ideas. In this poem, he links rape and chastity, imprisonment and freedom, violent death and entrance to heaven. Anthropomorphizing God, or making him out to have human characteristics, carried blasphemous consequences: unlike humans, God does not commit sins, and he definitely doesn't feel lust. Donne relies on the paradoxical juxtapositions to rescue the sonnet from blasphemy. Through the rape, the speaker will be made pure; through imprisonment, the speaker will become free; through violent death, the speaker will be made ready for heaven. With God, the speaker will be purified from any past sins, liberated from the sins of the world, and worthy of paradise. Ultimately, the sonnet praises God by showing the extent of his power: so great is God's authority that he makes the most violent and sinful activities virtuous.

JOHN DONNE

ALEXANDER
POPE

(1688–1744)

CONTEXT

Alexander Pope was born in London in 1688, the year of England's "Glorious Revolution." The revolution occurred when Parliament replaced the unpopular Catholic king James II with his Protestant daughter Mary and her husband, William of Orange. Anti-Catholic sentiment was extremely high, and laws were passed that severely limited the rights of Roman Catholics. As a Catholic, Pope was affected by the atmosphere and legislation prevalent in England at the time: he was not permitted to attend school, nor was he allowed to participate in political life. An eager scholar, he educated himself, including mastering several languages on his own. His early verses were often imitations of poets he admired. Pope's obvious talent was encouraged by well-read friends and by his father, a linen draper with whom he was very close. At the age of twelve, Pope contracted a form of tuberculosis that left him stunted and misshapen and caused him great pain for much of his life. He never married, although he formed a number of lifelong friendships in London's literary circles. Most notably, he became extremely close with the satirist Jonathan Swift.

In 1711, at the age of twenty-three, Pope published his first successful poem, *An Essay on Criticism*. After the revision and republication of the mock epic *The Rape of the Lock* in 1714, Pope spent many years translating the works of Homer. During the ten years he devoted to this arduous project, he produced few new poems of his own but refined his taste in literature, as well as his moral, social, and political opinions. His translation of the *Iliad* sold extremely well, and Pope became the first English poet who was able to live entirely off the sales of his poetry. His money allowed him to lease a comfortable villa with beautiful gardens, which he cultivated with great care. However, Pope's enemies continued to verbally attack him, his translations, and his poetry.

Pope wrote during what is often called the Augustan Age of English literature (it is actually Pope's career that defines the age, roughly 1690–1744). During this time, England had recovered from the English Civil Wars and the Glorious Revolution, and the new sense of political stability led to a resurgence of support for the arts. For this reason, many compared the period to the reign of Augustus in Rome, under whom the epic poet Virgil and the great critic Horace had found support for their work. Just as the scientists and philosophers of the day were turning to the thinkers of classical Greece and Rome for inspiration, eighteenth-century English writers admired and imitated classical writings—in fact, their aesthetic is known as **neoclassicism**. Neoclassical writers valued poetry that alluded to classical texts and adhered to classical rules and morals, setting less value on originality than the romantic poets would in the next century. Unlike the romantics, neoclassical writers were not particularly interested in poetry that expressed the experiences or emotions of individuals. Instead, they preferred literature with moral or political themes, privileging satire as the dominant mode of expression.

Both the government and the London literary world of Pope's era were rife with favoritism, factionalism, mudslinging, and backstabbing. During the reigns of Queen Anne (1702–1714) and King George I (1714–1727), political intrigue was common—people worked hard to flatter and conspire with the people in power, whether they were members of Parliament or the cabinet, and forming an alliance with the wrong person could have been disastrous. Since most authors could not make a living from the sale of their books, they relied on the patronage of wealthy noblemen or on government positions for income. Therefore, writers were constantly scrambling to win favor with patrons, government officials, and prominent poets who could introduce them to patrons or officials. Writers also had to make sure that the content of their poems did not insult or offend their patrons. The financial success of Pope's writing freed him from these concerns, but he still participated fully in the social aspects of life in literary London. Pope was part of a circle of brilliant satirists, many of them members of Queen Anne's Tory government who lost political favor when the Whig Party came to power. These friends, including Swift, the author of *Gulliver's Travels*, called themselves the Scriblerus Club, after Martinus Scriblerus, an absurd, pedantic character they created together as a satire of false learning and bad taste. Pope's willingness to satirize his contemporaries, coupled with his fame and his relative wealth, won him the enmity of many prominent English literary figures, including the famous Whig poet Joseph Addison and Pope's former friend Lady Mary Wortley Montagu, a renowned female writer and wit.

Meanwhile, the sweeping scientific and philosophical developments of the **Enlightenment**, or Age of Reason, were changing the way Europeans thought about politics, religion, and the universe in general. Instead of making assumptions about how the world worked and trying to explain events in nature using those assumptions, seventeenth- and eighteenth-century scientists followed the example set by the ancient Greek philosopher Aristotle. They observed nature, performed experiments, and derived their understanding of the universe from those observations. Sir Isaac Newton used these methods to develop his laws of physics. According to Newton, the universe was like a giant clock that worked in a predictable, rational way, according to mathematical laws.

Philosophers followed the scientists' example, questioning traditional assumptions about religion, humankind, and society. René Descartes proved the existence of God using reason and logic. Some philosophers, such as John Locke, tried to use reason to uncover natural laws that could improve society. Other philosophers distrusted the tyrannical power that the European monarchs wielded. Although they did not advocate democracy, these philosophers believed rulers should be guided by reason and should keep their subjects' best interests at heart. Their thinking influenced a generation of "enlightened despots" who ruled using Enlightenment ideals. In general, thinkers in the first half of the eighteenth century had enormous faith in the human ability to reason and stressed the importance of intellectual liberty and rational improvements to society. Pope tempers this emphasis on reason with a heavy dose of satire, particularly in the two long poems *An Essay on Criticism* and *An Essay on Man* (1733–1734).

Severe judgment and acrid satire characterize Pope's later works. Many of these later poems are angry or mocking responses to Pope's critics: in *The Dunciad* (1728), a scathing exposé, Pope skewers the bad writers and pseudo-intellectuals of his day, and in "An Epistle to Arbuthnot" (1735), Pope defends his life, particularly his choice of writing as a vocation, from harsh criticism. Pope died of asthma and dropsy in 1744, at the age of fifty-six.

THEMES, MOTIFS & SYMBOLS

THEMES

THE IMPORTANCE OF BALANCE AND HARMONY

This is perhaps the most important theme in Pope's writings—almost every person, scene, or situation critiqued in his poetry could be remedied with a more balanced perspective or a more harmonious blending of elements. Human beings must balance passion with reason and the body with the mind if they are to be happy and successful. Critics must balance honest judgment with good-natured tact. Poets and thinkers must balance their literary and intellectual ambition with a humble awareness of their own limits. Fear of death must be balanced with the miraculous ability to hope for the best. Generally, Pope distrusts extremes and believes that they should be avoided, advice he doles out in *An Essay on Criticism*. However, in many cases, instead of advising his readers to totally restrain their extreme impulses, he suggests that extremes should be tempered by other, opposite extremes. Balancing passion with reason, for example, is better than suppressing reason altogether. Working in harmony, the two forces retain their positive qualities while curbing each other's negative qualities.

Pope's model of how the universe functions—the Great Chain of Being—retains this sense of balance and harmony. In this model, each creature in the universe works (consciously or unconsciously) for the benefit of all the others. The harmonious blend of the different creatures' unique talents and abilities creates a world that is in accordance with God's divine plan, a philosophy thoroughly explored in *An Essay on Man*.

THE DANGERS OF PRIDE

Pope seems to regard pride as one of the most serious human sins, and he discusses it in his poetry more than he discusses any other sin or failing. According to Pope, pride is particularly dangerous because it blinds us to itself—and to our other sins as well. In part 2 of *An Essay on Criticism*, Pope claims that when we lack "wit" or intelligence, pride "steps in to our defense / And fills up all the

57

mighty Void of Sense!" (209–210). Thus, humans are proud of themselves even when they shouldn't be: they think they are brilliant, beautiful, and important when they are not. They set goals and ambitions that are beyond their abilities, neglecting tasks they are better suited to doing and making themselves look supremely foolish in the process.

In Pope's work, warnings against pride are not reserved for individuals. He also cautions his readers not to display too much pride in humankind's place in the universe. As humans, we think the universe revolves around us, but it doesn't. Humankind has limits and weaknesses, and those limits and weaknesses were prescribed by God. All humans should be aware of their own faults and weaknesses and should work within them. They should not try to study things beyond the scope of their understanding, such as the will of God; instead, they should limit their studies to the human experience. In the second epistle of *An Essay on Man*, Pope writes that "the proper study of mankind is Man" (2). Humans must display gratitude and humility to anyone who knows better than they do, but especially to God.

THE SUPERIORITY OF THE CLASSICAL ERA

As a neoclassical writer, Pope admired and imitated the great writers of the classical era, which included the ancient civilizations of Greece and Rome. These writers, including Horace, Virgil, Homer, and Cicero, whose works were mostly ignored during the Middle Ages, had been rediscovered in the Renaissance. Pope and his contemporaries believed that these writers had come as close to perfection in poetry and philosophy as is humanly possible. They also believed that the rules that governed classical writing and classical society were derived directly from nature. Therefore, all modern writers should follow classical rules when they write: Pope says of the classical poets that "to copy Nature is to copy them" (140) in *An Essay on Criticism*, part 1.

Pope's love and admiration for these ancient societies resulted in a very conservative attitude toward literature. Because he believed that the classical rules governing literature are so close to ideal and the classical writers so supremely gifted, Pope argued that it was presumptuous and prideful of modern writers to believe that they could achieve the heights already achieved by the classical writers. Pope also thought that violating classical rules was sacrilegious, and therefore he distrusted literary innovation. He did not see the literary developments of his own time as innovations but rather as a return to the classical ideals. Pope described political and historical developments in a similar way, claiming in *An Essay on Man* that the eighteenth-century ideal of enlightened, benevolent kings was not a new idea: it was simply a return to the purer, more natural political ideals of the ancients.

MOTIFS

ART

For Pope, the word *art* refers to the deliberate care and craftsmanship that goes into creation. A poet puts art into the creation of a poem; God put art into the creation of the earth. Good literature must be similarly artful—deliberately planned and extremely well crafted, using skills honed in years of study and practice. Pope did not have great faith in the idea that poetry flows naturally from a divine source of inspiration, an idea that flourished in the romantic period. However, he did think that the most artful literature concealed the art that went into it, so that the literature appeared spontaneous and natural. Examples of this kind of art abound in Pope's work, from nature's seamless creations in *An Essay on Man* to Belinda's flawless hairdressing skills in *The Rape of the Lock*.

THE GREAT CHAIN OF BEING

Pope subscribes to the Enlightenment ideal of the chain of being, a vast, cosmic chain that connects all forms of life in the universe. Every creature has its place on the chain, from the lowest, least-developed animals at the bottom of the chain to all-knowing, all-powerful God at the top. Humans are halfway up the chain, between the animals and the angels, which explains humans' dual nature: according to Pope, we possess an animal's body and animal passions but a divine and rational soul. In *An Essay on Man*, Epistle 1, the speaker notes the "strong connections, nice dependencies" (3) that make us what we are, and later he explains the interconnection between all beings on the chain: "Where, one step broken, the great scale's destroyed: / From Nature's chain whatever link you strike, / Tenth or ten thousandth, breaks the chain alike" (244–246).

ACCEPTANCE

Throughout his poems, Pope's characters struggle to accept limits, imperfections, seeming injustice, and the inevitability of death. In *An Essay on Criticism*, Pope cautions writers and critics to work

ALEXANDER POPE

within the limitations of their taste and their talents, as well as within the limits set by the great classical rules that govern literature. In addition, critics need to accept that no work on earth is totally perfect, and Pope extols them to make their judgments with that in mind. In *The Rape of the Lock*, Belinda needs to accept the loss of her curl, as well as the inevitable fact that her beauty will someday fade. In *An Essay on Man*, humans must accept the realities of being human. Humans will never have the powers of animals or of angels, not everyone gets to be rich or famous, life is brief and unpredictable, and we never know when death will come.

Pope saves his most searing satire for people who fail to accept limits and disappointments: the lousy poet who keeps on writing, the prideful man who wants to be "the god of God" (*An Essay on Man*, Epistle 1, 122). Nevertheless, Pope recognizes the difficulty of acceptance. In "Eloisa to Abelard" (1717), Eloisa knows she must accept her fate as a nun, but she cannot completely let go of her impossible desire for Abelard. In "Epistle to Doctor Arbuthnot" (1735), Pope imagines his speaker as a patient, virtuous man who tries to endure the attacks of his enemies but ultimately cannot resist the urge to respond in kind.

SYMBOLS

CHINA JAR

In *The Rape of the Lock*, Pope uses the image of a china jar to symbolize a young woman's virginity. Porcelain china was rare, expensive, and highly valued in the eighteenth century, as valued as virginity. China is also extremely delicate and easy to break, and Pope suggests that virginity was very easy for young women to lose: the flirtatious girls in *The Rape of the Lock* are constantly in danger of accidentally losing their heads at a dance or a masquerade and thus losing their chastity. However, although the china jar represents chastity, it also represents what the jar actually is—a decorative object. By associating chastity with such a decorative item, Pope equates the characters' concerns for women's chastity to their concern for frivolous material things, suggesting that the preservation of chastity is not motivated by morality as much as by the desire to keep up appearances.

HEAT AND COLD

In several of Pope's poems, heat represents intense passion and sexual desire and cold represents a suppression of those qualities. In "Eloisa to Abelard," for example, Pope uses imagery of heat and fire to describe Eloisa's intense sexual passion for Abelard. He contrasts these images of warmth with the images of cold associated with the church where Eloisa lives and the life of chaste religious seclusion she is supposed to lead there. In *An Essay on Man*, Pope uses images of cold to criticize stoic philosophers who completely ignore their passions rather than exercising them with restraint—these people have frozen their virtue. In both cases, the cold imagery is used to suggest a lack of participation in life. For Pope, human life requires some form of the fires of passion, tempered by chilly reason.

LIGHT AND DARKNESS

In the eighteenth century, the word *light* in a poem almost always symbolized reason and intelligence. Indeed, the labels "Enlightenment" and "the Age of Reason" are used interchangeably to describe the era. Light can also represent God, whose divine and perfect mind is the source of all human reason. Darkness, therefore, represents obstacles that block the light of reason: stupidity, ignorance, superstition, and pride. Pope uses these symbols throughout his work, but most extensively in *The Dunciad*, in which the darkness of Dulness opposes and eventually destroys the holy light of reason and learning.

BAY AND LAUREL LEAVES

Wreathes of bay leaves and laurel leaves were awarded to great poets in ancient times, and Pope uses the leaves as a symbol for modern poets, especially those who have been awarded the title of "poet laureate"—a phrase that refers to a poet who has been honored with laurel—or have received the patronage of rich nobles. Pope's attitude toward these poets was usually contemptuous since he disdained poets who flattered their wealthy patrons in order to get money and fame. The fact that Pope adorns them with the leaves associated with his beloved classical poets is ironic since Pope believed many poet laureates of his time to be laughably inferior to the ancient masters. In Book the Fourth of *The Dunciad*, Pope portrays the then-poet laureate of England, Colley Cibber, adorned with a wreath of bay leaves and reclining at the feet of the Goddess of Dulness.

SUMMARY & ANALYSIS

AN ESSAY ON CRITICISM

EXCERPT FROM AN ESSAY ON CRITICISM

'Tis hard to say, if greater want of skill
Appear in writing or in judging ill,
But, of the two, less dangerous is the offence,
To tire our patience, than mislead our sense:
Some few in that, but numbers err in this,
Ten censure wrong for one who writes amiss;
A fool might once himself alone expose,
Now one in verse makes many more in prose.
      'Tis with our judgments as our watches, none
Go just alike, yet each believes his own
In poets as true genius is but rare,
True taste as seldom is the critic's share;
Both must alike from Heaven derive their light,
These born to judge, as well as those to write.
Let such teach others who themselves excel,
And censure freely who have written well.
Authors are partial to their Wit, 'tis true,
But are not critics to their judgment too?
      Yet if we look more closely, we shall find
Most have the seeds of judgment in their mind;
Nature affords at least a glimmering light;
The lines, though touched but faintly, are drawn right.
But as the slightest sketch, if justly traced,
Is by ill coloring but the more disgraced,
So by false learning is good sense defaced.
Some are bewildered in the maze of schools,
And some made coxcombs nature meant but fools.
In search of wit these lose their common sense,
And then turn critics in their own defence.
Each burns alike, who can, or cannot write,
Or with a rival's or an eunuch's spite.
All fools have still an itching to deride,
And fain would be upon the laughing aide;

If *Maevius* scribble in *Apollo's* spight,
There are, who judge still worse than he can write.

.   .   .   .   .

Of all the causes which conspire to blind
Man's erring judgment, and misguide the mind,
What the weak head with strongest bias rules,
Is pride, the never failing vice of fools.
Whatever nature has in worth denied
She gives in large recruits of needful pride:
For as in bodies, thus in souls, we find
What wants in blood and spirits swelled with wind:
Pride, where wit fails, steps in to our deference,
And fills up all the mighty void of sense:
If once right reason drives that cloud away,
Truth breaks upon us with resistless day.
Trust not yourself; but your defects to know,
Make use of every friend—and every foe.
    A little learning is a dangerous thing;
Drink deep, or taste not the Pierian spring:
There shallow draughts intoxicate the brain,
And drinking largely sobers us again.
Fired at first sight with what the Muse imparts,
In fearless youth we tempt the heights of arts,
While from the bounded level of our mind
Short views we take, nor see the lengths behind:
But more advanced, behold with strange surprise
New distant scenes of endless science rise!
So pleased at first the towering Alps we try,
Mount o'er the vales, and seem to tread the sky;
The eternal snows appear already past,
And the first clouds and mountains seem the last:
But those attained, we tremble to survey
The growing labours of the lengthened way;
The increasing prospect tires our wandering eyes,
Hills peep o'er hills, and Alps on Alps arise!
    A perfect judge will read each work of wit
With the same spirit that its author writ;
Survey the whole, not seek slight faults to find
Where Nature moves, and Rapture warms the mind:
Nor lose, for that malignant dull delight,
The generous pleasure to be charmed with wit.

ALEXANDER POPE

SUMMARY

At the beginning of this long poem, the speaker says that criticism is as much of an art as writing and requires just as much talent. True taste in a critic, which enables him to judge well, is as rare as true genius in an author. Most people are born with the foundations of good taste, but their taste is spoiled by bad education or by ambitions to succeed beyond their abilities. For example, some people become critics because they are not talented enough to be poets and want to take out their frustrations on other writers. These critics are even worse than bad writers. The speaker advises aspiring critics to be aware of their own limitations: nature limits each person's abilities, and it is wisest to observe them. According to the speaker, critics should follow nature's example when they write. There are many beautiful things in nature, which were created by the "art" of a divine force, but the way in which they were created is not obvious. This lack of ostentation becomes a kind of restraint. The literary rules of ancient Greece, which call for a balance between artistic indulgence and restraint, are extremely close to the rules of nature.

In ancient times, the purpose of criticism was to enhance the reader's appreciation of literature. Over time, critics began to ruin literary texts by rewriting them or devising mechanical rules for the construction of dull poetry. To be a true critic, one must return to the ancient writers and study their work, which is so close to the rules of nature. The speaker notes that some brilliant classical writers got away with not following the rules. Their work is so good that it is beyond criticism. Modern critics should hesitate to pass judgment on the classical writers since the writers may be using techniques too brilliant and sophisticated for us to understand. In every way, modern writers and critics should defer to their classical predecessors.

Part 2 lists some impediments that can get in the way of good critical judgment. The first is pride, which can blind a person to his own stupidity. A good critic must not trust himself to judge his own intelligence. Instead, he must listen to his friends and even his enemies. Another problem is an incomplete education: according to the speaker, "a little learning is a dangerous thing" (215). In addition, critics should focus on the work as a whole, not on minor problems. According to the speaker, expecting any work to be perfect all the way through is absurd. "A faultless piece" of writing has never existed (253)—and never will exist. Critics should not place too much importance on any one aspect of writing, such as cleverness, use of language, or adherence to meter. Critics should also avoid extremes—only a foolish person is always wildly enthusiastic or negative. Finally, critics should try to remain unbiased, judging by merit rather than according to their political, intellectual, or national prejudices.

Critics should also avoid envy. When a critic writes negatively about a work because he is envious of it, it is the critic—and not the work itself—that winds up looking bad. The speaker reminds us that in ancient times the purpose of criticism was to praise good literature, even if it was not the best. The speaker says, "To err is human; to forgive, divine" (525). If a critic must show disdain and anger in his criticism, he should save it for serious literary crimes, such as obscenity and dullness or stupidity. The speaker recognizes that he lives in morally lax times, in which blasphemous writing prevails.

Part 3 begins with the speaker explaining that knowing good writing from bad is not enough. Critics must also have good manners, be truthful, and be good-natured, admitting errors when they make them. They must try to be honest without being blunt. They should not be afraid to criticize a good writer since people who deserve praise are also the best at handling criticism. It is less important to be honest with stupid, untalented people since critics will never be able to change how they write. The speaker reminds us that there are critics who are just as shamelessly inept as these stupid writers.

Then the speaker wonders where an unbiased, well-educated, well-bred, sincere man can be found, one who is humble and who enjoys giving praise within reason. He gives examples of critics of ancient Greece and Rome who were like this. According to the speaker, all this critical wisdom was lost when Rome fell and the Middle Ages began. It was not rediscovered until the Renaissance, when humanist scholars rediscovered classical texts. This interest in classics spread to seventeenth-century France, where critics revived the old classical poetic rules. Most English writers resisted those rules, except for some wise writers and critics, including William Walsh (Pope's early mentor).

At the end of the poem, the speaker addresses the dead Walsh, saying that Walsh taught the speaker to sing but also to restrain himself. Without his guide, the speaker no longer attempts to reach poetic heights and will be content if he can educate a few people without fearing derision or desiring fame. The speaker is happy to praise people but not afraid to blame them, and he says that he himself is not free from faults nor too vain to fix them.

ANALYSIS

An Essay on Criticism lays out the principles of the neoclassical movement in England. Above all else, this poem emphasizes the classical ideals of order, balance, and harmony. Many of Pope's major complaints about bad criticism center around the importance of order and the need of limiting extremes—and the lack of these traits in contemporary criticism. Critics and writers who overreach their limits, focus too much on one aspect of literature, favor one school of thought or nationality above another, write cruel or obsequious criticism, refuse to follow any rules, or follow rules too strictly are all flawed, and they could all benefit from a more balanced, harmonious outlook.

In his frequent references to the importance of "art," Pope emphasizes order. To Pope and his contemporaries, the word *art* had a slightly different meaning than it has today—back then, it referred to the craftsmanship that went into a piece of writing. To do something artfully meant years of practice and study, and good art was extremely well planned, well constructed, and consistent with established literary rules and practices. In many ways, Pope followed his own literary rules: it is no coincidence that Pope called this poem an "essay." Like the five-paragraph essays that modern high school students are taught to write, the poem is carefully crafted and presents clear, concise arguments. It is organized into three parts, which can be easily identified by the reader. The first part introduces the topic and identifies Pope's general points, the second identifies causes that hinder critical judgment, and the third gives rules for the manners of a critic.

The poem is also written in a very strict, orderly verse form. Pope wrote in *heroic couplets*, rhymed pairs of iambic pentameter lines (lines of ten syllables each, alternating stressed and unstressed syllables). Generally, these couplets were witty and concise, expressing a complete idea within the limited space of two lines. Many of Pope's couplets can stand alone, out of the context of the poem they are part of. For example, this couplet from *An Essay on Criticism* succinctly expresses one of the major ideas of the poem: "True ease in writing comes from art, not chance / As those move easiest who have learned to dance" (362–363).

Upon first reading, Pope's couplets seem very breezy and effortless. One of the most important—and difficult—aspects of "art" as Pope defines it is that art should be almost impossible to detect. The poet had to be so artful that he could hide the art he used to write his poem. This follows the classical ideal established by the famous Roman critic Horace, who said that "the art is to conceal the art."

Pope believed that to conceal craftsmanship was to follow the examples of nature and God. Some readers might imagine that because they valued artifice and craftsmanship so much, the neo-classical writers were not interested in the natural world. But Pope saw God, and the natural world God acted through, as the supreme artist. To Pope, God designed and maintained the ultimate work of art—the universe. At the beginning of the poem, Pope describes how nature creates things without making its craftsmanship felt. He sees this lack of "show" and "pomp" as a kind of restraint or modesty, which human writers should follow.

The qualities valued by classical writers—structure, craftsmanship, and restraint—came directly from nature, according to Pope. The classical rules governing writing and criticism, therefore, are almost as perfect as God's laws and should be followed almost as religiously. This belief is typical of the neoclassical period, which emphasized tradition as much as it emphasized order. Pope and other neoclassi-cal writers believed that the classical period was a golden age, with geniuses that the modern age could never hope to produce. This is one of the reasons why Pope warns against pride so much in the poem, as well as why he also encourages critics and writers alike to know the limits of their taste and abilities. It also explains his disgust with critics who made changes to classic literary texts.

Pope also distrusts innovation because he believes that any mod-ern advances will not improve on classical models. The classical writers have already figured out the best way to do things, and mod-ern writers shouldn't try to meddle with their system. "Moderns, beware!" (163) Pope writes, after comparing the classical writers to kings who can bend their own laws: modern writers are not elevated enough to experiment. Alternatively, if modern writers "must offend" against classical laws, they should only offend in a way that classical writers have already done. As the end of the poem, the speaker claims he will no longer make any attempt to "rise" poeti-cally without the guidance of his mentor. Pope believed it was pride-ful and foolish for modern poets to think they could reach poetic heights without the guidance of a mentor or of the classical masters themselves. It is more appropriate to set humbler, more realistic goals, trying the "short excursions" into verse Pope mentions at the end of the poem.

Despite his emphasis on the importance of rules, Pope recognizes that even limits have limits. His disapproval of excess extends to those critics who, when discussing a literary work, obsess over mechanical details, such as meter, or dissect a work to find minor flaws. These critics fail to understand that the value of a literary work rests in the effect it has as a whole, not in its minor problems. Since writers, especially modern writers, are only human, it is foolish to expect perfection from them.

THE RAPE OF THE LOCK

ALEXANDER POPE

EXCERPT FROM CANTO 1

And now, unveiled, the toilet stands displayed,
Each silver vase in mystic order laid.
First, robed in white, the nymph intent adores
With head uncovered, the cosmetic powers.
A heavenly image in the glass appears,
To that she bends, to that her eyes she rears;
The inferior priestess, at her altar's side,
Trembling, begins the sacred rites of pride.
Unnumbered treasures ope at once, and here
The various offerings of the world appear;
From each she nicely culls with curious toil,
And decks the goddess with the glittering spoil.
This casket India's glowing gems unlocks,
And all Arabia breathes from yonder box.
The tortoise here and elephant unite,
Transformed to combs, the speckled and the white.
Here files of pins extend their shining rows,
Puffs, powders, patches, Bibles, billet-doux.
Now awful beauty puts on all its arms;
The fair each moment rises in her charms,
Repairs her smiles, awakens every grace,
And calls forth all the wonders of her face;
Sees by degrees a purer blush arise,
And keener lightnings quicken in her eyes.
The busy sylphs surround their darling care;
These set the head, and those divide the hair,
Some fold the sleeve, while others plait the gown;
And Betty's praised for labours not her own.

SUMMARY

The poem begins with a letter to Arabella Fermor, the young lady to whom Pope has dedicated the poem. He tells her that the poem was written to amuse only a few people but was published against his will before it was finished. Since then, Pope has added the "machinery," which is the part played by gods, angels, or demons in a poem. Pope adds that he always mentions the loss of Miss Fermor's hair with reverence, and he says that Belinda resembles her "in nothing but in beauty."

Canto 1 begins with the announcement of the poem's topics: the trouble that love can cause and the way that "mighty contests" (2) or battles can arise from trivial things. He then addresses a few questions to his muse, asking her why a mannered nobleman would assault a beautiful woman and why such a woman would reject a lord. Then the action of the poem begins. It is late morning, but Belinda's "guardian Sylph" (20) keeps her asleep by sending her a "morning dream" (22).

In the dream, a handsome young man whispers in Belinda's ear. He uses poetic language to tell her that she is surrounded by countless magical sprites, which hang around her when she is at the theater or driving her carriage around the park. He also tells her the spirits were once women. When they die, women's frivolous interests, such as playing cards and riding in carriages, survive as spirits. These spirits then take the form of one of four elements, the one that is closest to their character. Argumentative women become fire spirits, or salamanders. Soft women become water nymphs. Serious, prudish women sink into mischievous earth spirits, or gnomes. Flirtatious coquettes become airy sprites called sylphs. Chaste, beautiful maidens are held by sylphs, who, now that they are spirits, can take on whatever shape and sex they please. The sylphs keep the maidens from giving in to sexual temptation at balls and masquerades. Women who are too vain, according to the dream, are embraced by gnomes. They are obsessed with the idea of breaking hearts and marrying rich noblemen.

The dream man goes on to explain that when a woman seems to act somewhat immorally, it is only her sylph keeping the woman virtuous: by making a girl flirtatious and easily distracted, the sylph keeps her from focusing on one man long enough to be seduced by him.

Next, the dream man reveals that he is Ariel, a sylph who watches over Belinda. He warns her that he has foreseen that a terrible event will happen that day, but he does not know the circumstances of it. Belinda must beware of everything, especially men.

Belinda is awakened when her lapdog, Shock, licks her face. The first thing she sees is a billet-doux, or love letter, and it makes her forget her vision. She begins to get dressed. The speaker compares Belinda's morning beauty ritual to the performance of a priestess at an altar—she is performing her "sacred rites of Pride" (128). He describes her maid as an "inferior priestess" (127) and her cosmetics as holy offerings from around the world. The sylphs all work to get her ready, some parting her hair or folding her dress, although her maid gets the credit for their work.

ANALYSIS

The letter that precedes the poem reveals that the poem is based on a real event: the event took place between two prominent Catholic families in Pope's social circle. Lord Petre cut off a lock of Arabella Fermor's hair, and the young people's families fell into strife as a result. Another member of Pope's circle asked Pope to write a light poem that would put the episode into a humorous perspective and reconcile the two families. The teasing but polite attitude Pope displays in his letter to Arabella shows that reconciliation is his goal— he wants Arabella to be able to laugh at the event, not to take offense at his mockery of her.

Canto 1 begins with an invocation to a muse, a poetic act that immediately establishes this poem in the epic tradition. Epic poems, such as the *Iliad* and *Odyssey*, by the ancient Greek poet Homer, always begin by calling forth, or invoking, the muse. The topics Pope proposes to cover—love and war—are grand, sweeping themes that were considered appropriate subjects for epic poetry. However, *The Rape of the Lock* is not a true epic, but a mock epic, a poem that uses the elaborate, formal conventions of the epic to describe a commonplace or insignificant subject. Indeed, Pope called his work "An Heroi-Comical Poem." In this case, the "am'rous causes" will not be the grand love of Greek heroes, but rather the flirtations between idle, privileged noblemen and noblewomen. The "contests" will be card games and flirtatious tussles, not the great battles of epic tradition. Belinda's beautiful face will not launch a thousand ships, as Helen of Troy's does in the *Iliad*; rather, it will inspire nonsensical arguments between fops and flirts. The poem satirizes the misguided values of a society that mistakes small matters for serious ones while failing to attend to issues of genuine importance.

With Belinda's dream, Pope introduces the "machinery" of the poem—the supernatural powers that influence the action from behind the scenes. Here, the sprites that watch over Belinda are meant to mimic the gods of the Greek and Roman traditions, who are sometimes benevolent and sometimes malicious but always intimately involved in earthly events. Of the four kinds of sprites that Ariel describes, the airy sylphs have a particular concern for Belinda because she is an "airy Coquette," just like they were in life. This will be the aspect of feminine nature with which the poem is most concerned.

Pope begins to sketch this character of the "coquette" in the first canto. He draws the portrait indirectly, using the characteristics of the sylphs rather than of Belinda herself. The sylphs' priorities reveal that the central concerns of womanhood, at least for women of Belinda's class, are social ones. Women's "joy in gilded Chariots" indicates an obsession with pomp and superficial splendor, while "love of Ombre," a fashionable card game, suggests frivolity. The erotic charge of this social world, in turn, prompts another crucial concern: the protection of chastity. These are women who value the prospect of marrying to advantage above all, and they have learned at an early age how to promote themselves and manipulate their suitors without compromising themselves. The sylphs become an **allegory** for the mannered conventions that govern female social behavior. Principles such as honor and chastity have become no more than another part of conventional interaction. Pope makes it clear that these women are not conducting themselves on the basis of abstract moral principles but are governed by an elaborate social mechanism. This mechanism is fittingly caricatured in the machinery of the sylphs.

While Pope's technique of employing supernatural machinery allows him to critique the societal idea of a coquette, it also helps to keep the satire light and to exonerate individual women from too severe a judgment. If Belinda has all the typical female foibles, it is only because she has been educated and trained to act in this way, a point Pope makes clear. Society as a whole is as much to blame as she is.

The portrayal of Belinda at her dressing table introduces some mock-heroic motifs that will run through the poem. The scene of her toilette is rendered first as a religious sacrament, in which Belinda herself is the priestess and her image in the looking glass is the goddess she serves. This parody of the religious rites before a battle then gives way to another kind of mock-epic scene, that of the ritualized arming of the hero. Combs, pins, and cosmetics take the place of weapons as "awful Beauty puts on all its arms."

Several years after the publication of *The Rape of the Lock*, Pope's friend Jonathan Swift would write a poem about a woman whose artificial beauty rituals help conceal her disgustingly hideous face. The poem displays the misogyny that Swift, Pope, and some of their contemporaries are often accused of displaying. Pope also uses the dressing table to expose feminine artificiality, but his judgment is less harsh than that of Swift. The lofty, stylized description of the dressing table accentuates the frivolity of Belinda's behavior, and Pope certainly disapproves of her turning vanity into a religion. But Belinda's cosmetics do not mask a hideous face. Rather, they show off her natural beauty, just as Pope believes that art can show the beauty of nature to its best effect.

EXCERPT FROM CANTO 2

> This nymph, to the destruction of mankind,
> Nourished two locks, which graceful hung behind
> In equal curls, and well conspired to deck
> With shining ringlets her smooth ivory neck.
> Love in these labyrinths his slaves detains,
> And mighty hearts are held in slender chains.
> With hairy sprindges we the birds betray,
> Slight lines of hair surprize the finny prey,
> Fair tresses man's imperial race ensnare,
> And beauty draws us with a single hair.

SUMMARY

Belinda and her friends—beautiful young ladies and young men—are taking a boat ride from London to Hampton Court Palace. The speaker describes Belinda's great beauty and her flirtatiousness. Her eyes are like the sun because they are bright but also because they "shine on all alike" (14). Belinda has two locks of hair hanging down her neck. The speaker says the locks will be the "destruction of mankind" (19), and he describes the locks as labyrinths and traps that imprison men with love.

One of Belinda's companions, the "adventurous Baron" (29), wants to capture the locks for himself and tries to decide whether to get them by deceit or by force. The speaker comments that when a lover is successful, few people wonder if he used deceit or force.

As Belinda enjoys her boat ride, the sylph Ariel directs the other spirits to protect her. They are invisible to mortal eyes, but Ariel explains to the fairies and spirits that they have various important tasks in the world: they guide planets, control weather, and even guard the British throne. But the primary role of Ariel and his servants is to attend and protect beautiful young women. They curl the girls' hair and inspire them in dreams with new beauty ideas. Today, though, omens warn of a disaster. Belinda may lose her virginity, staining her "honour" (107), or she may stain her gown. She might "forget her prayers, or miss a masquerade" (108). Each of the spirits is in charge of a different part of Belinda's outfit. One guards her fan, one her earrings, one her favorite lock of hair, one her lapdog. Fifty sylphs have the very important job of guarding her petticoat.

Ariel concludes by warning the spirits that if they neglect their posts, they will be punished—wedged into the eye of a needle or bound on the wheel of a hot-chocolate machine. The spirits take their posts and anxiously await the "dire event" (141) that Ariel foresaw.

ANALYSIS

From the first, Pope describes Belinda's beauty as divine. In a sense, this praise is ironic, reflecting negatively on a system of values in which external characteristics rank higher than moral or intellectual ones. But the speaker also shows a real reverence for his heroine's physical and social charms, and certainly Pope has some interest in flattering Arabella Fermor, the real-life woman on whom Belinda is based. In order for his poem to achieve the desired reconciliation, it must not offend.

Pope also exhibits his appreciation for the ways in which physical beauty is an art form. Throughout Pope's poetry, he emphasizes the importance of art and craftsmanship. In his description of Belinda's legendary locks of hair, Pope recognizes that the locks, which appear so natural, are actually carefully contrived, as elaborately constructed as a trap or a labyrinth. Despite the fact that he censures Belinda for her vanity and frivolity, Pope continues to admire her for her ability to use art or craftsmanship to complement her natural gifts. As he explains at length in *An Essay on Criticism*, Pope believes that craftsmanship and the care of true "art," or artifice, is essential to good literature. He especially appreciates art that although extremely well planned and well constructed seems natural and effortless, like the effect of Belinda's curls. In a sense, Pope may consider the machinations of the lady's dressing table similar to his own literary art.

But aesthetics are not everything for Pope. He also believes that art should serve a greater social or moral purpose, and Belinda's curls inspire nothing but shallow admiration. Pope suggests that the general human readiness to worship beauty amounts to a kind of sacrilege. The cross that Belinda wears around her neck serves an ornamental—rather than symbolic or religious—function. Because of this, the speaker says, it can be adored by "Jews" (8) and "infidels" (8) as readily as by Christians. And there is some ambiguity about whether any of the admirers are really valuing the cross itself or the "white breast" (7) on which it lies.

The most important worshiper of Belinda's beauty is the Baron. His ritual sacrifices performed in the predawn hours are another mock-heroic element of the poem, mimicking the epic tradition of sacrificing to the gods before an important battle or journey. In the Baron's case, the grandeur of the epic language only accentuates the triviality of his goals. The fact that he discards all his other love tokens in these preparations reveals his capriciousness as a lover. Earnest devotional prayer is replaced by the self-indulgent sighs of the lover in this parodic scene.

In Canto 1, the religious imagery surrounding Belinda's grooming rituals gives way to images taken from the military and warfare. Here, the same pattern holds. Her curls are compared to a trap perfectly calibrated to ensnare the enemy. Yet the character of female coyness is such that it seeks simultaneously to attract and repel, so the counterpart to the enticing ringlets is the formidable petticoat. The speaker describes this undergarment as a defensive armament comparable to the shield of Achilles in the *Iliad* and supported in its function of protecting the maiden's chastity by the invisible might of fifty sylphs. These sylphs are charged with protecting her not from failure but from too great a success in attracting men. This paradoxical situation dramatizes the contradictory values and motives implied in the era's sexual conventions.

Canto 2 emphasizes the poem's sexual allegory. The title of the poem already associates the cutting of Belinda's hair with a more explicit sexual conquest. In this section, Pope hints at the "rape" of the title by using words such as *ravish* and referring to the ways lovers use "fraud or force" to reach their sexual goals. When Ariel speculates about the possible forms the "dire event" (141) might take, he includes a breach of chastity ("Diana's law"). In the sylphs' defensive efforts, Belinda's petticoat becomes the battlefield that requires the most extensive fortifications. The rape of the lock thus stands in for a literal rape or at least represents a threat to Belinda's chastity more serious than just the mere theft of a curl.

Although the sylphs worry that Belinda might lose her chastity, they devote a good deal of concern to the prospect of much more trivial "disasters." They worry that the nymph might lose her virginity, but they also worry that she will mess up her dress. Belinda might "lose her heart" (109), but she might also lose her necklace; she could forget to pray or forget to attend a dance.

EXCERPT FROM CANTO 3

Just in that instant, anxious Ariel sought
The close recesses of the virgin's thought;
As on the nosegay in her breast reclined,
He watched the ideas rising in her mind,
Sudden he viewed, in spite of all her art,
An earthly lover lurking at her heart.
Amazed, confused, he found his power expired,
Resigned to fate, and with a sigh retired.

SUMMARY

Belinda, in search of fame, challenges two adventurous knights to a popular card game called ombre. Each of her sylphs takes charge of a card in her hand. The speaker describes the card game as a great battle, with the "velvet plain" (44) of the card table as a battlefield. The game begins with Belinda declaring, "Let spades be trumps!" (46). Her cards, described as soldiers, are initially successful. Then fate changes and favors the Baron. When the Baron's knave of diamonds triumphs over Belinda's queen of hearts, Belinda knows she's losing and turns pale and trembles. But then her king of hearts avenges the queen by destroying the Baron's ace of hearts. Belinda wins the game, and her shouts of triumph echo throughout the surrounding landscape. The speaker of the poem exclaims, "O thoughtless mortals!" (101) and laments that humans rejoice and despair too quickly, not knowing what fate has in store for them. He notes that soon Belinda's honors will be snatched away, and this day will be cursed forever.

After the game, the friends enjoy several cups of freshly brewed coffee. Belinda's sylphs hover around her as she drinks, protecting her dress from spills. According to the speaker, coffee is what gives politicians their crafty intelligence. This coffee induces the Baron to think up crafty new ways to gain possession of Belinda's lock of hair. The speaker warns the Baron to stop before it is too late—and to recall that Scylla, a princess from Greek mythology, was turned into a bird as punishment for stealing a lock of hair from her father.

Just then Clarissa, one of Belinda's friends, takes out a "two-edged" (128) weapon—a pair of scissors. The speaker compares Clarissa to a lady from a medieval romance who helps prepare her knight for battle by bringing him his weapons. The Baron takes the scissors. As Belinda bends over her coffee, he makes two attempts to cut her lock. Both times, the sylphs protect her by blowing away the hair and making her look behind her. Then Ariel looks into Belinda's heart and sees that she loves someone. Ariel is shocked and finds himself powerless to protect her.

The Baron tries a third time to cut the lock, and this time he succeeds. In the process he cuts in half a sylph who had interfered at the last moment. The sylph will grow back together, but the lock has been severed "forever and forever" (154).

A horrified Belinda screams louder than a woman does when she finds her husband or lapdog is dead or when a precious china jar breaks. The Baron proudly declares his victory, announcing that his fame will continue as long as fish swim in streams, as long as a little pillow decorates a lady's bed, and as long as other traditions and pastimes of high society, such as the driving of carriages around Hyde Park.

The speaker ends the canto by telling us that steel, which symbolizes military might, can destroy the works of gods and humans alike. He asks rhetorically, why should Belinda be surprised that her hair was conquered by steel?

ANALYSIS

This canto contains many classic examples of Pope's masterful use of **zeugma** (a figure of speech in which a word refers to two words in the same sentence), which demonstrate his blending of poetic style and comedic content. For example, Pope describes Hampton Court Palace as the place where Queen Anne "dost sometimes counsel take—and sometimes tea" (8). One does not "take" tea in the same way one takes counsel, and the effect of the zeugma is to show the royal residence as a place that houses both serious matters of state and frivolous social occasions. The reader is asked to contemplate that paradox and to reflect on the relative value and importance of these two different kinds of activity.

A similar point is made in the second and third stanzas of this canto. Here, against the gossip and chatter of the young lords and ladies, Pope opens a window onto more serious matters that are occurring "meanwhile" (19) and elsewhere, including criminal trials and executions and economic exchange. Although the judges and merchants Pope describes in this passage are not as idle as Belinda and her friends—they have careers and make important decisions that affect the nation—they may not be any less frivolous. The "hungry judges" (21), for example, hurry to give out death sentences so that they can get to lunch on time. The judges value their lunch breaks over the sanctity of human life, refusing to invest the time and deliberation that a matter of life and death demands. Clearly, the young lords and ladies on the boat are not the only ones who favor trivial subjects over serious moral matters. Their flaws reflect the flaws of society as a whole.

Pope's description of the card game evokes the battle scenes of the great epic poems. In doing so, Pope suggests that the energy and passion once applied to brave and serious purposes are now expended on such insignificant trials as games and gambling, which often become a mere front for flirtation. The structure of the three tries by which the lock is cut is a convention of heroic challenges, particularly in the romance genre. The romance is further invoked in the image of Clarissa arming the Baron—not with a real weapon, however, but with a pair of sewing scissors.

Unlike the armies clashing in the Trojan War, Belinda is not a real adversary, and Pope makes it plain that her resistance—and, by implication, her subsequent distress—is to some degree an affectation. He makes Belinda's grief seem even less authentic by using anticlimax to describe her screams. To achieve a powerful rhetorical effect, writers often make a list that builds toward a climax—each item in the list is grander and more significant than the last, culminating in a final item that is the grandest and most significant of all. For example, a writer might say a certain event has repercussions "for our city, for our state, for our nation, and for the world!" A list that builds to an anticlimax, however, places the concepts in the reverse order, raising the reader's expectations at the beginning with sweeping rhetoric and concluding with inanity. Pope compares

Belinda's shrieks to the cries a woman makes "when husbands or when lapdogs breathe their last, / Or when rich china vessels, fallen from high, in glittering dust and painted fragments lie" (158–159). If a broken piece of china gets the same number of screams—or more—than the death of a husband, the screams can hardly be considered heartfelt.

The elevation of the trivial to the heroic begun in the melodramatic descriptions of Belinda's screams continues in the ironic comparison of the Baron's feat to the conquest of nations, as well as in the speaker's assertion that the Baron has severed the lock forever. This line borrows its solemnity and its sense of the eternal from the Bible, in which the phrase *forever and ever* is frequently used to describe the lasting glory of God's kingdom. Thus, the loss of Belinda's lock (which will, of course, grow back) takes on the scope and significance of one of the most sacred teachings of Christianity. Similarly, Pope uses the phrase to skewer time: if the consequences of such a seemingly trivial action can last for eternity, how long can eternity be? This question is answered in the Baron's victorious speech at the end of the canto. The Baron's concept of eternity is as limited as his narrow social sphere. If he believes that lovely noblewomen will ride in coaches around Hyde Park for as long as fish swim in streams, perhaps "forever and forever" (154) is an appropriately banal phrase to describe the cutting of a lock of hair.

EXCERPT FROM CANTO 4

"For ever cursed be this detested day,
Which snatched my best, my favorite curl away!
Happy! ah, ten times happy had I been,
If Hampton-Court these eyes had never seen!
Yet am not I the first mistaken maid,
By love of courts to numerous ills betrayed.
Oh, had I rather unadmired remained
In some lone isle, or distant northern land;
Where the gilt chariot never marks the way,
Where none learn ombre, none ev'r taste bohea!
There kept my charms concealed from mortal eye,
Like roses that in deserts bloom and die.
What moved my mind with youthful lords to roam?
Oh, had I stayed, and said my prayers at home!
'Twas this, the morning omens seemed to tell;

Thrice from my trembling hand the patch-box fell;
The tottering china shook without a wind,
Nay, Poll sat mute, and Shock was most unkind!
A Sylph too warned me of the threats of fate,
In mystic visions, now believed too late!
See the poor remnants of these slighted hairs!
My hands shall rend what even thy rapine spares:
These, in two sable ringlets taught to break,
Once gave new beauties to the snowie neck.
The sister-lock now sits uncouth, alone,
And in its fellow's fate foresees its own;
Uncurled it hangs, the fatal sheers demands;
And tempts once more thy sacrilegious hands.
Oh, hadst thou, cruel! been content to seize
Hairs less in sight, or any hairs but these!"

SUMMARY

In this canto, the speaker begins by telling us that Belinda feels more rage, resentment, and despair about her stolen lock than kings feel when they are captured in battle or the virgin goddess Diana felt when her cloak was pinned wrong. Her feelings developed as a result of a gnome named Umbriel going deep into the earth to search for Spleen, a goddess who symbolizes vague, self-indulgent melancholy, at the moment when Ariel left Belinda.

Umbriel finds Spleen in a dark, gloomy cave, in which she spends her time sighing in bed, with a migraine headache and a pain in her side. She has two servants, Ill Nature and Affectation. Ill Nature is wrinkled and old, full of prayers and insults. Affectation has rosy cheeks but pretends to be delicate and weak, showing off her illnesses and her pretty nightgown. Spleen's cave is foggy and filled with hallucinatory images, including the images of angels in stage machinery and ordinary objects that can talk and walk.

The gnome brings Spleen an herb as an offering. He addresses her as a queen, who rules over women between the ages of fifteen and fifty. He says that Spleen is responsible for giving women fits of hysteria and fits of poetry. The gnome tells Spleen that there is one nymph who disdains Spleen's power and keeps many people happy. But, as the gnome continues, if Spleen can make Belinda upset, it will give the whole world the vague melancholy that Spleen represents. The gnome swears this is true by the acts he has performed in order to give girls the spleen, including giving beautiful girls pimples, making women commit adultery, and turning a lapdog sick.

Spleen grants the gnome's request, although she looks discontented and "seems to reject" (80) it. She gives him a bag filled with female "signs, sobs, and passions" (84), as well as a vial full of delicate sorrows and tears. Rejoicing, the gnome flies up to the surface with the gifts.

There the gnome finds Belinda being comforted by her friend Thalestris and empties the bag over Belinda's head. The contents of the bag fill Belinda with great anger. Thalestris encourages Belinda's anger. She asks Belinda if it was for this that Belinda took such good care of her hair, enduring the weight of her hair decorations. Thalestris wonders if the Baron, whom she describes as a rapist, will display the stolen lock for all to see. She says this is an insult to Belinda's honor, and honor is more important to women than comfort or even virtue. Thalestris envisions the horrible way in which people will gossip about Belinda, ruining her reputation. She wonders how she, Thalestris, could possibly help Belinda in that situation, noting further that it would be shameful to appear to be Belinda's friend. It would be better for the earth, sea, and air to fall into chaos and for fashionable people to stop driving around Hyde Park Circle so that grass grows upon it than for the Baron to display Belinda's hair as a trophy forever.

Thalestris turns to her boyfriend, Sir Plume, and insists that he get Belinda's lock back. Sir Plume, a vain fop, opens his snuffbox and makes a brief speech, which consists almost entirely of slang expressions and half-finished sentences. In the speech, he weakly demands that the Baron return the lock. The Baron replies with a long, dramatic speech. He swears by the "sacred Lock" (133) that for as long as he lives, he will display the lock on his own hand.

At this point, Umbriel the gnome breaks open another gift from Spleen, the vial of sorrows. Belinda becomes beautifully sad. She too makes a speech, in which she curses the day that took her favorite curl away from her. She says she wishes she had spent her life in some distant land, far from society, in which her beauty would have gone unobserved. She describes the omens she saw that morning—her pets were unkind to her, a china jar rattled although there was no wind, she dropped things during her morning toilette, a sylph gave her a warning in a dream. Now she believes these visions, but it is too late. In her grief, she says, she will pull out the hair that is left. Now the one remaining lock hangs down messy and vulnerable, tempting the Baron to cut it off too. Belinda ends her speech by wishing the Baron could have taken "hairs less in sight" than the lock he cut—"any hairs but these!" (175)

ANALYSIS

Canto 4 opens with another example of anticlimax. By following a description of the pathos of kings imprisoned in battle with the irritation of a woman whose dress is disheveled, Pope implies that Belinda's social world is unable to make distinctions between genuine disaster and trivial inconveniences. Umbriel's journey to the Cave of Spleen mimics another epic convention, the journey to the underworld. Similar journeys are made by the heroes of the *Odyssey* and the *Aeneid*. Since the spleen was once thought to be the cause of malaise and depression, Pope uses the allegorical figure of Spleen to explore the sources and nature of Belinda's feelings.

The presence of Spleen's two handmaidens reveals that despite her goddesslike status, Spleen does not inspire noble emotions. Instead, women who display spleen are ill-natured fakers. Because delicate women were considered feminine and desirable, it was fashionable for women to affect weakness or illness. Pope's portrait of Affectation shows that he thinks these women's maladies are just another form of feminine artifice, an excuse to show off a pretty new nightdress and a languid, sexy demeanor. The presence of Affectation reinforces the idea that Belinda's grief is less than pure—it is "affected," or put on, as decorative as her curl was.

During Pope's time, the idea that women were irrational, emotionally unstable, and liable to fits of malaise or spleen was accepted as medical fact. Indeed, Pope's description of Spleen and her handmaidens reflects the common eighteenth-century psychological and physiological stereotypes about women. Since he is no longer directly referring to Belinda but to women in general, Pope can afford to make harsher judgments. The darkness of the cave, as well as the strange, twisted visions that haunt it, represent women's irrational nature: while in the throes of spleen, women were certainly far from the light of reason. And, as Umbriel declares when he addresses Spleen, she rules all women "from fifty to fifteen" (58)—roughly the period during which women menstruate and bear children. This assertion links spleen even more closely to women's bodily rhythms. In addition, many of the images also reflect a fear of women's sexuality. The moistness and darkness of the cave suggest the mysterious territory of the female body, and at least one spleen-induced vision is a mocking reference to female sexual desire, which was thought to be uncontrollable and animalistic.

Another symptom of Spleen seems to be the desire to write poetry or plays. Throughout much of his work, Pope's contempt for women writers is strong. In this canto, he equates the desire to write poetry with a "hysteric fit" and implies that women write plays in order to rid themselves of some kind of unhealthy hysteria. When men write, it can be a rational activity, but when women write, it is merely a compulsion, brought on by a disturbance in their physical bodies that affects their minds.

Thalestris's speech invokes a courtly ethic. She encourages Belinda to think about the Baron's misdeed as an affront to her honor and draws on ideals of chivalry in demanding that Sir Plume challenge the Baron in defense of her friend's honor. Despite her highly moral tone, however, Thalestris is as preoccupied with appearances as any of the other characters. Her primary worry is the social embarrassment that the Baron will bring upon Belinda by showing off the lock. She seems less concerned with Belinda's feelings than she is with her own: if Belinda were to become the target of ridicule and shame, it would be "infamy" to be her friend. Despite her fierceness, Thalestris is not willing to risk her social position for the sake of her friendship with Belinda.

Sir Plume makes a muddle of the task Thalestris assigns to him, showing how far from courtly behavior this generation of gentlemen has fallen. He fills his speeches with foppish slang and has none of the logical, moral, or oratorical power that a knight should properly wield. It is, however, an example of Pope's ear for dialogue and his mastery of the verse form: Pope manages to give Sir Plume a unique, hilarious voice while still respecting the rigid meter of the poem.

Close attention to questions of honor underscores the sexual allegory of the poem. As Thalestris suggests, the real danger is that "the ravisher" (103) might display the lock and make it a source of public humiliation to Belinda and, by association, to her friends. Thus the real danger is a superficial one—a damaged public reputation—rather than a moral imperative to chastity. Belinda's words at the close of the canto corroborate this suggestion; she exclaims, "Oh, hadst thou, cruel! been content to seize / Hairs less in sight, or any hairs but these!" (175–176). The "hairs less in sight" suggest her pubic hair. This is an explicit statement of what Pope has been hinting at throughout the poem: Belinda is preoccupied with external appearances (whether beauty or reputation) above all else. She wants to keep chaste because her reputation relies on chastity, not because she is particularly virtuous. She would rather suffer a breach to her virtue, especially if it were unseen, than a breach to her appearance.

EXCERPT FROM CANTO 5

"Restore the Lock!" she cries; and all around
"Restore the Lock!" the vaulted roofs rebound.

ALEXANDER POPE

SUMMARY

Neither Belinda's pathetic speech nor Thalestris's anger moves the Baron. Next, Clarissa gives a speech. She asks why beautiful women receive so much attention and praise. A woman's beauty is useless if she does not also have the good sense she needs to hold on to the adoration her beauty gains her. If beauty were the only thing that mattered, no one would bother to be practical or virtuous. But beauty always fades, no matter what one does to preserve it. Therefore, women have to be able to maintain a pleasant nature no matter what happens to their appearance. Good humor, Clarissa says, is a more effective response to problems than screaming, scolding, or putting on airs. Physical attractiveness "strikes the sight, but merit wins the soul" (34).

No one is impressed by Clarissa's speech. Thalestris calls her a prude and, yelling, "To arms!" (37), begins a fight. The speaker of the poem compares the battling lords and ladies to the gods that battle each other in Homer's *Iliad*—the combat is fierce and thunderously loud. Umbriel the gnome contentedly watches the battle from above. The women use their eyes and frowns as weapons to metaphorically slay the men. Two men, Dapperwit and Sir Fopling, collapse as they compose metaphors about the lethal beauty of Thalestris's eyes.

In the skies, the Roman god Jove sits in divine judgment, weighing the men's wits against Belinda's hair. The scales tip in favor of the hair. Belinda attacks the Baron. He is not afraid to fight her, even though the odds are in her favor since his only goal is to "die" upon his enemy, Belinda. (In Pope's era, *dying* was a euphemism for orgasm.) Belinda throws a pinch of snuff in the Baron's face, causing him to sneeze. Then she takes a pin from her side. The speaker gives us a history of the bodkin, which has been in Belinda's family for generations. It started out as a signet ring belonging to her great-

great grandfather and has been melted down into different kinds of ornaments throughout the years.

The Baron cries that someday Belinda will be defeated by someone else, just as she defeats the Baron now. He says that all he fears is leaving her behind. Belinda cries, "Restore the lock!" (103). However, no one can find it. The speaker notes that people often argue over a prize for so long that the prize itself is lost before the conflict ends.

To conclude, the speakers says some think the lock went up to the moon, where all things that are lost on earth end up, including "heroes' wits," courtiers' promises, and sick man's prayers, / The smiles of harlots, and the tears of heirs" (119–120). As the speaker says, his muse knows the lock rose up to the sky and shot through the air like a star. Now society people can see it, lovers can swear by it, and astrologers can use it to make predictions. Belinda should not mourn her lost hair since it now adds glory to the heavens. After she is done killing people with her eyes, Belinda will die herself, and all her hair will turn to dust. But her one lost lock will be immortal and will write her name in the stars.

ANALYSIS

Some critics have interpreted Clarissa's speech as the voice of the poet expressing the moral of the story. Certainly, the goal of her oration is similar to Pope's goal of putting the dispute between the two families into a more reasonable perspective. But Pope's position achieves more complexity than Clarissa's speech since he has used the occasion of the poem to critically address a number of broader societal issues as well. And Clarissa's righteous stance loses authority in light of the fact that it was she who originally gave the Baron the scissors. Clarissa's failure to inspire a reconciliation proves that the quarrel is itself a kind of flirtatious game that all parties are enjoying. The description of the fight has a markedly erotic quality, as ladies and lords wallow in their mock agonies. Sir Plume "draw[s] Clarissa down" (67) in a sexual way, and Belinda "flies" (75) on her foe with flashing eyes and an erotic ardor. Lastly, the "death" the Baron seeks is sexual consummation.

This final battle is the culmination of the long sequence of mock-heroic military actions. Pope invokes by name the Roman gods who were most active in warfare, and he alludes as well to the *Aeneid*, comparing the stoic Baron to Aeneas ("the Trojan"), who had to leave his love to become the founder of Rome. Belinda's tossing of the snuff makes a perfect turning point, ideally suited to the scale of this trivial battle. The snuff causes the Baron to sneeze, a comic and decidedly unheroic thing for a hero to do. The bodkin too serves nicely: here a bodkin is a decorative hairpin, not the weapon of ancient days. Still, Pope gives the pin an elaborate history in accordance with the conventions of true epic.

The mock-heroic conclusion of the poem is designed to compliment the lady it alludes to (Arabella Fermor) while also giving the poet himself due credit for being the instrument of her immortality. This ending effectively indulges the heroine's vanity, even though the poem has functioned throughout as a critique of that vanity. No real moral development has taken place. Belinda is asked to come to terms with her loss through a kind of bribe or distraction that reinforces her basically frivolous outlook. But even in its most mocking moments, this poem is a gentle one, in which Pope shows a basic sympathy with the social world in spite of its folly and foibles. The searing critiques of his later satires would be much more stringent and less forgiving.

THE DUNCIAD[1]

EXCERPT FROM BOOK THE FOURTH

Yet, yet a moment, one dim ray of light
Indulge, dread Chaos, and eternal Night!
Of darkness visible so much be lent,
As half to shew, half veil the deep Intent.
Ye Powers! whose mysteries restored I sing,
To whom Time bears me on his rapid wing,
Suspend a while your force inertly strong,
Then take at once the poet and the song.

.   .   .   .   .

---

1. Pope published three books of *The Dunciad* in 1728. The fourth book, sometimes called *The New Dunciad*, was published in 1742—it was Pope's last major published work. In 1743, Pope revised *The Dunciad*, incorporating the 1742 version into the older version as Book the Fourth. Only the fourth book is included here, as that part of the poem is most commonly read and studied by contemporary critics and scholars.

ALEXANDER POPE

[THE TRIUMPH OF DULNESS]

Art after Art goes out, and all is Night.
See skulking Truth to her old cavern fled,
Mountains of casuistry heaped o'er her head!
Philosophy, that leaned on Heaven before,
Shrinks to her second cause, and is no more.
Physic of Metaphysic begs defense,
And Metaphysic calls for aid on Sense!
See Mystery to Mathematics fly!
In vain! they gaze, turn giddy, rave, and die.
Religion blushing veils her sacred fires,
And unawares Morality expires.
Nor public Flame, nor private, dares to shine;
Nor human Spark is left, nor Glimpse divine!
Lo! thy dread Empire, CHAOS! is restored;
Light dies before thy uncreating word:
Thy hand, great Anarch! lets the curtain fall;
And Universal Darkness buries All.

SUMMARY

The book begins with an invocation to "dread Chaos" and "eternal Night" (2). The speaker asks Night to allow him one "dim ray of light" (1) that he can use to describe the triumph of Goddess Dulness. After that, Night can take over. He goes on to describe the beginning of the age of Dulness: the goddess Dulness rises to her throne, in which her head is concealed within a cloud, but "all below" (18) is brilliantly revealed. Martinus Scriblerus, in a note, says that this describes the old adage, "The higher you climb, the more you shew your A—." Her son, the Laureate, reclines on her lap, wearing a wreath of bay leaves. Science, wit, logic, and rhetoric are imprisoned, exiled, or gagged and bound below her. The Muses are guarded by envy and flattery. Dulness's children and associates—including idiots, tasteless admirers, and the patrons of dunces—crowd around her.

One by one, Dulness's subjects approach her throne and tell her how they advance her cause. Schoolmasters tell her how they force students to memorize words and rhymes to keep them from acquiring real knowledge. A plant enthusiast complains about a butterfly enthusiast who has picked a rare flower, but Dulness commends both of them, encouraging men to study trifles, such as butterflies and flowers, but not to go beyond that study to learn anything about nature or

God. A philosopher assures her that looking at nature would never lead him to any such conclusions. Making a pun on the phrase *a priori*, which means making deductions from a known cause, he says that the "high priori" (471) road leads him and his colleagues to doubt God or to replace him with man, a "mechanic cause" (475), or other things.

Silenus, a drunken demigod from Greek mythology, brings the youth of England to the goddess and has them drink from a cup that makes them forget their obligations to God, their country, and everything else. Then Dulness gives out titles to all of her subjects. She reminds them to encourage the noblemen and politicians of England to ignore their real jobs and duties for trivial amusements and to "MAKE ONE MIGHTY DUNCIAD OF THE LAND" (604). Finally, she puts the whole world to sleep with one mighty yawn.

Even the Muse must succumb to the power of the yawn. Imagination, wit, and art are extinguished in the darkness of Dulness. Truth, philosophy, religion, and morality die out. The speaker calls out to Chaos that its empire has been restored and that "light dies before thy uncreating word" (654). Darkness covers everything.

ANALYSIS

The invocation that opens Book the Fourth inverts the second invocation in John Milton's *Paradise Lost*, which appears at the beginning of Book 3 of that poem. Milton's second invocation is to "holy light," which he asks to help him describe the glory of God in heaven. Pope invokes night and chaos. Milton, who was blind, asks the heavenly light to revisit his eyes long enough for him to describe God, while Pope asks the darkness to allow his own light to shine long enough for him to describe Dulness. The face of Milton's God is invisible because he is so surrounded by brightness, but the bottom of his robes is shaded by clouds so they can be seen. Dulness's face is obscured too but by dark clouds, and her lower parts are revealed by the light that shines on them—Dulness is so dull and dark that anything else in the world is brighter than she is. By giving Dulness the exact opposite characteristics from God, Pope shows how much the ignorance, bad taste, and foolishness he describes throughout the poem deviate from the glory of God and all the good things that God provides.

Dulness—and thus society at large—is rendered still more ridiculous by Martinus Scriblerus's absurd note. The note, which crudely implies that the more famous you get, the more you expose yourself to ridicule, has an earthy, scatological sensibility that reflects much of the satire written by Jonathan Swift, who co-created the character of Scriblerus with Pope. Pope uses quite a bit of scatological humor in *The Dunciad*: the winning diver in Book the Second meets up with a "nut-brown" mud nymph whose name, Merdamente, is derived from the French word for "excrement"; in Book the Fourth, an eager antiquities dealer agrees to go through another enthusiast's excrement to find some valuable coins he swallowed. Pope and Swift both used gross bodily humor in their satire as an antidote to the overweening pride of some of their targets.

In his description of Dulness's subjects and admirers, Pope makes it clear that no section of the intellectual world is immune from Dulness. Indeed, the very things that are supposed to promote knowledge—the school and university systems, scientific research, logical thinking—actually end up standing in the way of true knowledge. The schoolteachers fill students' brains with memorized facts and words, such that there is no room for intellectual growth, and the scientists and philosophers pay so much attention to the minute details of their research and their arguments that they lose sight of the big concern, God. As he does in so many of his poems, Pope stresses that real knowledge comes from using perspective and paying attention to the whole rather than the parts.

Pope's attack on the "a priori" philosophers, who treated philosophy and theology like a science experiment, trying to derive general rules from what they can observe for themselves, shows that reason is something more than mere logic for Pope. For all his emphasis on rational thought and his seemingly deep understanding of the science of his day, Pope thinks there is some element in reason that comes directly from God, which leads us to believe in the divine without logical evidence. Belief in God is part of humanity, a kind of divine common sense.

The poem's final four lines invert the beginning of the Bible. There, the first lines describe God as having and being "the Word," which is usually called Logos, its Greek name. *Logos* is the "creating word" of God, and it brings forth light first. The word of *Chaos* is the opposite of Logos's word: it is "uncreating," and it brings darkness. This inversion emphasizes the ungodliness of Dulness, Chaos, and darkness, but it also invests them with a terrifying power. That the darkness of dullness could "uncreate" so much of what God has created for humanity is painful. In the poem's final image of "Universal Darkness" (655), Pope attempts to shock and shame the reader into fighting against the encroaching power of Dulness.

WILLIAM BLAKE

(1757–1827)

CONTEXT

William Blake was born in London, England, on November 28, 1757. As a child, he was especially close to his younger brother, Robert. His father, James Blake, was a hosier, successful enough to keep his family in the middle class. Young William Blake began pursuing his artistic talents early on: at ten, he was sketching copies of Greek and Roman antiquities. The experience Blake gained as an engraver during his youth would not only provide an income throughout his adult life but would also become a source of poetic inspiration when he began writing in his twenties.

Blake's education was almost wholly in the arts. At the age of ten, he enrolled, at the behest of his father, in a nearby drawing school. There he learned to sketch the human figure by copying plaster casts. When he was fourteen, he left school and became an apprentice at the workshop of James Basire, who was the engraver for the prestigious Society of Antiquaries and Royal Society. Under Basire's tutelage, Blake learned the skill of copy engraving. At twenty-one, after Blake had finished his apprenticeship and made the transition into professional work, he began making a living by doing copy engravings for print and book publishers. In 1789 Blake was accepted into the Royal Academy of Art's School of Design, where he studied painting and learned about classical proportion in the works of artists, such as Michelangelo and Raphael.

In his youth, Blake began having the visions that would ultimately provide the impetus and content for much of his art. His first vision probably occurred at age nine, when he reported having seen a tree filled with angels while he was taking a walk. These visions would persist throughout his life, and they would become the basis for much of his poetry's complex mythology, which involved different personifications of the angels. His understanding of Christianity was similarly affected by the visions: Blake believed that his visions stemmed from direct personal revelation rather than from learning or the intervention of religious figures. Indeed, he believed so much in the revelatory power of his visions that he began working with a new method of engraving, called relief etching, after his dead brother Robert appeared and instructed Blake in this time-consuming, labor-intensive art. To create a relief etching, Blake would write the text backward on a copper plate, then place the plate in acid so that the unadorned copper would burn away; the designs and words of the adorned copper could then be printed on paper or cloth. Blake would go on to illustrate many of his books of poetry using relief etching. Because Blake included etchings with his poems, critics often refer to sections of the poems by citing the plate number.

At age twenty-four, Blake met an illiterate young woman named Catherine Boucher, who became his wife in 1782. Their marriage appears to have been very happy, and they were very close. During the course of their marriage, Blake taught Catherine rudimentary reading and writing skills, as well as trained her as an engraver so that she could help him with his work. They never had children. She also shared his particular view of religion—Christianity by individual revelation—and together they joined the Swedenborgian New Church in 1789. This church, based on the writings of theologian Emanuel Swedenborg, combined the Old and New Testaments and preached the omnipotence of Jesus Christ. Within the year, however, they broke with the church, believing that they should worship on their own, without the intervention of organized religion. Blake and Catherine remained together until Blake's death in 1827.

Much of Blake's life was troubled and turbulent. In the summer of 1780, for instance, the Gordon Riots, violent anti-Catholic demonstrations, broke out. In one such demonstration, Blake was involuntarily swept along in the crowd as they marched to and then burned down the local prison. Later that summer, while on a sketching trip with friends, Blake was arrested. Police mistakenly assumed the group were spies because they had come abnormally close to a naval base. In 1800, the Blakes moved to Felpham, Sussex, but in 1803, Blake found himself charged with sedition after an altercation with a soldier, John Scofield, in the Blakes' garden. Scofield charged Blake not only with assault but also with damning the king, which, at the time, carried severe penalties, as England was in the middle of the Napoleonic Wars with France. Eventually, Blake was acquitted. Although Blake's connections to fellow artists had always been strong, their various troubles with the society and the law bonded them further: William Godwin, author and husband of Mary Wollstonecraft, founded philosophical anarchism; Thomas Holcroft, the journalist and playwright, was charged with high treason; and Thomas Paine, author of *The Rights of Man*, had to flee England in order to avoid arrest.

WILLIAM BLAKE

Blake's poetry reflected the turbulence in his personal life, as well as the diversity of his friendships. His first book, *Poetical Sketches* (circa 1783), explicitly critiqued not only contemporary verse for "abandoning" the poetry of his precursors, such as Edmund Spenser, but also British imperialism. *The Marriage of Heaven and Hell* (1790), in which Swedenborg appears as a character, satirizes the Swedenborgian New Church. In the late 1790s, Blake developed his mythology, which relied on interlocked symbols and metaphors and which attempted to encompass all of human history. Blake composed *Visions of the Daughters of Albion* (1793), a long poem condemning sexual violence and rape, partly in supportive response to Wollstonecraft's *Vindication of the Rights of Woman* (1792). Like his literary friends, Blake thought about the role of the artist in the changing, increasingly modern world, and he invented the character Los to symbolize the artist's imagination. Later Blake began to prophesize about humanity and the course of human history in what he called the Prophetic Books, which included *The Four Zoas* (begun in 1796 or 1797) and *Jerusalem* (begun in 1804).

Throughout his work, Blake demonstrated consistency in his choice of **themes**, **motifs**, and **symbols**. Although his poetry increased in complexity as he matured as an artist, the main poetic thrusts remain similar: he explored cowardice, direct revelation, suffering, the rejection of morality, and the possibility of redemption while constantly reevaluating humanity's past, present, and future. He changed characters from book to book, eventually drawing many of his **personae** from the Bible and attempting to represent what he perceived to be the duality of humanity. Again and again, Blake retold the biblical stories of creation, the Fall, and the promised redemption of Judgment Day, but he added a unique spiritual, often ironic spin.

Despite receiving some amount of notoriety for his idiosyncratic verse and illustrations, Blake never achieved popular or critical success in his lifetime. In fact, he found it increasingly difficult to make a living, and he abandoned poetry for art while in his sixties. Around 1818, Blake met John Linnell, who would become his patron and would introduce him to several admirers. Blake died in 1827 and was buried in an unmarked grave in London. In the 1880s, W. B. Yeats began studying Blake's work, and he published an edited collection of Blake poems in 1893. Yeats even based some of his mythological symbols on those created by Blake. In the 1940s, Blake experienced a critical resurgence after the publication of *Fearful Symmetry: A Study of William Blake* (1947), by scholar Northrop Frye. American Beat writers of the 1950s, including Allen Ginsberg, envisioned Blake as an early role model. Rock group The Doors took their name from the following passage of Blake's *The Marriage of Heaven and Hell*:

> *If the doors of perception were cleansed every thing would appear to man as it is: Infinite.*

Today Blake is considered to be the most mystical and most visionary of English poets.

Themes, Motifs & Symbols

Themes

The Rejection of Morality

Blake uses his poetry to reject, and then attack, notions of morality. To Blake, morality serves as a restrictive code of conduct, impeding creativity and encouraging cowardice. Imagination and creativity were the axes on which Blake's life spun, and he summarily rejected any idea or sentiment perceived to be in opposition to either the imagination or creativity. In this way, Blake saw morality as a form of oppression, as it suppressed the freethinking necessary for imaginative and creative endeavors. This oppression was, in turn, a way for cowards—people too spiritually weak to have any thoughts or experience that transcended the standard, socially accepted codes—to essentially control people with different moral codes. He believed that no one system of morality, especially when codified into law, could justly apply to all. Codified morality was yet another form of tyranny, which Blake believed the poet, with the help of his imagination, had a duty to resist.

Although deeply Christian, Blake saw in morality something degraded and removed from a living spiritual experience, which emphasized sensual perception and the use of the imagination. Without a living experience, morality would be a form of state oppression. Blake's work demonstrates the destructive powers of morality: in *Jerusalem*, he portrays moral law as a murderer of spiritual life. Blake ironically adopts traditional Christian notions of good and evil in *The Marriage of Heaven and Hell* to argue that true good and a worthwhile life come from the unions of polar opposites—heaven and hell, good and evil, the "Prolific" and the "Devouring," as he explains in Plate 16. In Blake's formulation, conventional philosophies and religious beliefs, which usually constitute moral systems, suppress the innate human ability to experience spiritual transformation through direct, visionary revelation.

WILLIAM BLAKE

The Importance of Direct Revelation

Blake's belief in the importance of direct spiritual revelation appears in all of his poems, from the early lyrics to the later Prophetic Books. "The Chimney Sweeper," from *Songs of Innocence and of Experience* (1794), portrays the transformation of an orphaned little boy, forced into the dangerous profession of chimney sweeping, after he is visited by an angel. This angel shows the boy a world in which the dead rise and run in an idyllic scene, and he tells the boy about the love of the Christian God. Enraptured with the new vision of the world, the boy returns to his difficult life "happy & warm" (23). Blake's belief in direct revelation was due, in part, to his own visions, which began at age nine and featured angels, ghosts, and other transcendental creatures. Direct revelation was also another way of avoiding the strict, conservative morality that prevailed in late eighteenth- and early nineteenth-century England. During this time, England instituted a series of repressive domestic measures, including stiff laws against sedition, to protect itself from what the English government perceived to be a revolutionary spirit of rebellion spreading across Continental Europe.

According to Blake, direct revelation is an antidote to the **Enlightenment** philosophies, which privileged reason over imagination, so prevalent in his lifetime. In Blake's formulation, imagination leads to new understandings of reason, which could then help institute social change. In *America* (1793), Blake uses the character of Orc to stand in for the spirit of the power of revelation and the capabilities of a person who chooses to use his or her newfound knowledge. After experiencing a revelation that America is self-sufficient, Orc incites a revolt to overthrow its oppressive colonial government. According to the poem, the American Revolution becomes an example to other nations, in which people also begin having revelations, inciting revolutions, and following innovative ways of ordering society and of living. These people, including those in "France Spain & Italy" (Plate 16, line 16), have each had insight that their spiritual experience is more valuable than what could be gleamed by an oppressive regime. Thus Blake saw political action as a result of spiritual or imaginative awakening: he attributed very real revolutions in eighteenth- and nineteenth-century France, Spain, and Italy to hypothetical causes, namely the revelations of the revolutionary participants. To Blake, revelations lead to knowledge, which then lead to action.

THE OVERCOMING OF HISTORICAL CIRCUMSTANCE

Blake believed that people are capable of overcoming their individual circumstances, as well as larger historical forces, and the idea of transcendence is central to his poetry. According to Blake, people could transcend morality through direct revelation, and visionaries could overcome history using their prophecies and imagination. In the "Introduction" to *Songs of Experience*, Blake introduces the figure of the Bard, a poet capable of describing the past, the present, and the future because his imagination gives him a place outside of history. Using his powers of imagination, the Bard has overcome his own circumstances and is now able to float freely from moment to moment into and out of history. He has seen it all, in effect, and his omniscient sight allows him to describe history in song or verse. To Blake, the person who overcomes history, like the Bard, can guide others, helping to lead them beyond their social and historical circumstances into a world in which people are liberated and allied with one another in love.

In Blake's conception of history, the promise of a better world sometimes necessitates the sacrifice of individuals, either literally or figuratively. But since the individual is capable of direct revelation and can envision a better future, the individual will not be bothered by his or her sacrifice to larger forces. Rather, he or she will see it as necessary for the future. Perhaps the best example of a sacrificed individual is Jesus, whom Blake introduces as a character in *Jerusalem*: here, as in the New Testament, from which Blake drew inspiration, Jesus dies but is resurrected for eternity and given eternal life. Aside from his role as a savior, Jesus has also overcome both morality and history. He knows the past, the present, and the future, and he stands outside the course of normal time. When a person can envision a better world, he or she will stoically bear whatever problems might be encountered in daily life. This idea had significant meaning in Blake's late eighteenth- and early nineteenth-century England, a time in which individual freedoms were greatly restricted, including the dissolution of habeas corpus and the right to gather in groups. Belief in an improved future allows individuals to handle—and overcome—suffering.

MOTIFS

OPPOSITES

Blake constantly lets characters transform into their opposites. For instance, in *The Marriage of Heaven and Hell*, Blake transforms a devil into an angel. Elsewhere in the long poem, the **speaker**, or the Voice of the Devil, explains that energy represents evil and reason represents good. These transformations speak to the power of individual thinking, or direct revelation, as well as to the individual's ability to transcend historical and social circumstances. The person with the capacity to transform into her or his opposite, or even just to imagine this transformation, is, for Blake, the person most capable of envisioning and creating the new, improved world. Furthermore, the union of opposites, particularly in *The Marriage of Heaven and Hell*, will help bring about this new world. Blake also uses poems themselves to echo and reflect one another. In *Songs of Innocence and of Experience*, "The Divine Image" aligns with "The Human Abstract": the former portrays the good traits of humanity, while the latter enumerates the negative traits. Throughout his work, Blake blended contradictory forces, including spirituality and politics, Christianity and atheism, even art and writing, as he included text in his etchings and published drawings with his poems, to create an improved, stronger whole.

CONTRADICTION AND IRONY

Characters contradict themselves constantly throughout Blake's work, and their verbal backtracking and physical transformations allowed Blake to directly comment on the social, religious, and political events of his time. His oblique, contradictory references shrouded his arguments inside his poetry. Blake frequently employed **irony**, a literary technique in which words mean something other than their literal meanings. *The Marriage of Heaven and Hell* is probably Blake's most ironic poem since here he pretends to praise traditional Christian concepts of good, evil, and morality. Contradiction also occurs when a character or idea is used against itself, as in *America*. Over the long poem's three parts, Blake first praises America for its instigation of the American Revolution, then contradicts his original position by criticizing the use of violent force and by waxing pessimistic about the society's potential after the war. Orc, the poem's protagonist, calls himself a "terror" (Plate 8, line 1), a label in stark contrast to his heroic stand against repression, as represented by the godlike Urizen. Within the larger framework of the poem, Blake twists the political positions of the United States and England, contrasting and contradicting, in order to analyze revolution, conflict, and politics as pure states, removed from actual historical circumstances and readers' preconceived notions.

THE LONG SPEECH

Within their ubiquitous long speeches, Blake's characters express their circumstances, their moralities, their histories, and their religious views. The long speech gives characters an opportunity to verbalize themselves as both agents of change and victims of circumstance, and thus the literary technique demonstrates Blake's belief that all of humanity possesses the potential to become articulate. According to Blake's schema, most people live in a "fallen," or denigrated, state, in which they are subject to religious rules and codified laws. Through direct revelation, people can transcend social morality and historical circumstance—and these revelations often take the form of speeches in which the speakers argue, prophesize, and reveal. In *America*, Orc, the poem's protagonist, tells Albion that time has come to an end in a fiery apocalypse, but humanity, as symbolized by Orc, still retains its powers of speech. Even as the world ends, Orc speaks. Most of the *Visions of the Daughters of Albion* consist of the monologues of the three main characters, including a concluding speech by Oothoon in which she extols the benefits of sexual freedom.

SYMBOLS

ORC AND URIZEN

Blake contrasts the rebel Orc with the repressive god Urizen. In *America*, Blake employs Orc as a demon rebel. Although Albion's Angel, the speaker of several the poem's plates, calls him an "antichrist" and a "transgressor of God's Law" (Plate 7, lines 5–6), he becomes the poem's hero, renowned for his fight against repression. Orc fights for humankind, and he symbolizes human imagination and the desire for freedom. He transcends his negative portrait to become a force for good. Also appearing in *Europe* (1794), *The Four Zoas*, and *The Book Urizen* (1794), Orc embodies the spirit of revolution, eventually personifying the American and French Revolutions, while Urizen symbolizes repression—and the passionate fights between Orc and Urizen occur throughout Blake's poetry.

While Blake portrays Orc as a vivacious young man, Urizen usually appears as an old man with a beard. The figure of Urizen comes from the Old Testament, but Blake reimagines him as a repressive god who uses huge nets to suppress people and their desires for personal liberty and sexual fulfillment.

ALBION

Albion, a character in *America*, *Visions of the Daughters of Albion*, and *Jerusalem*, generally symbolizes a state of passivity. The word *Albion* means "whiteness" and was used by ancient Greek and Roman writers as another name for England. Sometimes Blake employs Albion as a representation of the oppressive nature of the British government and sometimes as an embodiment of the British people, who willingly accept the oppressive policies. In *America*, Albion becomes an oppressor to rebel against, whereas in *Jerusalem* he personifies the biblical Jews. Elsewhere Albion symbolizes the mental block of conformity and spiritual cowardice that any person must overcome in order to become more fully human—that is, no longer confined by morality and history. In *Visions of the Daughters of Albion*, Albion symbolizes England, and the daughters are late eighteenth-century Englishwomen. England as Albion shackles its women and men in chains that limit their thoughts, imaginations, and perceptions. Like all of Blake's characters, the persona of Albion is flexible, changing as the poem and its arguments change.

THE FIGURE OF THE POET

Throughout his work, Blake uses characters of poets to symbolize the freethinking visionary ideal to which all humans should aspire. *Songs of Experience* begins with an "Introduction," in which the speaker extols readers to "hear the voice of the Bard!" (1). This Bard, or poet, transcends history and exists outside of regular time. Familiar with the Bible, this Bard prophesizes about the past, the present, and the future. Los, a character from *Jerusalem*, also symbolizes the poet. Los speaks the lines that perhaps constitute Blake's most famous quotation: "I must Create a System or be enslaved by another Man's." Los symbolizes the hope that humanity would stand in imaginative, prophetic defiance to all types of oppression. To Blake, the poet does not simply record or describe but rather creates a new way of thinking in order to overcome society's oppressive systems. Similarly, poetry could encompass the poet's imaginings and prophesies, which would be received during visionary direct revelation.

SUMMARY & ANALYSIS

SONGS OF INNOCENCE AND OF EXPERIENCE

"THE TYGER," FROM SONGS OF EXPERIENCE

Tyger Tyger, burning bright,
In the forests of the night:
What immortal hand or eye,
Could frame thy fearful symmetry?

In what distant deeps or skies   5
Burnt the fire of thine eyes!
On what wings dare he aspire!
What the hand, dare seize the fire?

And what shoulder, & what art,
Could twist the sinews of thy heart?   10
And when thy heart began to beat,
What dread hand? & what dread feet?
What the hammer? what the chain,
In what furnace was thy brain?
What the anvil? what dread grasp,   15
Dare its deadly terrors clasp!

When the stars threw down their spears
And water'd heaven with their tears:
Did he smile his work to see?
Did he who made the Lamb make thee?   20

Tyger, Tyger burning bright,
In the forests of the night:
What immortal hand or eye,
Dare frame thy fearful symmetry?

SUMMARY

Songs of Innocence and of Experience consists of two individual manuscripts: *Songs of Innocence* (1789), which was combined with

WILLIAM BLAKE

additional poems to form *Songs of Innocence and of Experience* (1794). The speaker of the poems is a Bard, or poet, who assumes the persona of different characters. Many of the poems are spoken from a child's perspective, and the "Introduction" plainly states that the book was intended for children. Perhaps the most significant poems from *Songs of Innocence* are the "Introduction," "The Lamb," "The Chimney Sweeper," and "The Divine Image"; these poems are summarized in the following paragraph. These poems directly deal with or engage children, Blake's concept of a Christian God, or a combination of both. "Introduction" explains that the poems are happy songs, meant to bring joy to children. The speaker/ Bard remembers one day when he encountered a child sitting on a cloud, who asked him to play a song about a lamb. After he played the song, much to the child's delight, the child told him to drop his pipe and instead sing cheerful songs. The child then instructs the speaker to write down his songs, at which point the child disappears and the speaker proceeds to write.

"The Lamb," addressed directly to a lamb and spoken in the voice of a child, asks in the first stanza whether the lamb knows how he was made, given life, fed, clothed, and given the power to bleat. In the second stanza, the Bard answers the questions posed in the first stanza: a modest and gentle man, who is sometimes also called a lamb, made the lamb and the child. Both stanzas fairly directly invoke God, who made both the lamb and the child in his image, as a dedication. "The Chimney Sweeper" tells the story of young Tom Darce, an unhappy chimney sweeper who is visited by an angel as he sleeps. Upon awakening, he feels contented by his nocturnal vision of the resurrection and Eden and ready to face his difficult work because his faith shrouds and protects him. "The Divine Image," a hymnlike poem of five stanzas, explicates the four virtues of humanity: "Mercy, Pity, Peace, and Love" (1). These four virtues are the embodiment of God, manifested by humans in their faces, hearts, and bodies when they live within these virtues. The final stanza concludes by stating that all humans, regardless of race, religion, or creed, carry God within themselves because all humans carry the capacity to express and live within these virtues.

Key poems from *Songs of Experience* include the "Introduction," "The Earth's Answer," "The Tyger," and "The Human Abstract," summarized below. "Introduction" commands listeners to hear the poet, who simultaneously sees all moments in time and who knows the Bible as it was originally presented in Eden. The second stanza addresses the fallen, and the poet calls upon Earth to intervene in the affairs of the world. Earth replies to the poet in "Earth's Answer." Angrily, Earth criticizes the "selfish father of men" (11) and explains that she has been imprisoned, much as chaste young women are imprisoned. She implores the poet to break her chains, which repress freedom, sexual desire, and boundless natural energy. "The Tyger," one of Blake's most famous poems, asks a tiger about his creator. The speaker describes the creator in increasingly disparaging terms, drawing the imagery from blacksmithing, and finally concludes by wondering how the creator could fashion both a lamb and a tiger. "The Human Abstract" explores cruelty and deceit, two states that, according to the poem, are not found in heaven but are found in humanity. As the poem explains, pity and mercy are both dependent on conditions opposed to them: poverty and unhappiness. Here humanity is not made in God's image, as it is in other poems, but rather exists narcissistically, stamping out humility and cultivating deceit.

ANALYSIS

Blake's inaugural poem in *Songs of Innocence*, "Introduction," functions literally as an introduction to easy-to-understand, religious verse for children. According to the first poem, the Bard writes to make children happy with his lines. The speaker spies a child on a cloud in the first stanza, an angel who commands him to play a song about Jesus Christ, traditionally referred to as a "lamb." As the angel departs from the scene, the speaker begins transcribing and thus assumes the persona of a messenger, one who has important knowledge to impart to his listeners/readers. The messenger role accords with Blake's belief that divinity is experienced through direct revelation: an angel instructs the speaker to write down the religious songs so that others may be given religious instruction. Singing the songs allows humans to experience God and worship more directly, without the intervention of a figure of organized religion.

Throughout the poems in *Songs of Innocence and of Experience*, Blake creates dramatic distance between himself and his writings by employing the Bard as his speaker. Blake then further distances himself by having the Bard assume other personae, including that of children. The switching of personae is another manifestation of Blake's belief in individual relationships with God: all individuals— from children to poets to chimney sweepers—were capable of directly interacting with God. "The Lamb" functions as a **hymn**, with a simple structure of rhyming **couplets**. Blake intended the Bard's songs to replace church hymnals, which he thought represented only a degraded version of religion, not one based in lived experience. Indeed, the speaker of "Introduction," from *Songs of Experience*, directly addresses his words to "the lapsèd Soul" (6), people who either have not known or have forgotten the divinity that exists within every human being. The inborn, individual embodiment of God was a major tenet of Blake's radical Christianity.

According to Blake, direct revelation was accessible to all, and all stood to benefit from visions and faith. In "The Chimney Sweeper," the appearance of an angel and the revelation of Eden comfort a young boy as he goes about his dangerous profession. In the eighteenth and nineteenth centuries, families sometimes sold their children as apprentices to various professional masters, including master sweeps, who would then force the children into the chimneys for cleaning. At the time, there were no safety regulations or child labor laws to protect the young workers, and the life was difficult, dirty, and dangerous. Blake believed in faith as an antidote to despair: through a belief in God and the potential for a perfect world, individuals can transcend their circumstances, including very real, very nasty historical and social conditions. By devoting one's faith to the qualities of "Mercy, Pity, Peace, and Love" (1), as explained in "The Divine Image," one could not only embody the divine but also help humanity. If everyone practiced these virtues, the world would be transformed and would become ideal.

An angry yet beloved God emerges from several of Blake's poems, and Blake urges humanity to embrace both sides of God. In "Earth's Answer," Earth complains that God keeps her in bondage. According to this poem, God is selfish, mean-spirited, and cruelly omnipotent: God has the power to free Earth and her humans, yet chooses not to. The speaker of "The Tyger" marvels that God could create the peaceful, loving lamb and the vicious, violent tiger. Like humans, God has two sides: a good side and an evil side. Blake more fully explores the union of dichotomies in *The Marriage of Heaven and Hell*, but even these earlier poems illustrate an interest in opposites. "The Tyger," with its rhyming couplets and questions addressed to an animal, invokes the earlier poem "The Lamb," which also consists of rhyming couplets and asks questions of an animal. In "The Human Abstract," Blake rebuts the lovely qualities explored in "The Divine Image": humans are capable of great mercy and tenderness, but these qualities stem from a sense of superiority over the less fortunate.

The poems in *Songs of Innocence and of Experience* portray the human soul as it moves from purity or innocence to wisdom or experience. To have a rich life, humans need to embrace both innocence and experience. Blake first completed *Songs of Innocence*, then added several poems to create *Songs of Experience* and eventually combined the two manuscripts into *Songs of Innocence and of Experience* in 1794. He subtitled the new book "shewing the two contrary states of the human soul." "The Divine Image" exemplifies the innocent initial stage of life, whereas the jaded cynicism of "The Human Abstract" exemplifies the latter stage. The innocence poems are full of pastoral imagery, simple language and rhymes, children as speakers and listeners, and expressions of faith. These poems are generally set in an idyllic wonderland, as imagined in "The Echoing Green." In contrast, the experience poems deal with contemporary social ills and evils, including poverty, child labor, disease, sexual repression, and political oppression. These poems are set in overcrowded urban areas, in which every person shows "marks of weakness, marks of woe" (4), as portrayed in "London." Poems echo one another and act as mirror images: "The Lamb" calls to mind "The Tyger," "Infant Joy" resonates with "Infant Sorrow."

THE MARRIAGE OF HEAVEN AND HELL

"THE ARGUMENT," THE POEM THAT BEGINS THE MARRIAGE OF HEAVEN AND HELL

Rintrah roars & shakes his fires in the burden'd air;
Hungry clouds swag on the deep.

Once meek, and in a perilous path,
The just man kept his course along
The vale of death. 5
Roses are planted where thorns grow.
And on the barren heath
Sing the honey bees.

Then the perilous path was planted:
And a river, and a spring 10
On every cliff and tomb;

And on the bleached bones
Red clay brought forth.

Till the villain left the paths of ease,
To walk in perilous paths, and drive   15
The just man into barren climes.

Now the sneaking serpent walks
In mild humility.
And the just man rages in the wilds
Where lions roam.   20

Rintrah roars & shakes his fires in the burden'd air;
Hungry clouds swag on the deep.

SUMMARY

This long work of many poems and plates begins with the introduction of the characters Rintrah and the devil, as well as other characters. Rintrah angrily yells and fusses as deceitful villains ruin the route of righteous men. Another plate introduces the character of Swedenborg: although he is a devil, he disguises himself as an angel. This section also contains the poem's most famous quotations: "Without Contraries is no progression. Attraction and Repulsion, Reason and Energy, Love and Hate, are necessary to Human existence." The Voice of the Devil speaks in the next section, in which he lists and corrects the erroneous parts of the Bible, including the idea that humans contain a separate body and soul. This voice also invokes John Milton's *Paradise Lost* (1674) and uniquely interprets the earlier long poem by praising only those parts that deal with Satan.

Often titled "A Memorable Fancy," many plates describe the speaker's multiple descents into hell and transcribe the aphorisms and parables he heard there. "Proverbs from Hell" includes such counterintuitive phrases as "drive your cart and your plow over the bones of the dead" and "the lust of the goat is the bounty of God" (Plate 8). In another section, the speaker describes eating with Isaiah and Ezekiel, who recount their prophetic visions and answer the speaker's questions about argument, persuasion, rhetoric, and motivation. Elsewhere, the speaker goes to visit a publishing house in hell, in which he sees a dragon man, a viper, an eagle, a lion, and unknown entities hard at work. These entities, the so-called Giant

Forms, created the earth once upon at time but are now imprisoned by those with small, weak minds, who resist the natural energy of the world. Along with an angel who wants to save him, the speaker visits a dark abyss in another section of the poem. Later he hears a man sing about the necessity of freeing one's mind and altering one's opinion. Over several sections, the speaker and the devil argue with the angel about their versions of Christianity: traditional (the angel) versus unique (the speaker and the devil). The devil argues that Jesus broke the commandments and acted impulsively. "A Song of Liberty" concludes the prophetic book. The poem consists of a numbered list, which describes an apocalyptic vision of fire, tears, and death that ends with the dissolution of empires. It ends by stating that all living things are sacred.

ANALYSIS

The Marriage of Heaven and Hell describes Blake's vision of the world, of humanity, and of a beneficial life as a series of unions of opposites. Blake employs personae, including the prophetlike Rintrah and the Voice of the Devil, to distance himself from the sentiments expressed. Perhaps fearful of charges of sedition or treason, Blake buried his criticisms beneath layers of complex symbols and myths. He also satirizes the traditional Christian concepts of good and evil, as well as heaven and hell; rails against self-righteousness; and criticizes those who docilely believe in organized religion and social law rather than thinking for themselves and developing independent, idiosyncratic systems of morality. Blake advocates freethinking and encourages readers to develop their own opinions, as well as unique relationships with God. He envisioned the poems as a response to the theological teachings of Emanuel Swedenborg, to whose New Church both Blake and his wife had once belonged and who emphasized the worship of Jesus Christ. Less than a year after joining, however, the Blakes broke with the church and devised their own unique systems of devotional prayer. In his writings, Swedenborg imagines fictional trips to heaven, which Blake parodies in his own poem's descriptions of fictional trips to hell.

Blake's book opens with a vision of the impending apocalypse, meant to destroy stable, staid humanity and introduce a new world of creativity and imagination. According to Blake's formulations, genius, personified by the Giant Forms who created the world, resides in hell. There, genius is chained by small minds incapable of thinking freely for themselves—that is, those who blindly follow the dictates of society and organized religion. Evil represents energy needed to produce visions, interpret those visions, and institute social change on the basis of those visions. In other words, evil is a fundamental component of the creative process. Blake situates genius and energy in hell as a way of emphasizing the importance of wholeness. Rather than pretend that all humans are entirely good, Blake encourages readers to accept the positive and the negative aspects of humanity and history. Written in the 1790s, Blake's work explicitly invoked the spirit of revolution sweeping the United States and Europe. Like his fellow romantic poets—William Wordsworth, Samuel Taylor Coleridge, John Keats, and Percy Bysshe Shelley— Blake fervently believed that the revolutions, despite their violence, would usher in a golden age. Blake co-opts the conventional Christian concepts of apocalypse and judgment and rewrites stories from the Bible in order to imagine a world freed from the shackles of tyranny and a people who equally employ their reason and their imagination—but, as in the Bible, this freedom could only come after a period of pain.

Throughout his work, Blake urges individuality, independence, and libertarianism as antidotes to the bland submissiveness of his day—and he does so by blending literary styles. Free thinkers, including the Beat writers of the 1950s, elevated Blake to the status of a visionary mystic, a slightly crazy man capable of creative feats of art and writing. Over the length of his career, Blake ceased writing the **lyrics** that constitute *Songs of Innocence and of Experience* and began writing the so-called Prophetic Books, of which *The Marriage of Heaven and Hell* is an example. The lack of coherent order and narrative within *The Marriage of Heaven and Hell* encourages readers to flip around the work rather than reading each section sequentially. Although "Proverbs of Hell" satirizes clichéd sayings, Blake reminds readers of his views with aphorisms of his own, including "All deities reside in the human breast" (Plate 11) and "One Law for the Lion & Ox is Oppression" (Plate 24). His final poem of the book, "A Song of Liberty," concludes with a prose paragraph, called the Chorus. This paragraph mimics the language of metaphysical and political tracts of his day, but it also extols priests and tyrants to let the "sons of joy" live freely, a radical idea couched in a familiar form.

WILLIAM BLAKE

AMERICA: A PROPHECY

EXCERPT FROM PLATE 6

*The morning comes, the night decays, the watchmen leave their
stations;
The grave is burst, the spices shed, the linen wrapped up;
The bones of death, the cov'ring clay, the sinews shrunk & dry'd,
Reviving shake, inspiring move, breathing! awakening!
Spring like redeemed captives when their bonds & bars are burst.
Let the slave grinding at the mill run out into the field:
Let him look up into the heavens & laugh in the bright air;
Let the inchained soul shut up in darkness and in sighing,
Whose face has never seen a smile in thirty weary years,
Rise and look out; his chains are loose, his dungeon doors are
open.
And let his wife and children return from the opressor's scourge.
They look behind at every step & believe it is a dream,
Singing, "The Sun has left his blackness, & has found a fresher
morning
And the fair Moon rejoices in the clear & cloudless night;
For Empire is no more, and now the Lion & Wolf shall cease."*

EXCERPT FROM PLATE 8

*The terror answerd: "I am Orc, wreath'd round the accursed
tree:
The times are ended; shadows pass, the morning 'gins to break;
The fiery joy, that Urizen perverted to ten commands,
What night he led the starry hosts thro' the wide wilderness:
That stony law I stamp to dust: and scatter religion abroad
To the four winds as a torn book, & none shall gather the leaves;
But they shall rot on desart sands, & consume in bottomless
deeps,
To make the desarts blossom, & the deeps shrink to their
fountains,
And to renew the fiery joy, and burst the stony roof,
That pale religious letchery, seeking Virginity,
May find it in a harlot, and in coarse-clad honesty
The undefil'd, tho' ravish'd in her cradle night and morn:
For every thing that lives is holy, life delights in life;*

Because the soul of sweet delight can never be defil'd.
Fires inwrap the earthly globe, yet man is not consumed;
Amidst the lustful fires he walks: his feet become like brass,
His knees and thighs like silver, & his breast and head like gold."

SUMMARY

The poem begins with the "Preludium." The virginal daughter of Urthona brings Orc food for two weeks until he forces himself on her on the fourteenth day. Orc tells her that he hates her father, who keeps him chained. Eventually, Orc breaks the chains. In the final stanza, the young girl promises to stay with Orc in their embrace, which she likens to "eternal death." Titled "A Prophecy," the rest of the long poem details scenes from the American Revolution, as well as the fictional trials of the prince of Albion. While the prince sits in his tent, General George Washington, across the Atlantic, rallies his troops by describing the weakening of the colonial chains. The Atlantic Ocean churns, while Albion the country (i.e., England) grows sicker, America becomes enervated, and even the heavenly bodies react angrily to the scenes in America. Orc's rebellion is compared to a comet, which threatens to spread across the earth. A disembodied voice then describes an impending apocalypse. Albion's Angel asks the voice whether it belongs to Orc, and the voice affirms his identity, going on to portray more scenes of suffering and violence. The angel begins to cry.

Albion declares war. The speaker next describes thirteen angels, who live in an imaginary place between America and Albion. Alive with Orc's spirit, the Boston angel wonders who has determined the social order, which blocks people from having unique experiences and which everyone is forced to obey. All thirteen angels then tear off their special heavenly clothes and go to America. Meanwhile, thirteen English governors rush to Washington and beg mercy, while British soldiers abandon ranks and disappear. Albion's Angel commands a plague and other natural disasters to descend on America, frightening everyone, from sailors in Boston to builders in Virginia. America disappears in Orc's wrathful destruction, which blends with the natural disorders and spreads to England. Some citizens are feeling awakened and renewed. Urizen, a god in the heavens, emerges, crying. Other nations begin to notice the shackles of Urizen oppressing Albion, and they begin to feel Orc's spirit. Revolution spreads.

WILLIAM BLAKE

ANALYSIS

In this poem, Blake retells the story of the American Revolution and comments on the French Revolution, which was happening as he wrote, using a series of symbols, characters, and allegories. Blake's central characters include Orc, or the spirit of revolution; Urthona, or the possibilities of the imagination; and Albion, or England. Albion's thirteen angels are actually the thirteen American colonies, and Albion's Angel is King George III, ruler of England during the colonial rebellion. Urizen symbolizes a repressive god, similar to the vengeful god described in the biblical Old Testament. As in other works, here Blake employs heavily veiled symbols as a way of distancing himself from the political opinions expressed therein. Blake wrote and published in England during a time of repressive domestic policies: expressing praise for the American Revolution, as well as support for the French revolutionaries during a time in which England and France were fighting each other in the Napoleonic Wars, was fraught with potential consequences, including imprisonment and hanging. Thus Blake's mythology had a creative component, since the mythology allowed him to detail his wild visions of the world, as well as a political component, since the mythology allowed him to directly criticize contemporary actors and situations.

The poem begins with the sexual union, possibly a rape, between Orc and the daughter of Urthona—that is, the figurative marriage of the spirit of rebellion and imagination. This combination of rebellion and imagination sparks the American Revolution, the French Revolution, and the political upheaval in Spain and Italy, according to the poem and according to Blake's unique belief system. Orc's rebellion symbolizes America's desire for self-sufficiency and independence from England, its colonizer, who keeps America chained. Urthona's daughter lists several nation-specific symbols of revolution in the final stanza of "Preludium," including a serpent in Canada and a lion in Peru, and thus emphasizes the naturalness of rebellion. Despite the horrible pain, she explains, the violence is destiny and "the torment long foretold." Orc's shackled state represents the natural state of humans: fallen, degraded, chained by ignorance. In his brutal taking of the virginal girl, Orc overcomes his natural state and eventually goes beyond his previous limits. Likewise, Blake believed that humans needed to metaphorically transcend their present circumstances, which included an overarching sense of political tyranny, as well as the smallness of their own minds as they blithely follow society's dicta. To do so, they needed to employ a combination of their imagination and a fiery, passionate spirit.

"A Prophecy" uses oblique and heightened language and biblical symbols to not only describe the aftermath of the American Revolution, but also to detail Blake's hope for the revolutionary spirit to spread throughout Europe, overhauling contemporary, staid society and instituting a new world. Blake's use of the imagery of slavery, including chains, shackles, and heated iron, both invokes the plight of the biblical Jews enslaved in Egypt and signifies the relationship between England and America. Blake drew his symbolism and stories from the Bible to demonstrate his knowledge that informed his opinions: his was not a crackpot, haphazard system, but rather a carefully thought-out retooling of Christianity. Albion's Angel calls forth the plague and pestilence to stop the rebellion from spreading through Europe. As in the Bible, the poem's plague afflicts the innocent and the guilty alike. Called "blasphemous Demon, Antichrist, hater of Dignities" by Albion's Angel, Orc is the direct opposite of Christ, who stands for loving kindness. In his rebelliousness, Orc lashes out against English rule and the English god, or Urizen, who imprisons his worshipers and, according to Orc, perverts the Ten Commandments. After the rebellion, in the new world formed by the violent apocalypse, Blake envisioned the worship of both sides of God—the violent side symbolized by Orc and the peaceful side represented by Christ.

VISIONS OF THE DAUGHTERS OF ALBION

EXCERPT FROM PLATE 2

The lark does rustle in the ripe corn, and the eagle returns
From nightly prey, and lifts his golden beak to the pure east,
Shaking the dust from his immortal pinions to awake
The sun that sleeps too long. Arise, my Theotormon! I am pure,
Because the night is gone that clos'd me in its deadly black.
They told me that the night and day were all that I could see;
They told me that I had five senses to enclose me up;
And they enclos'd my infinite brain into a narrow circle,
And sunk my heart into the Abyss, a red, round globe, hot
*   burning,*

Till all from life I was obliterated and erasèd.
Instead of morn arises a bright shadow, like an eye
In the eastern cloud; instead of night a sickly charnel-house,
That Theotormon hears me not. To him the night and morn
Are both alike; a night of sighs, a morning of fresh tears;
And none but Bromion can hear my lamentations.

SUMMARY

This long work begins with an epigram, "The Eye sees more than the Heart knows," and "The Argument," a short poem that details the love of Oothoon for Theotormon. Hiding in Leutha's valley, the young virgin speaker is raped by "terrible thunders." The remainder of the work consists of several poems grouped under the heading "Visions." These visions begin by describing the enslaved daughters of Albion, looking toward the soul of America, embodied by Oothoon, for help in their imprisonment. Oothoon wanders into a valley and plucks a marigold, putting it between her breasts. Flying to Theotormon, with whom she is in love, Oothoon is attacked and raped by Bromion. Furious, Theotormon binds Bromion back-to-back with Oothoon, imprisons them in Bromion's cave, and sits, crying, at the threshold. He hears Oothoon's cries but does not help, even as Oothoon beseeches his eagles to pluck her clean. Acting as a chorus, the daughters of Albion hear Oothoon and sigh with her.

The remainder of the poem intertwines speeches from Oothoon, Theotormon, and Bromion with the daughters' plaintive chorus. Oothoon begins a monologue in which she bewails Theotormon's lack of help and ultimate rejection. She explains that she is made pure by her love, drawing examples from nature to illustrate her point, and she makes claims for her innocence. Theotormon answers her in a short monologue of his own, in which he claims to have lost all his love and joy. Bromion defends himself and his actions by appealing to tradition and nature through a series of rhetorical questions. Finally, in her long concluding monologue, Oothoon appeals to Urizen, the "creator of men" (Plate 5), to find out whether he condones this behavior from men, who are supposed to be endowed with greater intelligence than animals. She criticizes a society in which raped virgins are labeled "whore," and she admits to having felt sexual desire for Theotormon, who has been made almost insane by jealousy. Oothoon ends by praying for love, imagining a pre-rape world in which she and Theotormon could live together in harmony. In this world, all living things would feel the holiness that lives within them, helping and loving one another.

ANALYSIS

Visions of the Daughters of Albion directly engages the political and social issues of the late eighteenth century and proposes new methods of social interaction. According to Blake's formulations, England enslaved America, men enslaved women, and all people were enslaved by organized religion, tyranny, and pervasive small-mindedness. As such, Blake often portrays Oothoon as an American black slave and Bromion as her vicious master. Engravings Blake made at this time also demonstrate his belief in the equality of all. Similarly, in "The Little Black Boy," from *Songs of Innocence and of Experience*, the young speaker explains that while his skin is black, his soul is white and he worships the Christian God. Although we might now find this formulation distasteful or racist, at the time Blake was trying to express what he perceived to be a fundamental similarity between people: the capacity of the human soul, regardless of race or color, to believe in and manifest God. Bromion attempts to defend himself by drawing examples from the natural world, in which one law exists for lions and oxen and the strong always dominate the weak. Ironically using Bromion as a mouthpiece, Blake parrots the proslavery rhetoric of his day, which attempted to use evidence from nature to defend slavery.

The most revolutionary aspect of the poem is its free expression of sexual desire and its vision of a world in which the sexes were equal. Blake imagined his poem as a response to Mary Wollstonecraft's *Vindication of the Rights of Woman* (1792), a nonfiction book in which Wollstonecraft argued for female equality and effectively launched the modern feminist movement. As in Wollstonecraft's work, here Blake argues against the imprisonment of women in the domestic sphere. Oothoon freely expresses sexual desire for Theotormon, decorating her breast with flowers and eagerly anticipating their reunion. The daughters of Albion, or Englishwomen, second Oothoon's arguments. In her concluding monologue, sex becomes a positive expression of love between two people—and Oothoon argues that people turn toward organized religion to suppress their desires rather than forgoing prescribed worship and reveling in the body's natural urges. Furthermore, Oothoon claims that those who do not feel sexual desire will be unable to create or express themselves, a groundbreaking connection that demonstrates Blake's belief in the importance of and potential for individual transcendence of historical and social circumstances. Working together, all members of English society could liberate themselves from outdated rules that limited their potential for free expression and experience.

WILLIAM WORDSWORTH

(1770–1850)

CONTEXT

William Wordsworth was born on April 7, 1770, in Cockermouth, a small town in the rural Lake District of northern England. His mother died when Wordsworth was eight, and his father died when he was thirteen. Somewhat unruly as a child, Wordsworth enjoyed wandering around the land. In 1787, when Wordsworth was seventeen, he entered Cambridge University. At school, Wordsworth became interested in radical political causes, becoming an early supporter of the French Revolution. In 1790, Wordsworth and a friend visited France and the Alps on a walking tour, and Wordsworth returned to France after his graduation from Cambridge in 1791. While there, Wordsworth had an affair with a Frenchwoman named Annette Vallon. She became pregnant and gave birth to a daughter named Caroline in December 1792.

In 1793, Wordsworth published two poems, "An Evening Walk" and "Descriptive Sketches," possibly hoping to earn enough money to return to Annette and Caroline. But less than a month later, England declared war on France and he was prevented from returning. Gradually, Wordsworth became disillusioned with the revolutionary cause. At this point, the French Revolution had turned bloody and chaotic during the Reign of Terror, and the philosophers he once read struck him as too rational and emotionless. He felt depressed and full of despair. In 1794, however, Wordsworth reunited with his beloved younger sister Dorothy, and they moved in together. He also developed an influential friendship with Samuel Taylor Coleridge around 1795. Together, Wordsworth and Coleridge began formulating a new theory of poetry, which would lead to the development of **romanticism** in England. They jointly published *Lyrical Ballads* in 1798, a collection of poems that laid out the tenets of romanticism.

Critics now consider *Lyrical Ballads* to be one of the most important books of poetry ever published, though it achieved little success in 1798. Coleridge and Wordsworth decided that the cure for society's ills lay not in the rationalism of the eighteenth-century **Enlightenment**, which praised classical ideals and objective knowledge, but in a devotion to nature. Eighteenth-century poets followed the classical model of verse: they used only elevated diction and chose only nobly born characters as their subjects. In contrast, Coleridge and

Wordsworth used colloquial diction—the language of everyday life—and sought their subjects in the country people they saw in the Lake District. These everyday people lived their lives close to nature. Both Coleridge and Wordsworth valued nature for the meditation and knowledge it sparked in human consciousness. They also esteemed the supernatural and mysterious aspects of existence over the neoclassical emphasis on reason.

In 1800, a second edition of *Lyrical Ballads* was published, which included a preface written by Wordsworth. This preface was later expanded and revised for the third edition, published in 1802. The essay summarizes Wordsworth's poetic project. To Wordsworth, "all good poetry is the spontaneous overflow of powerful feelings," and the goal of poetry is to communicate those feelings to the reader. Eighteenth-century poets emphasized artifice and action, so Wordsworth's ideas about spontaneous, abundant emotions were quite revolutionary, as was his use of everyday speech and country characters. By suggesting that rural laborers could be a fit subject for poetry, Wordsworth elevated the lower classes to the level of the nobility, thereby demonstrating in poetry a sympathy for the radical French Revolution. Democratic ideals also appear in the emphasis Wordsworth placed on the importance of individuals and the powers of the individual mind. He entreated his readers to decide for themselves whether the poems in *Lyrical Ballads* were any good, based on their own personal reactions and not based on the comments of critics. Throughout the essay, intellectual independence is held up as the only way to achieve pleasure and truth.

Along with Coleridge, Wordsworth is usually credited with founding the romantic movement in English. Today, scholars consider six poets to constitute the major romantics: Wordsworth, Coleridge, William Blake, Percy Bysshe Shelley, Lord Byron, and John Keats. Though they were not all friends with one another, and though they had different artistic goals and political ideals, their shared emphasis on emotion and intuition, their interest in the powers of the human mind and in nature, their belief in the individual, and their rejection of many of the rules and conventions of eighteenth-century English poetry binds the men together as a group. The younger generation of romantics—Shelley, Keats, and Byron—were inspired by *Lyrical Ballads* to embrace new forms of verse and to further explore the relationship between the individual and nature. In many ways, these poets took Wordsworth's ideas to more radical conclusions, and they criticized Wordsworth as he aged for betraying the radicalism of his youth.

WILLIAM WORDSWORTH

Around the beginning of the nineteenth century, Wordsworth had begun working on a long poem, which he hoped would illustrate Coleridge's theories regarding love for nature. A "prelude" to this planned work would become his autobiographical poem *The Prelude*. Wordsworth expanded and revised this poem for many years, and it would not be published until a few months after his death in 1850. Critics generally consider *The Prelude* to be one of the most extraordinary long poems in English. Its fourteen books take Wordsworth as its hero and describe the spiritual and intellectual development of his mind from childhood to adulthood. The poem examines key experiences, focusing on the workings of memory and the impact of the imagination on nature. According to Wordsworth's formulations, the mind uses its powers of creativity to impose itself on nature; this imposition allows the mind to uncover nature's mysteries.

A brief peace with France allowed Wordsworth to leave England in 1802 and travel to meet his daughter Caroline for the first time. Upon returning to England, Wordsworth married his childhood friend Mary Hutchinson, with whom he would have five children. In his later years, Wordsworth became more conservative. Around 1810, Wordsworth and Coleridge had a bitter falling-out; they only resumed their friendship almost two decades later. In 1813, Wordsworth took the job of tax gatherer for the region of Westmorland, which gained him a reliable salary for a minimal amount of work and allowed him to move his family and Dorothy into a stately house. By the 1820s, he was an established and respectable figure in English poetry. In 1843, Wordsworth was appointed poet laureate of England, a position he held until his death in 1850.

THEMES, MOTIFS & SYMBOLS

THEMES

THE BENEFICIAL INFLUENCE OF NATURE

Throughout Wordsworth's work, nature provides the ultimate good influence on the human mind. All manifestations of the natural world—from the highest mountain to the simplest flower—elicit noble, elevated thoughts and passionate emotions in the people who observe these manifestations. Wordsworth repeatedly emphasizes the importance of nature to an individual's intellectual and spiritual development. A good relationship with nature helps individuals connect to both the spiritual and the social worlds. As Wordsworth explains in *The Prelude*, a love of nature can lead to a love of humankind. In such poems as "The World Is Too Much with Us" (1807) and "London, 1802" (1807) people become selfish and immoral when they distance themselves from nature by living in cities. Humanity's innate empathy and nobility of spirit becomes corrupted by artificial social conventions as well as by the squalor of city life. In contrast, people who spend a lot of time in nature, such as laborers and farmers, retain the purity and nobility of their souls.

THE POWER OF THE HUMAN MIND

Wordsworth praised the power of the human mind. Using memory and imagination, individuals could overcome difficulty and pain. For instance, the **speaker** in "Lines Composed a Few Miles Above Tintern Abbey" (1798) relieves his loneliness with memories of nature, while the leech gatherer in "Resolution and Independence" (1807) perseveres cheerfully in the face of poverty by the exertion of his own will. The transformative powers of the mind are available to all, regardless of an individual's class or background. This democratic view emphasizes individuality and uniqueness. Throughout his work, Wordsworth showed strong support for the political, religious, and artistic rights of the individual, including the power of his or her mind. In the 1802 preface to *Lyrical Ballads*, Wordsworth explained the relationship between the mind and poetry. Poetry is "emotion recollected in tranquility"—that is, the mind transforms the raw emotion of experience into poetry capable of giving plea-sure. Later poems, such as "Ode: Intimations of Immortality" (1807), imagine nature as the source of the inspiring material that nourishes the active, creative mind.

THE SPLENDOR OF CHILDHOOD

In Wordsworth's poetry, childhood is a magical, magnificent time of innocence. Children form an intense bond with nature, so much so that they appear to be a part of the natural world, rather than a part of the human, social world. Their relationship to nature is passion-ate and extreme: children feel joy at seeing a rainbow but great ter-ror at seeing desolation or decay. In 1799, Wordsworth wrote several poems about a girl named Lucy who died at a young age. These poems, including "She dwelt among the untrodden ways" (1800) and "Strange fits of passion have I known" (1800), praise her beauty and lament her untimely death. In death, Lucy retains the innocence and splendor of childhood, unlike the children who grow up, lose their connection to nature, and lead unfulfilling lives. The speaker in "Ode: Intimations of Immortality" believes that children delight in nature because they have access to a divine, immortal world. As children age and reach maturity, they lose this connection but gain an ability to feel emotions, both good and bad. Through the power of the human mind, particularly memory, adults can rec-ollect the devoted connection to nature of their youth.

MOTIFS

WANDERING AND WANDERERS

The speakers of Wordsworth's poems are inveterate wanderers: they roam solitarily, they travel over the moors, they take private walks through the highlands of Scotland. Active wandering allows the characters to experience and participate in the vastness and beauty of the natural world. Moving from place to place also allows the wanderer to make discoveries about himself. In "I travelled among unknown men" (1807), the speaker discovers his patriotism only after he has traveled far from England. While wandering, speakers uncover the visionary powers of the mind and understand the influence of nature, as in "I wandered lonely as a cloud" (1807). The speaker of this poem takes comfort in a walk he once took after he has returned to the grit and desolation of city life. Recollecting his wanderings allows him to transcend his present circumstances.

WILLIAM WORDSWORTH

Wordsworth's poetry itself often wanders, roaming from one subject or experience to another, as in *The Prelude*. In this long poem, the speaker moves from idea to idea through digressions and distractions that mimic the natural progression of thought within the mind.

MEMORY

Memory allows Wordsworth's speakers to overcome the harshness of the contemporary world. Recollecting their childhoods gives adults a chance to reconnect with the visionary power and intense relationship they had with nature as children. In turn, these memories encourage adults to re-cultivate as close a relationship with nature as possible as an antidote to sadness, loneliness, and despair. The act of remembering also allows the poet to write: Wordsworth argued in the 1802 preface to *Lyrical Ballads* that poetry sprang from the calm remembrance of passionate emotional experiences. Poems cannot be composed at the moment when emotion is first experienced. Instead, the initial emotion must be combined with other thoughts and feelings from the poet's past experiences using memory and imagination. The poem produced by this time-consuming process will allow the poet to convey the essence of his emotional memory to his readers and will permit the readers to remember similar emotional experiences of their own.

VISION AND SIGHT

Throughout his poems, Wordsworth fixates on vision and sight as the vehicles through which individuals are transformed. As speakers move through the world, they see visions of great natural loveliness, which they capture in their memories. Later, in moments of darkness, the speakers recollect these visions, as in "I wandered lonely as a cloud." Here, the speaker daydreams of former jaunts through nature, which "flash upon that inward eye / which is the bliss of solitude" (21–22). The power of sight captured by our mind's eye enables us to find comfort even in our darkest, loneliest moments. Elsewhere, Wordsworth describes the connection between seeing and experiencing emotion, as in "My heart leaps up" (1807), in which the speaker feels joy as a result of spying a rainbow across the sky. Detailed images of natural beauty abound in Wordsworth's poems, including descriptions of daffodils and clouds, which focus on what can be seen, rather than touched, heard, or felt. In Book Fourteenth of *The Prelude*, climbing to the top of a mountain in Wales allows the speaker to have a prophetic vision of the workings of the mind as it thinks, reasons, and feels.

WILLIAM WORDSWORTH

SYMBOLS

LIGHT

Light often symbolizes truth and knowledge. In "The Tables Turned" (1798), Wordsworth contrasts the barren light of reason available in books with the "sweet" (11) and "freshening" (6) light of the knowledge nature brings. Sunlight literally helps people see, and sunlight also helps speakers and characters begin to glimpse the wonders of the world. In "Expostulation and Reply" (1798), the presence of light, or knowledge, within an individual prevents dullness and helps the individual to see, or experience. Generally, the light in Wordsworth's poems represents immortal truths that can't be entirely grasped by human reason. In "Ode: Imitations of Immortality," the speaker remembers looking at a meadow as a child and imagining it gleaming in "celestial light" (4). As the speaker grows and matures, the light of his youth fades into the "light of common day" (78) of adulthood. But the speaker also imagines his remembrances of the past as a kind of light, which illuminate his soul and give him the strength to live.

THE LEECH GATHERER

In "Resolution and Independence," the ancient leech gatherer who spends his days wandering the moors looking for leeches represents the strong-minded poet who perseveres in the face of poverty, obscurity, and solitude. As the poem begins, a wanderer travels along a moor, feeling elated and taking great pleasure in the sights of nature around him but also remembering that despair is the twin of happiness. Eventually he comes upon an old man looking for leeches, even though the work is dangerous and the leeches have become increasingly hard to find. As the speaker chats with the old man, he realizes the similarities between leech gathering and writing poetry. Like a leech gather, a poet continues to search his or her mind and the landscape of the natural world for poems, even though such intense emotions can damage one's psyche, the work pays poorly and poverty is dangerous to one's health, and inspiration sometimes seems increasingly hard to find. The speaker resolves to think of the leech gatherer whenever his enthusiasm for poetry or belief in himself begins to wane.

WILLIAM WORDSWORTH

SUMMARY & ANALYSIS

"WE ARE SEVEN"

———A simple Child,
That lightly draws its breath,
And feels its life in every limb,
What should it know of death?

I met a little cottage Girl: 5
She was eight years old, she said;
Her hair was thick with many a curl
That clustered round her head.

She had a rustic, woodland air,
And she was wildly clad: 10
Her eyes were fair, and very fair;
—Her beauty made me glad.

"Sisters and brothers, little Maid,
How many may you be?"
"How many? Seven in all," she said   15
And wondering looked at me.

"And where are they? I pray you tell."
She answered, "Seven are we;
And two of us at Conway dwell,
And two are gone to sea.   20

"Two of us in the church-yard lie,
My sister and my brother;
And, in the church-yard cottage, I
Dwell near them with my mother."

"You say that two at Conway dwell,   25
And two are gone to sea,
Yet ye are seven!—I pray you tell,
Sweet Maid, how this may be."

WILLIAM WORDSWORTH

Then did the little Maid reply,
"Seven boys and girls are we;
Two of us in the church-yard lie,
Beneath the church-yard tree."

       30

"You run about, my little Maid,
Your limbs they are alive;
If two are in the church-yard laid,
Then ye are only five."

       35

"Their graves are green, they may be seen,"
The little Maid replied,
"Twelve steps or more from my mother's door,
And they are side by side.

       40

"My stockings there I often knit,
My kerchief there I hem;
And there upon the ground I sit,
And sing a song to them.

"And often after sunset, Sir,
When it is light and fair,
I take my little porringer,
And eat my supper there.

       45

"The first that died was sister Jane;
In bed she moaning lay,
Till God released her of her pain;
And then she went away.

       50

"So in the church-yard she was laid;
And, when the grass was dry,
Together round her grave we played,
My brother John and I.

       55

"And when the ground was white with snow,
And I could run and slide,
My brother John was forced to go,
And he lies by her side."

       60

WILLIAM WORDSWORTH

"How many are you, then," said I,
"If they two are in heaven?"
Quick was the little Maid's reply,
"O Master! we are seven."

"But they are dead; those two are dead!   65
Their spirits are in heaven!"
'Twas throwing words away; for still
The little Maid would have her will,
And said, "Nay, we are seven!"

SUMMARY

The speaker begins by wondering what a child, who is so healthy and full of life, could possibly understand about death. For the remaining sixteen **stanzas** of the poem, the speaker narrates a conversation he has with an eight-year-old country girl. She has thick, curly hair; pretty eyes; and a "rustic, woodland air" (9). He finds the little girl beautiful. The speaker asks the girl how many brothers and sisters she has, and the girl replies that there are seven children in her family. At the speaker's request, the girl tells him where her siblings are: two live in Conway, a town in Wales; two are in the navy; and one sister and one brother are lying in their graves. The little girl lives near the graveyard, in a cottage with her mother.

Confused, the speaker asks the little girl how two children in Conway, two in the navy, and one at home can add up to seven. The girl answers that the two children in the graveyard bring the total number of children to seven. But the speaker insists that the girl count only the living number of children in her family, even as the girl stubbornly claims that her dead brother and sister still exist. She can see their graves, and she still spends time with them, sitting nearby as she sews or eats her dinner and sometimes singing them a song. Next the girl describes their deaths. Her sister Jane was the first to die, suffering from a painful illness until God released her from death. After Jane was buried, the little girl and her brother John often played together around the grave. But when winter came, and the little girl was able to frolic on the snow, John died too and was buried beside Jane.

Now that the little girl has made it clear that she knows her brother and sister are dead, the speaker repeats his question: if two of the children are in heaven, how many children are left in her family? The little girl repeats her answer: "O Master! we are seven"

(64). In a final outburst, the exasperated speaker cries that two children are dead. But in the final three lines of the poem, he acknowledges that all his explanations and protests are useless because the little girl refuses to admit there is any truth to his logic. She insists on claiming that there are seven children in her family.

ANALYSIS

First published in *Lyrical Ballads*, "We Are Seven" seems to be a straightforward and sentimental illustration of an innocent child's inability to understand death. Like many of the poems in *Lyrical Ballads*, this poem has a rural setting and features rustic people who live and work in the country. The poem's **quatrains** rely on simple, everyday language and use an *abab* rhyme scheme. Finally, the poem's meter, which alternates between **iambic trimeter** and **iambic tetrameter**, gives the poem a singsong quality and thus emphasizes the girl's young age. The unnamed girl speaks without using **figures of speech**, such as **metaphors**, and she uses the vocabulary of childhood: she talks about running and playing, and she does simple chores, such as sewing and knitting. Nonetheless, Wordsworth imbues the little girl with earnestness and dignity, thereby lending credence to her views on death.

Wordsworth demonstrates that children have an innate, mystical relationship to the world that operates outside the boundaries of logic. While the adult in the poem persists in his belief that the girl's family only contains five children, the girl remains steadfast in her view that there are seven children. She understands that two siblings have died, but she nevertheless includes them in her count. The adult, in contrast, believes that the girl cannot understand the abstract concept of death: because she can see the graves that contain her siblings' bodies, she imagines that their spirits still exist. She only understands what she can see with her own eyes. Although the adult may be charmed by the girl's rustic beauty and her sweet, cheerful devotion to her dead siblings, he clearly believes that when the child grows older, she will have to confront the realities of life and death—as an adult, she will understand that there are only five children left in her family. Because she believes her siblings are still with her, she does not grieve over their deaths.

The poem demonstrates two equally legitimate ways of viewing death. In the adult's view, death eradicates the individual and the soul. In the child's view, death takes the individual's body but leaves the individual's soul. The girl clearly understands that her siblings have died, but she argues that they remain a significant part of her life: their graves are "green, they may be seen" (37), and she feels an emotional connection to them. Frustrated, the speaker finds he cannot argue with her peculiar logic. He can only say that the souls of the dead children are in heaven, but he cannot prove them to be there. She, in contrast, can prove that she feels connected to her dead siblings by talking about how she spends time at their graves, sewing and eating. By the end of the poem, the speaker seems to have the more naive view of death and the more simplistic view of life. By stubbornly dividing the world into living people and dead people, the adult ignores the subtle, complex emotional relationship between everything in the universe.

LINES COMPOSED A FEW MILES ABOVE TINTERN ABBEY

EXCERPT FROM "LINES COMPOSED A FEW MILES ABOVE TINTERN ABBEY"

> These beauteous forms,
> Through a long absence, have not been to me
> As is a landscape to a blind man's eye:
> But oft, in lonely rooms, and 'mid the din
> Of towns and cities, I have owed to them
> In hours of weariness, sensations sweet,
> Felt in the blood, and felt along the heart;
> And passing even into my purer mind,
> With tranquil restoration:—feelings too
> Of unremembered pleasure: such, perhaps,
> As have no slight or trivial influence
> On that best portion of a good man's life,
> His little, nameless, unremembered, acts
> Of kindness and of love. Nor less, I trust,
> To them I may have owed another gift,
> Of aspect more sublime; that blessed mood,
> In which the burthen of the mystery,
> In which the heavy and the weary weight
> Of all this unintelligible world,
> Is lightened:—that serene and blessed mood,
> In which the affections gently lead us on,—
> Until, the breath of this corporeal frame

And even the motion of our human blood
Almost suspended, we are laid asleep
In body, and become a living soul:
While with an eye made quiet by the power
Of harmony, and the deep power of joy,
We see into the life of things.

SUMMARY

The speaker begins by explaining that he last visited the area five years ago. This is the second time he has seen the landscape around him, with its precipitous crags, unobtrusive orchards, wild-looking bushes, farms of green pastures, and smoke that rises up from between the trees. Looking at the smoke, the speaker imagines that gypsies live in the woods or that a hermit lives in the caves. Although it has been a long time since the speaker has been here, he says he has frequently remembered the landscape, particularly when he was far away from nature. His memory brought him happiness and peace when he was lonely or caught in stressful circumstances. He suspects that the feelings the memory inspired in him are the kinds of feelings that influence a person to perform small, everyday acts of benevolence and adoration. These feelings are also probably responsible for bringing on a "blessed mood" (37)—a trancelike state in which the harmony and joy he feels transforms him into a visionary capable of seeing deeply into the heart and soul of all living things.

But, the speaker says, he might be wrong about these feelings. However, he repeats that he has found solace in his memories of the Wye landscape, and now his memory is being refreshed as he looks upon the scene again. His pleasure comes not only from his current enjoyment of the scene but also from the idea that he will be able to remember this moment in the future, as he was able to remember his previous visit. The speaker hopes that this will be true, even though he is different than he was five years ago. Then he ran through the woods like a deer, acting like a man who was running away from something, rather than toward something he adored. At that time, nature was everything to him. He was deeply passionate about every natural object that he saw, and his delight came entirely from his senses. Back then, he didn't have to analyze his feelings or give them deeper intellectual or spiritual meaning.

Although that time of the speaker's life has gone by, the speaker does not regret losing his passionate, ecstatic relationship to nature. Now he has learned a new way to interact with nature, which more than compensates for the loss of the old way. The speaker understands the presence of humanity within the natural landscape, which can humble and subdue him, despite its gentleness. In these moments, the speaker senses a sublime "presence" (94) that runs through all of nature, from the sun to the ocean to the human mind. He still loves the natural world and everything his senses perceive because he recognizes a moral and spiritual force in them that can guide his heart and mind.

In the final stanza, the speaker says that he would still retain his vitality and creativity, even if he were not aware of this spiritual force in nature. He would retain his imaginative powers simply because his friend sits with him on the banks of the river. In the eyes and the voice of his "dear, dear Sister" (121), the speaker sees shades of his former self and of the passionate pleasure he took in nature. The speaker declares that nature will never wound those who worship her, and he prays that nature will guide them through their lives, filling their minds with elevated thoughts and aesthetic pleasures. These thoughts and pleasures will keep them cheerful and grateful for the blessings of life, even as they encounter nasty, evil people or the dullness of everyday life. He encourages his sister to indulge in rapturous experiences with nature so that later in life she can remember these experiences with her mature mind. If she feels lonely, afraid, or sad, she can remember what the speaker said to her today and find comfort in the memory. She will remember how the speaker, who once worshiped nature in a simple way, came to worship it in a deeper, holier way. Finally, the speaker extols his sister to remember the immense pleasure he received on his second visit to the Wye River, not only because the landscape remained beautiful but also because her pleasure in the landscape made him doubly glad to revisit the area.

ANALYSIS

Published in the 1798 edition of *Lyrical Ballads*, "Lines Composed a Few Miles Above Tintern Abbey" depicts the ways in which nature enriches and shapes people's lives, even as their relationships with nature alter with age. A visit to the Wye River prompts the speaker to recollect his first visit there, five years before, and to compare his interaction with nature then to his interaction with nature now. As a youth, the speaker actively wandered around the landscape with "glad animal movements" (74), and he compares his young self to a deer who climbed hills and crossed creeks. As a young man, the speaker passionately remembered the landscape with "dizzy rap-tures" (85) like an adolescent in the first flush of love. Finally, as an adult, the speaker combines his powers of thought with his powers of sensory perception: now he enjoys the beauty of the landscape while simultaneously mediating on the passage of time and the sub-sequent maturation of his association with the natural world.

"Tintern Abbey" uses the relationship between the speaker and nature as a springboard from which to discuss the larger relation-ship between society and nature. Detailed images of the quiet land-scape open the poem: water flows down the mountain, crags rise up, landscape blends into sky. In the distance, smoke rises from houses the speaker cannot see. The smoke and the cultivated pastures dem-onstrate human involvement with the natural world. These woods have human dwellers. Rather than tame nature and bend it to human will, the inhabitants of the area have let nature continue on its own course and have seamlessly blended their society into nature. Orchards planted by humans grow harmoniously among the indigenous trees that grow without human intervention. Bushes, also planted by humans, grow in "little lines / of sportive wood run wild" (15–16), so that even the ornamentation planted by the land's human inhabitants reflects the natural growth nearby. The poem portrays an ideal relationship between humans and nature, in which humans respect nature and nature, in turn, provides humans with bountiful resources with which to live and enjoy.

In addition to providing sustenance, nature also provides balm for the human soul. The speaker explains that he has fondly recalled the Wye landscape over the past few years during times of stress and pain in the noisiness of urban areas. These memories comforted him, enabled him to treat others with care and gentleness, and trans-formed him into a kinder, more humane man. At the end of the poem, the speaker praises nature not just for its beauty but for its ability to bond him even more deeply to his sister. Knowing that she will now have the memory of Wye to bring her solace on dark days brings the speaker significant, altruistic happiness. But nature also has more mysterious powers: recollecting the beauty of the natural world helps the speaker understand the metaphysical link between everything in the universe. As an adult, the speaker now realizes that he does not have to separate himself from society or shut off his intellect to enjoy nature because a current runs through every-thing—himself, other people, and every object in the natural world. This current keeps him constantly connected to nature and to all of humanity.

"COMPOSED UPON WESTMINSTER BRIDGE, SEPTEMBER 3, 1802"

Earth has not anything to show more fair:
Dull would he be of soul who could pass by
A sight so touching in its majesty:
This City now doth, like a garment, wear
The beauty of the morning; silent, bare,   5
Ships, towers, domes, theatres, and temples lie
Open unto the fields, and to the sky;
All bright and glittering in the smokeless air.
Never did sun more beautifully steep
In his first splendour, valley, rock, or hill;   10
Ne'er saw I, never felt, a calm so deep!
The river glideth at his own sweet will:
Dear God! the very houses seem asleep;
And all that mighty heart is lying still!

SUMMARY

In this **sonnet**, the speaker stands on the Westminster Bridge and imagines that he looks upon one of the most beautiful sights in the world. As he looks at London, the city "wear[s] / the beauty of the morning" (4–5). Everything—from the buildings to the boats to the byways—lies quiet and still and bright. The sun has never touched anything so beautiful, and the speaker believes that he has never felt so calm as now. Even the houses seem to be sleeping, and the city's very core stays quiet.

ANALYSIS

Written in 1802 and published in 1807, "Composed Upon Westminster Bridge" expresses great love for the city of London. As the city sleeps in the early morning, the speaker imagines that the sun has never touched anything so attractive as London's man-made structures. These structures produce in the speaker a sense of peace, and they are as lovely as anything in nature. "Westminster Bridge" and its praise of urban life stand out from the rest of Wordsworth's poems, which tend to dismiss urban life in favor of country life and in favor of a close relationship with the natural world. Like many romantic poets, Wordsworth blamed the city for separating adults from the close relationship with nature they cultivated as children.

WILLIAM WORDSWORTH

Urban life bred despair, loneliness, and isolation. Critics often read "Westminster Bridge" alongside "London, 1802," a sonnet that expresses deep disgust with the city. But the speaker in "Westminster Bridge" feels buoyed by the quiet city and peaceful River Thames. Rather than alienating him, the city feels welcoming and makes him content.

The speaker praises the man-made structures of London in order to pay tribute to the economic and artistic achievements of humanity. During the eighteenth and nineteenth centuries, England rapidly industrialized. As a result of the changing economy, people abandoned rural life for the factory and service jobs of the city. Generally, Wordsworth lamented the Industrial Revolution because it divided people from nature. In this poem, however, Wordsworth sees the city as being a part of nature. The speaker favorably compares the city to the natural world and also points out how closely linked the city is to the countryside. Nevertheless, the speaker values the city only as a product of human ingenuity: the air is "smokeless" (8) because the factories are closed, and the poem ends by reiterating the city's quiet and stillness. Awake and alive, with smoking factories and bustling people, the city would disgust the speaker with its noise, crowds, and working life.

"I WANDERED LONELY AS A CLOUD"

I wandered lonely as a cloud
That floats on high o'er vales and hills,
When all at once I saw a crowd,
A host, of golden daffodils;
Beside the lake, beneath the trees,   5
Fluttering and dancing in the breeze.

Continuous as the stars that shine
And twinkle on the milky way,
They stretched in never-ending line
Along the margin of a bay: 10
Ten thousand saw I at a glance,
Tossing their heads in sprightly dance.

The waves beside them danced; but they
Out-did the sparkling waves in glee:
A poet could not but be gay,   15

In such a jocund company:
I gazed—and gazed—but little thought
What wealth the show to me had brought:

For oft, when on my couch I lie
In vacant or in pensive mood,   20
They flash upon that inward eye
Which is the bliss of solitude;
And then my heart with pleasure fills,
And dances with the daffodils.

SUMMARY

The speaker begins by saying that he took a walk as aimlessly as a cloud that moves across the sky. All of a sudden, he came upon a multitude of daffodils moving in the breeze. He compares the roughly 10,000 daffodils growing next to a lake to a long line of shining stars and then to a dancing mass of people. While the water of the lake ruffles and shimmies, the daffodils do their own joyous dance, which fills the speaker with tremendous joy. The speaker looked and looked at the flowers, but at the time, he had no idea what a worthwhile gift he had just been given. Now, however, the speaker knows how priceless the vision was: he explains that sometimes, while he is just lying around and daydreaming, the image of the daffodils will flash through his mind. His ability to remember brings him happiness. When he sees the flowers swaying in his memory, his heart fills with pleasure and sways along with them.

ANALYSIS

Written in 1802, "I wandered lonely as a cloud" demonstrates the importance of nature to human happiness. The simple sight of fluttering flowers brings the speaker two types of joy: the immediate elation he expresses in stanza 3 and the emotional consolation he expresses in stanza 4. Like the daffodils, his heart moves with pleasure whenever he remembers the scene. The speaker has absorbed some of the daffodils' joy as he committed the sight to memory. Happiness thus comes from both witnessing the sights of nature and being a part of nature: the speaker compares himself to a cloud in stanza 1, then compares the flowers to people in stanza 2. Nature is like people, and people are like nature. Daydreaming in stanza 4, the speaker takes pleasure in remembering the interconnectedness

WILLIAM WORDSWORTH

of all living things, even as he lies alone in the city. The daffodils have triggered the speaker's imaginative power, thereby making him a better thinker even as they make him a happier person.

Wordsworth uses "I wandered lonely as a cloud" to describe the relationship between nature and poetry. The first three stanzas describe one of the simple, everyday experiences that Wordsworth argued make excellent material for poetry: walking along aimlessly, the speaker comes across a field of daffodils blowing in the breeze, and the sight of them makes him happy. As a poet, the speaker "could not but be gay" (15), nor could he help but use **similes** to describe the scene: although the speaker realizes that wind makes the daffodils move, he willfully chooses to believe that the daffodils move from an inner happiness, much like a mass of people moving to music. In this way, the poem becomes an exercise in uncovering figures of speech capable of describing the effects of the natural world. By the fourth stanza, the speaker describes the value of this vision: the speaker explicitly states that the vision has given him solace in times of solitude, while Wordsworth implicitly states that the true value of the vision has been the poem itself.

SAMUEL TAYLOR COLERIDGE

(1772–1834)

CONTEXT

Samuel Taylor Coleridge was born in 1772 at Ottery St. Mary, in Devonshire, England. Although his father, John Coleridge, held the prestigious position of parish vicar at the Church of Ottery St. Mary, the Coleridge family was quite poor. As the youngest of four-teen children, Coleridge was often bullied by his brothers and ignored by his mother, Ann Bowden. At age seven, Coleridge endured a particularly gruesome fight with his brother Francis, after Francis maliciously attacked Coleridge's cheese sandwich. Coleridge reacted in a burst of rage, lunging quickly at Francis with a knife and then fleeing the kitchen before his parents could properly intervene. Coleridge spent the following night at the bottom of a hill nearly a mile away from his home, repeating prayers from his little shilling book. That morning, the local baronet found Coleridge and carried him home to his anxious parents. He was nearly dead from prolonged exposure to the cold. The imagery of this traumatic incident would later appear and reappear in Coleridge's poetry, particularly "Monody on the Death of Chatterton" (1829).

In 1781, Coleridge's father died, just before Coleridge's ninth birthday. Coleridge then left Devonshire for London, where he attended boarding school at Christ's Hospital as a charity scholar. The move was intensely traumatic for Coleridge, and his resentment over being plucked from the countryside and imprisoned in the city would resurface later in his poetry. In 1791, Coleridge enrolled in Jesus College at Cambridge, living off a small allowance provided by his brother George. During his school years, Coleridge was plagued by illness and frequently given laudanum (opium dissolved in alcohol) to relieve the feverish symptoms. The addictive proper-ties of opium were not yet understood, and the drug was widely and casually prescribed for pain. Over the course of his treatment, Coleridge developed an addiction to opium that he would describe in an 1814 letter as an "accursed habit." Most scholars presume that Coleridge composed many of his poems under the influence of the drug, even as he spent many years attempting to stop his ingestion of it altogether.

Although he was a brilliant scholar, Coleridge abandoned Cambridge and his studies for London in December 1793. There he joined the Light Dragoons, under the pseudonym Silas Tomkyn

Comerbacke. Coleridge was unsuccessful as a solider, having never properly learned how to ride a horse. Soon, his brothers discovered what he had done and convinced Coleridge to return to Cambridge. Coleridge complied but spent the following summer alongside the poet Robert Southey, dreaming of the utopian "Pantisocracy" that the pair planned to establish on the banks of the Susquehanna River in Pennsylvania. In 1795, Coleridge again left Cambridge without completing his studies and moved to Bristol. Because the utopian movement required offspring in order to continue and flourish as a lifestyle, Coleridge became engaged to Sara Fricker, the younger sister of Southey's fiancée, Edith. Pantisocracy failed, but Sara and Coleridge were married anyway on October 31, 1795, and moved to Somerset, England. Nearly a year later, on November 19, 1796, Coleridge's first son, Hartley, was born. Coleridge published his first collection of poetry, *Poems on Various Subjects*, in 1797.

Around 1795, Coleridge struck up a friendship with the poet William Wordsworth and his sister Dorothy, thus igniting an artistic collaboration that would eventually revolutionize poetry and birth an entirely new literary movement in England: **romanticism**. Wordsworth and Coleridge jointly published *Lyrical Ballads*, a collection of poems credited with solidifying the tenets of romanticism that contained Coleridge's much-lauded poem "The Rime of the Ancient Mariner." Upon its publication in 1798, *Lyrical Ballads* received little fanfare, but critics now consider the volume to be one of the most influential books of poetry ever published. The poems reject the rationalism of the eighteenth-century **Enlightenment**, which praised classical ideals and objective knowledge, in favor of subjective experience, sensory perception, and a reverence for the mystical power of nature. They also demonstrate a commitment to the social and political ideals of the late eighteenth century, including liberty, justice, equality, and social progress. Finally, *Lyrical Ballads* proposed using colloquial diction—the language of everyday life—in poetry and valued nature for the meditation and knowledge it sparked in human consciousness.

As an artistic movement, romanticism began in the late 1780s in Germany and England and flourished in England until the 1830s. William Blake, often considered a precursor to the romantics, emphasized individual expression and emotion, as well as the idea of the poet as a visionary, in his late eighteenth-century work. Wordsworth and Coleridge expanded Blake's views: they too rejected the calm, balanced rationality that marked the work of the Enlighten-

SAMUEL T. COLERIDGE

ment. Instead, the romantics, including John Keats, Percy Bysshe Shelley, and Lord Byron, created subjective, emotional, spontaneous poetry that celebrated the individual and praised the outcast. The romantics favored sensory experience over intellectual appreciation, and they valued a strong creative spirit rather than a poet's ability to follow formal structures and rules, which the neoclassical period that preceded romanticism had emphasized. Imagination became a doorway to transcendence and spiritual enlightenment. In general, romantic poets expressed interest in the exotic and mysterious, inner passions and struggles, and the supreme beauty of the natural landscape.

Lyrical Ballads and the other work done in the late eighteenth century, including "Kubla Khan" (1797–1798) and *Christabel* (1798–1800), marked the highpoint of Coleridge's literary career. Although Coleridge and Wordsworth wrote *Lyrical Ballads* together, Wordsworth received more praise and Coleridge suffered in his shadow. Constantly berating himself and his work, Coleridge quickly became an extraordinarily insecure writer. After 1805, he essentially gave up poetry in favor of different forms of writing, including plays, periodicals, and philosophical prose. By 1806, after a two-year sojourn in Malta, Coleridge had returned to England damaged, deeply addicted to opium, separated from his wife, and tormented by terrible nightmares. He quarreled bitterly with Wordsworth in 1810 and later moved in full-time with a London doctor, with whom he lived until his death, in an attempt to curb his drug use. Although Coleridge wrote several important works in the nineteenth century, including the two-volume prose work *Biographia Literaria* (1817), he also began lifting passages from other writers and splicing them into his essays without credit. Regardless of his carelessness or insecurities, Coleridge profoundly influenced poetry, philosophy, and theology. He died on July 25, 1834.

THEMES, MOTIFS & SYMBOLS

THEMES

THE TRANSFORMATIVE POWER OF THE IMAGINATION

Coleridge believed that a strong, active imagination could become a vehicle for transcending unpleasant circumstances. Many of his poems are powered exclusively by imaginative flights, wherein the **speaker** temporarily abandons his immediate surroundings, exchanging them for an entirely new and completely fabricated experience. Using the imagination in this way is both empowering and surprising because it encourages a total and complete disrespect for the confines of time and place. These mental and emotional jumps are often well rewarded. Perhaps Coleridge's most famous use of imagination occurs in "This Lime-Tree Bower My Prison" (1797), in which the speaker employs a keen poetic mind that allows him to take part in a journey that he cannot physically make. When he "returns" to the bower, after having imagined himself on a fantastic stroll through the countryside, the speaker discovers, as a reward, plenty of things to enjoy from inside the bower itself, including the leaves, the trees, and the shadows. The power of imagination transforms the prison into a perfectly pleasant spot.

THE INTERPLAY OF PHILOSOPHY, PIETY, AND POETRY

Coleridge used his poetry to explore conflicting issues in philosophy and religious piety. Some critics argue that Coleridge's interest in philosophy was simply his attempt to understand the imaginative and intellectual impulses that fueled his poetry. To support the claim that his imaginative and intellectual forces were, in fact, organic and derived from the natural world, Coleridge linked them to God, spirituality, and worship. In his work, however, poetry, philosophy, and piety clashed, creating friction and disorder for Coleridge, both on and off the page. In "The Eolian Harp" (1795), Coleridge struggles to reconcile the three forces. Here, the speaker's philosophical tendencies, particularly the belief that an "intellectual breeze" (47) brushes by and inhabits all living things with consciousness, collide with those of his orthodox wife, who disapproves of his unconventional ideas and urges him to Christ. While his wife lies untroubled, the speaker agonizes over his spiritual conflict, caught between Christianity and a unique, individual spirituality that equates nature with God. The poem ends by discounting the pantheist spirit, and the speaker concludes by privileging God and Christ over nature and praising them for having healed him from the spiritual wounds inflicted by these unorthodox views.

NATURE AND THE DEVELOPMENT OF THE INDIVIDUAL

Coleridge, Wordsworth, and other romantic poets praised the unencumbered, imaginative soul of youth, finding images in nature with which to describe it. According to their formulation, experiencing nature was an integral part of the development of a complete soul and sense of personhood. The death of his father forced Coleridge to attend school in London, far away from the rural idylls of his youth, and he lamented the missed opportunities of his sheltered, city-bound adolescence in many poems, including "Frost at Midnight" (1798). Here, the speaker sits quietly by a fire, musing on his life, while his infant son sleeps nearby. He recalls his boarding school days, during which he would both daydream and lull himself to sleep by remembering his home far away from the city, and he tells his son that he shall never be removed from nature, the way the speaker once was. Unlike the speaker, the son shall experience the seasons and shall learn about God by discovering the beauty and bounty of the natural world. The son shall be given the opportunity to develop a relationship with God and with nature, an opportunity denied to both the speaker and Coleridge himself. For Coleridge, nature had the capacity to teach joy, love, freedom, and piety, crucial characteristics for a worthy, developed individual.

MOTIFS

CONVERSATION POEMS

Coleridge wanted to mimic the patterns and cadences of everyday speech in his poetry. Many of his poems openly address a single figure—the speaker's wife, son, friend, and so on—who listens silently to the simple, straightforward language of the speaker. Unlike the descriptive, long, digressive poems of Coleridge's classicist predecessors, Coleridge's so-called conversation poems are short, self-contained, and often without a discernable poetic form. Colloquial, spontaneous, and friendly, Coleridge's conversation poetry is also highly personal, frequently incorporating events and details of his domestic life in an effort to widen the scope of possible poetic content. Although he sometimes wrote in **blank verse**, unrhymed **iambic pentameter,** he adapted this metrical form to suit a more colloquial rhythm. Both Wordsworth and Coleridge believed that everyday language and speech rhythms would help broaden poetry's audience to include the middle and lower classes, who might have felt excluded or put off by the form and content of neoclassicists, such as Alexander Pope, Lady Mary Wortley Montagu, and John Dryden.

DELIGHT IN THE NATURAL WORLD

Like the other romantics, Coleridge worshiped nature and recognized poetry's capacity to describe the beauty of the natural world. Nearly all of Coleridge's poems express a respect for and delight in natural beauty. Close observation, great attention to detail, and precise descriptions of color aptly demonstrate Coleridge's respect and delight. Some poems, such as "This Lime-Tree Bower My Prison," "Youth and Age" (1834), and "Frost at Midnight," mourn the speakers' physical isolation from the outside world. Others, including "The Eolian Harp," use images of nature to explore philosophical and analytical ideas. Still other poems, including "The Nightingale" (ca. 1798), simply praise nature's beauty. Even poems that don't directly deal with nature, including "Kubla Khan" and "The Rime of the Ancient Mariner," derive some symbols and images from nature. Nevertheless, Coleridge guarded against the **pathetic fallacy,** or the attribution of human feeling to the natural world. To Coleridge, nature contained an innate, constant joyousness wholly separate from the ups and downs of human experience.

PRAYER

Although Coleridge's prose reveals more of his religious philosophizing than his poetry, God, Christianity, and the act of prayer appear in some form in nearly all of his poems. The son of an Anglican vicar, Coleridge vacillated from supporting to criticizing Christian tenets and the Church of England. Despite his criticisms, Coleridge remained defiantly supportive of prayer, praising it in his notebooks and repeatedly referencing it in his poems. He once told the novelist Thomas de Quincey that prayer demanded such close attention that it was the one of the hardest actions of which human hearts were capable. The conclusion to Part 1 of *Christabel* portrays Christabel in prayer, "a lovely sight to see" (279). In "The Rime of the Ancient

Mariner," the mariner is stripped of his ability to speak as part of his extreme punishment and, consequently, left incapable of praying. "The Pains of Sleep" (1803) contrasts the speaker at restful prayer, in which he prays silently, with the speaker at passionate prayer, in which he battles imaginary demons to pray aloud. In the sad poem, "Epitaph" (1833), Coleridge composes an epitaph for himself, which urges people to pray for him after he dies. Rather than recommend a manner or method of prayer, Coleridge's poems reflect a wide variety, which emphasizes his belief in the importance of individuality.

SYMBOLS

THE SUN

Coleridge believed that symbolic language was the only acceptable way of expressing deep religious truths and consistently employed the sun as a symbol of God. In "The Rime of the Ancient Mariner," Coleridge compares the sun to "God's own head" (97) and, later, attributes the first phase of the mariner's punishment to the sun, as it dehydrates the crew. All told, this poem contains eleven references to the sun, many of which signify the Christian conception of a wrathful, vengeful God. Bad, troubling things happen to the crew during the day, while smooth sailing and calm weather occur at night, by the light of the moon. Frequently, the sun stands in for God's influence and power, as well as a symbol of his authority. The setting sun spurs philosophical musings, as in "The Eolian Harp," and the dancing rays of sunlight represent a pinnacle of nature's beauty, as in "This Lime-Tree Bower My Prison."

THE MOON

Like the sun, the moon often symbolizes God, but the moon has more positive connotations than the sun. In "The Rime of the Ancient Mariner," the sun and the moon represent two sides of the Christian God: the sun represents the angry, wrathful God, whereas the moon represents the benevolent, repentant God. All told, the moon appears fourteen times in "The Rime of the Ancient Mariner," and generally favorable things occur during night, in contrast to the horrors that occur during the day. For example, the mariner's curse lifts and he returns home by moonlight. "Dejection: An Ode" (1802) begins with an epitaph about the new moon and goes on to describe the beauty of a moonlit night, contrasting its beauty with

SAMUEL T. COLERIDGE

the speaker's sorrowful soul. Similarly, "Frost at Midnight" also praises the moon as it illuminates icicles on a winter evening and spurs the speaker to great thought.

DREAMS AND DREAMING

Coleridge explores dreams and dreaming in his poetry to communicate the power of the imagination, as well as the inaccessible clarity of vision. "Kubla Khan" is subtitled "A Vision in a Dream." According to Coleridge, he fell asleep while reading and dreamed of a marvelous pleasure palace for the next few hours. Upon awakening, he began transcribing the dream-vision but was soon called away; when he returned, he wrote out the fragments that now comprise "Kubla Khan." Some critics doubt Coleridge's story, attributing it to an attempt at increasing the poem's dramatic effect. Nevertheless, the poem speaks to the imaginative possibilities of the subconscious. Dreams usually have a pleasurable connotation, as in "Frost at Midnight." There, the speaker, lonely and insomniac as a child at boarding school, comforts himself by imagining and then dreaming of his rural home. In his real life, however, Coleridge suffered from nightmares so terrible that sometimes his own screams would wake him, a phenomenon he details in "The Pains of Sleep." Opium probably gave Coleridge a sense of well-being that allowed him to sleep without the threat of nightmares.

SAMUEL T. COLERIDGE

Summary & Analysis

"The Rime of the Ancient Mariner"

Excerpt from "The Rime of the Ancient Mariner"

The ship driven by a storm toward the south pole.

"And now the storm-blast came, and he
Was tyrannous and strong:
He struck with his o'ertaking wings,
And chased us south along.

With sloping masts and dipping prow,
As who pursued with yell and blow
Still treads the shadow of his foe,
And forward bends his head,
The ship drove fast, loud roared the blast,
The southward aye we fled.

And now there came both mist and snow,
And it grew wondrous cold:
And ice, mast-high, came floating by,
As green as emerald.

The land of ice, and of fearful sounds where no living thing was
to be seen.

And through the drifts the snowy clifts
Did send a dismal sheen:
Nor shapes of men nor beasts we ken—
The ice was all between.

The ice was here, the ice was there,
The ice was all around:
It cracked and growled, and roared and howled,
Like noises in a swound!

Till a great sea-bird, called the Albatross, came through the
     snow-fog, and was received with great joy and hospitality.

At length did cross an Albatross,
Thorough the fog it came;
As if it had been a Christian soul,
We hailed it in God's name.

It ate the food it ne'er had eat,
And round and round it flew.
The ice did split with a thunder-fit;
The helmsman steered us through!

And lo! the Albatross proveth a bird of good omen, and
     followeth the ship as it returned northward through fog and
     floating ice.

And a good south wind sprung up behind;
The Albatross did follow,
And every day, for food or play,
Came to the mariners' hollo!

In mist or cloud, on mast or shroud,
It perched for vespers nine;
Whiles all the night, through fog-smoke white,
Glimmered the white Moon-shine."

The ancient Mariner inhospitably killeth the pious bird of good
     omen.

"God save thee, ancient Mariner!
From the fiends, that plague thee thus!—
Why look'st thou so ?"—With my cross-bow
I shot the Albatross.

SUMMARY: PART I

Three young men are walking together to a wedding when one is
stopped by an old seaman, the "ancient mariner" of the title.
Annoyed at being detained by the mariner's grasp, the wedding
guest explains that he is related to the groom and must hurry to the
wedding. The mariner releases the guest, but the guest becomes

entranced by the mariner's "glittering eye" (13) and sits down to listen. The mariner begins his tale by describing the sailing of his ship out from the native harbor into a sunny sea. Simultaneously, the guest hears the music of the bassoon, which signals that the bride has entered the wedding hall. Even though the guest wants to attend the wedding, he feels strangely compelled to stay and listen to the mariner's story.

Continuing with his tale, the mariner explains that while the voyage started out pleasantly, it very quickly became dark and scary. A violent storm rose up and forced the ship off course toward the South Pole. The ship sailed into ice and snow as blocks of green ice, as high as the ship's mast, floated by. Soon, the ship entered a barren land, devoid of any life and filled with shifting ice. Suddenly, a giant seabird, called an albatross, flew out of the snow and fog. Delighted to see another living creature, the crew cheered the bird; considering it a good omen, they fed and played with the bird. As the bird flew around the ship, the ice continued to crack. The ship was able to turn itself north, through more fog and floating ice, propelled by a strong southern wind. Every day, the albatross followed the ship, looking for food or to play. Concerned, the guest interrupts to ask the mariner why he looks so sad. The mariner admits that he killed the albatross with his crossbow.

SUMMARY: PART II

Although the albatross had been killed, the sun rose as the ship sailed north, propelled by gentle wind but shrouded in fog. Onboard the ship, the sailors were furious with the mariner for killing the albatross—and for destroying the good omen. As the fog cleared, however, the crew relented and admitted that the bird also brought with it the terrible weather. It was right, they claimed, to kill such birds, which brought cloudy, wet conditions. Soon, the wind died down, and the ship was left in a silent sea, idle and unmoving. Days passed with no movement under a hot sun. The ocean thickened as the ship's water became depleted and the sailors became increasingly thirsty. While the night sky danced, the sea appeared as if it were rotting, with unpleasant, slippery creatures swimming around the ship. At night, the ocean burst forth in many colors, like a painting composed by a witch. Some members of the crew began to dream that an invisible spirit, neither a ghost nor an angel, had begun to follow the ship on its journey. Soon all of the sailors lost the power of speech. Blaming the mariner for their bad luck, the crew hung the rotting corpse of the albatross around the mariner's neck.

SUMMARY: PART III

Time passed. Everyone onboard the ship suffered from weariness, dry throats, and cloudy eyes. Looking toward the west, the mariner spied something moving across the sky. At first, the object appeared to be something minuscule, then it looked like a fog, and finally the object transformed into a ship as it moved closer and closer. Too dry-mouthed to speak, the mariner bit his arm and sucked his own blood, wetting his mouth enough to cry out. Everyone onboard the ship cheered because they believed that they were about to be saved, ignoring or not noticing that the mysterious ship was moving without wind. But as the ship drew closer, blocking the sun, the sailors saw its ghostly, ghastly skeleton. The mariner spotted the ship's two inhabitants: death and his companion, a pale, blond woman with red lips called Night-mare Life-in-Death.

Death and Life-in-Death began throwing dice to determine the fate of the mariner and the crew. Life-in-Death won and whistled three times, which caused the sun to instantly sink into the horizon and stars and moon to appear in the sky. One after another, the other sailors cursed the mariner with their eyes, then dropped dead. Two hundred men died silently, without a sign or a moan. The only noise came from the sound of bodies falling, and the mariner watched the dead men's souls rise up and speed past him like arrows shot from a crossbow.

SUMMARY: PART IV

Part IV opens with the wedding guest admitting that he fears the mariner because he believes the mariner to be a ghost, with long, skinny hands and sparkling eyes. But the mariner tells the guest not to be afraid since the mariner did not die on the ship. Instead, he was punished: the mariner was left alone on the ship, surrounded by two hundred corpses and the disgusting, creature-riddled sea. The mariner repeatedly attempted to pray, but he was ultimately silenced by an evil voice that turned his heart to stone. He closed his eyes so as not to look at the corpses or the creatures, but his eyes pulsed in agony. For seven days and seven nights, he lived among the dead bodies, which did not rot or decay but rather cursed him silently with their fixed eyes. Lonely and despairing, the mariner yearned for home and the familiar sky. Finally, the moon rose, casting a shadow across the ship and the sea. Where the ship's shadow met the sea, the water turned red. Watching ugly snakes move through the water in the moonlight, the mariner felt overcome with love for the creatures, and he called them beautiful. At that moment, the albatross fell from his neck and the mariner realized he could now pray.

SUMMARY: PART V

The mariner continues telling his tale to the wedding guest. Finally freed from the curse of the albatross, the mariner fell asleep. He dreamt of water and awoke to find the ship's buckets filled. Rain began to fall, relieving his dehydration. Filled with water, the mariner felt somehow light—and thought he had died in his sleep. As the moon rose and the winds kicked up, spirits descended from the sky and began to reenter the dead sailors' bodies. In an amazing display, the men once again began to move about the ship, performing their daily tasks. They were silent and did not speak to or look at the mariner. The mariner joined them in their work, and the ship began to move forward.

At this point, the guest once again interjects to express his fear of the mariner. In response, the mariner claims that the men's bodies were actually inhabited by blessed spirits—not cursed souls. At dawn, the men clustered around the mast of the ship, singing sweetly. Their song—the sound of their souls exiting their bodies— rose upward toward the sun, then returned to the ship. Driven by the spirits, the ship moved forward. At noon, the ship suddenly stopped, twitching back and forth as if caught in a tug-of-war. As the ship broke free of the tugging, the mariner lurched to one side and fell off the ship's deck. He heard two far-off, disembodied voices coming from the sky. One spirit asked the other if the mariner was the man who killed the albatross. The other spirit answered affirmatively, then explained that although the mariner had paid for his crime, he would still continue to pay.

SUMMARY: PART VI

Part VI features a dialogue between the two voices as they discuss the fate of the mariner. The first voice asks how the ship is able to move so quickly, and the second responds by explaining that the moon has overpowered the sea and an angelic power is moving the ship north at such a quick rate. Meanwhile, the mariner has fallen into a trance, as the ship's speed turns out to be more than humans can bear. As he awakened, the mariner spied the dead men and realized that the curse and his punishment would continue. At night, the men lined up and stared at the mariner. The mariner could neither look away nor pray. Suddenly, the curse ended. A breeze kicked up and propelled the ship toward the mariner's home.

Slowly, the mariner began to recognize distant objects: the lighthouse, the hill, the church. The mariner, crying, prayed that he really was returning home. As the ship neared the bay, the spirits once again left the bodies of the sailors, and the mariner saw silent figures of pure light rising from the corpses. As they rose, each figure waved to the mariner. Soon after, he heard the sound of oars and turned to see a boat coming toward him, containing a pilot, the pilot's son, and a hermit. He rejoiced, believing that the hermit could absolve the mariner of his sins and wash the blood of the albatross from the mariner's soul.

SUMMARY: PART VII

Part VII opens by describing the hermit, who prays three times a day and enjoys talking with sailors from distant lands. As the small boat approached the ship, the hermit encouraged the pilot and his son to remain unafraid, even as the hermit commented on the strange condition of the ship. Just as the boat reached the ship, the ship began to sink, and the mariner was rescued. The pilot was frightened, and his son became hysterical, laughing crazily and calling the mariner the devil. Finally back on land, the mariner immediately asked the hermit to absolve him. The hermit asked the mariner to tell his tale, and as he spoke, the mariner felt relieved and free from the pain of his guilt. After some time passes, though, the guilt returns, prompting him to search out someone else to whom to tell his tale. Now, the mariner explains, he roams around until he spies a man destined to hear him out. The wedding guest was one such man. At this moment, the doors of the wedding hall are thrown open, and the wedding party wanders outside.

The mariner explains that his experiences were so frightening that there were times when he doubted the existence of God. He tells the wedding guest that the person who offers love and reverence to all God's creatures—humans and birds and beasts—will lead a far better life. The mariner leaves, and the despondent wedding guest wanders away from the party, only to wake the next morning a sadder and wiser man.

ANALYSIS

"The Rime of the Ancient Mariner" underwent numerous revisions and reprints—some quite drastic—after it first appeared in print in 1798 as part of *Lyrical Ballads*. Coleridge originally conceived of the poem after hearing about a friend's dream, and the poem was once meant to be a collaboration between Coleridge and Wordsworth. As they planned their joint volume, *Lyrical Ballads*, Wordsworth decided to contribute poems on everyday life, while Coleridge would contribute work with a supernatural edge. Although Coleridge ultimately wrote the poem unassisted, Wordsworth did suggest a few plot details, including the albatross's death. Adapted from a 1692 book of philosophy by Thomas Burnet, the Latin epigraph that opens the poem states that both visible and invisible forces roam the earth. It also encourages readers to stretch their minds by imagining a better world but reminds them to maintain a balance between fantasy and reality. The epigraph obliquely urges readers of the poem to pay attention more to the poem's concluding moral than to whether the story could actually have happened.

Much as the mariner's suspenseful content captivates the wedding guest, the poem's form and meter have a magnetic, mesmerizing effect. Over its seven parts, the poem employs a variety of so-called ballad **stanzas**. Like most of the **ballads** written in the late eighteenth and early nineteenth centuries, the poem employs **alliteration**, repetition, quintets (five-line stanzas), and **quatrains** (four-line stanzas), in which the first and third lines are written in **iambic tetrameter** and the rhyming second and fourth lines are written in **iambic trimeter**. In the Advertisement, or preface, to the first edition of *Lyrical Ballads*, Coleridge and Wordsworth explain that their new poems were meant to be considered experiments in whether they could write successfully using traditional forms but including colloquial speech and quotidian content—hence the title "lyrical ballads." Unlike traditional ballads, "The Rime of the Ancient Mariner" also includes glosses, often published alongside or preceding parts of the poem. These glosses explicate the poem's text, thereby moving the story along and letting the poem itself revel in its rhyme and **meter**.

Narrative ambiguity dominates the text of "The Rime of the Ancient Mariner": without the glosses, readers could not be entirely sure about what happens to the ship, the crew, or the mariner. Several key facts are missing from the poem's story. For instance, the mariner's nautical rank is never revealed, nor is the original destination of the ship explained. The ship appears not to have any captain, unless the mariner himself helms the ship. Perhaps the most significant question of the poem is why the mariner shoots the albatross—an act made all the more puzzling by the crew's heralding of the bird as a good-luck omen. The absence of answers to these questions heightens the poem's supernatural tension. While the glosses help readers understand the action of the poem, an otherworldly aura shrouds the both the poem and the glosses. From a formal perspective, the absence of answers emphasizes the poem's concluding moral: like the wedding guest, the poem's readers leave the tale sadder, wiser, and more aware of the interlocking relationships between humans, creatures, nature, and God.

The poem contains multiple speakers and listeners. At least six people or beings speak in "The Rime of the Ancient Mariner": the wedding guest; the mariner; the scholarly figure who voices the glosses; the two disembodied voices that discuss the mariner's sins and punishments at the end of Part V and the beginning of Part VI; and an unnamed, omnipresent figure capable of making grand proclamations, such as the poem's ending **couplet**, which describes the internal state of the young man. Similarly, the wedding guest listens to the mariner, the mariner becomes a listener to the voices debating his future, the voices listen to each other, and we as readers listen to everyone or everything that speaks. Like the wedding guest, the poem's readers are forced to decide whether to trust what they are hearing from these multiple perspectives. Unlike a traditional **lyric**, in which one speaker voices the entire poem, this poem does not contain a single unified perspective to latch onto and analyze.

The importance of listening and storytelling is one of the poem's major themes. Without a listener, the mariner cannot tell his tale—and cannot absolve himself of the guilt and pain he carries, like an albatross around his soul. His entire penance rests on the willingness of someone, such as the wedding guest, to hear his story. One of the mariner's punishments dries out his mouth, crippling his ability to speak or pray. When he spies a ship, the mariner must moisten his mouth with his blood before he can alert the crew. As readers, we might align ourselves with the wedding guest, the poem's most prominent listener and the one who expresses concern about the truthfulness of the mariner's tale and who wonders whether the mariner is dead. The act of prayer always assumes a listener, regardless of whether the listener might be the traditional Judeo-Christian God, a divine being, or a figure of the penitent's own invention. Like a god, the wedding guest—and any other listener the mariner chooses—has the power to forgive the mariner simply by hearing his story.

In "The Rime of the Ancient Mariner," Coleridge portrays his version of the romantic **archetype**, a character or **symbol** that reoccurs throughout literature and that stands for a significant aspect of

a culture or human experience. Coleridge's mariner echoes the biblical figure of Cain, doomed to walk the earth alone after he murders
his brother, Abel; both Cain and the mariner are wanderers, alienated figures who exist outside the bounds of society. The figure of
the wanderer appears throughout Western literature: from the travels of Odysseus in Homer's *Odyssey* (ca. 800 B.C.E.) to the journeys
of Victor Frankenstein and his monster in Mary Shelley's *Frankenstein* (1818) through T. S. Eliot's *The Waste Land* (1922). Cursed
but heroic, the romantic wanderer—an exile and an outcast—constantly searched for self-discovery, both literally and figuratively.
Romantic poetry celebrates the outcast. Frequently, the romantics
linked the wanderer to the ideal of the romantic individual, another
figure separated from society, questing for discovery and understanding, closely aligned with nature, and capable of producing
important moral truths.

Critics debate the meaning of the albatross. Some see the symbol
and the poem itself as a Christian **allegory**, in which the mariner
symbolizes Christ and the albatross symbolizes the shackles binding
Christ to the cross. Another religious interpretation argues that the
albatross symbolizes a soul weighted down with sin, which is
relieved through the act of confessing to a priest in Catholicism. As
the bird flies, with its wings outstretched, it makes a cross, a fact
highlighted by the line "at length did cross an albatross" (63). In the
poem, only after the mariner recognizes the beauty of all living
things, including the slimy snakes that surround the boat, and
silently blesses them does the bird's rotting corpse fall from his neck
and into the sea. Finally, the albatross might also stand for God's
favor, which ebbs and flows according to the beliefs of the pious.
Those who fear God and abide by his rules, like the crew, which
feeds and plays with the bird, will have lives filled, metaphorically,
with good weather and smooth sailing. Those who do not fear God
or abide by his rules, like the mariner, who unnecessarily shoots the
bird, will have lives filled with extreme punishments, including the
inability to pray.

As a romantic poem, "The Rime of the Ancient Mariner" is
somewhat atypical in its length, its narrative meanderings, its figure
of the wanderer, its bizarre glosses, and its moral agenda. On the one
hand, given the poem's complex story, its concluding lesson also
seems rather simplistic. The mariner tells the wedding guest that all
of God's creatures, from giant birds to humans to the oceans'
snakes, deserve love and respect. But on the other hand, the poem

SAMUEL T. COLERIDGE

contains simple rhymes and simple images, as in these famous lines: "Water, water, every where / And all the boards did shrink; / Water, water every where, / Nor any drop to drink" (119–122). In its use of uncomplicated literary techniques, the poem prepares readers for its uncomplicated conclusion—and demonstrates the romantic philosophy of Wordsworth and Coleridge that poetry could be simultaneously simple, sincere, and profound.

"Frost at Midnight"

> The frost performs its secret ministry,
> Unhelped by any wind. The owlet's cry
> Came loud—and hark, again! loud as before.
> The inmates of my cottage, all at rest,
> Have left me to that solitude, which suits   5
> Abstruser musings: save that at my side
> My cradled infant slumbers peacefully.
> 'Tis calm indeed! so calm, that it disturbs
> And vexes meditation with its strange
> And extreme silentness. Sea, hill, and wood,   10
> This populous village! Sea, and hill, and wood,
> With all the numberless goings-on of life,
> Inaudible as dreams! the thin blue flame
> Lies on my low-burnt fire, and quivers not;
> Only that film, which fluttered on the grate,   15
> Still flutters there, the sole unquiet thing.
> Methinks, its motion in this hush of nature
> Gives it dim sympathies with me who live,
> Making it a companionable form,
> Whose puny flaps and freaks the idling Spirit   20
> By its own moods interprets, every where
> Echo or mirror seeking of itself,
> And makes a toy of Thought.
>
>   But O! how oft,
> How oft, at school, with most believing mind,   25
> Presageful, have I gazed upon the bars,
> To watch that fluttering stranger! and as oft
> With unclosed lids, already had I dreamt
> Of my sweet birth-place, and the old church-tower,
> Whose bells, the poor man's only music, rang   30

From morn to evening, all the hot Fair-day,
So sweetly, that they stirred and haunted me
With a wild pleasure, falling on mine ear
Most like articulate sounds of things to come!
So gazed I, till the soothing things, I dreamt,   35
Lulled me to sleep, and sleep prolonged my dreams!
And so I brooded all the following morn,
Awed by the stern preceptor's face, mine eye
Fixed with mock study on my swimming book:
Save if the door half opened, and I snatched   40
A hasty glance, and still my heart leaped up,
For still I hoped to see the stranger's face,
Townsman, or aunt, or sister more beloved,
My play-mate when we both were clothed alike!

   Dear Babe, that sleepest cradled by my side,   45
Whose gentle breathings, heard in this deep calm,
Fill up the interspersèd vacancies
And momentary pauses of the thought!
My babe so beautiful! it thrills my heart
With tender gladness, thus to look at thee,   50
And think that thou shalt learn far other lore,
And in far other scenes! For I was reared
In the great city, pent 'mid cloisters dim,
And saw nought lovely but the sky and stars.
But thou, my babe! shalt wander like a breeze   55
By lakes and sandy shores, beneath the crags
Of ancient mountain, and beneath the clouds,
Which image in their bulk both lakes and shores
And mountain crags: so shalt thou see and hear
The lovely shapes and sounds intelligible   60
Of that eternal language, which thy God
Utters, who from eternity doth teach
Himself in all, and all things in himself.
Great universal Teacher! he shall mould
Thy spirit, and by giving make it ask.   65

   Therefore all seasons shall be sweet to thee,
Whether the summer clothe the general earth
With greenness, or the redbreast sit and sing
Betwixt the tufts of snow on the bare branch

Of mossy apple-tree, while the nigh thatch   70
Smokes in the sun-thaw; whether the eave-drops fall
Heard only in the trances of the blast,
Or if the secret ministry of frost
Shall hang them up in silent icicles,
Quietly shining to the quiet Moon.   75

Summary

"Frost at Midnight" begins with an evocation to the evening frost, which performs its duties without the help of any breeze. Somewhere, an owl cries twice. Everyone else in the country house is asleep, while the speaker sits up, watching the fire—a situation that suits his meandering, meditating mind. By his side, a baby sleeps peacefully in a cradle. The speaker comments on the calmness that has descended on the ocean, the lands, and the forest, but he also states that the evening's silence is so total, perfect, and complete as to become distracting to the speaker. Everything surrounding him, including the nearby town, seems hallucinatory and fascinating. In the fire's grate, only a piece of soot moves; even the blue flame stands low unmoving. The speaker sympathizes with "the sole unquiet thing" (16), moving in an otherwise perfectly still landscape. Watching the soot flutter, the speaker comments that a lazy, quiet soul always seeks a reflection or companion of itself, making a plaything out of rational thought.

In the second stanza, the speaker remembers watching a grate as a child at a school, when he would close his eyes and dream about his childhood home and church, whose bells sounded all day long. As a child, the speaker found the bell's sounds extremely pleasant, and they stirred within him promises and hopes of a marvelous future. Thinking of these things, the speaker sometimes would pretend to study and would even fall asleep over his schoolwork. He would rouse himself whenever the door opened, hoping that a family member or friend had entered.

The speaker addresses the sleeping baby in the third stanza, whose breathing punctuates the speaker's thoughts. Looking at the infant fills the speaker with deep joy. Next the speaker expresses his happiness that his child shall have many opportunities that the speaker did not since the speaker was imprisoned in the city and unable to see nature, except for the sky and stars. Unlike the speaker, the child shall grow up in the country, exploring mountains, lakes, and beaches. He shall be able to see and hear God's language as it reverberates through nature, and his soul shall be molded by God's teachings. In the fourth stanza, the speaker tells the baby that because of God's direct influence on him through his experience of nature, he shall enjoy all the seasons, whether the summer shrouds the earth in green or winter piles up snow and icicles are hung secretly in the midnight frost and still moonlight.

ANALYSIS

First composed in 1798 but not published until 1829, "Frost at Midnight" takes place at Coleridge's house in rural Nether Stowey, England. The baby addressed in the poem is Coleridge's seventeen-month-old son Hartley. A typical conversation poem written in blank verse, "Frost at Midnight" examines several contrasts that consistently appear in Coleridge's work: childhood versus adulthood, night versus day, dreams versus reality, and the country versus the city. The poem also responds to Wordsworth's long-held assumption that all children naturally achieve a unity with nature and that this unity can be resurrected in adulthood simply by recollecting one's childhood. As evidenced in "Frost at Midnight," Coleridge did not have an opportunity to commune with nature as a child, and thus he is excluded by Wordsworth's hypothesis. In response, Coleridge explains how communing with nature contributes to the development of a complete soul but does not imply that this communion automatically occurs during childhood.

Of all the poem's conflicts, the conflict between the country and the city produces the most tension. Reacting to the Industrial Revolution, which began in Britain around 1750, and the increased mechanization of labor, romantic poets frequently praised the natural world and criticized cities as overpopulated and polluted. Through nature, individuals could become most fully themselves, in contrast to the throbbing undifferentiated masses that inhabited urban areas. In "Frost at Midnight," as the speaker recollects his childhood, he implies that the city itself kept him from nature and thus from himself. While at boarding school, the speaker could only just see the sky and the stars. Here the city becomes an evil place, which hampers the development of the soul and damages its residents. In contrast to the speaker's childhood—and to Coleridge's own youth—the speaker's child shall be reared in the country, a place filled with beauty and with God, and far away from the stifling, dirty city.

"Frost at Midnight" also contrasts the possibilities of healing through dreams and imaginings with the possibilities inherent in the natural world. Deeply engrossed in watching the fire, the speaker falls into a dreamlike state, in which he recollects his childhood dreams and daydreams, as well as prophesizes about his child's future. According to the speaker's experiences, dreams allow us to renew through the powers of our imagination: much as the speaker once took joy from his remembrances of his childhood home, dreams allow us to escape a difficult or troubling reality. In contrast to the speaker, however, his son shall experience nature directly, not through dreams or imaginings. Indeed, nature shall become the child's "Great universal Teacher!" (64). He will therefore be able to directly rejuvenate simply by exploring nature's mountains or streams—not just by dreaming. The speaker clarifies this point when he explains that his son shall experience and enjoy the seasons, from the bounty of summer to the dead of winter.

Coleridge emphasizes the workings of the imagination throughout "Frost at Midnight," and the poem's form mirrors its content. The poem begins by describing the night's frost but quickly halts with a "hark" (3) as the cry of an owl startles the speaker. Riled by the sudden noise, the speaker then remarks on the eeriness of the quiet nocturnal world. After a few moments, however, the speaker has calmed down and starts to meditate on a fluttering piece of soot, and his mind moves from a focus on the present to a focus on the past, symbolized by the extra space and the exclamation "But O!" (24). Watching the soot in the present reminds him of fires in the past, an act that highlights the ability of the human mind to be simultaneously in multiple places in time. Over the course of the poem, the speaker's mind wanders from the present to the past to the future to the present. By the end of the poem, the speaker has returned from his recollections to speak to his child and to describe icicles dangling outside.

SAMUEL T. COLERIDGE

"KUBLA KHAN"

In Xanadu did Kubla Khan
A stately pleasure-dome decree:
Where Alph, the sacred river, ran
Through caverns measureless to man
   Down to a sunless sea.   5
So twice five miles of fertile ground
With walls and towers were girdled round:
And there were gardens bright with sinuous rills,
Where blossomed many an incense-bearing tree;
And here were forests ancient as the hills,   10
Enfolding sunny spots of greenery.
But oh! that deep romantic chasm which slanted
Down the green hill athwart a cedarn cover!
A savage place! as holy and enchanted
As e'er beneath a waning moon was haunted   15
By woman wailing for her demon-lover!
And from this chasm, with ceaseless turmoil seething,
As if this earth in fast thick pants were breathing,
A mighty fountain momently was forced:
Amid whose swift half-intermitted burst   20
Huge fragments vaulted like rebounding hail,
Or chaffy grain beneath the thresher's flail:
And 'mid these dancing rocks at once and ever
It flung up momently the sacred river.
Five miles meandering with a mazy motion   25
Through wood and dale the sacred river ran,
Then reached the caverns measureless to man,
And sank in tumult to a lifeless ocean:
And 'mid this tumult Kubla heard from far
Ancestral voices prophesying war!   30
   The shadow of the dome of pleasure
   Floated midway on the waves;
   Where was heard the mingled measure
   From the fountain and the caves.
It was a miracle of rare device,   35
A sunny pleasure-dome with caves of ice!

A damsel with a dulcimer
In a vision once I saw:
It was an Abyssinian maid,
And on her dulcimer she played,   40
Singing of Mount Abora.
Could I revive within me
Her symphony and song,
To such a deep delight 'twould win me,
That with music loud and long,   45
I would build that dome in air,
That sunny dome! those caves of ice!
And all who heard should see them there,
And all should cry, Beware! Beware!
His flashing eyes, his floating hair!   50
Weave a circle round him thrice,
And close your eyes with holy dread,
For he on honey-dew hath fed,
And drunk the milk of Paradise.

SUMMARY

In a brief explanatory note written on the poem's publication in 1816, Coleridge remarks that he composed the poem in 1797 on awakening from a strange dream, in the English countryside. At the time, he was suffering from dysentery and in ill health, and his doctors prescribed opium to ease his ailments. One day, Coleridge fell asleep while reading a seventeenth-century travel book, and he cites in full the sentence he read immediately before he dropped off. It concerns the garden and house of Kubla Khan, also known as Cublai Can, the thirteenth-century founder of the Chinese Mongol dynasty and a grandson of Genghis Khan. During his sleep, Coleridge dreamed he was writing a poem of 200 to 300 lines. When he awoke, he anxiously scribbled down fifty-four lines—the poem we now know as "Kubla Khan"—before being called away. By the time he returned to write, he had forgotten the other lines. Regarding the poem, he reminds readers that it consists of only "fragments" rather than a finished work. Coleridge also explains that he decided to publish the poem as a "psychological curiosity" at the request of another poet, Lord Byron.

Coleridge opens "Kubla Khan" by describing a vision of the construction of the palatial home of Kubla Khan in Xanadu. Khan has amassed a massive, exotic paradise to be built near the fictional river

Alph, which runs through immeasurably large caves and feeds into a dark ocean. The compound, with round towers and walls, encloses ten miles of lush ground, filled with bright gardens, blossoming trees, and ancient forests. A structure made of cedar sits at the bottom of a green hill. According to the speaker, the scene is both "savage" and "enchanted" (14), like a woman crying for a "demon-lover" (16). From deep within this chasm, turbulence rises, as if the earth itself were bound up and trying to breathe. Suddenly, a tumultuous geyser bursts forth from the ground, rumbling and shaking. Big bits of rock fly upward and rain down upon the landscape, splashing into the river. The river carries the rocks through a maze of trees and underground caverns, finally depositing them into a body of water about five miles away. In the middle of this uproar, Khan hears the voices of his ancestors, predicting war. Shadows from the palace are cast onto the ocean. A "miracle of rare device" (35), the palace contains both sunlight and structures of ice.

In the second stanza, the speaker switches perspective and begins commenting on his dream rather than just describing it. He remembers a young Abyssinian woman with an instrument, playing a song about Mount Abora, whom he had seen in an earlier dream. Next he admits that if he could bring this woman and her song back, he would give himself great pleasure—and could thus be able to construct a palace such as the one he imagined being built by Khan. If he could conjure such a palace out of thin air, everyone around him would become quite frightened and would consider him a madman. Scared onlookers would draw three circles around him to protect themselves from his possessed state. The speaker ends by commanding the fictional onlookers to shut their eyes in his presence because the speaker has consumed food and drink meant not for mortals but for gods.

ANALYSIS

Scholars have long doubted the truthfulness of Coleridge's 1816 prefatory note. When "Kubla Khan" first appeared in *Christabel and Other Poems* (1816), readers obeyed his directive and promptly dismissed the poem as unfinished and meaningless. Over the years, however, readers began paying attention, discovering a poem both finished and full of meaning. Some scholars attribute Coleridge's opening story to his own insecurities, fueled by the praise lauded on Wordsworth after the first publication of *Lyrical Ballads*. Regardless of Coleridge's reasons for writing such a preface, historical fact disproves much of its content: at the time of composition, Coleridge was living in Nether Stowey, nearly twenty-five miles from the alleged site of writing. Back then, journeys of even short distances were difficult, particularly for an admittedly ill man. Similarly, the book Coleridge claims to have been reading, *Purchas's Pilgrimage*, was close to 1,000 pages, making it unlikely that he had brought such a tome with him to a lonely farmhouse in the countryside. Finally, Coleridge offers no explanation for the mysterious "person from Porlock" who interrupts him, and the phrase "person from Porlock" has now become synonymous with anything that interrupts artistic creation.

Whereas "Frost at Midnight" provides a snapshot of a mind at rest, "Kubla Khan" chronicles a mind at work, racing from one image to the next. Written in iambic tetrameter, the poem has a hypnotic, mesmerizing sound that befits its fantastical subject matter. Its staggered rhymes and couplets create a singsong effect, as in its opening lines: "In Xanadu did Kubla Khan / A stately pleasure dome decree" (1–2). The poem moves from a careful description of the palace and its gardens to a frightening image of a woman and bursting geyser to ominous echoes of war and concludes with an analysis of visions and their effects. Coleridge highlights the poem's revelry with a profusion of exclamation points. He also uses several similes in an effort to demonstrate an imagination processing an object or aspect of nature. For example, the cedar structure reminds the speaker of a mournful scene, while the water pressure sounds like labored breathing.

The poem's final stanza transforms the work from a fantastical dream to a persuasive analysis of poetry and poets. Here, the speaker laments his inability to adequately reconstruct a vision he once had of a young woman playing an instrument. Were he able to recall the vision, he claims, he could transfix crowds of anxious listeners. References to Book 4 of John Milton's *Paradise Lost* (1667) heighten the poem's self-referentiality, emphasizing the idea that this poem is a poem about writing poems. According to Coleridge's preface, the act of creation begins somewhere deep in the mind, unconsciously, and the poet must rouse himself or herself from the hallucinatory vision to begin writing. There, Coleridge claims that the poem came to him in a dream, but he was called away before he could complete the poem's transcription. All poems are therefore attempts to transcribe this unconscious process of creation. "Kubla Khan" remains somewhat disjointed and unclear precisely because Coleridge, like the speaker, couldn't quite remember his earlier dream-vision.

Contemporary politics obliquely appear in "Kubla Khan," even though generally Coleridge tended to focus on supernatural, ethereal themes and figures in his poetry, saving political commentary for prose. Like his fellow romantics, including Percy Bysshe Shelley and Lord Byron, Coleridge closely followed the revolutionary spirit sweeping Europe in the late eighteenth century. He supported the ideals of "Liberty, Equality, Fraternity" that first motivated the French Revolution in 1789 and believed in the capacity of individuals to alter society and political systems. As a youth, Coleridge had even tried to begin a utopian community. Although he mostly rejected the extreme politics of his youth as an adult, "Kubla Khan" retains traces of these radical ideals. Kubla hears "ancestral voices prophesying war" (30), and these voices sound like a geyser pushing up from the earth—an implication that violent revolution is a normal, natural part of the social and historical order. The pleasure palace contains both sunlight and ice, becoming a metaphor for a balanced, utopian society capable of housing extremes in equal measure. Likewise, the palace's surrounding gardens, with their lush greenery and rivers, symbolize a harmonious Eden.

PERCY BYSSHE SHELLEY

(1792–1822)

CONTEXT

Percy Bysshe Shelley was born in England on August 4, 1792. His father was a wealthy minor nobleman and member of Parliament. Because of his privileged background, Shelley received an excellent education: first, at prestigious Eton College, where he began writing poetry and became interested in radical politics, interests that he combined throughout his life. Later he matriculated at Oxford University but was expelled after writing a pamphlet called *The Necessity of Atheism* in 1811. His disbelief in the existence of God—another lifelong concern—led to an estrangement from his father. A few months later, Shelley eloped with sixteen-year-old Harriet Westbrook and was disinherited by his family.

Shelley found a mentor in the philosopher William Godwin, who believed that government could be replaced by personal morality, individual responsibility, and rational thought. Eventually, Shelley fell in love with Godwin's brilliant teenage daughter, Mary, whose mother was the feminist thinker Mary Wollstonecraft, author of *The Vindications of the Rights of Women*. Although he was still married to Harriet, Shelley ran off with Mary in 1814. Mary's stepsister, Claire Clairmont, also came along. In the spring of 1816, Claire had an affair with the poet Lord Byron, and Shelley, Mary, Claire, and Byron spent the summer together in Switzerland. It was an artistically productive, collaborative time: inspired by a trip he took to the Alps with Mary, as well as by discussions with Mary and Byron, Shelley wrote the poems "Mont Blanc" and "Hymn to Intellectual Beauty." Byron produced a few sections of his long work *Childe Harold*, and Mary composed her famous novel *Frankenstein* in response to a competition proposed by Byron in which each friend was required to compose a ghost story.

Like their friend John Keats, Shelley and Byron were influenced by the poets William Wordsworth and Samuel Taylor Coleridge. The publication of *Lyrical Ballads* (1798), a collaboration between Wordsworth and Coleridge that outlined their ideals of poetry, transformed the pair into the spokesmen for **romanticism**, a literary movement popular in England from the late eighteenth to the early nineteenth centuries. Their book became the movement's manifesto. Its poems reject the rationalism of the eighteenth-century **Enlightenment**, which praised classical ideals and objective knowl-

PERCY BYSSHE SHELLEY

edge, in favor of subjective experience, sensory perception, and a reverence for the mystical power of nature. The poems also demonstrate a commitment to the social and political ideals of the late eighteenth century, including liberty, justice, equality, and social progress. Finally, *Lyrical Ballads* proposed using colloquial diction—the language of everyday life—in poetry and sought to replace organized religion with pantheism, the belief that divine powers run through everything in the universe. Along with these poetic characteristics, Shelley and Byron were also attracted to the emphasis placed on individual experience and the visionary power of the human mind, and they imagined the poet as a Christ-like figure capable of changing the world through verse. In their work, the younger romantic poets Shelley, Keats, and Byron called for the dramatic overthrow of oppressive governments, and Byron eventually died while fighting for these ideals in 1824, during the Greek war against the Ottomans.

The younger romantics became more extreme versions of Wordsworth and Coleridge, their literary predecessors. Shelley rejected conventional religion more dramatically than Wordsworth. Also, Shelley sometimes called himself an atheist, sometimes a pantheist, but always declared his position as one of "awful doubt" about the existence of a divine being. He remained awed by the power of nature but skeptical of its divinity. Byron, Shelley, and Keats also rejected conventional morality: Shelley used drugs and advocated free love, while Byron's shocking sexual exploits were the talk of Europe. The modern perception of a poet as passionate, irrational, idealistic, egocentric, and unstable—that is, our conception of the mad artistic genius—developed in the early years of the nineteenth century and was based on the real-life antics of Byron and Shelley.

Romanticism as a movement was greatly affected by the political and social upheaval of the late eighteenth and early nineteenth centuries. The French Revolution began in 1789, when the peasants and middle class rose up against the monarchy and aristocracy. The slogan of the revolutionaries—"Liberty, Equality, Fraternity"—exemplified the ideals of many eighteenth-century philosophers, as well as those belonging to the leaders of the 1776 American Revolution. These intellectuals believed that all men were created equal and capable of governing themselves without the tyranny of kings and queens. In 1793, the revolutionary government killed the king of France. Fearful that the French spirit of revolution would spread, the ruling powers of Europe went to war against France. These liberal ideals did eventually spread to other nations, including Greece, in whose revolution Byron was killed. Romantic poets were generally sympathetic to the revolutionary ideals and incorporated the abstract concepts of liberty, justice, and equality into their work.

Partially in response to the French Revolution, England changed its domestic policies and became increasingly repressive. Measures were undertaken in an effort to suppress dissent: rallies were made illegal, advocates for social reform were charged with treason, and people were jailed for criticizing the English government or sympathizing with the French cause. This repressive atmosphere was not enough to quell thoughts of liberty or revolution, and debates raged about the emancipation of slaves, as well as the Irish struggle for home rule and freedom from British colonization. Philosophers, such as Godwin, and poets, such as Wordsworth, spoke out in support of the ability of everyday, ordinary people to govern themselves. At the time, the king of England was clinically insane and the crown prince was a decadent fop, leading many to lose faith in the monarchy. In 1819, 60,000 workers gathered on St. Peter's Field near Manchester to demand parliamentary reform. Troops on horseback charged into the crowds, killing or injuring many. Shelley, among others, was enraged by this incident and regarded it as proof that England was in the grip of tyranny and ripe for revolutionary change.

Shelley expressed his strong political views in his poetry. He composed "Ode to the West Wind" (1820) and *Prometheus Unbound* (1820), revolutionary poems that display his belief that humans can triumph over tyranny and oppression. In late 1816, after Harriet's suicide, Shelley and Mary were married, but Shelley lost custody of the children from his previous marriage. Troubled by health problems and increasingly disgusted with the English government, Shelley moved permanently to Italy in 1818, along with Mary and their children. In 1821, after the deaths of two of his children with Mary and the death of his friend John Keats, Shelley wrote *Adonais*, in which he transforms the character of Keats into a visionary martyr murdered by the harsh words of his critics. Shelley died tragically in 1822, drowned while sailing off the coast of Italy.

THEMES, MOTIFS & SYMBOLS

THEMES

THE HEROIC, VISIONARY ROLE OF THE POET

In Shelley's poetry, the figure of the poet (and, to some extent, the figure of Shelley himself) is not simply a talented entertainer or even a perceptive moralist but a grand, tragic, prophetic hero. The poet has a deep, mystic appreciation for nature, as in the poem "To Wordsworth" (1816), and this intense connection with the natural world gives him access to profound cosmic truths, as in "Alastor; or, The Spirit of Solitude" (1816). He has the power—and the duty—to translate these truths, through the use of his imagination, into poetry, but only a kind of poetry that the public can understand. Thus, his poetry becomes a kind of prophecy, and through his words, a poet has the ability to change the world for the better and to bring about political, social, and spiritual change. Shelley's poet is a near-divine savior, comparable to Prometheus, who stole divine fire and gave it to humans in Greek mythology, and to Christ. Like Prometheus and Christ, figures of the poets in Shelley's work are often doomed to suffer: because their visionary power isolates them from other men, because they are misunderstood by critics, because they are persecuted by a tyrannical government, or because they are suffocated by conventional religion and middle-class values. In the end, however, the poet triumphs because his art is immortal, outlasting the tyranny of government, religion, and society and living on to inspire new generations.

THE POWER OF NATURE

Like many of the romantic poets, especially William Wordsworth, Shelley demonstrates a great reverence for the beauty of nature, and he feels closely connected to nature's power. In his early poetry, Shelley shares the romantic interest in pantheism—the belief that God, or a divine, unifying spirit, runs through everything in the universe. He refers to this unifying natural force in many poems, describing it as the "spirit of beauty" in "Hymn to Intellectual Beauty" and identifying it with Mont Blanc and the Arve River in "Mont Blanc." This force is the cause of all human joy, faith, goodness, and pleasure, and it is also the source of poetic inspiration and divine truth. Shelley asserts several times that this force can influence people to change the world for the better. However, Shelley simultaneously recognizes that nature's power is not wholly positive. Nature destroys as often as it inspires or creates, and it destroys cruelly and indiscriminately. For this reason, Shelley's delight in nature is mitigated by an awareness of its dark side.

THE POWER OF THE HUMAN MIND

Shelley uses nature as his primary source of poetic inspiration. In such poems as "The Mask of Anarchy Written on the Occasion of the Massacre at Manchester" (1819) and "Ode to the West Wind," Shelley suggests that the natural world holds a sublime power over his imagination. This power seems to come from a stranger, more mystical place than simply his appreciation for nature's beauty or grandeur. At the same time, although nature has creative power over Shelley because it provides inspiration, he feels that his imagination has creative power over nature. It is the imagination—or our ability to form sensory perceptions—that allows us to describe nature in different, original ways, which help to shape how nature appears and, therefore, how it exists. Thus, the power of the human mind becomes equal to the power of nature, and the experience of beauty in the natural world becomes a kind of collaboration between the perceiver and the perceived. Because Shelley cannot be sure that the sublime powers he senses in nature are only the result of his gifted imagination, he finds it difficult to attribute nature's power to God: the human role in shaping nature damages Shelley's ability to believe that nature's beauty comes solely from a divine source.

MOTIFS

AUTUMN

Shelley sets many of his poems in autumn, including "Hymn to Intellectual Beauty" and "Ode to the West Wind." Fall is a time of beauty and death, and so it shows both the creative and destructive powers of nature, a favorite Shelley theme. As a time of change, autumn is a fitting backdrop for Shelley's vision of political and social revolution. In "Ode to the West Wind," autumn's brilliant colors and violent winds emphasize the passionate, intense nature of the poet, while the decay and death inherent in the season suggest the sacrifice and martyrdom of the Christ-like poet.

Ghosts and Spirits

Shelley's interest in the supernatural repeatedly appears in his work. The ghosts and spirits in his poems suggest the possibility of glimpsing a world beyond the one in which we live. In "Hymn to Intellectual Beauty," the speaker searches for ghosts and explains that ghosts are one of the ways men have tried to interpret the world beyond. The speaker of "Mont Blanc" encounters ghosts and shadows of real natural objects in the cave of "Poesy." Ghosts are inadequate in both poems: the speaker finds no ghosts in "Hymn to Intellectual Beauty," and the ghosts of Poesy in "Mont Blanc" are not the real thing, a discovery that emphasizes the elusiveness and mystery of supernatural forces.

Christ

From his days at Oxford, Shelley felt deeply doubtful about organized religion, particularly Christianity. Yet, in his poetry, he often represents the poet as a Christ-like figure and thus sets the poet up as a secular replacement for Christ. Martyred by society and conventional values, the Christ figure is resurrected by the power of nature and his own imagination and spreads his prophetic visions over the earth. Shelley further separates his Christ figures from traditional Christian values in *Adonais*, in which he compares the same character to Christ, as well as Cain, whom the Bible portrays as the world's first murderer. For Shelley, Christ and Cain are both outcasts and rebels, like romantic poets and like himself.

Symbols

Mont Blanc

For Shelley, Mont Blanc—the highest peak in the Alps—represents the eternal power of nature. Mont Blanc has existed forever, and it will last forever, an idea he explores in "Mont Blanc." The mountain fills the poet with inspiration, but its coldness and inaccessibility are terrifying. Ultimately, though, Shelley wonders if the mountain's power might be meaningless, an invention of the more powerful human imagination.

THE WEST WIND

Shelley uses the West Wind to symbolize the power of nature and of the imagination inspired by nature. Unlike Mont Blanc, however, the West Wind is active and dynamic in poems, such as "Ode to the West Wind." While Mont Blanc is immobile, the West Wind is an agent for change. Even as it destroys, the wind encourages new life on earth and social progress among humanity.

THE STATUE OF OZYMANDIAS

In Shelley's work, the statue of the ancient Egyptian pharaoh Ramses II, or Ozymandias, symbolizes political tyranny. In "Ozymandias," (1817) the statue is broken into pieces and stranded in an empty desert, which suggests that tyranny is temporary and also that no political leader, particularly an unjust one, can hope to have lasting power or real influence. The broken monument also represents the decay of civilization and culture: the statue is, after all, a human construction, a piece of art made by a creator, and now it—and its creator—have been destroyed, as all living things are eventually destroyed.

Summary & Analysis

"Hymn to Intellectual Beauty"

I

The awful shadow of some unseen Power
   Floats though unseen among us; visiting
   This various world with as inconstant wing
As summer winds that creep from flower to flower;
Like moonbeams that behind some piny mountain shower,   5
      It visits with inconstant glance
      Each human heart and countenance;
Like hues and harmonies of evening,
      Like clouds in starlight widely spread,
      Like memory of music fled,   10
      Like aught that for its grace may be
Dear, and yet dearer for its mystery.

2

Spirit of BEAUTY, that dost consecrate
   With thine own hues all thou dost shine upon
   Of human thought or form, where art thou gone?   15
Why dost thou pass away and leave our state,
This dim vast vale of tears, vacant and desolate?
      Ask why the sunlight not for ever
      Weaves rainbows o'er yon mountain-river,
Why aught should fail and fade that once is shown   20
      Why fear and dream and death and birth
      Cast on the daylight of this earth
      Such gloom, why man has such a scope
For love and hate, despondency and hope?

3

No voice from some sublimer world hath ever   25
   To sage or poet these responses given:
   Therefore the names of Demon, Ghost, and Heaven,
Remain the records of their vain endeavour:
Frail spells whose utter'd charm might not avail to sever,

From all we hear and all we see,   30
    Doubt, chance and mutability
Thy light alone like mist o'er mountains driven,
        Or music by the night-wind sent
        Through strings of some still instrument,
        Or moonlight on a midnight stream,   35
Gives grace and truth to life's unquiet dream.

                                    4
Love, Hope, and Self-esteem, like clouds depart
    And come, for some uncertain moments lent.
    Man were immortal and omnipotent
Didst thou, unknown and awful as thou art,   40
Keep with thy glorious train firm state within his heart.
        Thou messenger of sympathies,
        That wax and wane in lovers' eyes;
Thou, that to human thought art nourishment,
        Like darkness to a dying flame!   45
        Depart not as thy shadow came,
        Depart not—lest the grave should be,
Like life and fear, a dark reality.

                                    5
While yet a boy I sought for ghosts, and sped
    Through many a listening chamber, cave and ruin,   50
    And starlight wood, with fearful steps pursuing
Hopes of high talk with the departed dead.
I call'd on poisonous names with which our youth is fed;
        I was not heard; I saw them not;
        When musing deeply on the lot   55
Of life, at that sweet time when winds are wooing
        All vital things that wake to bring
        News of birds and blossoming,
        Sudden, thy shadow fell on me;
I shriek'd, and clasp'd my hands in ecstasy!   60

                                    6
I vow'd that I would dedicate my powers
    To thee and thine: have I not kept the vow?
    With beating heart and streaming eyes, even now
I call the phantoms of a thousand hours

PERCY BYSSHE SHELLEY

Each from his voiceless grave: they have in vision'd bowers   65
    Of studious zeal or love's delight
    Outwatch'd with me the envious night:
They know that never joy illum'd my brow
    Unlink'd with hope that thou wouldst free
    This world from its dark slavery,   70
    That thou, O awful LOVELINESS,
Wouldst give whate'er these words cannot express.

7

The day becomes more solemn and serene
    When noon is past; there is a harmony
    In autumn, and a lustre in its sky,   75
Which through the summer is not heard or seen,
As if it could not be, as if it had not been!
    Thus let thy power, which like the truth
    Of nature on my passive youth
Descended, to my onward life supply   80
    Its calm, to one who worships thee,
    And every form containing thee,
    Whom, SPIRIT fair, thy spells did bind
To fear himself, and love all human kind.

SUMMARY

In the first **stanza**, the **speaker** states that an invisible, dark, powerful specter moves among humans, traveling the world like moonlight or balmy breezes and touching everyone and everything inconsistently. The specter visits every being, and the speaker compares these visits to nighttime colors and clouds, to the memory of musical sound that echoes in one's mind long after the music has stopped, and to something made special because of its grace and mystery.

The speaker, in the second stanza, asks the aesthetic force that beautifies all it touches where it has gone. He wonders why the force has departed, leaving humanity empty and alone. Everything that exists must fade, a fact that saddens the speaker, causing him to wonder why human life and emotion cause such despair. He concludes by asking rhetorically why humans are capable of such strong feelings as love and hate.

No being from beyond has ever answered these questions posed by a wise person or a poet, as the speaker points out in the third

PERCY BYSSHE SHELLEY

stanza, and thus the wise people and poets have attempted to answer the questions themselves, relying on superstition and religion. Superstitious and religious incarnations are weak and do not dispel the doubt, uncertainty, and sadness that motivate humanity to ask such questions. Only the aesthetic force from the second stanza—an effervescence that flits like dew over mountains, the frets of an instrument, or the moon on water—can quiet such questions and comfort the questioners.

Continuing to address this effervescent force of splendor, the speaker begins the fourth stanza by musing on the nebulous comings and goings of positive emotions and feelings, such as hope. If splendor resided permanently within the human core, humans would be all-powerful and alive forever. This sense of splendor nourishes humans as the dark nourishes a fire, and the speaker begs the force not to leave as rapidly as it came. If this force leaves, the speaker fears he might discover death to be as full of despair as life.

In the fifth stanza, the speaker recalls his youth, when he would scamper about caverns, ravines, and forests, searching for these forces of beauty. Although he yelled their names, they did not hear him, and he never sighted any. But one day in spring, while he contemplated life, the specters appeared to him, and he shouted with delight.

After his joyful exclamation, the speaker vowed to dedicate his life to the forces, which he directly addresses in the opening of the sixth stanza. He asks these forces whether he has kept his vow to them, then states that he has summoned these forces from their graves as his heart raced and eyes watered. These specters watched him during the night as he studied or loved, and they knew that any joy he felt was connected to his desire that these forces of splendor release the world from its darkness—and give the world what cannot be expressed by poetry.

Finally, in the seventh stanza, the speaker observes that afternoon has come and the day is calmer. He notes that autumn has a peacefulness and beauty not apparent in summer. Then he asks the aesthetic force, which descended upon him in his youth, to bring some peace to his later life since he has loyally served and venerated the force and all its manifestations throughout his life. He concludes the poem by addressing the force, noting that its enchantments have made the speaker dread himself but adore all others.

PERCY BYSSHE SHELLEY

ANALYSIS

"Hymn to Intellectual Beauty" is an ode to the "spirit of beauty"—
the pure, intellectual idea of beauty that humans can discover, or
abstract, from the thousands of beautiful things in the world.
Throughout the poem, the speaker addresses this aesthetic force in
an evocative, pleading way. It may seem odd that Shelley, a self-
described atheist, would write a semi-religious **hymn**, particularly
since hymns are usually written in praise of God. But although Shelley rejected the Christian God, he often embraced mystic, spiritual
experience and, like many romantic poets, found in nature something
divine. By calling his poem a "hymn," Shelley elevates intellectual
beauty to the status of a god and himself to a worshiper of that god.

Shelley uses religious language and imagery to emphasize the
poem as a hymn and to cement the divine status of intellectual
beauty. The speaker calls intellectual beauty a "spirit," suggesting
that beauty is not merely a collection of objects that are pleasing to
the eye but an otherworldly presence. In the second stanza, he
claims that the spirit can "consecrate," or bless, all creation. Later,
in the fourth stanza, he says that the spirit has the ability to make
humans all-powerful and capable of living forever. This ability suggests that the spirit is as powerful as the Christian God and can exert
the same moral influence. By repeating certain phrases and sentences structures, such as the list of similes in the first stanza, the
poem develops an incantatory quality that echoes a prayer.

This poem is Shelley's answer to the human desire to reach a
world beyond our own, a desire that is often satisfied by religion. As
a child, the speaker sought to communicate with the beyond by
looking for ghosts. Poets and sages try to access a "sublimer world"
but receive no answer, and so they invent their own answers, represented by the concepts of God, ghosts, and heaven. According to
Shelley, the sages, the poets, and the child are equally wrong—clinging
to conventional religion is as false and immature as looking for
ghosts in caves. In the poem, the only person to successfully achieve
contact with the sublime is the speaker, who is possessed by the
spirit of beauty while walking amid the natural world in a glorious
springtime. Therefore, the abstract concept of intellectual beauty is
only accessible through interaction with the tangible, physical
beauty of nature.

To emphasize the interconnectedness of the spiritual and physical
worlds, Shelley uses an inspired literary technique: he begins by

PERCY BYSSHE SHELLEY

invoking the spirit of beauty as an abstraction of natural beauty, then constantly describes the spirit in physical, natural terms, using similes to compare it to things in nature—clouds, winds, rainbows, and so on. This reinforces the link between the poem's abstract and concrete ideas, namely that the spirit cannot be accessed without the forms of nature. The spirit of beauty is beyond the world, but at the same time it is of the world.

Like his fellow romantic poets, Shelley favored sensory perception and subjective experience over objective knowledge and organized religion. The speaker's ecstatic experience in the fifth stanza does not—and probably could not—take place in a conventional house of worship. The sheer exuberance of the solitary experience is partly due to Shelley's love of nature, but it also reveals his convictions about the power of personal experience, independent of the beliefs and doctrines of others. Also, the speaker does not adhere to conventional Christian morality. For example, he describes sexual love as an inspired, almost religious experience, witnessed by the spirit of beauty. Instead of being in awe or worshiping the Christian God, he has learned to be in awe of, and revere, himself.

Worship does not occur unquestioningly. Throughout the poem, the speaker expresses doubt about the spirit's benevolence and even its power. He describes the spirit as "inconstant" and undependable, suggesting that nature's grace is random or even cruel. He hopes that the spirit will free humanity from its darkness, but he is not certain—he worries that death might, after all, be nothing but a "dark reality." In the last stanza, the speaker tries to come to grips with the darker side of nature: by alluding to the peaceful balance of autumn, a time of loveliness and peace but also a harbinger of death, Shelley foreshadows his great later poem, "Ode to the West Wind," in which he embraces nature as a destructive and creative force.

PERCY BYSSHE SHELLEY

"Mont Blanc"
Lines Written in the Vale of Chamouni

Excerpt from "Mont blanc"

The everlasting universe of things
Flows through the mind, and rolls its rapid waves,
Now dark — now glittering — now reflecting gloom —
Now lending splendor, where from secret springs
The source of human thought its tribute brings
Of waters, — with a sound but half its own,
Such as a feeble brook will oft assume
In the wild woods, among the mountains lone,
Where waterfalls around it leap forever,
Where woods and winds contend, and a vast river
Over its rocks ceaselessly bursts and raves.

.   .   .   .   .

Mont Blanc yet gleams on high — the power is there,
The still and solemn power of many sights,
And many sounds, and much of life and death.
In the calm darkness of the moonless nights,
In the lone glare of day, the snows descend
Upon that Mountain — none beholds them there,
Nor when the flakes burn in the sinking sun,
Or the star-beams dart through them — Winds contend
Silently there, and heap the snow with breath
Rapid and strong, but silently! Its home
The voiceless lightning in these solitudes
Keeps innocently, and like vapor broods
Over the snow. The secret Strength of things
Which governs thought, and to the infinite dome
Of Heaven is as a law, Inhabits thee!
And what were thou, and earth, and stars, and sea,
If to the human mind's imaginings
Silence and solitude were vacancy?

SUMMARY

"Mont Blanc" begins by comparing thoughts, perceptions, and imaginings—the mind's consciousness—to a river. This river shifts, sometimes reflecting light and sometimes reflecting darkness. At other times, the river rolls and reveals the starting place of thought, a tributary of this larger river. This tributary makes a small sound and moves gently in contrast to the rollicking, fast-moving river.

In the second stanza, the speaker addresses the ravine of the Arve River. He describes it as full of colors and echoes and the river as powering down from glaciers to cut the mountains into a ravine, lined with pine trees that make music as wind rustles their branches. A waterfall, full of motion, hides part of the ravine and makes its own loud sound. The speaker says that the awe-inspiring landscape throws him into an ecstatic trance and makes him think about his own mind, and his thoughts range from the view in front of him to the cave of poetry. His mind submissively receives outside influences but also transforms them, creating an endless interchange with the "universe of things" (1). Inside the poetry cave, he searches for images and shades, and he finds the ravine in there.

According to the speaker, some claim that visions of a world beyond this one visit us when we sleep. As the speaker looks up, overwhelmed by the view, he wonders if some powerful being has lifted the curtain between death and life or if he is asleep, dreaming. He spies Mont Blanc, a calm, snowy mountain, surrounded by ice and smaller mountains, its landscape a desert populated only by storms, an occasional eagle, and wolves. The speaker wonders if the scary, high mountains were the playthings of young earthquakes or if they were once covered by fire. No one knows. The wild landscape now seems eternal and can inspire awestruck skepticism or serene belief. Only this belief can reunite man with nature. At the end of the stanza, the speaker addresses Mont Blanc, claiming that it can speak and can repeal false and cruel laws. Not everyone comprehends its voice, but the sage and the good can decipher the voice, feel it themselves, or help other people feel it.

In stanza 4, the speaker declares that almost everything on earth is born and dies, from fields to hurricanes to human beings and their accomplishments. However, power exists apart from this cycle, "remote, serene, and inaccessible" (97). The speaker says that he can learn something from the ancient mountains before him. Glaciers creep, like a decaying city built to mock mortal power. But a glacier is not a city but a "flood of ruin" (107), which destroys everything

PERCY BYSSHE SHELLEY

in its path, including the homes of animals and humans. Beneath the glacier rushes water from vast caves; the waters meet in the valley, forming one magnificent river that rolls forever to the ocean.

Mont Blanc sits high above, full of amazing views, noises, and "much of life and death" (129). The speaker describes how at night snow falls on the mountain, wind blows, and lightning strikes, and no one witnesses these acts. Instead, the strength, which governs both thinking and heaven, inhabits it. The speaker concludes by wondering what the mountain, as well as the earth, stars, and oceans, would be if the human mind interpreted quiet and isolation as emptiness.

ANALYSIS

In this five-stanza, meditative poem, Shelley describes emotional and intellectual reactions to a landscape in order to illustrate the relationship between nature and the human mind. This subject is similar to William Wordsworth's 1798 poem "Tintern Abbey," which was a strong influence on Shelley's work. Both poems describe an exchange between the mind and nature: a natural landscape instills the speaker with visionary power and moral strength, but the speaker has creative power over the landscape since he can perceive it different ways.

The first lines of the poem portray the mind and everything outside the mind as equal partners. Inside the mind runs "the everlasting universe of things," which gives the mind pleasure and alleviates some of its sadness. Thought, a smaller, weaker tributary of the river, nevertheless adds to its flow. Shelley develops this relationship between the mind and the world outside it throughout the poem. The arresting sight of the powerful mountain and the river sends the speaker into "a trance sublime and strange" (35). Then Shelley personifies the mountain, giving it a voice capable of righting injustice. But the speaker is powerful too, holding the mountain captive in his own thoughts, within the cave of "Poesy," until he can find the right words to describe the mountain in a poem.

Awestruck by the power of the landscape, Shelley ascribes to it an even more impressive divinity than he gave to the spirit of beauty in "Hymn to Intellectual Beauty." In this poem, the mountain seems to keep the secrets of the universe beneath its snow. But Shelley recognizes that its power, like all power in nature, is destructive as well as creative. The landscape is beautiful but also desolate and frightening. Similarly, the Arve River can bring life and inspire poetry, but it

PERCY BYSSHE SHELLEY

can also destroy all living things. As for Mont Blanc, although it is beautiful and able to influence humanity for the better, it is also "remote, serene, and inaccessible." It has lasted forever, immune and indifferent to the suffering and death of generations of living things. Although some people are able to reconcile themselves to the sinister side of nature through religious belief, the speaker cannot. Rather, the speaker feels both a great awe for nature's power and a doubt that it is benevolent or even meaningful.

A sense of doubt appears again at the end of the poem, when the speaker wonders what the mountain—and other elements of nature—would be if, instead of interpreting their "silence and solitude" (144) as power and wisdom, humans read them as emptiness. This musing also mirrors the sentiments in "Hymn to Intellectual Beauty," when the speaker fears that death is not a spiritual journey but merely a "dark reality," like life and dread. A world in which nature is nothing but empty forms is truly the world of an atheist, and it could be seen as cause for despair. Shelley, however, believes in the human mind. In the last lines of the poem, Mont Blanc becomes vacant because the human mind drains it of its power. The mountain is only powerful in a spiritual sense because the human mind perceives it as powerful. Thus, the mind seems to have gained the upper hand in the relationship between mind and nature that begins the poem—it is an incredible creative force, able to change the world at will.

Since the mind's power lies in its creativity, the greatest human mind must belong to the artist, and the greatest artist is the poet, as only the poet can articulate imaginings. One of the most striking characteristics of Shelley's poetry is his faith in the poet as visionary and revolutionary. In the third stanza, Shelley makes it clear that not everyone can understand the just, revolutionary voice of the mountain. Only the moral and intellectual elite—"the wise, and great, and good" (82)—can "deeply feel" (83) the mountain's message and interpret it for the rest of humanity. The real power may not be the mountain's power to convey meaning or even the human power to interpret, but rather the poet's power to take inspiration from the mountain and convey meaning. Thus, the poet becomes the ideal messenger of truth, and Shelley believes that poetry can change both the natural and the political world.

"Ode to the West Wind"

1

O wild West Wind, thou breath of Autumn's being,
Thou, from whose unseen presence the leaves dead
Are driven, like ghosts from an enchanter fleeing,

Yellow, and black, and pale, and hectic red,
Pestilence-stricken multitudes: O thou,   5
Who chariotest to their dark wintry bed

The wingèd seeds, where they lie cold and low,
Each like a corpse within its grave, until
Thine azure sister of the Spring shall blow

Her clarion o'er the dreaming earth, and fill   10
(Driving sweet buds like flocks to feed in air)
With living hues and odours plain and hill:

Wild Spirit, which art moving everywhere;
Destroyer and Preserver; hear, O hear!

2

Thou on whose stream, 'mid the steep sky's commotion,   15
Loose clouds like Earth's decaying leaves are shed,
Shook from the tangled boughs of Heaven and Ocean,

Angels of rain and lightning: there are spread
On the blue surface of thine airy surge,
Like the bright hair uplifted from the head   20

Of some fierce Maenad, even from the dim verge
Of the horizon to the zenith's height,
The locks of the approaching storm. Thou dirge

Of the dying year, to which this closing night
Will be the dome of a vast sepulchre   25
Vaulted with all thy congregated might

Of vapours, from whose solid atmosphere
Black rain, and fire, and hail will burst: O hear!

3
Thou who didst waken from his summer dreams
The blue Mediterranean, where he lay,   30
Lulled by the coil of his crystalline streams,

Beside a pumice isle in Baiae's bay,
And saw in sleep old palaces and towers
Quivering within the wave's intenser day,

All overgrown with azure moss and flowers   35
So sweet, the sense faints picturing them! Thou
For whose path the Atlantic's level powers

Cleave themselves into chasms, while far below
The sea-blooms and the oozy woods which wear
The sapless foliage of the ocean, know   40

Thy voice, and suddenly grow grey with fear,
And tremble and despoil themselves: O hear!

4
If I were a dead leaf thou mightest bear;
If I were a swift cloud to fly with thee;
A wave to pant beneath thy power, and share   45

The impulse of thy strength, only less free
Than thou, O Uncontrollable! If even
I were as in my boyhood, and could be

The comrade of thy wanderings over Heaven,
As then, when to outstrip thy skiey speed   50
Scarce seemed a vision; I would ne'er have striven

As thus with thee in prayer in my sore need.
Oh! lift me as a wave, a leaf, a cloud!
I fall upon the thorns of life! I bleed!

A heavy weight of hours has chained and bowed   55
One too like thee: tameless, and swift, and proud.

                                    5
Make me thy lyre, even as the forest is:
What if my leaves are falling like its own!
The tumult of thy mighty harmonies

Will take from both a deep, autumnal tone,   60
Sweet though in sadness. Be thou, Spirit fierce,
My spirit! Be thou me, impetuous one!

Drive my dead thoughts over the universe
Like withered leaves to quicken a new birth!
And, by the incantation of this verse,   65

Scatter, as from an unextinguished hearth
Ashes and sparks, my words among mankind!
Be through my lips to unawakened Earth

The trumpet of a prophecy! O Wind,
If Winter comes, can Spring be far behind?   70

Summary

This poem consists of five sections, each fourteen lines long. In the first stanza of the first section, the speaker addresses the West Wind: the wind, which acts as autumn's air, removes multicolored dead leaves from the trees and takes tree kernels (from which will sprout saplings in the spring) to their winter resting place. The speaker likens the leaves to diseased people but claims that spring, the wind's sister, will awaken the earth with sweetness, color, and pleasant smells by moving buds from place to place like a shepherd moves his animals. This section concludes with the speaker calling the West Wind an untamed force that both destroys and preserves and urging it to listen to his cries.

Continuing to address the West Wind, the speaker describes fierce autumn storms in the second stanza. Like the breeze that moves the dead leaves, clouds dump rain and lightning in the sky and on the sea. The speaker compares the clouds stretched across the sky to hair: the coming bad weather is like bright hair standing up on the head of a distraught woman. He then compares the wind to a lamenting hymn signaling the end of the year and compares the end of the night to the cover of a tomb. The combined power of the wind's vapors will create the vault of the tomb, and black rain, fire, and hail will burst from the tomb. Again, the speaker concludes by urging the wind to listen to his cries.

In the third section, the speaker discusses the wind's effect on the Mediterranean Sea. The wind woke the sea from summer dreams, in which it had been lulled to sleep by the sounds of its streams, alongside an island in a bay, dreaming of ancient ruins covered in sweet moss and flowers and shimmering beneath waves. According to the speaker, the Atlantic Ocean opens its surface to let the West Wind pass through. Beneath the surface, underwater plants tremble at the sound of the wind's voice and lose their leaves. The speaker concludes by asking the wind to listen to his cries.

The speaker spends the fourth section explaining that he would not have prayed to the West Wind had he been something that could be controlled by the wind and thus share in its power—a leaf, a cloud, a wave, or even a child like he once was. He longs to accompany the wind on its journey across the sky and begs the wind to raise him as it does the waves, clouds, and leaves. Instead, the speaker is wounded by the roughness of life. Like the wind, he is fast, unable to be tamed, and arrogant, but he is imprisoned and weighed down by time.

In the fifth section, the speaker asks to be made into the wind's instrument, like the forest. He says that he doesn't care if he loses bits of himself as the trees lose their leaves because the wind will produce a pleasant, lamenting sound from both the speaker and the forest. The speaker addresses the wind directly—calling it "impetuous" (62)—and passionately asks to be its spirit. He longs to be reborn and calls for the wind to rid him of his lifeless ideas as it rids trees of dead leaves. The speaker then asks the wind to take his poem and scatter it around humankind so that he might become a prophet, heralding the coming of spring. He concludes by wondering how long it might be until spring, after winter arrives.

ANALYSIS

"Ode to the West Wind" describes Shelley's view of nature as simultaneously awe inspiring and morally ambiguous. In earlier poems, Shelley struggled to reconcile nature's power to give life, inspiration, and enlightenment with its capacity for merciless destruction. He seems to have reconciled the two sides of nature in "Ode to the West

Wind," a poem that celebrates nature as a revolutionary force that creates as it destroys. The wind is an all-pervading natural force, which ranges over the earth and can inspire humans to change the world politically, socially, and artistically—but these changes cannot be undertaken without suffering and sacrifice.

To illustrate the fusion of pain and exultation inherent in both nature and change, Shelley uses autumnal imagery. The poem is set in autumn, a time when the living things that flourished in summer are beginning to die, anticipating the inhospitable cold of winter. Trees lose their leaves, a violent wind stirs up strong storms, and the year itself seems to die. However, while there is restlessness and mourning in these autumn scenes, there is also great beauty and passion: the leaves are brilliant with colors, filled with a feverish intensity. Clouds resemble "angels" (18) and the luminous hair of a maenad, one of the violent, sensual, decadent women who followed the Greek god of wine, continually in a state of ecstasy and abandon. Throughout the poem, the speaker begs the West Wind to bestow upon him some of this ecstatic, almost sexual energy. Longing to be possessed by the wind, the speaker wishes the wind would fill his body. Along with sexuality, passion, and rebirth the images also suggest death: while the wind disperses dead leaves, these leaves distribute the seeds that will grow into plants next spring.

The cycle of death and rebirth in nature becomes a metaphor for human progress: Shelley sees the wind as an imaginative force that can change the world, but not without violence. Right now, humankind is as sleepy and unresponsive as the summertime Mediterranean, unable to recognize that change is needed until the West Wind stirs it up. The decaying leaves represent the masses of humanity: only after the furious wind relieves them of their dead ideas can humans be reborn as agents of change.

Through the dissemination of his incantatory poem, the speaker believes he can help humanity achieve this new birth, but he too will have to suffer. The speaker feels paralyzed, weighed down by conventional morality and social injustice, so he asks the wind to possess him, to give him strength, and to allow him to spread his ideas. In this way, the speaker becomes a Christ-like visionary, sacrificed to the cruelties of life: "I fall upon the thorns of life! I bleed!" (54). His thorns resemble the crown of thorns worn by Christ at the Crucifixion, and the speaker considers himself a prophet like Christ, martyred but resurrected to spread his message of rebirth to all. By comparing

PERCY BYSSHE SHELLEY

himself to Christ, the speaker glorifies the status of the poet and highlights Shelley's image of the heroic, prophetic artist.

In his poetry, Shelley frequently uses religious **imagery** to resolve the tension between the creative powers of the poet and the creative powers of nature. While Shelley is in awe of nature's ability to create, he tends to ascribe the greatest creative power to the poet. In "Ode to the West Wind," the speaker, himself a poet, asks to be an instrument of the West Wind. In other words, the speaker wants to do with words what the wind does as a natural force: he wants to spread his message from person to person as the wind removes dead leaves and spreads seeds, thus causing rebirth. The speaker wants to serve nature in the same way that Christ serves—and receives power from—God. Similarly, the speaker asks the wind to hear his cries, much as the pious and penitent ask God to hear their prayers. However, although the wind gives the poet life and power, the speaker's thoughts are his own, and they come from his own lips. Shelley resolves the tension by linking the speaker and the wind, much as Christian doctrine links Christ and God. For Shelley, the poet and nature are one ecstatic, revolutionary force that will see humankind through the winter of its suffering and into a new spring.

ADONAIS

EXCERPT FROM ADONAIS

I weep for Adonais—he is dead!
O, weep for Adonais! though our tears
Thaw not the frost which binds so dear a head!
And thou, sad Hour, selected from all years
To mourn our loss, rouse thy obscure compeers,
And teach them thine own sorrow, say: "With me
Died Adonais; till the Future dares
Forget the Past, his fate and fame shall be
An echo and a light unto eternity!"

. . . . . .

To that high Capital, where kingly Death
Keeps his pale court in beauty and decay,
He came; and bought, with price of purest breath,
A grave among the eternal.—Come away!
Haste, while the vault of blue Italian day

Is yet his fitting charnel-roof! while still
He lies, as if in dewy sleep he lay;
Awake him not! surely he takes his fill
Of deep and liquid rest, forgetful of all ill.

He will awake no more, oh, never more!—
Within the twilight chamber spreads apace
The shadow of white Death, and at the door
Invisible Corruption waits to trace
His extreme way to her dim dwelling-place;
The eternal Hunger sits, but pity and awe
Soothe her pale rage, nor dares she to deface
So fair a prey, till darkness, and the law
Of change, shall o'er his sleep the mortal curtain draw.

.   .   .   .   .

Lost Echo sits amid the voiceless mountains,
And feeds her grief with his remembered lay,
And will no more reply to winds or fountains,
Or amorous birds perched on the young green spray,
Or herdsman's horn, or bell at closing day;
Since she can mimic not his lips, more dear
Than those for whose disdain she pined away
Into a shadow of all sounds:—a drear
Murmur, between their songs, is all the woodmen hear.

.   .   .   .   .

Alas! that all we loved of him should be,
But for our grief, as if it had not been,
And grief itself be mortal! Woe is me!
Whence are we, and why are we? of what scene
The actors or spectators? Great and mean
Meet massed in death, who lends what life must borrow.
As long as skies are blue, and fields are green,
Evening must usher night, night urge the morrow,
Month follow month with woe, and year wake year to sorrow.

.   .   .   .   .

The splendours of the firmament of time
May be eclipsed, but are extinguished not;
Like stars to their appointed height they climb,
And death is a low mist which cannot blot
The brightness it may veil. When lofty thought
Lifts a young heart above its mortal lair,
And love and life contend in it, for what
Shall be its earthly doom, the dead live there
And move like winds of light on dark and stormy air.

.   .   .   .   .

That Light whose smile kindles the Universe,
That Beauty in which all things work and move,
That Benediction which the eclipsing Curse
Of birth can quench not, that sustaining Love
Which through the web of being blindly wove
By man and beast and earth and air and sea,
Burns bright or dim, as each are mirrors of
The fire for which all thirst, now beams on me,
Consuming the last clouds of cold mortality.

SUMMARY

This fifty-five-stanza poem is dedicated to the poet John Keats. The first stanza begins with the speaker lamenting Adonais's death and asking time to mourn with him, as well as to remember Adonais in perpetuity. In the second stanza, the speaker addresses Adonais's mother, Urania. He asks her to answer for her whereabouts during Adonais's death and accuses her of being in paradise while her son let go of the music of life. The speaker continues to address Urania in the third stanza, commanding her to awaken and mourn. But then he shifts sentiments and tells her to be as stoic as her dead son, for all living things must die and death mocks our mourning rituals. By stanza 4, the speaker again urges Urania to wail loudly, this time to mourn the death of another poet, who, though blind and old, went as boldly into death as he practiced poetry during a time when his country was being ruled by tyrants. His spirit still walks among humans, along with those of two other poets. In the fifth stanza, the speaker asks the mourners to cry again, as not every poet dares to achieve those heights. Minor poets who are remembered are luckier than those great poets whose brilliance is forgotten, extinguished by jealousy. But some great poets survive in the world's memory, taking a difficult path to fame.

Stanzas 6 through 10 continue to describe Adonais's death and urge mourners to grieve. In stanza 6, the speaker addresses Urania and tells her that her youngest child, who was like a flower fed with love, has died. The speaker compares Adonais to a blooming flower and explains that this child was to sustain his mother through her widowhood. The speaker describes Adonais in death in the seventh stanza: he looks as if he's sleeping under the Italian sky. But in death he rests, away from evil. In stanza 8, the speaker explains that Adonais will now sleep forever, as the spirits of decay wait to devour his body. These spirits will wait until night, though, out of respect. Stanza 9 continues to discuss Adonais in death: his dreams and his thoughts no longer flow throughout his body, once motivated by love and now silenced by death. A winged mourner clutches Adonais's cold body and, in his beauty, believes him to still be alive. Crying, she calls Adonais "our love, our hope, our sorrow."

In the next few stanzas, until stanza 15, the speaker portrays Adonais's many mourners. Stanza 11 describes some of the acts of mourning performed by the ethereal beings hovering around Adonais: one spirit washes his body in an urn while another makes a funereal wreath from her cut hair, and another mourner breaks her bow and arrow in grief. Still another spirit lands on Adonais's cold lips in stanza 12, from where Adonais once drew in air and gained strength. But death took away Adonais's breath and removed the fire from his body. Desires, Sorrow, Pleasure, and everything Adonais loved or wrote about come to pay their respects in stanzas 13 and 14. Even the oceans rest and the weather stays calm to mourn him too. Stanza 15 elaborates on the impact of Adonais's death: mountains' echoes cease repeating the sounds of birds or instruments and instead become a dreary mumble.

Stanzas 16 through 20 continue describing the effects of Adonais's death on the world. Spring acted like autumn and refused to bloom, and Phoebus, the sun, refused to shine on its flowers in stanza 16. A nightingale, sister in spirit to Adonais, does not mourn the death of her mate as sorrowfully as England mourns for Adonais. Stanza 17 closes by cursing the man who killed Adonais. In stanza 18, the speaker explains that despite the arrival of spring and its wondrous trappings, he still feels sad. The speaker compares spring and its effect on earth to the creation of the world in stanza 19: "baser things" come alive with love and lust for life. Spring touches even the decaying corpse, and from the corpse bloom flowers in stanza 20, but these flowers are tinged with death. Everything, even brief flashes of light, must die.

In stanza 21, the speaker, resigned to the presence of death, wonders why we exist if we are to experience grief, as night follows day, and eventually die. In stanza 22, the speaker repeats that Adonais will never again wake, then personifies misery and has Misery tell Urania to wake up. After hearing calls to wake from dreams and echoes, the aging Urania awakens at the beginning of stanza 23. She arrives, grieving, shrouded in sorrow, at Adonais's death chamber; the speaker compares her arrival to the descent of darkness during the fall. Stanza 24 describes Urania's arrival from her heavenly home through the industrial world and the human core, which wounded her with its steeliness and sharp speech. Upon the arrival of Urania, Death, ashamed at having taken her child, leaves Adonais's chamber, and life briefly returns to Adonais in stanza 25.

Most of stanzas 26 through 30 cover Urania's speech to Adonais. In stanza 26, she urges her son to remain with her and give her a kiss so that the kiss might linger now that he is dead. She exclaims that she would die too if she could, but her time for death has not yet arrived. In stanza 27, Urania despairingly asks Adonais why he dared to fight a dragon when he was still so young and inexperienced. She chastises him for not using wisdom to protect himself. In stanza 28, Urania claims that carnivorous, morbid animals such as wolves and vultures fled when Adonais was killed. In stanza 29, Urania describes the passage of day and night: the sun rises, creatures copulate; the sun sets, and creatures die. This pattern, Urania explains, occurs with humans too: during the day, a person's imagination roams, but night dims the day's great thoughts. In stanza 30, the speaker resumes as Urania finishes her speech. He lists the various human mourners, including shepherds and poets, who transform their grief into verse and song.

Throughout stanzas 31 through 35, the speaker focuses on one particular mourner, "a phantom among men" (272) walking alone just after a storm, as the speaker describes him in stanza 31. The speaker describes his beauty and power in the next stanza, comparing him to strong objects surrounded by weakness, such as a flickering flame. The mysterious figure wears a crown of flowers and carries a spear, as described in stanza 33, and stands alone, crying for his fate as well as for Adonais's death in stanza 34. Urania asks the stranger to identify himself; in reply, he bares his head and shows a mark that resembles that of Cain or Christ. The speaker speculates about the effect of having Christ mourn Adonais in stanza 35: if it is Christ, the speaker decides to accept—without question—Adonais's death.

In stanzas 36 through 40, the speaker wonders about Adonais's murder to the mourners. The speaker muses about how the murder could have ended Adonais's short life and silenced his song. He then curses the murderer to live in shame and remorse in stanza 37; the murder will be remembered only as a stain on Adonais's name. The rant continues into the next stanza, in which the speaker explains that the murderer shall eventually die but shall not join Adonais, who has joined the Eternal and is thus not dead. In his eternal rest, Adonais is free from the passion and pain of life. Those who live decay each day, eaten up by terror and sadness. Death has freed Adonais from the struggles of life, which we misidentify as joy, as the speaker explains in stanza 40.

Stanzas 41 through 45 imagine Adonais in death. In stanza 41, the speaker commands the mourners, human and otherwise, to cease grieving, as Adonais resides now with nature, including the dew that drapes over everything on earth. Adonais's voice can be heard in nature's music, and he can be seen in nature's shadows and sun, as explained in stanza 42. Stanza 43 continues to describe Adonais's presence in nature, making it more beautiful than it was before his death. Although time may dim nature's light, it will never completely extinguish it, according to stanza 44, because thought and poetry renders its thinkers and writers above the mortality of life: as they are read, the poets live on in the bodies of their readers. The speaker mentions various poets in stanza 45 who have been made immortal through their works, including Chatterton and Sidney.

In stanza 46, the speaker describes Adonais as being welcomed to the afterlife by famous poets who died before fulfilling their potential. In stanza 47, the speaker asks mourners to stop being sad and to kindle hope, and in stanza 48, he tells mourners to go to Rome to visit Adonais's grave. Stanzas 49 and 50 describe Rome: even though empires and religions lie buried there, Adonais is more glorious than they are since the art he created is immortal. In Rome, a place like paradise, flowers grow over ruins, and nature battles time.

The poem's final five stanzas deal with death and Rome. In stanza 51, the speaker stops to examine the graves of those who died too young and asks mourners why they fear death. In stanza 52, the speaker reminds mourners that with death comes eternity and glory:

PERCY BYSSHE SHELLEY

heaven is eternal, whereas the earth is transitory. In stanza 53, the speaker addresses his heart and asks that it let him join Adonais in death, from where Adonais calls him. In stanza 54, the speaker claims that light that sustains and inspires the universe shines on him, burning away the last traces of his mortality. Finally, in stanza 55, the speaker himself is traveling away from the earth, far from the crowds, toward the soul of Adonais, which shines from the land of the immortal.

ANALYSIS

Adonais is Shelley's eulogy in verse for John Keats, a friend and a fellow romantic poet. In 1821, at the age of twenty-six, Keats died of tuberculosis in Rome. *Adonais* glorifies Keats as a great poet and as a martyr who died too soon, as well as vilifies Keats's critics: Shelley claims that it was their unfair attacks, and not tuberculosis, that killed Keats. The poem also ruminates about death and the promise of immortality through art.

The poem is an **elegy**, or a formal poem of lament for a specific person, and follows the tradition of the **pastoral epic**, or a long poem that takes place in an idealized classical setting. Much of the poem occurs in Rome, among the ruins of ancient civilizations. The name Adonais is an adaptation of the name of Adonis, a figure from Greek mythology. A beautiful young man who was beloved by Aphrodite, the Greek goddess of love, Adonis died early and tragically. Adonais's mother, Urania, is a Muse, and figures representing the Greek gods Apollo and Dionysus are among Adonais's mourners.

Shelley employs the **pathetic fallacy** (the attribution of human characteristics to nature or inanimate objects) throughout the poem to underscore the significance of Keats. In addition to immortal mourners, nature also mourns Adonais. Portraying the effect of human activity on nature is another convention of the pastoral epic, and it is particularly appropriate for a poem written by Shelley and written for Keats. Like Shelley, Keats wrote primarily about the power and beauty of nature, and in this poem the natural world mourns Keats not only because he was young and innocent but also because he made nature more beautiful through his verse. Shelley refers to specific Keats poems, including Keats's famous "Ode to a Nightingale," in stanza 17.

The speaker of *Adonais* mourns Adonais's early death, in particular the tragedy of his untapped potential. The poet dead too young is a common motif in romantic poetry. Since the romantics valued emotional responses and personal impulses, they idealized youth, a time when people are more impulsive and emotional than they are in maturity. Shelley sees Adonais/Keats as a beautiful, idealized figure whose brilliant future is destroyed by the hatred and jealousy of older and wiser but less gifted individuals, as in stanza 36. Adonais becomes a martyr to the cause of youth, passion, and poetry.

Transforming Keats into a martyr, as opposed to portraying him as a tuberculosis victim, supports one of Shelley's main artistic goals: to elevate poets to heroic status. Throughout Shelley's poetry, the figure of the poet is a passionate, tragic savior of humanity, someone who understands great truths and takes great risks to communicate them to others. One of Shelley's favorite **metaphors** for the poet is the figure of Prometheus, who was punished by eternal torture for stealing fire from the gods and giving it to humans. To Shelley, Keats's death provided a real-life example of this kind of martyrdom, and Shelley imagines Adonais as taking magnificent risks. For instance, he describes the brave but inexperienced Adonais confronting a wild dragon in its den in stanza 27.

By association, Shelley shares in the dead poet's grandeur: some of the glory being written about rubs off on the writer. In the poem, Shelley transforms the speaker into a vocal mourner at Adonais's funeral and imagines him as sharing qualities with the wild, mysterious Greek god of wine, Dionysus; the exiled wanderer and murderer, Cain; and the ultimate martyr, Christ. At the end of the poem, Shelley foresees a lifetime of wandering for the speaker/poet, who will become isolated from humanity. He will achieve immortality through his own version of martyrdom. Interestingly enough, Shelley himself died young, in a storm at sea.

Traditionally, pastoral elegies end with a consolation: the speaker ceases to mourn because he realizes that the dead man has now achieved eternal life. For Christian poets, this immortality is with God in heaven, but Shelley imagines a more secular, aesthetic immortality, based on the glorification of the poet. In the heaven he describes, poets live on in the hearts of their readers. For Shelley, this is the only true immortality. Political figures and religious leaders may seem to have the most power in the world, but, as Shelley demonstrates in "Ozymandias," an earlier poem, the immortal work of artists outlasts the work of rulers and popes.

The triumph of the poet is not simply artistic immortality but political power: through their art, poets can enact social change. Early in the poem, the speaker explains that although the seventeenth-century poet John Milton died in a time of political corruption, he survived the horrors of his age to become as a beloved poet. Shelley believed that the English political situation in his time was similarly corrupt. By associating Keats/Adonais with Milton, Shelley suggests that the work of the romantic poets will not only outshine their critics, but will outlast, and eventually conquer, the tyranny and injustice of their age.

JOHN KEATS

(1795–1821)

CONTEXT

John Keats had the shortest writing career of any major English poet: he lived to be only twenty-five years old. The eldest son of a livery stable manager, Keats was born on October 31, 1795, in London. By all accounts, he lived in a warm, lively household along with his parents, two brothers, and one sister. Life in the Keats house centered around the stable, which was managed with great success by Keats's father, Thomas Keats, and Keats grew up surrounded by horses and riding gear. Although the Keats family wasn't wealthy, they were comfortable, and like his two younger brothers Keats was educated privately. However, Keats left home for school at age eight. Soon after, the Keats family fell upon misfortune: Keats's father died in a riding accident in April 1804, and for the next few years, the family moved around, ultimately settling in Edmonton, a small town outside of London, where they lived happily enough for a time. In March 1810, Keats's mother died of tuberculosis.

During his teenage years, from roughly 1811 to 1816, Keats studied to become a doctor, eventually passing his medical examinations after spending a year in training at Guy's Hospital, in London. Around this time, Keats also began writing poetry. He wrote his first poem, "Imitation of Spenser," in 1814, and was published for the first time in a magazine in May 1816, two months before passing his medical exams. Although his exams qualified him to practice as an apothecary surgeon, Keats abandoned medicine for poetry. Critics generally agree that Keats reached his poetic maturity in 1818–1819. That year, he also fell in love with Fanny Brawne; nursed his brother Tom, who would die of tuberculosis that December; and went on a walking tour of the English Lake District, Ireland, and Scotland. Although Brawne reciprocated Keats's affections, his devotion to poetry and eventual terminal illness made marriage impossible. In his travels, Keats saw England's great natural beauty, as well as its appalling rural poverty. He also became sick with a sore throat, which forced him to cut his travels short and to return home early—a possible indication of the tuberculosis that would kill him only a few years later.

In 1819, at age twenty-four, Keats wrote his most famous poems: "The Eve of St. Agnes," "La Belle Dame sans Merci," "Ode to Psyche," "Ode to a Nightingale," "Ode on a Grecian Urn," "Ode on Melancholy," and "To Autumn," as well as the long poems *Lamia* and *The Fall of Hyperion*. The next year Keats developed a severe hemorrhage of the lungs and left England for Rome, in the hopes that a warmer climate would lead to recovery. He died there of tuberculosis on February 23, 1821. Although he'd had been writing poetry for just a short time, his output was prolific. During his lifetime, critics and other poets often looked down on Keats, probably because of his relatively humble class origins. Today, however, his poetry provides many outstanding examples of romantic verse.

Along with Percy Bysshe Shelley and Lord Byron, Keats comprised the younger generation of English romantic poets. Shelley, Byron, and Keats succeeded William Blake, William Wordsworth, and Samuel Taylor Coleridge, the three poets most responsible for creating the romantic literary movement in England. In 1798, the publication of *Lyrical Ballads*, a book of poems composed by Wordsworth and Coleridge, catapulted those authors into the literary limelight. As a movement, **romanticism** began in England in the late eighteenth century and lasted until roughly the mid-nineteenth century. Romantic poets rejected the rationalism of the eighteenth-century **Enlightenment** in favor of emotional subjectivity and sensory perception. They also valued transcendent experiences, including mysticism, communion with nature, the innocence of childhood, and other events or situations that lead the individual to self-discovery and change. Like other romantic poets, Keats looked to nature as a route to transcendence, and he valued dreams, visions, memories, and fantasies for their transformative power.

Keats's poetry and prose tries to overcome the divide between ordinary life and transcendent experience. In an 1817 letter to his brothers, Keats developed the notion of "negative capability," an idea that animates his poetry as well. According to Keats, negative capability occurs when a writer becomes a passive observer and transcribes only what she or he sees, without adding commentary or trying to understand present experience in light of the past. Writers should rid themselves of bias, facts, and knowledge in order to chronicle their observations—and in order to pursue and describe beauty. They should feel comfortable dwelling in "uncertainties, Mysteries, doubts," as Keats explains in the letter. By losing ourselves in experience, without trying to understand the experience or rationalize our feelings, we can grow, change, and develop as individuals. Negative capability demands close attention to the world, which bridges the gap between ordinary life and transcendent experience. Focusing on the outside world heightens our experiences and brings us to new knowledge.

Romantic poetry praises a life devoted to beauty and experience as a way of coping with contemporary political revolutions and great social change. The French Revolution began in 1789, when the peasants and middle class rose up against the aristocracy. Romantic poets incorporated the revolution's ideals of "Liberty, Equality, Fraternity" into their verse. Indeed, Shelley, Keats, and Byron called for the dramatic overthrow of oppressive governments, and Byron eventually died while fighting for these ideals in 1824, during the Greek war against the Ottomans. These poets also reacted to the Industrial Revolution, which began in England around the middle of the eighteenth century. Industrialization threatened to separate individuals from nature, as labor became increasingly mechanized and people were forced to abandon rural hamlets for cities. Keats's work manifests a deep devotion to nature, as well as a struggle to understand how to make one's life meaningful and worthwhile when confronted with poverty, evil, and suffering. In his short life, Keats created a remarkable body of work, one that simultaneously demonstrates the characteristics of romantic poetry and illuminates the intellectual and imaginative processes of a profound, singular mind.

THEMES, MOTIFS & SYMBOLS

THEMES

THE INEVITABILITY OF DEATH
Even before his diagnosis of terminal tuberculosis, Keats focused on death and its inevitability in his work. For Keats, small, slow acts of death occurred every day, and he chronicled these small mortal occurrences. The end of a lover's embrace, the images on an ancient urn, the reaping of grain in autumn—all of these are not only symbols of death, but instances of it. Examples of great beauty and art also caused Keats to ponder mortality, as in "On Seeing the Elgin Marbles" (1817). As a writer, Keats hoped he would live long enough to achieve his poetic dream of becoming as great as Shakespeare or John Milton: in "Sleep and Poetry" (1817), Keats outlined a plan of poetic achievement that required him to read poetry for a decade in order to understand—and surpass—the work of his predecessors. Hovering near this dream, however, was a morbid sense that death might intervene and terminate his projects; he expresses these concerns in the mournful 1818 **sonnet** "When I have fears that I may cease to be."

THE CONTEMPLATION OF BEAUTY
In his poetry, Keats proposed the contemplation of beauty as a way of delaying the inevitability of death. Although we must die eventually, we can choose to spend our time alive in aesthetic revelry, looking at beautiful objects and landscapes. Keats's **speakers** contemplate urns ("Ode on a Grecian Urn"), books ("On First Looking into Chapman's Homer" [1816], "On Sitting Down to Read *King Lear* Once Again" [1818]), birds ("Ode to a Nightingale"), and stars ("Bright star, would I were stedfast as thou art" [1819]). Unlike mortal beings, beautiful things will never die but will keep demonstrating their beauty for all time. Keats explores this idea in the first book of *Endymion* (1818). The speaker in "Ode on a Grecian Urn" envies the immortality of the lute players and trees inscribed on the ancient vessel because they shall never cease playing their songs, nor will they ever shed their leaves. He reassures young

lovers by telling them that even though they shall never catch their mistresses, these women shall always stay beautiful. The people on the urn, unlike the speaker, shall never stop having experiences. They shall remain permanently depicted while the speaker changes, grows old, and eventually dies.

MOTIFS

DEPARTURES AND REVERIES

In many of Keats's poems, the speaker leaves the real world to explore a transcendent, mythical, or aesthetic realm. At the end of the poem, the speaker returns to his ordinary life transformed in some way and armed with a new understanding. Often the appearance or contemplation of a beautiful object makes the departure possible. The ability to get lost in a reverie, to depart conscious life for imaginative life without wondering about plausibility or rationality, is part of Keats's concept of negative capability. In "Bright star, would I were stedfast as thou art," the speaker imagines a state of "sweet unrest" (12) in which he will remain half-conscious on his lover's breast forever. As speakers depart this world for an imaginative world, they have experiences and insights that they can then impart into poetry once they've returned to conscious life. Keats explored the relationship between visions and poetry in "Ode to Psyche" and "Ode to a Nightingale."

THE FIVE SENSES AND ART

Keats imagined that the five senses loosely corresponded to and connected with various types of art. The speaker in "Ode on a Grecian Urn" describes the pictures depicted on the urn, including lovers chasing one another, musicians playing instruments, and a virginal maiden holding still. All the figures remain motionless, held fast and permanent by their depiction on the sides of the urn, and they cannot touch one another, even though we can touch them by holding the vessel. Although the poem associates sight and sound, because we see the musicians playing, we cannot hear the music. Similarly, the speaker in "On First Looking into Chapman's Homer" compares hearing Homer's words to "pure serene" (7) air so that reading, or seeing, becomes associating with breathing, or smelling. In "Ode to a Nightingale," the speaker longs for a drink of crystal-clear water or wine so that he might adequately describe the sounds of the bird singing nearby. Each of the five senses must be involved in worthwhile experiences, which, in turn, lead to the production of worthwhile art.

The Disappearance of the Poet and the Speaker

In Keats's theory of negative capability, the poet disappears from the work—that is, the work itself chronicles an experience in such a way that the reader recognizes and responds to the experience without requiring the intervention or explanation of the poet. Keats's speakers become so enraptured with an object that they erase themselves and their thoughts from their depiction of that object. In essence, the speaker/poet becomes melded to and indistinguishable from the object being described. For instance, the speaker of "Ode on a Grecian Urn" describes the scenes on the urn for several stanzas until the famous conclusion about beauty and truth, which is enclosed in quotation marks. Since the poem's publication in 1820, critics have theorized about who speaks these lines, whether the poet, the speaker, the urn, or one or all the figures on the urn. The erasure of the speaker and the poet is so complete in this particular poem that the quoted lines are jarring and troubling.

Symbols

Music and Musicians

Music and musicians appear throughout Keats's work as **symbols** of poetry and poets. In "Ode on a Grecian Urn," for instance, the speaker describes musicians playing their pipes. Although we cannot literally hear their music, by using our imaginations, we can imagine and thus hear music. The speaker of "To Autumn" reassures us that the season of fall, like spring, has songs to sing. Fall, the season of changing leaves and decay, is as worthy of poetry as spring, the season of flowers and rejuvenation. "Ode to a Nightingale" uses the bird's music to contrast the mortality of humans with the immortality of art. Caught up in beautiful birdsong, the speaker imagines himself capable of using poetry to join the bird in the forest. The beauty of the bird's music represents the ecstatic, imaginative possibilities of poetry. As mortal beings who will eventually die, we can delay death through the timelessness of music, poetry, and other types of art.

JOHN KEATS

NATURE

Like his fellow romantic poets, Keats found in nature endless sources of poetic inspiration, and he described the natural world with precision and care. Observing elements of nature allowed Keats, Wordsworth, Coleridge, and Shelley, among others, to create extended meditations and thoughtful odes about aspects of the human condition. For example, in "Ode to a Nightingale," hearing the bird's song causes the speaker to ruminate on the immortality of art and the mortality of humans. The speaker of "Ode on Melancholy" compares a bout of depression to a "weeping cloud" (12), then goes on to list specific flowers that are linked to sadness. He finds in nature apt images for his psychological state. In "Ode to Psyche," the speaker mines the night sky to find ways to worship the Roman goddess Psyche as a muse: a star becomes an "amorous glow-worm" (27), and the moon rests amid a background of dark blue. Keats not only uses nature as a springboard from which to ponder, but he also discovers in nature **similes**, symbols, and **metaphors** for the spiritual and emotional states he seeks to describe.

THE ANCIENT WORLD

Keats had an enduring interest in antiquity and the ancient world. His longer poems, such as *The Fall of Hyperion* or *Lamia*, often take place in a mythical world not unlike that of classical antiquity. He borrowed figures from ancient mythology to populate poems, such as "Ode to Psyche" and "To Homer" (1818). For Keats, ancient myth and antique objects, such as the Grecian urn, have a permanence and solidity that contrasts with the fleeting, temporary nature of life. In ancient cultures, Keats saw the possibility of permanent artistic achievement: if an urn still spoke to someone several centuries after its creation, there was hope that a poem or artistic object from Keats's time might continue to speak to readers or observers after the death of Keats or another writer or creator. This achievement was one of Keats's great hopes. In an 1818 letter to his brother George, Keats quietly prophesied: "I think I shall be among the English poets after my death."

SUMMARY & ANALYSIS

"ON FIRST LOOKING INTO CHAPMAN'S HOMER"

Much have I travell'd in the realms of gold,
    And many goodly states and kingdoms seen;
    Round many western islands have I been
Which bards in fealty to Apollo hold.
Oft of one wide expanse had I been told   5
    That deep-brow'd Homer ruled as his demesne:
    Yet did I never breathe its pure serene
Till I heard Chapman speak out loud and bold:
Then felt I like some watcher of the skies
    When a new planet swims into his ken;   10
Or like stout Cortez, when with eagle eyes
    He stared at the Pacific—and all his men
Look'd at each other with a wild surmise—
    Silent, upon a peak in Darien.

SUMMARY

The sonnet begins with the speaker talking about his travels. He claims to have visited myriad countries and realms and to have spent time on islands whose poets were loyal to Apollo, the Greek god of sun, light, truth, and poetry. The speaker then explains that he had often heard about one particular place, which was ruled by the Greek poet Homer. But, he says, he had never truly been to such a place until he read the translation of Homer's work into English by Chapman. He compares the effect of hearing Chapman's version to the way an astronomer feels upon discovering a new planet or the way Cortez felt when he and his crew saw the Pacific Ocean for the first time: high on a mountaintop in Darien, incapable of speech.

ANALYSIS

The sonnet "On First Looking into Chapman's Homer" expresses a love for reading and a belief in the transformative power of words. George Chapman, an English scholar, modernized and re-translated Homer's *Iliad* (ca. eighth century B.C.E.), which had first been trans-

JOHN KEATS

203

lated into English by Alexander Pope in the eighteenth century. One night in October 1810, Keats stayed up late with some friends to read portions of Chapman's translation aloud to one another. According to legend, when the friends awoke the next morning, Keats had gone home—and "On First Looking into Chapman's Homer" was waiting on the breakfast table. The **octet**, or the first eight lines, recounts the speaker's past experience of poetry, while the **sestet**, or final six lines, recounts the speaker's joy and elation upon reading the new translation of Homer. A **conceit**, or extended metaphor, of exploration and discovery weaves through the two groups of lines and unites the poem.

Metaphors of exploration and discovery appear throughout the sonnet to emphasize the wonders of reading. The speaker begins by talking about his travels, implying that he has physically journeyed to the various "realms of gold" (1). By the fifth line, however, we realize that the speaker has only metaphorically taken these journeys through reading; the realms of gold are actually realms of words. Hearing and reading the words of Chapman's translation causes the speaker to feel like an astronomer, who searches the sky, and an explorer, who searches the sea and the land. Keats incorrectly invokes Cortez in line 11: actually, Balboa reached the Pacific Ocean in 1513. Through his imaginative explorations, the speaker discovers new horizons and new vistas as magnificent and as transformative as the discovery of new planets or the first European sighting of the New World. Even the title of the poem echoes the idea of exploration and discovery: the speaker looks into the poem, as if the poem itself were a vista or horizon.

Keats also explores the imaginative roles of the senses, particularly sight. Over the course of the poem, the speaker looks, travels, sees, hears, and breathes. The speaker uses his senses throughout his imaginative journeys. Rather than simply and passively letting the words wash over him, the speaker acts as he reads, becoming involved and feeling as if he had actually taken a journey and touched these strange lands. In particular, reading Chapman's Homer has caused the speaker to see differently. Whereas before he had traveled and employed his senses, after reading the new translation, he begins to experience previously unimaginable sensations, which he likens to discovering planets and oceans. He sees—and senses—differently after having read the new translation. The poem emphasizes sight over the other senses due to the link between seeing and reading. Nevertheless, the other senses matter to the imagination. When a work grips all of our senses, as opposed to affecting just one, the work possesses and inhabits us, ultimately causing us to act, feel, and perceive in new ways.

"On First Looking into Chapman's Homer" blurs the distinction between art and nature. Like a magnificent landscape seen for the first time, great art has the power to render its readers or viewers totally silent. While the conquistadores sought gold, Keats and his speaker seek the beauty of the natural world rendered even more beautiful by an accurate poem. In lines 5 and 6, the speaker notes that Homer has "ruled" over a "wide expanse." These lines imply that the writers can control—and own—nature simply by describing it. Art, in the form of Keats's sonnet, helps readers see nature differently. Not only do words take us on transformative journeys, but they also return us to our daily world with heightened powers of observation.

"BRIGHT STAR, WOULD I WERE STEDFAST AS THOU ART"

Bright star, would I were stedfast as thou art—
   Not in lone splendor hung aloft the night,
And watching, with eternal lids apart,
   Like nature's patient, sleepless eremite,
The moving waters at their priestlike task   5
   Of pure ablution round earth's human shores,
Or gazing on the new soft-fallen mask
   Of snow upon the mountains and the moors;
No—yet still stedfast, still unchangeable,
   Pillow'd upon my fair love's ripening breast,   10
To feel for ever its soft swell and fall,
   Awake for ever in a sweet unrest,
Still, still to hear her tender-taken breath,
And so live ever—or else swoon to death.

JOHN KEATS

SUMMARY

This sonnet begins with the speaker addressing a star he sees in the night sky. He tells the star that he wishes that he could be as steady and as permanent as the star above. Then the speaker clarifies his wish, explaining that while the star is beautiful, it is also alone. He likens the star to an eye and to a sleepless hermit, both of which can only watch from afar and cannot participate in what they see. The star watches the oceans wash the shores of continents, and it watches the snow fall on mountains and plains. "No," the poet concludes in line 9: he wants to be similar to the star and wants to possess the star's steadfastness, but he does not want to be exactly like the star. Steadfast as a star, he could remain forever with his lover, using her breast as a pillow. He rests his head against it as he looks up at the star in the sky. He would like to lie there, feeling her chest rise and fall, hearing her soft breathing, forever—or else he would rather die at this moment of perfect bliss.

ANALYSIS

"Bright star" expresses a love of thinking and imagining. Unlike traditional romantic sonnets, it does not praise a beloved or idealize a woman. Although a lover does appear at the end of the poem, the poem itself focuses on imagining the life of a star. In the poem's octet, the speaker describes the star's life, whereas the poem's sestet describes the speaker's life as a human lover. As the speaker points out, being a star has advantages and disadvantages. Its main advantage is its unchanging nature. Stars stay constant and steadfast. Its disadvantages include its solitary condition, its isolation, its remoteness, and its cold, unemotional existence. Ultimately, the speaker prefers to remain human. Even though humans are subject to change and impermanence, being human also means being connected to a community and living a warm, emotional life. Unlike humans, stars are passionless and sexless. Although imagining himself to be a star proves to be a fun exercise, the speaker concludes by expressing pleasure at his humanity, including his ability to feel passion and desire.

Throughout the poem, Keats sets up a series of contrasts in the descriptions and comparisons made by the speaker. First, the speaker begins by comparing himself to the steadfast star. As he lies against his lover's breast, the speaker describes it as "ripening" (10). The word *ripening* invokes the cycle of life: objects are born, they ripen and mature, they decay, and they die. Unlike the immortal star, humans are mortal. Another contrast occurs in lines 5 and 6 when the speaker describes "priestlike" oceans lapping against "human shores." Here the waters remove sins from the earth, much like religious figures absolve worshipers of their wrongdoings and guilt. Finally, the speaker contrasts sleeping and dreaming with a constant state of observation. Stars stay permanently awake, never closing

JOHN KEATS

their eyes and never drifting off into a fantasy or daydream. Unlike poets or lovers, stars have no imagination. In the final lines of the poem, the speaker explains that he would rather stay half awake on his lover's breast, lazily gazing up at the stars, than be transformed into an ever-watchful being like a star.

As a sonnet, "Bright star" idealizes the human ability to think and imagine. The narrative situation sets up the poem as an elaborate experiment in thinking and imagining. Comfortable, the lover-speaker looks up at the stars and begins to wonder what it might be like to be a star. Once he expresses this desire, he immediately begins qualifying it by thoughtfully listing the disadvantages of the star's life. He challenges himself to come up with reasons and descriptions, so that a layer of snow becomes a "soft-fallen mask" (7) and flowing water brings forgiveness to banks. Lines possess a kind of languor in keeping with the narrative situation. Half asleep, half awake, the speaker ends some lines with punctuation and some with **enjambment** so that a thought runs over multiple lines, as in lines 5–6 and 7–8. **Alliteration** further emphasizes the speaker's thoughtfulness: the **poetic diction** not only shapes the poem's content, but it also affects the poem's form. The thoughtful crafting of tone and diction further emphasizes the poem's praise of thought and imaginative reason.

"ODE ON A GRECIAN URN"

1

Thou still unravish'd bride of quietness,
    Thou foster-child of Silence and slow Time,
Sylvan historian, who canst thus express
    A flowery tale more sweetly than our rhyme:
What leaf-fringed legend haunts about thy shape   5
    Of deities or mortals, or of both,
        In Tempe or the dales of Arcady?
    What men or gods are these? What maidens loth?
What mad pursuit? What struggle to escape?
    What pipes and timbrels? What wild ecstasy?   10

2

Heard melodies are sweet, but those unheard
    Are sweeter; therefore, ye soft pipes, play on;
Not to the sensual ear, but, more endear'd,

JOHN KEATS

Pipe to the spirit ditties of no tone:
Fair youth, beneath the trees, thou canst not leave   15
    Thy song, nor ever can those trees be bare;
        Bold Lover, never, never canst thou kiss,
Though winning near the goal—yet, do not grieve;
    She cannot fade, though thou hast not thy bliss,
For ever wilt thou love, and she be fair!   20

                          3
Ah, happy, happy boughs! that cannot shed
    Your leaves, nor ever bid the Spring adieu;
And, happy melodist, unwearièd,
    For ever piping songs for ever new;
More happy love! more happy, happy love!   25
    For ever warm and still to be enjoy'd,
        For ever panting, and for ever young;
All breathing human passion far above,
    That leaves a heart high-sorrowful and cloy'd,
        A burning forehead, and a parching tongue.   30

                          4
Who are these coming to the sacrifice?
    To what green altar, O mysterious priest,
Lead'st thou that heifer lowing at the skies,
    And all her silken flanks with garlands drest?
What little town by river or sea-shore,   35
    Or mountain-built with peaceful citadel,
        Is emptied of its folk, this pious morn?
And, little town, thy streets for evermore
    Will silent be; and not a soul, to tell
        Why thou art desolate, can e'er return.   40

                          5
O Attic shape! fair attitude! with brede
    Of marble men and maidens overwrought,
With forest branches and the trodden weed;
    Thou, silent form! dost tease us out of thought
As doth eternity: Cold Pastoral!   45
    When old age shall this generation waste,
        Thou shalt remain, in midst of other woe
Than ours, a friend to man, to whom thou say'st,

"Beauty is truth, truth beauty,"—that is all
Ye know on earth, and all ye need to know.   50

Summary

Standing before a Grecian urn, the speaker begins addressing the ancient relic in the first stanza. Frustratingly, the urn remains silent about the story depicted in pictures on its surface. The speaker asks a series of questions: who are the men, women, and deities painted on the urn? Why are some figures chasing others, and why are some figures trying to escape? What music is being played? What unbridled joy is taking place? In stanza 2, the speaker tries to answer his questions by examining each scene in greater detail. He looks at a picture of a musician playing on the pipes—of course he cannot hear their music. Next, he looks at a young man pursuing a maiden. Although the young man will never win her heart, and although they will never consummate their passion, the maiden will never grow old and the lover's love will never fade.

The speaker looks to another part of the urn in stanza 3. Here he addresses the trees depicted there, noting that they will never lose their leaves and spring will never change to fall. In this scene, the musicians will never grow tired, the lovers will never grow fickle, and the trees will never lose their leaves. The speaker moves to still another scene in stanza 4, in which a cow is being sacrificed at an altar. He ruminates on the deserted, small hilltop town depicted there, and he wonders where the inhabitants have gone to and what they might be able to tell him should they reappear and speak. In the final stanza, the speaker again addresses the urn. He explains that the urn provides viewers with a glimpse of eternity in its deserted rural imagery. When his generation has died, he thinks, the urn will still live on, saying to those who look upon it, "Beauty is truth, truth beauty" (49)—the only axiom that humans must understand.

Analysis

In a nine-month period during 1819, Keats composed several significant **odes**, including perhaps his most famous poem, "Ode on a Grecian Urn." Certainly this ode stands as his most-often critiqued poem, with many scholars focusing their analyses on the enigmatic quotation in stanza 5 about beauty and truth. Critics differ about who speaks these lines—whether the speaker, one or all of the figures, the urn's creator, or even the urn itself. Similarly, critics disagree about the lines' significance: first, is truth beauty? Second, is such a statement worth dealing with, or is it actually a profound summation of the relationship between aesthetics and reality? Finally, critics wonder who the "ye" refers to in the final line, and what exactly this person or group of people needs to know: the statement about truth and beauty or the entire fifth stanza, including the lines about the mortality of humans and immortality of art? How we as readers answer these questions and understand the fifth stanza largely depends on our interpretation of the poem and our readings of the previous four stanzas.

At first, the urn and its mysteries beguile the speaker, but by the end of the poem, the speaker feels repelled by the impenetrability of the urn and its secrets. In the first stanza, the speaker calls the urn a "sylvan historian" (3), or a chronicler of bucolic scenes. He compares the urn to a storyteller who speaks more ably than any poet. Also the speaker ends the first stanza with several rhetorical questions that he intends to answer in the remaining stanzas. By the fifth stanza, however, the speaker criticizes the urn for being "overwrought" (42) and "cold" (45). Rather than tell stories, the pictures depicted on the urn instead lead to unanswerable questions. According to the speaker in line 44, the urn has become a "silent form." The urn's silence frustrates the speaker, much as a difficult poem or complex painting might frustrate a reader or viewer. Although admiring a work is easy, interpreting and understanding a work is quite difficult. "Ode on a Grecian Urn" depicts this difficulty of interpreting art and the critical thinking that we as readers or viewers must do in order to adequately understand art.

To penetrate the urn's meaning, the speaker engages with the urn and its pictures three times in stanzas 1 through 4. Stanza 1 depicts the speaker asking the urn various questions that it cannot, of course, literally answer. The urn's original meaning has been lost since its creators and the society from which it came are dead. Although we can guess or theorize, we can never really know who the men are or why they are chasing the women. Stanzas 2 and 3 describe the musician and ever-blooming trees. Here the speaker imagines himself as part of the urn, and at first he feels joy at having connected to the figures and their conditions. Eventually, however, he remembers the negative aspects of being in love. He then imagines being subjected to this state, including nervousness and hot flashes, for all of eternity, and he abandons his identification. Finally, in stanza 4, the speaker tries to imagine the figures actually worshiping and living their lives, offscreen and away from the urn's pictures. But he realizes in line 39 that there's not a "soul to tell" him why the town has been abandoned and what the figures might be doing away from the urn's images.

The speaker's interaction with the silent urn contrasts mortality and immortality. At some point in time, someone created the urn, shaping the clay and drawing the figures. Though this person has long since died, his or her work lives on. Despite the mortality of the artist, the artwork is immortal. Unlike the figures on the urn, real people experience many emotions, including love. Although the beauty of the woman on the urn will never fade, the man will never consummate his love nor will he ever receive a kiss from her. In exchange for their ability to experience, kiss, and live, real people must eventually die. Directly addressing the urn in stanza 5 allows the speaker to comment on the eternity of art: he claims that the urn will live on, even as his generation grows old and passes on.

Keats emphasizes the eternal beauty of art in the final stanza, but he also questions whether beauty actually is eternal. The poem's first four stanzas describe the urn's scenes, but these descriptions are fleeting. We as readers cannot remain locked in their descriptions forever because we must eventually put down the poem and return to the real world. In the fifth stanza, someone or something—perhaps the speaker, the figures, or the urn—claims that "'beauty is truth, truth beauty'" (49). Readers of the poem, however, probably realize that this statement might not apply to their lives because human life requires all sorts of knowledge. The urn may not need to know more than this statement, but we do. Nevertheless, the urn will be beautiful forever, even if those who view it might not understand exactly what the pictures are trying to communicate. In this sense, the beauty of the urn is as real today as it was when it was first created—its beauty has remained true over the centuries.

"To Autumn"

I

Seasons of mists and mellow fruitfulness,
   Close bosom-friend of the maturing sun;
Conspiring with him how to load and bless
   With fruit the vines that round the thatch-eves run;
To bend with apples the moss'd cottage-trees,   5
   And fill all fruit with ripeness to the core;
     To swell the gourd, and plump the hazel shells

JOHN KEATS

> With a sweet kernel; to set budding more,
> And still more, later flowers for the bees,
> Until they think warm days will never cease,   *10*
>   For Summer has o'er-brimm'd their clammy cells.

2

> Who hath not seen thee oft amid thy store?
>   Sometimes whoever seeks abroad may find
> Thee sitting careless on a granary floor,
>   Thy hair soft-lifted by the winnowing wind;   *15*
> Or on a half-reap'd furrow sound asleep,
>   Drows'd with the fume of poppies, while thy hook
>   Spares the next swath and all its twined flowers:
> And sometimes like a gleaner thou dost keep
>   Steady thy laden head across a brook;   *20*
>   Or by a cyder-press, with patient look,
>   Thou watchest the last oozings hours by hours.

3

> Where are the songs of Spring? Ay, where are they?
>   Think not of them, thou hast thy music too, —
> While barred clouds bloom the soft-dying day,   *25*
>   And touch the stubble plains with rosy hue;
> Then in a wailful choir the small gnats mourn
>   Among the river sallows, borne aloft
>   Or sinking as the light wind lives or dies;
> And full-grown lambs loud bleat from hilly bourn;   *30*
>   Hedge-crickets sing; and now with treble soft
>   The red-breast whistles from a garden-croft;
>   And gathering swallows twitter in the skies.

JOHN KEATS

Summary

Addressed to autumn, this ode begins with the speaker personifying the season, giving it human characteristics and abilities. He imagines fall plotting with the sun to ripen fruits and set flowers budding. Fall also plots with the sun to convince the bees, whose honeycombs are filled with honey, that the days will always be temperate and pleasant. In the second stanza, the speaker continues to address fall. He rhetorically wonders who hasn't witnessed this particular season, which is now in the act of harvest. Autumn rests among her store of fruit and crops. The speaker next imagines Autumn as a woman, sitting on the floor of a granary, with her hair blowing in the wind. Then he pictures her on a half-reaped field, sleeping, having not yet mowed a swath of grain entwined with flowers. Finally, he pictures Autumn next to a cider press, watching the cider drip out for hours. Autumn is sleepy and disconsolate. The speaker begins the final stanza by asking, "Where are the songs of Spring?" (23). He decides that Autumn, like Spring, has her songs, which he lists in the remaining lines. As the autumn suns plays over the harvested grasses, the speaker hears the noises and sounds of gnats, river swallows, lambs, crickets, redbreasts, and other birds gathering in the sky.

ANALYSIS

Keats wrote "To Autumn" at the end of an extremely fertile period of creativity in 1819. Like his other odes, this ode explores the idea of death. Critics consider it to be Keats's most philosophical and mature meditation on the inevitability of dying. With autumn comes the harvest and decay, which seems particularly brutal after the abundance of summer. Winter—the season of death and infertility—follows autumn. Much of autumn is thus spent missing the bounty of summer and dreading the cold of winter. Rather than focus on these aspects of the season, the poem chooses to portray fall's beauty as realistically as possible. Images are lovely, not depressing, and the speaker extols readers and the season itself to remember that autumn has its own peculiar music. By recognizing the beauty of autumn, readers can come to terms with their own mortality and begin to see death as a natural, necessary part of the life cycle that contains its own music.

Throughout the poem, the speaker uses **personification**, which gives the inhuman season of autumn human characteristics. In stanza 1, autumn acts: it conspires, loads, blesses, rounds, runs, bends, fills, swells, and plumps. Later autumn sits, sleeps, and watches. Transformed into a person, autumn becomes soothing and gentle, not frightening or decaying. Rather than chop down flowers with its scythe, autumn leaves the blossoms and rests instead because the flowers' smells have made autumn sleepy and relaxed. Our knowledge of and direct experience with autumn make the poem mournful and sad: we know that winter follows autumn, just like we know that flowers decay and trees lose their leaves throughout the fall. The personification of the season contributes to the mournful tone by imagining autumn as benevolent and life affirming. Along with the speaker, we know that autumn is, in fact, detrimental and potentially nasty. After all, when autumn has completed its cycle, the grass will be buried in snow, the lambs sheared or slaughtered, and the birds silenced. But the lovely images and personified figure of autumn temper the mournful tone.

In the third stanza, Keats invokes the **lyric** poetic tradition in English by contrasting the songs of spring with the songs of fall. Many poems, from Geoffrey Chaucer's *The Canterbury Tales* (1387–1400) to T. S. Eliot's *The Waste Land* (1922), imagine spring, particularly April, as a bountiful, beautiful time. Keats chooses instead to address fall, deeming it worthy of a poem and describing its ability to make music and bring pleasure. Like spring, fall is capable of inspiring poetry. Romantic poets deemed all of nature worthy of observation, and careful attention to nature in any season rewards any observer. Personified into a woman, autumn herself is a figure of steadfast attention: she not only reaps the harvest but also works in the granary. She not only gathers apples but patiently presses them into cider. "To Autumn" reassures readers about the life cycle and about middle age, or the autumnal stage of life, by showing them that even autumn contains splendor and harmonies.

ALFRED, LORD TENNYSON

(1809–1892)

CONTEXT

Alfred Tennyson was born in the northern English village of Somersby in 1809, the fourth of twelve children in a large and troubled family. His father, George Tennyson, was the local rector, or village minister; he was a sometimes violent alcoholic. Of Tennyson's three older brothers, one died in infancy, one fled England to live in Italy, and the third became an opium addict. Tennyson's younger brother Edward went permanently insane when Tennyson was in his early twenties. Family troubles and tragedy affected Tennyson, whose poetry is characterized by gloom and melancholy. Despite these disadvantages, he demonstrated a talent for writing poetry even as a child. As a teenager, Tennyson began publishing his verse. While a student at Cambridge University, Tennyson received his first serious recognition when he won a major prize for his poem "Timbuctoo." This prize gained him entry into a campus literary group known as "the Apostles."

Family and money troubles forced Tennyson to leave Cambridge without taking a degree in 1831. He published two volumes of poetry, in 1830 and 1832, and both suffered from severe criticism. In 1833, Tennyson's best friend and the leader of the Apostles, Arthur Henry Hallam, suddenly died while vacationing in Austria. Hallam had been engaged to marry Tennyson's younger sister Emily, and his public praise of Tennyson's poetry had helped establish Tennyson's reputation and solidify Tennyson's self-confidence. Many scholars at Cambridge expected Hallam to become the greatest literary critic of his generation. For the next decade, Tennyson did not publish any poems and lived in relative poverty. He became engaged in 1836 but was not able to marry until 1850, in large part because of his finances. That year also saw the publication of *In Memoriam*, a long elegiac poem dedicated to Hallam that catapulted Tennyson into critical favor and financial comfort. Queen Victoria so admired the poem that she asked Tennyson to serve as poet laureate of England.

From 1850 until the end of his life, Tennyson was the preeminent living English poet. His books were read widely, and he grew very rich. In addition to further collections of his personal work, he regularly wrote and published official poems as poet laureate to commemorate state occasions. Possibly more than any other poet who had ever lived, Tennyson became a popular celebrity and cultural icon. During this later period, he also wrote a number of longer works. Most notable among these is *Maud* (1855), a long **monologue**, and *Idylls of the King* (1859), a linked series of short poems set in the mythical England of King Arthur. Later poetry tended to be more narrative than his earlier lyrical verse. Around 1875, Tennyson began publishing plays in both prose and **blank verse**. All of them were, essentially, disastrous failures, both financially and critically. In 1883, Queen Victoria made Tennyson a baron—hence the name he is now known by: Alfred, Lord Tennyson. After his death in 1892, Tennyson was buried in Westminster Abbey.

Tennyson's life coincided with the reign of Queen Victoria, a time we now call the **Victorian era**. Victoria ruled from 1837 to 1901. Her reign was marked by rapid industrialization and scientific progress, as well as vast social and economic change. A large and newly affluent middle class arose. For the first time, high culture—literature, art, music, and so on—became the culture of the middle class rather than solely the purview of the upper class. The cost of printing fell, literacy expanded, and the novel replaced poetry as the dominant form of literature. Poets were thus forced to compete with novels, which led to the development of the **dramatic monologue** and other types of experimental narrative verse. Thus, unlike earlier major poets, Tennyson's audience was largely middle class, and he was forced to define and defend poetry for his age since its importance could no longer be taken for granted. He did this by writing poetry that was clearly connected to an older literary tradition, particularly the classical tradition, and by choosing subjects and settings out of England's past or out of ancient history. In this way, he helped his readers view Victorian culture and Victorian life as part of a continuing trajectory of cultural and historical progress, not as unsettlingly revolutionary.

In Memoriam, Tennyson's greatest work, reconciled religious faith with scientific discoveries, thereby providing a model for other Victorian thinkers grappling with similar issues. Tennyson published his long poem at a time when discoveries in biology, geology, and astronomy had already seemed to disprove the view of nature laid out in the Bible, and less than a decade before Charles Darwin made his theory of evolution public in *On the Origin of Species* (1859). Pieced together from fragments written over the course of seventeen years, Tennyson's poem expresses grief at Hallam's death and depicts the struggle to overcome despair. Eventually, the poem affirms faith in God and life after death. The poem equates human grief over deaths of loved ones with a religious despair fueled by new scientific evidence, which, at the time, seemed to possess the potential to prove definitely that God did not exist. Resolving the personal problem of grief allowed Tennyson to resolve the larger problem of religious faith, and his individual journey becomes a metaphor for the necessity, value, and reality of human progress. Elsewhere in his poetry, Tennyson finds technological advancements and scientific discoveries deeply alluring and worthy of examination.

Chronologically and thematically, Tennyson falls between the romantic poets, such as William Wordsworth and John Keats, and the modernist poets, such as Ezra Pound and T. S. Eliot. The romantics praised a life devoted to beauty and experience as a way of coping with contemporary political revolutions and great social change. Like the romantics, Tennyson thoughtfully considered the position of the social outcast, particularly in poems such as *Maud*. Tennyson also shared with the romantics a deep interest in the past, particularly the mythology of England and the ancient world. Consciously trying to reconnect to the literary past led Tennyson to utilize older metrical forms, as well as archaic language that evoked earlier English or even classical verse. For instance, he based the *Idylls of the King* on the fifteenth-century writer Sir Thomas Malory's *Le Morte D'Arthur* (*The Death of Arthur*, 1469–1470). This poem depicts the rise and fall of King Arthur's Camelot in order to show how corruption, betrayal, and deceit ruin an idealized English society. It also marks a return to **allegory**, a literary mode used by neither the romantics nor the modernists. Today, many contemporary poets and critics praise Tennyson's work for containing some of the finest examples of **meter** in English poetry.

THEMES, MOTIFS & SYMBOLS

THEMES

THE RECONCILIATION OF RELIGION AND SCIENCE

Tennyson lived during a period of great scientific advancement, and he used his poetry to work out the conflict between religious faith and scientific discoveries. Notable scientific findings and theories of the Victorian period include stratigraphy, the geological study of rock layers used to date the earth, in 1811; the first sighting of an asteroid in 1801 and galaxies in the 1840s; and Darwin's theory of evolution and natural selection in 1859. In the second half of the century, scientists, such as Fülöp Semmelweis, Joseph Lister, and Louis Pasteur, began the experiments and work that would eventually lead to germ theory and our modern understanding of microorganisms and diseases. These discoveries challenged traditional religious understandings of nature and natural history.

For most of his career, Tennyson was deeply interested in and troubled by these discoveries. His poem "Locksley Hall" (1842) expresses his ambivalence about technology and scientific progress. There the **speaker** feels tempted to abandon modern civilization and return to a savage life in the jungle. In the end, he chooses to live a civilized, modern life and enthusiastically endorses technology. *In Memoriam* connects the despair Tennyson felt over the loss of his friend Arthur Hallam and the despair he felt when contemplating a godless world. In the end, the poem affirms both religious faith and faith in human progress. Nevertheless, Tennyson continued to struggle with the reconciliation of science and religion, as illustrated by some of his later work. For example, "Locksley Hall Sixty Years After" (1886) takes as its protagonist the speaker from the original "Locksley Hall," but now he is an old man, who looks back on his youthful optimism and faith in progress with scorn and skepticism.

THE VIRTUES OF PERSEVERANCE AND OPTIMISM

After the death of his friend Arthur Hallam, Tennyson struggled through a period of deep despair, which he eventually overcame to begin writing again. During his time of mourning, Tennyson rarely wrote and, for many years, battled alcoholism. Many of his poems are about the temptation to give up and fall prey to pessimism, but they also extol the virtues of optimism and discuss the importance of struggling on with life. The need to persevere and continue is the central theme of *In Memoriam* and "Ulysses" (1833), both written after Hallam's death. Perhaps because of Tennyson's gloomy and tragic childhood, perseverance and optimism also appear in poetry written before Hallam's death, such as "The Lotos-Eaters" (1832, 1842). Poems such as "The Lady of Shalott" (1832, 1842) and "The Charge of the Light Brigade" (1854) also vary this theme: both poems glorify characters who embrace their destinies in life, even though those destinies end in tragic death. The Lady of Shalott leaves her seclusion to meet the outer world, determined to seek the love that is missing in her life. The cavalrymen in "The Charge of the Light Brigade" keep charging through the valley toward the Russian cannons; they persevere even as they realize that they will likely die.

THE GLORY OF ENGLAND

Tennyson used his poetry to express his love for England. Although he expressed worry and concern about the corruption that so dominated the nineteenth century, he also wrote many poems that glorify nineteenth-century England. "The Charge of the Light Brigade" praises the fortitude and courage of English soldiers during a battle of the Crimean War in which roughly 200 men were killed. As poet laureate, Tennyson was required to write poems for specific state occasions and to dedicate verse to Queen Victoria and her husband, Prince Albert. Nevertheless, Tennyson praised England even when not specifically required to do so. In the *Idylls of the King*, Tennyson glorified England by encouraging a collective English cultural identity: all of England could take pride in Camelot, particularly the chivalrous and capable knights who lived there. Indeed, the modern conception of Camelot as the source of loyalty, chivalry, and romance comes, in part, from Tennyson's descriptions of it in the *Idylls of the King* and "The Lady of Shalott."

MOTIFS

TRAGIC DEATH

Early, tragic death and suicide appear throughout Tennyson's poetry. Perhaps the most significant event of his life was the untimely death of his best friend Arthur Hallam at age twenty-two,

TENNYSON

which prompted Tennyson to write his greatest literary work, *In Memoriam*. This long poem uses the so-called *In Memoriam* stanza, or a **quatrain** that uses **iambic tetrameter** and has an *abba* rhyme scheme. The formal consistency expresses Tennyson's grief and links the disparate stanzas together into an elegiac whole. The speaker of "Break, Break, Break" (1834) sees death even in sunsets, while the early "Mariana" (1830) features a woman who longs for death after her lover abandons her. Each of that poem's seven stanzas ends with the line "I would that I were dead." The lady in "The Lady of Shalott" brings about her own death by going out into an autumn storm dressed only in a thin white dress. Similarly, the cavalrymen in "The Charge of the Light Brigade" ride to their deaths by charging headlong into the Russian cannons. These poems lyrically mourn those who died tragically, often finding nobility in their characters or their deaths.

SCIENTIFIC LANGUAGE

Tennyson took a great interest in the scientific discoveries of the nineteenth century, and his poetry manifests this interest in its reliance on scientific language. "The Kraken" (1830), which describes an ancient, slumbering sea beast, mentions a "cell" (8) and "polypi" (9). Section 21 of *In Memoriam* alludes to the 1846 discovery of Neptune. There, a traveler tells the speaker not to grieve for his friend. Rather than grieve, the traveler says, the speaker should rejoice in the marvelous possibilities of science. Section 120, in contrast, features the speaker wondering what good science might do in a world full of religious doubt and despair. Other poems praise technological discoveries and inventions, including the steamships and railways discussed in "Locksley Hall," or mention specific plants and flowers, as does "The Lotos-Eaters" (1832, 1842). Taking **metaphors** and **poetic diction** from science allowed Tennyson to connect to his age and to modernize his sometimes antiquarian language and archaic verse forms.

THE ANCIENT WORLD

Like the romantic poets who preceded him, Tennyson found much inspiration in the ancient worlds of Greece and Rome. In poems such as "The Lotos-Eaters" and "Ulysses," Tennyson retells the stories of Dante and Homer, which described the characters of Ulysses, Telemachus, and Penelope and their adventures in the ancient world. However, Tennyson slightly alters these mythic stories, shifting the time frame of some of the action and often adding more

TENNYSON

descriptive **imagery** to the plot. For instance, "Ulysses," a dramatic monologue spoken by Homer's hero, urges readers to carry on and persevere rather than to give up and retire. Elsewhere Tennyson channels the voice of Tithonus, a legendary prince from Troy, in the eponymous poem "Tithonus" (1833, 1859). He praises the ancient poet Virgil in his **ode** "To Virgil" (1882), commenting on Virgil's choice of subject matter and lauding his ability to chronicle human history in meter. Tennyson mined the ancient world to find stories that would simultaneously enthrall and inspire his readers.

Symbols

King Arthur and Camelot

To Tennyson, King Arthur symbolizes the ideal man, and Arthurian England was England in its best and purest form. Some of Tennyson's earliest poems, such as "The Lady of Shalott," were set in King Arthur's time. Indeed, Tennyson rhymes *Camelot*, the name of King Arthur's estate, with *Shalott* in eighteen of the poem's twenty stanzas, thereby emphasizing the importance of the mythical place. Furthermore, our contemporary conception of Camelot as harmonious and magnificent comes from Tennyson's poem. *Idylls of the King*, about King Arthur's rise and fall, was one of the major projects of Tennyson's late career. Queen Victoria and Prince Albert envisioned themselves as latter-day descendents of Arthur and the Knights of the Round Table, and their praise helped popularize the long poem. But King Arthur also had a more personal representation to Tennyson: the mythic king represents a version of his friend Arthur Henry Hallam, whose death at twenty-two profoundly affected Tennyson. Hallam's death destroyed his potential and promise, which allowed Tennyson to idealize Hallam. This idealization allows Tennyson to imagine what might have been in the best possible light, much as he does when describing King Arthur and his court.

The Imprisoned Woman

The imprisoned woman appears throughout Tennyson's work. In "Mariana," a woman abandoned by her lover lives alone in her house in the middle of desolate country; her isolation imprisons her, as does the way she waits for her lover to return. Her waiting limits her ability and desire to do anything else. "The Lady of Shalott" is likewise about a woman imprisoned, this time in a tower. Should she leave her prison, a curse would fall upon her. Tennyson, like many other Victorian poets, used female characters to symbolize the artistic and sensitive aspects of the human condition. Imprisoned women, such as these Tennyson characters, act as **symbols** for the isolation experienced by the artist and other sensitive, deep-feeling people. Although society might force creative, sensitive types to become outcasts, in Tennyson's poems, the women themselves create their own isolation and imprisonment. These women seem unable or unwilling to deal with the outside world.

Summary & Analysis

"The Kraken"

Below the thunders of the upper deep,
Far, far beneath in the abysmal sea,
His ancient, dreamless, uninvaded sleep
The Kraken sleepeth: faintest sunlights flee
About his shadowy sides; above him swell   5
Huge sponges of millennial growth and height;
And far away into the sickly light,
From many a wondrous and secret cell
Unnumbered and enormous polypi
Winnow with giant fins the slumbering green.   10
There hath he lain for ages, and will lie
Battening upon huge sea-worms in his sleep,
Until the latter fire shall heat the deep;
Then once by man and angels to be seen,
In roaring he shall rise and on the surface die.   15

Summary

This short **lyric** describes a kraken, a great sea monster that sleeps far beneath the surface of the ocean. He has slept for ages beneath the noise of stormy, crashing waves and below even the deepest part of the water. Only the barest glimmer of sunlight reaches him as he sleeps, and gigantic, ancient sponges cover him. Enormous sea creatures live in caves in this part of the ocean, searching for food with their large tentacles. (Tennyson probably uses the word *polypi* in its scientifically accurate sense—that is, to mean sea creatures, such as hydras and sea anemones, that are permanently attached to a rocky surface on one end, but he might also have meant to suggest squids or octopi.) The kraken has slept for a long, long time, and he will continue to sleep there, growing fat on the sea worms he eats, until the apocalypse comes. When the apocalyptic fires warm the deep ocean, the kraken shall awaken and rise to the surface. There, on the hot surface, as it dies from the heat, the kraken will finally be seen by men and angels alike.

TENNYSON

ANALYSIS

Written when Tennyson was just twenty-one, "The Kraken" gloomily predicts a distant future event: the death of the kraken during the apocalypse. The word *kraken* comes from Scandinavian folklore, but Tennyson takes the poem's events from the Bible's Book of Revelations. According to the Bible, a sea monster, or leviathan, will rise to the surface of the ocean in which it lives during the apocalypse. Revelations also says that a mountain of fire will be thrown into the sea and that everything living in the water will then die. The poem synthesizes the Christian story with the Scandinavian story. Critics differ about what the kraken might symbolize. Some argue that the monster represents the corruption or decay at the heart of society, and they claim that the monster symbolizes the violent rage that lies coiled within all humans and threatens to destroy civilization. Other critics point to Tennyson's abysmal family life and see the kraken as a symbol of broken-down family bonds.

One of Tennyson's great strengths as a poet was his ability to sustain a mood or feeling throughout a poem using **poetic diction** and **tone**. "The Kraken" triumphantly sustains a feeling of gloom, terror, and barely suppressed violence. In this poem, Tennyson represents the sublime, a spooky mixture of fear, excitement, anticipation, and potential destruction. Romantic poets, writing a generation before Tennyson, were also very interested in the sublime and its ability to simultaneously terrify and excite. They represented it in nature, most typically by describing dramatic landscapes, such as high mountains, and the ways these landscapes overwhelm the senses. In romantic poetry, descriptions of the sublime usually coincide with a story about some sort of epiphany or an intellectual argument about life, nature, or God. In contrast, Tennyson frequently evokes the sublime for purely aesthetic purposes, rarely as part of an intellectual argument. As a result, Tennyson has sometimes been criticized as anti-intellectual and merely ornamental in his verse.

TENNYSON

"THE LADY OF SHALOTT"

EXCERPT FROM "THE LADY OF SHALOTT"

In the stormy east-wind straining,
The pale yellow woods were waning,
The broad stream in his banks complaining.
Heavily the low sky raining
　　　Over towered Camelot;
Down she came and found a boat
Beneath a willow left afloat,
And around about the prow she wrote
　　　The Lady of Shalott.

And down the river's dim expanse
Like some bold seer in a trance,
Seeing all his own mischance—
With a glassy countenance
　　　Did she look to Camelot.
And at the closing of the day
She loosed the chain, and down she lay;
The broad stream bore her far away,
　　　The Lady of Shalott.

Lying, robed in snowy white
That loosely flew to left and right—
The leaves upon her falling light—
Thro' the noises of the night,
　　　She floated down to Camelot:
And as the boat-head wound along
The willowy hills and fields among,
They heard her singing her last song,
　　　The Lady of Shalott.

Heard a carol, mournful, holy,
Chanted loudly, chanted lowly,
Till her blood was frozen slowly,
And her eyes were darkened wholly,
　　　Turned to towered Camelot.
For ere she reached upon the tide
The first house by the water-side,

Singing in her song she died,
       The Lady of Shalott.

Under tower and balcony,
By garden-wall and gallery,
A gleaming shape she floated by,
Dead-pale between the houses high,
       Silent into Camelot.
Out upon the wharfs they came,
Knight and Burgher, Lord and Dame,
And around the prow they read her name,
       The Lady of Shalott.

Who is this? And what is here?
And in the lighted palace near
Died the sound of royal cheer;
And they crossed themselves for fear,
       All the Knights at Camelot;
But Lancelot mused a little space
He said, "She has a lovely face;
God in his mercy lend her grace,
       The Lady of Shalott."

SUMMARY

Part 1 begins with a description of an English country scene. A river runs through fields of barley and rye, and next to the river lies the road to Camelot. The location of the poem also gives us a sense of the time period: Camelot was the legendary capital of medieval King Arthur. All day, people travel along this road. Next, the speaker describes a small island in the middle of the river and on that island, a tower. Inside the tower is a mysterious woman, the Lady of Shalott. Barges and sailboats travel the river, but who, asks the speaker, has ever seen the lady? Does anyone know whether she even exists? Only peasants working in the fields have seen her, and only because they have sometimes heard her singing early in the morning or late at night. To them, she is "the fairy Lady of Shalott" (35–36)—a magical, otherworldly creature.

In part 2, the speaker further describes the Lady of Shalott. Living in her tower, she works night and day weaving a fantastical tapestry. Voices have told her that she will be cursed if she ever stops weaving to look out toward Camelot, but she does not know what form the curse will take. Rather than look out the window and risk the curse, she looks at the mirror hanging in front of her, in which she can see reflections of the world outside her tower window. She sees the countryside and all the people who travel the road below—sometimes knights, sometimes ladies, sometimes peasants. But no knight loves the lady. Nevertheless, the lady remains happy. She weaves pictures of all the things she sees outside into her tapestry. Sometimes she sees a funeral progress toward Camelot during the night, and sometimes she sees lovers meeting in the moonlit fields. However, this part ends with an expression of her unhappiness: she claims she is "half sick" (71) of watching reflections.

A description of Sir Lancelot begins part 3. He rides past the lady's tower on his way to Camelot. (According to legend, Sir Lancelot was the greatest of King Arthur's knights, although he also betrayed King Arthur by becoming the lover of Queen Guinevere, King Arthur's wife.) The speaker spends the next seven stanzas describing Lancelot's beauty and splendor. Lancelot travels very close to the tower, and all of his armor is encrusted with jewels and gleams in the sun. He rides night and day, through good weather and bad weather. The Lady of Shalott sees him in her mirror, and his beauty overwhelms her. She immediately falls in love with him and leaves her tapestry to gaze on him directly from the window. In an instant, just as she ceases to weave, the curse comes into effect. The loom and the tapestry are blown out the window by a sudden wind and the mirror cracks in two.

The lady leaves her tower during an autumnal storm at the start of part 4. As the wind blows and the rain falls, she finds a boat, writes her name on its prow, and sets out for Camelot, dressed only in a loose white dress. In a trancelike state, she glides down the river. All through the night she sings a sad song and lies in her boat. Just before she passes the first houses of Camelot, she dies of exposure, "her blood frozen slowly" (147). Everyone in the city comes out to the wharves to see her dead body floating through the water, and they are mystified by her name on the boat. The revelry in King Arthur's palace dies down, and everyone feels afraid. But Sir Lancelot sees her and offers a prayer, asking God to lend the lady grace.

ANALYSIS

Many critics think that "The Lady of Shalott" is about the dilemma faced by artists. Artists—whether poets, painters, sculptors, musicians, or, in this case, weavers—spend their lives making representations of the world around them. However, their creativity and acute sensitivity to experience makes it difficult for them to be active participants in everyday life. In part 2, the speaker describes the lady's tapestry as a "magic web" (38), into which she weaves "the mirror's magic sights" (65). The repeated use of the word *magic* emphasizes the idea that the woman, as an artist, has a special, superior vision of people and objects outside her tower. But this special ability comes with a high price: not only must she live isolated from society and community, she also risks incurring an unknown curse if she leaves the tower and stops making her art. She can only depict the people she sees reflected; she cannot talk or interact with them in any way. When she does lay down her craft and leave her tower, she cannot deal with the realities of the outside world and she becomes paralyzed in a trance. The heightened powers of observation of the artist, which allow him or her to depict and create, might also sometimes make the artist unfit for human company.

"The Lady of Shalott" establishes a connection between death, love, and desire. The tower protects the lady from death: she watches funerals go by, but she does not grieve or feel sad. But watching lovers meet in the moonlight eventually saddens her, and in part 2 she claims that she has tired of watching the world pass by in a mirror. Although she has her art to sustain her, she does not have a lover or any type of social interaction. Her art keeps her safe, but it also makes her lonely. When the lady first sees Lancelot in the mirror, she is so taken with his figure that she must turn around and see him straight on, even though she knows that leaving her work will bring on the curse. Familiar with the stories of King Arthur and Camelot, readers would know that Lancelot wasn't an honest knight since he once slept with another man's wife, Guinevere. Unfamiliar with the legend, however, the lady is overwhelmed by physical desire, falls in love, and sets out in a storm, wearing only a thin dress. Tennyson links her desire, her love, and her death. Thus the poem serves as a cautionary tale about letting desire overpower our will and confusing reason with emotions.

In the nineteenth century, many artists and writers aestheticized, or found beauty, in death, particularly in depictions of women's death. "The Lady of Shalott" evocatively describes a beautiful dead woman floating beneath the houses of mythical Camelot. Many artists, including John William Waterhouse in 1888, found inspiration in the poem and represented its lines in their paintings. This, in turn, led to the popular conception of women as powerless and prone to

TENNYSON

fits of fainting and hysteria. Victorians generally feared powerful, sexually aggressive women, and depicting women as beautiful yet dead rendered them harmless and safe. As actual women began agitating for rights in the late nineteenth-century social and political arenas, these artistic depictions became a way of suppressing independent women and preventing other young women from getting any rebellious ideas. Cultural and artistic representations of women as weak and quiet encouraged real-life women to also be weak and quiet, much the same as contemporary women might want to emulate an actor or singer they see on television or read about in magazines.

"ULYSSES"

It little profits that an idle king,
By this still hearth, among these barren crags,
Matched with an aged wife, I mete and dole
Unequal laws unto a savage race,
That hoard, and sleep, and feed, and know not me.   5
   I cannot rest from travel: I will drink
Life to the lees: all times I have enjoyed
Greatly, have suffered greatly, both with those
That loved me, and alone; on shore, and when
Through scudding drifts the rainy Hyades   10
Vexed the dim sea: I am become a name;
For always roaming with a hungry heart
Much have I seen and known; cities of men
And manners, climates, councils, governments,
Myself not least, but honored of them all;   15
And drunk delight of battle with my peers;
Far on the ringing plains of windy Troy.
I am part of all that I have met;
Yet all experience is an arch wherethrough
Gleams that untravelled world, whose margin fades   20
For ever and for ever when I move.
How dull it is to pause, to make an end,
To rust unburnished, not to shine in use!
As though to breath were life. Life piled on life
Were all too little, and of one to me   25
Little remains: but every hour is saved
From that eternal silence, something more,
A bringer of new things; and vile it were

For some three suns to store and hoard myself,
And this grey spirit yearning in desire   30
To follow knowledge like a sinking star,
Beyond the utmost bound of human thought.

   This is my son, mine own Telemachus,
To whom I leave the scepter and the isle—
Well-loved of me, discerning to fulfill   35
This labor, by slow prudence to make mild
A rugged people, and through soft degrees
Subdue them to the useful and the good.
Most blameless is he, centered in the sphere
Of common duties, decent not to fail   40
In offices of tenderness, and pay
Meet adoration to my household gods,
When I am gone. He works his work, I mine.

   There lies the port; the vessel puffs her sail:
There gloom the dark broad seas. My mariners,   45
Souls that have toiled, and wrought, and thought with me—
That ever with a frolic welcome took
The thunder and the sunshine, and opposed
Free hearts, free foreheads—you and I are old;
Old age hath yet his honor and his toil;   50
Death closes all: but something ere the end,
Some work of noble note, may yet be done,
Not unbecoming men that strove with Gods.
The lights begin to twinkle from the rocks:
The long day wanes: the slow moon climbs: the deep   55
Moans round with many voices. Come, my friends,
'Tis not too late to seek a newer world.
Push off, and sitting well in order smite
The sounding furrows; for my purpose holds
To sail beyond the sunset, and the baths   60
Of all the western stars, until I die.
It may be that the gulfs will wash us down:
It may be we shall touch the Happy Isles,
And see the great Achilles, whom we knew
Tho' much is taken, much abides; and though   65
We are not now that strength which in old days
Moved earth and heaven; that which we are, we are;

> One equal temper of heroic hearts,
> Made weak by time and fate, but strong in will
> To strive, to seek, to find, and not to yield.   70

SUMMARY

In this poem, Tennyson channels the voice of Ulysses, also known as Odysseus, the hero of Homer's *Odyssey* (ca. eighth century B.C.E.). According to Homer's poem, Odysseus and his crew wander the seas for ten years on their way home to Ithaca after the end of the Trojan War. Tennyson's poem takes place after Ulysses has returned home to his wife, Penelope, and son, Telemachus, and has regained leadership of the island of Ithaca.

The poem is a dramatic monologue spoken by Ulysses. He begins by explaining that he no longer feels content with his life back in Ithaca. It does little good, he says, for him to be an inactive ruler married to an old wife, trying to set forth laws that are too advanced for the "savage race" (4) of Ithaca, who act like animals and don't even recognize him. He has experienced a great deal in life and claims that he cannot be idle and at rest. Instead, he wants to live life to the fullest. After many years of wandering, he now belongs to the broader world he has encountered on his voyages, not in his original home of Ithaca. Next, Ulysses explains his personal philosophy. All of his life's experiences have simply shown him how much there is left to see and do. To rest and accept that his adventures are over would be dull and against his nature, so he plans to make the most of every hour of the little time remaining before death. He still wants to explore and chase after new experiences and insights.

In the next section of the poem, Ulysses explains that he will leave the leadership of Ithaca to his son, Telemachus, who will do the necessary work to gradually civilize and advance the unsophisticated inhabitants of Ithaca. Unlike Ulysses, Telemachus is focused on the world of ordinary affairs, and he will be a kind and pious ruler after Ulysses leaves. Ulysses acknowledges the different natures of father and son in the last lines of this stanza: "He works his work, I mine" (43). Father and son have disparate dispositions. Ulysses must wander the world, while Telemachus must stay behind and rule Ithaca.

Ulysses addresses his crew of sailors in the final section of the poem. His mariners have always worked alongside him, meeting all the challenges they faced with good cheer. They are loyal, having forgone individuality and instead put Ulysses and the collective group first. He rallies them, acknowledging that they all have aged and that death is near. But, he says, they still have time for more adventures appropriate to men like them, who have walked among the gods. Noting that the sun is setting and the moon is rising, Ulysses says that the time has come to set sail. Together they shall sail westward, beyond the end of the earth, until Ulysses dies. Death may come from drowning, but then again, they might also reach the Happy Isles, where the Greeks believed that dead heroes went after they died. There they might see Achilles, the greatest hero of the Trojan War. Although they are not as mighty as they once were, they retain some powers. They are what they are, Ulysses realizes. He concludes by saying that though they have grown old, they are determined to continue, to explore, and to not give up.

ANALYSIS

Written shortly after the death of his friend Arthur Hallam, "Ulysses" simultaneously expresses world-weariness and urges its readers to persevere. Throughout the poem, the tone conveys a sense of exhaustion and hopelessness, as Ulysses realizes that he has grown old. The imagery contributes to the tired tone: the landscape is "barren" (2), the ocean is "dim" (11), and the sun has begun to set and "the long day wanes" in the final stanza. This sounds less like an incitement to action than a description of aging and death. Nevertheless, Ulysses rallies his sailors—and the readers—in the final stanza by alluding to their shared past and their future adventures. He acknowledges that they are old but also tells them that they can still experience, travel, and live. To stay in Ithaca, retired and resting, would be a slow, painful death—for him and for them. The poem expresses his wish to die in action, on the high seas, and to continue living until the very end. The tired tone thus becomes a tone of acceptance, as Ulysses makes difficult realizations about himself as a ruler, husband, and father.

Tennyson demonstrates the complexity of Ulysses as a character. Although Ulysses's never-give-up attitude is very appealing, Ulysses is also quite selfish and egotistical. After all, despite having been away from his family for several years, he would rather go back to his travels than to rest and relax with Penelope and Telemachus. Ulysses prefers his adventures to his family and eagerly refuses his responsibilities as king. He values the possibilities of new experiences and knowledge over both the protection of Ithaca's citizens and the bonds of his family. On the one hand, Ulysses humbly accepts the limitations of his age: he realizes that he and his crew

TENNYSON

have grown old and cannot perform the way they once did. On the other hand, he wants to convince them to travel once again and longs to sail beyond the edge of the world, to the mythical Happy Isles, home of immortal Greek heroes. Even as he acknowledges the progress of nature and his own maturity, he wants to go beyond nature's rules and live forever among other powerful warriors and travelers. Ulysses is both humble and arrogant, willing to accept his age but unwilling to accept the infirmities that come with age.

"Ulysses" portrays the pleasures and pains of the human condition. As a character, Ulysses longs for adventure because adventure brings new insights and ideas. He longs "to follow knowledge like a sinking star" (31), even though this search will probably end in his death. This search for knowledge, which motivates many human pursuits, has the potential to bring wisdom. With this wisdom, though, comes both joy and sadness. To expand his intellect, Ulysses must abandon his family. While he seeks to re-establish bonds with his crew, itself a form of community, he also realizes that this quest will probably be their last, given their age. In his longing to fill the hours of his life with action, Ulysses expresses his doubts about the possibilities of an afterlife. He does not trust in the Christian idea that death will bring him to heaven or paradise. Instead, he likens death to "eternal silence" (27), in which he can neither act nor feel. Ulysses seeks to fill his life with experience in order to overcome his doubts about what happens after death.

"THE CHARGE OF THE LIGHT BRIGADE"

1

Half a league, half a league,
Half a league onward,
All in the valley of Death
      Rode the six hundred.
"Forward, the Light Brigade!   5
Charge for the guns!" he said:
Into the valley of Death
      Rode the six hundred.

2

"Forward, the Light Brigade!"
Was there a man dismayed?   10
Not tho' the soldier knew

Some one had blundered:
Theirs not to make reply,
Theirs not to reason why,
Theirs but to do and die: 15
Into the valley of Death
Rode the six hundred.

3

Cannon to right of them,
Cannon to left of them,
Cannon in front of them   20
Volleyed and thundered;
Stormed at with shot and shell,
Boldly they rode and well,
Into the jaws of Death,
Into the mouth of Hell   25
Rode the six hundred.

4

Flashed all their sabers bare,
Flashed as they turned in air
Sab'ring the gunners there,
Charging an army, while   30
All the world wondered:
Plunged in the battery-smoke
Right thro' the line they broke;
Cossack and Russian
Reeled from the saber stroke   35
Shattered and sundered.
Then they rode back, but not
Not the six hundred.

5

Cannon to right of them,
Cannon to left of them,   40
Cannon behind them
Volleyed and thundered;
Stormed at with shot and shell,
While horse and hero fell,
They that had fought so well
Came thro' the jaws of Death,   45

TENNYSON

Back from the mouth of Hell,
All that was left of them,
   Left of six hundred.

      6

When can their glory fade?
O the wild charge they made!   *50*
   All the world wondered.
Honor the charge they made!
Honor the Light Brigade,
   Noble six hundred!

SUMMARY

As the poem begins, the brigade has begun their charge. The Russian guns are a little less than two miles away, and the commanding officer urges the men forward. Rhetorically, the speaker wonders if any of the men were nervous or worried. No, the speaker answers, the men were not, even as they realized that "some one had blundered" (12) in urging them to go forward. In charging forward, the men are following orders and doing their duty as soldiers. Cannons and guns fire as the men move through the valley. Still, they ride unafraid, even as conditions worsen and men begin to die.

With swords raised, the men ride into the line of guns and attack the Russians, a feat that amazes the world. After the attack, the remaining men retreat. And as they retreat, the cannons and guns begin to fire again, and more men perish. A small percentage of the original brigade retreat and return; the rest have died. In the final stanza, the speaker wonders if the sense of the brigade's heroism could ever be lost. The speaker concludes by urging readers to remember the brigade and their bravery.

ANALYSIS

After Tennyson became the poet laureate of England in 1850, he frequently wrote poems from that office, commemorating state events, praising worthy Englishmen and Englishwomen, and dedicating poems to Queen Victoria and Prince Albert. "The Charge of the Light Brigade" is representative of these poems: while the poem is technically and formally excellent, it also expresses a straightforward patriotic enthusiasm that might seem suspicious or hollow to modern readers. Tennyson wrote the poem to commemorate a disastrous military defeat during the Crimean War, in which some 673

English cavalrymen charged through a narrow valley directly into a Russian artillery entrenchment. Close to 200 men died as a result of one of the stupidest mistakes in British military history. The poem only obliquely alludes to this mistake with the line "some one had blundered" (12), and generally the poem turns the tragic error into a heroic exploit. It concludes by reminding readers to remember the courage and sacrifice of the men.

The poem describes the charge and the men's heroism using several literary techniques. Naturally, the poem's content literally describes the men as they head into the Russian fire, but the poem's use of rhyme and meter also describe their hellish ride and retreat. Many phrases and words are repeated several times, including "half a league" in stanza 1 and "cannon" in stanzas 3 and 5. This repetition echoes the sounds of horses galloping and the sounds of guns firing. When the cavalrymen break the Russian lines, Tennyson uses a series of sibilant words to suggest the slashing sounds of the sabers, including "Cossack," "Russian," "saber stroke," "shattered," and "sundered." Stanzas 3 and 5 are almost perfectly symmetrical, which reflects the horror of rushing into gunfire and then retreating through even more gunfire. These patterns of repetition and symmetry end in the sixth stanza, which switches from describing the charge to extolling the reader to remember. As the shortest stanza, stanza 6 reflects the loss of men and the silence that swirls around the remaining men as they return, grieving, broken, and battered. After their deaths, speaker and reader alike can do nothing but remember.

ROBERT BROWNING

(1812–1889)

CONTEXT

Robert Browning was born in a suburb of London called Camberwell in 1812. He grew up in a suburban cottage with one sister and devoted middle-class parents. As a child, Browning was precocious and largely self-educated. Despite limited formal schooling, Browning received a very thorough education at home, mostly due to his own independent and often idiosyncratic reading. Throughout his early adulthood, he lived with his parents, dressed expensively, and refused to look for a job. While in his twenties, he published several long poems and wrote two verse plays for the stage. But his plays were failures, closing after only a few nights, and critics mostly dismissed his poetry as obscure. Playwriting led Browning to develop a sense of characters and to think about the relationship between character and **poetic diction**, two skills that would be crucial to his development as a poet of **dramatic monologues**. Although he demonstrated great potential as a youth, he did not achieve much public success until middle age.

In 1842, Browning published *Dramatic Lyrics*, a collection of shorter dramatic monologues, which included "My Last Duchess" and "Soliloquy of the Spanish Cloister." Dramatic monologues are poems spoken by a fictional or historical character to a silent audience of at least one person. These poems reveal the thoughts and feelings of the character as he or she expresses himself or herself to the audience. As such, the characters tend to be untrustworthy and unreliable: they show us only those sides of themselves that they want us to see. *Dramatic Lyrics*, along with *Dramatic Romances and Lyrics*, which he published in 1845, established the dramatic monologue as Browning's preferred poetic form and began to win him some critical praise. Browning's life changed dramatically in 1845, when he fell in love with the poet Elizabeth Barrett, who had praised his work in print. She was several years older than he, much more famous, and almost an invalid. Nevertheless, they eloped in 1846 and ran off to Italy, where they lived until her death. Along with their one son, they lived on money that Elizabeth had inherited. Despite Elizabeth's ongoing health problems, their life was mostly happy.

During his marriage to Elizabeth, Browning did not write much, but he did publish *Men and Women* in 1855, which included "Fra

Lippo Lippi," "Andrea del Sarto," and "Childe Roland to the Dark Tower Came." Modern critics generally consider this to be his best volume of poetry, but it was not successful at the time. Elizabeth's reputation, in contrast, continued to increase during their years abroad, and she was suggested as a candidate for poet laureate of England when William Wordsworth died in 1850 (ultimately that honor went to Alfred, Lord Tennyson). After a long decline, Elizabeth died in 1861. Browning hastily moved with his son back to London. There Browning's reputation quickly transformed. He published an edition of his collected works in 1863 and a new volume of poems, *Dramatis Personae*, in 1864. Both were tremendous successes, and he quickly became a celebrity, widely regarded as one of the greatest minds of the age.

From 1868 to 1869, he serially published *The Ring and the Book*, which retold in long monologues the true story of a seventeenth-century Italian murder trial from the perspectives of all of the parties involved. The length (22,000 lines) and difficulty of the work lost the poem its readership in the twentieth century, but at the time of its publication, the poem won Browning comparisons to Shakespeare and established him as second only to Tennyson among living poets. He continued to be productive for the next twenty years, writing long poems, publishing collections, and translating Greek tragedies. In 1889, he died during a trip to Venice. His body was returned to England, and he was buried in Westminster Abbey.

During the reign of Queen Victoria, from 1837 to 1901, England enjoyed a long period of domestic prosperity, stability, and peace. But nineteenth-century Continental Europe was much different. Beginning in 1848, a wave of revolutions swept across the Continent. These revolutions and the other small wars that were also occurring around that time disrupted and, in some cases, overthrew the aristocracies and political orders of many countries. In addition, new countries, including modern-day Germany and Italy, were being created, as networks of city-states and principalities became increasingly united. As a resident of Italy from 1846 to 1861, Browning witnessed many of these changes firsthand. His exposure to the revolutions and history of Europe helps explain the realistic, complex portrayals of medieval and Renaissance European settings in his work. For some Victorian poets, such as Tennyson, historical Europe and the ancient world were mythical realms, in which good and evil were sharply delimited and many of the complexities of modern life were stripped away. But for Browning, European history was filled with dirt and danger and moral ambiguity, which made it a more appropriate setting for his characters than comparatively bland Victorian England. The distant settings also allowed Browning to comment on contemporary issues without appearing to preach or moralize.

Romanticism, especially the poetry of Percy Bysshe Shelley, strongly influenced Browning in his youth. A cousin gave Browning a volume of poems by Shelley, and he soon traded his parents' evangelical Christianity for Shelley's atheism and followed Shelley in his vegetarianism and radical politics. Only a few years later, Browning explicitly rejected atheism in his first published work, *Pauline; a Fragment of a Confession* (1833), a sort of autobiographical poem in which Shelley appears as a poet called the "Sun-treader." Eventually Browning regained his faith in God, but he never fully reaccepted Christian doctrine. More important, Browning moved away from romanticism, which emphasizes lyricism, subjective experience, and sensory perception. Instead, Browning populated his poems with interesting characters who have shocking, perceptive things to say. Whereas the romantic poets sought truth by seeking the most intense and pure experiences—particularly the terrifying, exciting, sublime feelings often found in nature—Browning attempted to capture as wide a variety of human experiences as possible in his poetry, creating a huge number of **speakers** and putting them in different times, places, and dramatic contexts. In this way, his literary project was more akin to that of contemporary novelists, such as Charles Dickens, than that of his romantic predecessors.

THEMES, MOTIFS & SYMBOLS

THEMES

MULTIPLE PERSPECTIVES ON SINGLE EVENTS

The dramatic monologue verse form allowed Browning to explore and probe the minds of specific characters in specific places struggling with specific sets of circumstances. In *The Ring and the Book*, Browning tells a suspenseful story of murder using multiple voices, which give multiple perspectives and multiple versions of the same story. Dramatic monologues allow readers to enter into the minds of various characters and to see an event from that character's perspective. Understanding the thoughts, feelings, and motivations of a character not only gives readers a sense of sympathy for the characters but also helps readers understand the multiplicity of perspectives that make up the truth. In effect, Browning's work reminds readers that the nature of truth or reality fluctuates, depending on one's perspective or view of the situation. Multiple perspectives illustrate the idea that no one sensibility or perspective sees the whole story and no two people see the same events in the same way. Browning further illustrated this idea by writing poems that work together as companion pieces, such as "Fra Lippo Lippi" and "Andrea del Sarto." Poems such as these show how people with different characters respond differently to similar situations, as well as depict how a time, place, and scenario can cause people with similar personalities to develop or change quite dramatically.

THE PURPOSES OF ART

Browning wrote many poems about artists and poets, including such dramatic monologues as "Pictor Ignotus" (1855) and "Fra Lippo Lippi." Frequently, Browning would begin by thinking about an artist, an artwork, or a type of art that he admired or disliked. Then he would speculate on the character or artistic philosophy that would lead to such a success or failure. His dramatic monologues about artists attempt to capture some of this philosophizing because his characters speculate on the purposes of art. For instance, the speaker of "Fra Lippo Lippi" proposes that art heightens our pow-

244 ❦ THEMES, MOTIFS & SYMBOLS

ers of observation and helps us notice things about our own lives. According to some of these characters and poems, painting idealizes the beauty found in the real world, such as the radiance of a beloved's smile. Sculpture and architecture can memorialize famous or important people, as in "The Bishop Orders His Tomb at Saint Praxed's Church" (1845) and "The Statue and the Bust" (1855). But art also helps its creators to make a living, and it thus has a purpose as pecuniary as creative, an idea explored in "Andrea del Sarto."

THE RELATIONSHIP BETWEEN ART AND MORALITY
Throughout his work, Browning tried to answer questions about an artist's responsibilities and to describe the relationship between art and morality. He questioned whether artists had an obligation to be moral and whether artists should pass judgment on their characters and creations. Unlike many of his contemporaries, Browning populated his poems with evil people, who commit crimes and sins ranging from hatred to murder. The dramatic monologue format allowed Browning to maintain a great distance between himself and his creations: by channeling the voice of a character, Browning could explore evil without actually being evil himself. His characters served as **personae** that let him adopt different traits and tell stories about horrible situations. In "My Last Duchess," the speaker gets away with his wife's murder since neither his audience (in the poem) nor his creator judges or criticizes him. Instead, the responsibility of judging the character's morality is left to readers, who find the duke of Ferrara a vicious, repugnant person even as he takes us on a tour of his art gallery.

MOTIFS

MEDIEVAL AND RENAISSANCE EUROPEAN SETTINGS
Browning set many of his poems in medieval and Renaissance Europe, most often in Italy. He drew on his extensive knowledge of art, architecture, and history to fictionalize actual events, including a seventeenth-century murder in *The Ring and the Book*, and to channel the voices of actual historical figures, including a biblical scholar in medieval Spain in "Rabbi Ben Ezra" (1864) and the Renaissance painter in the eponymous "Andrea del Sarto." The remoteness of the time period and location allowed Browning to critique and explore contemporary issues without fear of alienating his readers. Directly invoking contemporary issues might seem didactic

and moralizing in a way that poems set in the thirteenth, fourteenth, and fifteenth centuries would not. For instance, the speaker of "The Bishop Orders His Tomb at Saint Praxed's Church" is an Italian bishop during the late Renaissance. Through the speaker's pompous, vain musings about monuments, Browning indirectly criticizes organized religion, including the Church of England, which was in a state of disarray at the time of the poem's composition in the mid-nineteenth century.

PSYCHOLOGICAL PORTRAITS

Dramatic monologues feature a solitary speaker addressing at least one silent, usually unnamed person, and they provide interesting snapshots of the speakers and their personalities. Unlike soliloquies, in dramatic monologues the characters are always speaking directly to listeners. Browning's characters are usually crafty, intelligent, argumentative, and capable of lying. Indeed, they often leave out more of a story than they actually tell. In order to fully understand the speakers and their psychologies, readers must carefully pay attention to word choice, to logical progression, and to the use of **figures of speech**, including any **metaphors** or analogies. For instance, the speaker of "My Last Duchess" essentially confesses to murdering his wife, even though he never expresses his guilt outright. Similarly, the speaker of "Soliloquy of the Spanish Cloister" inadvertently betrays his madness by confusing Latin prayers and by expressing his hate for a fellow friar with such vituperation and passion. Rather than state the speaker's madness, Browning conveys it through both what the speaker says and how the speaker speaks.

GROTESQUE IMAGES

Unlike other Victorian poets, Browning filled his poetry with images of ugliness, violence, and the bizarre. His contemporaries, such as Alfred, Lord Tennyson, and Gerard Manley Hopkins, in contrast, mined the natural world for lovely images of beauty. Browning's use of the grotesque links him to novelist Charles Dickens, who filled his fiction with people from all strata of society, including the aristocracy and the very poor. Like Dickens, Browning created characters who were capable of great evil. The early poem "Porphyria's Lover" (1836) begins with the lover describing the arrival of Porphyria, then it quickly descends into a depiction of her murder at his hands. To make the image even more grotesque, the speaker strangles Porphyria with her own blond hair. Although "Fra Lippo Lippi" takes place during the Renaissance in Florence, at the height of its wealth and power, Browning sets the poem in a back alley beside a brothel, not in a palace or a garden. Browning was instrumental in helping readers and writers understand that poetry as an art form could handle subjects both lofty, such as religious splendor and idealized passion, and base, such as murder, hatred, and madness, subjects that had previously only been explored in novels.

SYMBOLS

TASTE

Browning's interest in culture, including art and architecture, appears throughout his work in depictions of his characters' aesthetic tastes. His characters' preferences in art, music, and literature reveal important clues about their natures and moral worth. For instance, the duke of Ferrara, the speaker of "My Last Duchess," concludes the poem by pointing out a statue he commissioned of Neptune taming a sea monster. The duke's preference for this sculpture directly corresponds to the type of man he is—that is, the type of man who would have his wife killed but still stare lovingly and longingly at her portrait. Like Neptune, the duke wants to subdue and command all aspects of life, including his wife. Characters also express their tastes by the manner in which they describe art, people, or landscapes. Andrea del Sarto, the Renaissance artist who speaks the poem "Andrea del Sarto," repeatedly uses the adjectives *gold* and *silver* in his descriptions of paintings. His choice of words reinforces one of the major themes of the poem: the way he sold himself out. Listening to his monologue, we learn that he now makes commercial paintings to earn a commission, but he no longer creates what he considers to be real art. His desire for money has affected his aesthetic judgment, causing him to use monetary vocabulary to describe art objects.

EVIL AND VIOLENCE

Synonyms for, images of, and **symbols** of evil and violence abound in Browning's poetry. "Soliloquy of the Spanish Cloister," for example, begins with the speaker trying to articulate the sounds of his "heart's abhorrence" (1) for a fellow friar. Later in the poem, the speaker invokes images of evil pirates and a man being banished to hell. The diction and images used by the speakers expresses their evil thoughts, as well as indicate their evil natures. "Childe Roland to the Dark Tower Came" (1855) portrays a nightmarish world of dead horses and war-torn landscapes. Yet another example of evil and violence comes in "Porphyria's Lover," in which the speaker sits contentedly alongside the corpse of Porphyria, whom he murdered by strangling her with her hair. Symbols of evil and violence allowed Browning to explore all aspects of human psychology, including the base and evil aspects that don't normally appear in poetry.

SUMMARY & ANALYSIS

"MY LAST DUCHESS"

FERRARA

That's my last duchess painted on the wall,
Looking as if she were alive. I call
That piece a wonder, now; Fra Pandolf's hands
Worked busily a day, and there she stands.
Will't please you sit and look at her? I said   5
"Fra Pandolf" by design, for never read
Strangers like you that pictured countenance,
That depth and passion of its earnest glance,
But to myself they turned (since none puts by
The curtain drawn for you, but I)   10
And seemed as they would ask me, if they durst,
How such a glance came there; so not the first
Are you to turn and ask thus. Sir, 'twas not
Her husband's presence only, called that spot
Of joy into the Duchess' cheek: perhaps   15
Fra Pandolf chanced to say "Her mantle laps
Over my lady's wrist too much" or "Paint
Must never hope to reproduce the faint
Half-flush that dies along her throat": such stuff
Was courtesy, she thought, and cause enough   20
For calling up that spot of joy. She had
A heart—how shall I say?—too soon made glad,
Too easily impressed: she liked whate'er
She looked on, and her looks went everywhere.
Sir, 'twas all one! My favor at her breast,   25
The dropping of the daylight in the West,
The bough of cherries some officious fool
Broke in the orchard for her, the white mule
She rode with round the terrace—all and each
Would draw from her alike the approving speech,   30
Or blush, at least. She thanked men—good! but thanked
Somehow—I know not how—as if she ranked
My gift of a nine-hundred-years-old name

> With anybody's gift. Who'd stoop to blame
> This sort of trifling? Even had you skill   35
> In speech—(which I have not)—to make your will
> Quite clear to such a one, and say, "Just this
> Or that in you disgusts me; here you miss
> Or there exceed the mark"—and if she let
> Herself be lessoned so, nor plainly set   40
> Her wits to yours, forsooth, and made excuse
> —E'en then would be some stooping; and I choose
> Never to stoop. Oh sir, she smiled, no doubt,
> Whene'er I passed her; but who passed without
> Much the same smile? This grew; I gave commands;   45
> Then all smiles stopped together. There she stands
> As if alive. Will't please you rise? We'll meet
> The company below, then. I repeat,
> The Count your master's known munificence
> Is ample warrant that no just pretence   50
> Of mine for dowry will be disallowed;
> Though his fair daughter's self, as I avowed
> At starting is my object. Nay, we'll go
> Together down, sir. Notice Neptune, though,
> Taming a sea-horse, thought a rarity,   55
> Which Claus of Innsbruck cast in bronze for me!

SUMMARY

The poem begins with the duke speaking to an unnamed guest as he takes the guest on a tour of his art gallery. First, the duke shows him a painting of his wife, the previous duchess, who is now dead. Next the duke mentions the name of the artist, Fra Pandolf, and explains that the artist was quite busy painting the portrait. He asks the guest to sit and look at the painting, which he then begins to analyze in more detail. Addressing the guest, the duke asks if he is wondering about the duchess's blushing cheeks. Shouldn't it be only the duke who could bring about such emotion in his wife?

Now the duke keeps the painting covered so that he might be the only one who looks on it. The duke suggests that the guest might be wondering whether Fra Pandolf flattered the duchess in order to make her blush. No, the duke explains, the duchess had a "heart . . . too soon made glad" (22). She became happy and emotional too easily. Everything she saw made her happy, and she looked at everything. The duchess was equally pleased by a token of the duke's affection, by watching the sunset, by cherries from the orchard, and by riding her pet mule around the terrace; each of these objects or activities would win her compliments or some show of emotion. Although the duke approved of her courtesy, he disliked the fact that she seemed to appreciate any trifling present or pleasure as much as she appreciated the duke and his gift to her of his title and noble status.

But then the duke wonders what type of person would deign to make a big deal out of such an insignificant insult. He says that one would be "stooping" (42) by addressing the matter, even if one had the rhetorical abilities to say exactly what about such behavior was inappropriate. The duke denies that he has that type of rhetorical ability. Also, it would be deigning or stooping even if the duchess corrected her behavior and apologized after being reprimanded, and the duke "choose[s] / Never to stoop" (42–43). Every time he passed her, the duke acknowledged that she smiled at him, but everyone who passed her received a similar smile. As the problem grew worse, the duke gave orders and the smiling stopped. Apparently, the duke ordered her killed. "There she stands / As if alive" (46–47), says the duke.

We now learn that the duke's guest is an envoy from a count whose daughter the duke plans to marry. Politely, the duke asks his guest to rise so that they can rejoin some other guests nearby. The duke states that the count's reputation for generosity leads him to trust that the count will not object to his request for a dowry, a large gift of money or land that traditionally was given by the parents of the bride to the bridegroom. Having mentioned the dowry, the duke then says he seeks the count's daughter—and not her fortune. He stops the guest from preceding him downstairs, protesting that they should descend together. In doing so, he demonstrates his courtesy because he treats the guest as an equal. As they leave the duke's gallery, the duke points out an unusual statue that he had commissioned, which portrays Neptune riding and taming a half-fish, half-human creature.

ANALYSIS

Browning based this poem on Alfonso II, the fifth duke of Ferrara, Italy, who lived from 1533 to 1597. He married a young girl in 1558, who died three years later under mysterious circumstances. "My Last Duchess" is probably Browning's most famous dramatic monologue. Like a play, this poem has a setting (an art gallery), characters (the duke and the count's envoy), and an advanced plot;

these qualities make the poem dramatic. Set in Renaissance Italy, the poem describes the duke as he takes the guest on a tour of his house while they negotiate the dowry for the duke's next marriage. Since only one character speaks, the poem is a monologue. Critics differ about the purpose of the duke's speech. Some argue that the duke tells the guest about his last wife so that the guest will warn the duke's future wife to behave and obey the duke. Other critics suggest that the duke has gone insane and his story unwittingly betrays his murderous, corrupt nature. By confessing that he has killed his last wife, he dooms his marriage prospects and commits himself to living alone with the portrait of his last duchess.

The poem's word choice illustrates the duke's demented nature and role in his wife's death. Although the duke knows a lot about art, and although he politely offers his guest a seat in front of the painting, he is also selfish, proud, and glibly and unapologetically amoral. He shows no guilt or remorse for his wife's death, even as he admires her portrait and explains his role in making her smiles cease. Too proud to correct her behavior, he resorts to ordering her death. No one but he looks on her painting because "none puts by / the curtain" (9–10) he uses to cover it. Interestingly, what he loves in the painting, he detested in real life—that is, he loves the blush and smile that has been captured by Fra Pandolf, but he hated the way his duchess blushed and smiled at all she saw when she lived. Now, in death, his wife has become an object, much like the statute he points out as he and the guest exit the gallery.

"THE BISHOP ORDERS HIS TOMB AT SAINT PRAXED'S CHURCH"

EXCERPT FROM "THE BISHOP ORDERS HIS TOMB AT SAINT PRAXED'S CHURCH"

Vanity, saith the preacher, vanity!
Draw round my bed: is Anselm keeping back?
Nephews—sons mine . . . ah God, I know not! Well—
She, men would have to be your mother once,
Old Gandolf envied me, so fair she was!
What's done is done, and she is dead beside,
Dead long ago, and I am Bishop since,
And as she died so must we die ourselves,
And thence ye may perceive the world's a dream.

Life, how and what is it? As here I lie
In this state-chamber, dying by degrees,
Hours and long hours in the dead night, I ask,
"Do I live, am I dead?" Peace, peace seems all.
Saint Praxed's ever was the church for peace;
And so, about this tomb of mine. I fought
With tooth and nail to save my niche, ye know:
—Old Gandolf cozen'd me, despite my care;
Shrewd was that snatch from out the corner south
He graced his carrion with, God curse the same!

SUMMARY

The bishop begins by quoting the biblical book Ecclesiastes as he summons his heirs to his bedside. He addresses them as nephews and as sons because he does not know which they are. Years ago, he had an affair with their mother, before she died and before he became a bishop. His rival, Gandolf, envied him because the woman was so beautiful. But now he doesn't know which of the woman's sons, if any, might actually be his children, so he calls them all to him. Lying on his deathbed, the bishop wonders if he might be awake or dead. He has summoned the young men there to give them instructions for his tomb, which he wants built within the church after he dies. Unfortunately, Gandolf stole the space the bishop had picked out for himself because Gandolf died first.

Even though Gandolf got the prime spot, the bishop's place will nevertheless suit him. From his spot in the church, the bishop will be able to see the altar, part of the choir, and a section of the dome. There he'll rest for eternity, beneath a tomb of basalt and marble and surrounded by columns. His tomb will be much better than Gandolf's, whose tomb was made from a lesser-quality marble. He reminds his heirs to place his tomb such that it faces Gandolf's resting place. Next he urges his heirs to come closer so that he can explain what else he wants buried in the tomb. Once, during a fire at his church, the bishop stole a large piece of the precious stone lapis lazuli. Now he instructs his heirs on how to retrieve the stone from its hiding place in a vineyard. He reminds his heirs that he has bequeathed to them property and houses, so he asks that they bury the stone with him, rather than keeping it for themselves. Gandolf will explode with jealousy when he sees the stone.

The bishop reminds his heirs that he wants them to use black stone for his tomb. They should have the bishop's image carved into this stone, along with some images from paganism and Christianity. Suddenly, the bishop becomes convinced that his heirs are not paying attention and thus won't follow his wishes. He asks one heir, Anselm, what the others are conversing about. The bishop begins criticizing the heirs, and he imagines that they will destroy his houses after he dies. Then Gandolf will laugh at him. Should the heirs fulfill his wishes, the dead bishop will use his influence with Saint Praxed to give the heirs wealth, knowledge, and beautiful women. But, as the bishop reminds the heirs, he will only watch over them after death if the heirs do everything he asks. Fulfilling his wishes includes, among other things, choosing and carving the epitaph correctly.

At night, the bishop practices being dead. He lies in state, with his arms crossed, and pretends that he has already died. As the candles drip, the bishop thinks over his life, fondly remembering the woman with whom he had an affair—the mother of the heirs. His mind then begins to wander as he speaks to the heirs: he cites commonplace and biblical pieces of wisdom about the inevitability of death and the futility of man's time on earth. The bishop also babbles about Gandolf's tomb and reminds his heirs to follow his wishes. But he remains convinced that his heirs hate him and will betray him after he dies. He imagines that his heirs wish him dead, and he thinks that they will bury him in cheap sandstone surrounded by ugly sculptures. Finally, he tells the heirs to leave him alone. He asks them to walk out facing him, as if he were still a powerful clergymen and they were his pious servants. The bishop asks his heirs to let him lie there on his deathbed, imagining that he has already died and been placed in his tomb. As he dies, he thinks, he will recall Gandolf's jealousy over the woman's great beauty.

ANALYSIS

A visit to the medieval Roman church of Santa Prassede inspired Browning to write this dramatic monologue. Although the church exists, the bishop is fictional, yet another of Browning's complex, but entirely made up, creations. Not entirely lucid, the bishop has summoned some young men to his deathbed to explain his funereal wishes. Over the course of the poem, the bishop jumps from topic to topic, with few transitions, and demonstrates a perverse hatred for his rival, Gandolf. He also confesses to both an affair with the married mother of the young men and to having stolen a precious stone from his church, two more instances of the bishop's unchristian character. As in other Browning monologues, this speaker betrays his damaged personality and demented psychology through his words and the way he chooses to recollect the past. The only voice we hear in the poem belongs to the bishop, but that voice shows us all we need to know about the miserable depths of his soul.

Through his rambling, sometimes incoherent speech, the bishop betrays not only his true character but also mocks Christianity. Catholic priests and monks are supposed to take vows of poverty, chastity, and obedience. In contrast, the bishop is rich, owning many villas, and is completely consumed by a desire for a luxurious and expensive tomb. Blasphemously, the bishop compares himself to God as he asks his heirs to bury him with the lapis lazuli stone. Once upon a time, in his role as an officer of the church, the bishop probably had to give speeches about lofty ideals or against sin, and he probably quoted heavily from the Bible to do so. He also probably encouraged his followers and listeners to obey the Ten Commandments. Now on his deathbed, the bishop confesses his sins, rather than speak against sin. He confusedly invokes and interprets biblical passages from Ecclesiastes in line 1 and Job in line 51. The bishop has shrugged off any pretense of piety or virtue. Instead, he reveals himself to be base, vain, and competitive.

The bishop lacks a clear sense of the past, present, and future. He frequently wonders if he has already died but also pretends that his deathbed has become his tomb. In his muddled state, the bishop reveals that he does not believe in the one of the central premises of Christianity, namely that he will be saved and reborn in heaven. Instead, he believes only in an earthy afterlife: he will lie forever in his tomb, watching to make sure that Gandolf doesn't make fun of him and enjoying the sensual pleasures of the smell of incense smoke and the sounds of mass. He even wants a stone buried with him, a desire that harks back to the pre-Christian era, in which many cultures buried objects along with their dead. His desire for a mix of pagan and Christian iconographies to be carved into his tomb reveals his beliefs, or lack thereof, in the afterlife: although he believes that he will be conscious in death, he does not believe in heaven.

Using the bishop's voice, the poem subtly criticizes organized religion in general. Browning knew that his fictional bishop had real-life historical precedents: many Renaissance-era Catholic priests, bishops, and even popes had mistresses and illegitimate children, became very rich, and capriciously wielded great political power. The bishop's obsessive focus on his tomb also indicts organized religion for privileging beauty over religious feeling. Throughout the poem, the bishop specifies the material to be used for his tomb, the carvings and sculptures to be inscribed or created, and even what should be buried with him. At no point does he ask his heirs to pray for his soul, a request we might expect from a religious figure. Like the bishop himself, ornate churches that emphasize aesthetics seem to speak more to vanity than piety. True religious piety comes from a committed, devoted soul and not from the trappings of wealth or the symbols of religion.

"CHILDE ROLAND TO THE DARK TOWER CAME"

EXCERPT FROM "CHILDE ROLAND TO THE DARK TOWER CAME"

For, what with my whole world-wide wandering,
*   What with my search drawn out thro' years, my hope*
*   Dwindled into a ghost not fit to cope*
With that obstreperous joy success would bring,
I hardly tried now to rebuke the spring
*   My heart made, finding failure in its scope.*

As when a sick man very near to death
*   Seems dead indeed, and feels begin and end*
*   The tears and takes the farewell of each friend,*
And hears one bid the other go, draw breath
Freelier outside ("since all is o'er," he saith,
*   "And the blow fallen no grieving can amend")*

While some discuss if near the other graves
*   Be room enough for this, and when a day*
*   Suits best for carrying the corpse away,*
With care about the banners, scarves and staves:
And still the man hears all, and only craves
*   He may not shame such tender love and stay.*

Thus, I had so long suffered in this quest,
*   Heard failure prophesied so oft, been writ*
*   So many times among "The Band"—to wit,*
The knights who to the Dark Tower's search addressed

Their steps—that just to fail as they, seemed best,
*   And all the doubt was now—should I be fit?*

.   .   .   .   .

There they stood, ranged along the hillsides, met
*   To view the last of me, a living frame*
*   For one more picture! in a sheet of flame*
I saw them and I knew them all. And yet
Dauntless the slug-horn to my lips I set,
*   And blew.* "Childe Roland to the Dark Tower came."

SUMMARY

This poem begins with a description of an ugly, old, handicapped man standing at a fork in the road. Roland, the speaker of the poem, becomes convinced that the man is evil and out to deceive him, as he tries to deceive all the travelers who pass him and ask him for directions. The man tells Roland to take the road toward the ominous Dark Tower. Roland feels nothing but joy at the prospect of his long journey coming to an end, even as he senses maliciousness in the man and in the idea of the tower. Next, Roland describes his "whole world-wide wandering" (19): he has been searching for the tower for a long time, even as his friends have abandoned him or failed in their quest. He compares the end of his journey to someone suffering from an illness but nearing death. Like the sick man who knows death is near but who has not yet died, Roland has continued on his journey, even as others have predicted his failure or have left him. Now, as Roland comes closer to the end of his travels, he wonders if he is even worthy of finding the tower.

Gently, Roland leaves the man and goes down the road the man has gestured toward. After just a few steps, Roland turns: he can no longer see the man or the area where he had been standing. He continues on, through a desolate, blighted landscape, barren of life except for weeds. As he walks through the barrenness, he comes upon an old, sick horse. Roland immediately hates the horse, even as he sees how much the horse suffers. He decides that the horse was once evil and thus deserves its sores and suffering. To solace himself, Roland conjures memories of happier times and places. He tries to remember the friendship of his band of knights, for comfort, but his mind just turns to a memory of how one of them was disgraced and hung for treason. Night descends, and nothing moves or stirs.

Suddenly, a gross, foamy river appears in front of Roland. He describes the river as "petty yet so spiteful" (115), but he must cross it. Roland feels something in the water, which he thinks could equally be a dead person as a rat. The other side of the river is just as vile as the first side: the trampled turf looks if a war has just been waged. He continues, past an arena and broken farming equipment, past a bog, and into an area surrounded by mountains. An enormous bird flies by him. Then, as in a nightmare, he suddenly sees that he has arrived at the Dark Tower. Perhaps he hadn't been able to see it before because the sun has set, but some last rays of sunlight now illuminate the tower from a break in the surrounding mountains. Roland begins to hear the names of his fallen fellow knights, and he sees them standing on nearby hills. Resolute, he picks up his trumpet and sounds a battle cry to announce his presence. The poem ends here, and we do not learn Roland's fate.

ANALYSIS

Browning claimed to have written this poem in one day, while in a trancelike state. He took the title of the poem from a song sung by Edgar, King Lear's son, in Shakespeare's *King Lear*. Disguised as a beggar, Edgar sings, "Childe Rowland to the dark tower came, / His word was still, 'Fie, foh, and fum, / I smell the blood of a British man'" (act III, scene iv, 169–171). Like the tower of the song, the poem's tower is a sinister, dangerous place. We don't know Roland's fate, but we sense that he too dies, surrounded by the dead knights who have risen from the grave to watch Roland perish. The thirty-four **stanzas** of **iambic pentameter** that make up this poem have a peculiar hold on contemporary consciousness: T. S. Eliot's poem *The Waste Land* (1922) borrows some imagery of barren, scarred fields from Browning's work, and Stephen King has created a successful series of novels, called *The Dark Tower*, also based on this poem.

Like Eliot would some seventy years later, Browning used his poetry to express his concerns about the barren state of modern life. Browning's speaker, Roland, journeys on a quest that has no real significance. As readers, we don't know why he's on this journey or what reasons he might have for going to the Dark Tower. His life seems to lack purpose or meaning. We meet him on the last leg of his journey, which takes him through war-torn fields and across a debris-filled river. On this walk, Roland sees only a malicious man and a dying horse. During the mid-nineteenth century, English cities became increasingly overpopulated and polluted as people fled the country for the industrial jobs promised by urban life. Roland's disconnection to the land echoes the separation between humans and Earth wrought by the eighteenth- and nineteenth-century Industrial Revolution. Also, the land itself stands for infertile urban life. Roland hallucinates as he travels, imagining that his dead knights have come back to help him. His abnormal psychic state symbolizes the disconnection and horror of the modern city. Roland does not care whether he lives or dies—he only wants to come to the end of his travels.

"Childe Roland to the Dark Tower Came" demonstrates the usefulness and relevance of art to modern life. Browning took not just his title but also much of his imagery and symbolism from Shakespeare's *King Lear*. He then shaped the early seventeenth-century material into a commentary on nineteenth-century life. His ability to bend past work to fit the circumstances of contemporary life shows the potential relevance of literary work. But Browning's poem also explores how literature speaks—and lies. In the first line of the poem, Roland comments about the old man he meets on the road: "My first thought was, he lied in every word." The unreliability of the old man reminds us of the imaginative engine that drives all of literature: fiction is not the truth, but merely a version of the truth reflected and refracted through the eyes of the writer and the eyes of the reader. One of literature's purposes is to help readers understand the multiplicity of perspectives that make up reality.

"FRA LIPPO LIPPI"

EXCERPT FROM "FRA LIPPO LIPPI"

I drew men's faces on my copy-books,
Scrawled them within the antiphonary's marge,
Joined legs and arms to the long music-notes,
Found eyes and nose and chin for A's and B's,
And made a string of pictures of the world
Betwixt the ins and outs of verb and noun,
On the wall, the bench, the door. The monks looked black.
"Nay," quoth the Prior, "turn him out, d'ye say?
In no wise. Lose a crow and catch a lark.
What if at last we get our man of parts,
We Carmelites, like those Camaldolese
And Preaching Friars, to do our church up fine

And put the front on it that ought to be!"
And hereupon he bade me daub away.
Thank you! my head being crammed, the walls a blank,
Never was such prompt disemburdening.
First, every sort of monk, the black and white,
I drew them, fat and lean: then, folk at church,
From good old gossips waiting to confess
Their cribs of barrel-droppings, candle-ends,—
To the breathless fellow at the altar-foot,
Fresh from his murder, safe and sitting there
With the little children round him in a row
Of admiration, half for his beard and half
For that white anger of his victim's son
Shaking a fist at him with one fierce arm,
Signing himself with the other because of Christ
(Whose sad face on the cross sees only this
After the passion of a thousand years)
Till some poor girl, her apron o'er her head,
(Which the intense eyes looked through) came at eve
On tiptoe, said a word, dropped in a loaf,
Her pair of earrings and a bunch of flowers
(The brute took growling), prayed, and so was gone.
I painted all, then cried "'Tis ask and have;
Choose, for more's ready!"—laid the ladder flat,
And showed my covered bit of cloister-wall.
The monks closed in a circle and praised loud
Till checked, taught what to see and not to see,
Being simple bodies,—"That's the very man!
Look at the boy who stoops to pat the dog!
That woman's like the Prior's niece who comes
To care about his asthma: it's the life!"
But there my triumph's straw-fire flared and funked;
Their betters took their turn to see and say:
The Prior and the learned pulled a face
And stopped all that in no time. "How? what's here?
Quite from the mark of painting, bless us all!
Faces, arms, legs, and bodies like the true
As much as pea and pea! it's devil's-game!
Your business is not to catch men with show,
With homage to the perishable clay,
But lift them over it, ignore it all,

Make them forget there's such a thing as flesh.
Your business is to paint the souls of men—
Man's soul, and it's a fire, smoke . . . no, it's not . . .
It's vapor done up like a newborn babe—
(In that shape when you die it leaves your mouth)
It's . . . well, what matters talking, it's the soul!
Give us no more body than shows the soul!"

SUMMARY

Fra Lippo Lippi, the speaker of this dramatic monologue, was a fifteenth-century Italian painter. Raised from a young age as a monk,
he eventually eloped with a nun, breaking his vow of chastity. This
poem is set in Florence, where he worked for a while for Cosimo de'
Medici, an extremely rich and powerful man. The action begins in
the middle of the night: the city's night guardsmen have just caught
Lippo Lippi outside a back-alley brothel. Lippo Lippi makes various arguments to try to convince the guardsmen to release him.

Lippo Lippi begins by introducing himself, explaining that he
belongs to the order of Santa Maria del Carmine, and he asks that
the guardsmen stop choking him. Then he says that he is staying
with Cosimo de' Medici. At the mention of this important man's
name, the guards unhand Lippo Lippi and an officer begins grovel-
ing and apologizing. Lippo Lippi offers the guards some money for
a drink but then acknowledges that he is the renowned painter and
asks some of the guards, who know his work, to sit down for a
while. Slightly drunk, excited by the night's revelry, Lippo Lippi
wants to talk. He has left his house during the celebrations before
Lent, drawn out by the crowds singing in the streets below. After
fashioning a ladder out of sheets, Lippo Lippi climbed down from
his room and went outside. Now, he claims, he was on his way home
to get some sleep before morning when the guards caught him.

Although the guards seem sympathetic, they refuse to release
Lippo Lippi because he is a monk. To try to convince the guards to
let him go, Lippo Lippi explains that he is only a monk because of
circumstances: orphaned at age eight, he had no choice but to join
the order. Had he not, he would have starved. At the time, he did not
realize the strict, chaste life he had chosen. After taking the monk's
vows, including those of chastity and the renunciation of wealth,
Lippo Lippi began his education. As he explains, he was no good at
his lessons, but he was always doodling, and other monks soon recognized his potential as a painter. Lippo Lippi claims that his early

life on the streets honed his powers of observation. The head of his convent, the Prior, asked him to decorate their church, so Lippo Lippi painted everything he saw, including all the monks, the congregation, and the Prior's niece, just as he saw them.

When Lippo Lippi finished his realistic work, all the monks gathered around and remarked at how well Lippo Lippi had captured people's faces, gestures, and demeanors. But the Prior disapproved of Lippo Lippi's painting of worldly things. "Your business is to paint the soul's of men" (183), the Prior tells Lippo Lippi. The Prior claims that Lippo Lippi should paint stylized saints, souls, and other religious themes and tells Lippo Lippi to destroy what he has painted. Now, though, Lippo Lippi works for de' Medici and can paint whatever he wants. Sometimes he paints to please his religious superiors, and sometimes the world and earthly life seem too important to pass up in favor of painting heavenly scenes. Lippo Lippi appeals to the guardsmen's own experience. They aren't educated in the ways of the church, but they've seen the world in all its beauty. Like Lippo Lippi, they understand that God has created everything, and thus every painting of every thing in some way represents God.

Next, Lippo Lippi explains his artistic credo. He rhetorically asks the guardsmen whether they are thankful for all of this ordinary, worldly beauty or whether this beauty should be passed over and despised. Of course, he says, the guardsmen will say that the beauty should be dwelt upon and wondered at. But Lippo Lippi expects too that the guards will also question the point of trying to reproduce nature since nature already exists for everyone to see. Lippo Lippi imagines that the guardsmen will tell him to create works more beautiful than anything found in nature by painting scenes of higher things, such as heaven and angels, which people cannot see with their own eyes. In Lippo Lippi's view, human beings were made so that their attention is drawn to things they see painted, and they will love something in a painting that they have passed many times in life and never noticed. God uses artists to help people become more attuned to the everyday beauty around them.

Some people, such as the Prior, argue that the purpose of art is to remind people of God, prayer, and religious belief. But, Lippo Lippi reasons, anything can serve as a reminder, including a skull and crossbones or a bell. Six months ago, he painted the martyrdom of a saint. Lippo Lippi then asks a fellow monk how the painting turned out. This monk explains that devout churchgoers have nearly destroyed the painting by scratching out the faces of the figures killing the saint. Angrily, Lippo Lippi says that these churchgoers deserve to be hanged for their destructive act. At this, the guardsmen get angry again, so Lippo Lippi offers to paint a devotional altarpiece in the next six months. He goes on to describe this new painting: it will depict God, the Madonna, Baby Jesus, many beautiful angels, and a few saints.

This hypothetical painting will contain many religious figures, but it will also depict himself, Lippo Lippi, wearing his monk's clothes and a rope belt. An angel will stop him from leaving the painting by telling Lippo Lippi that he belongs there: God made him, just like he made everyone else. The angel says that Lippo Lippi must paint because he has a talent that others lack. So, Lippi says, there he will be in the bottom right-hand corner of his painting, happy and contented. This promise convinces the guardsmen, and they release Lippo Lippi just as the sky begins to become light.

ANALYSIS

In "Fra Lippo Lippi," Browning presents a complex psychological portrait of a monk caught after a night of partying and debauching. As the monk tries to talk himself out of getting arrested by the guards of Florence, he not only narrates his autobiography but also presents his unique theories of art. In his sympathetic portrait, Browning creates a charming, generous character who believes passionately in art but who nevertheless possesses a self-destructive streak that includes rebelliousness and sexual promiscuity. He uses this character to think about the relationship between art, responsibility, and morality. In the poem, Fra Lippo Lippi explains that he wants his art to delight, which causes him to clash with the Prior and other church leaders, who believe that art must instruct and preach. Lippo Lippi just wants to paint what he sees. Like Lippo Lippi, Browning was interested in **realism** in art, and he used his poetry to probe the often-unpleasant undersides of human psychology, including the human capacity for evil, violence, and other sins.

Lippo Lippi's artistic credo represents the cataclysmic shift in art that occurred during the Renaissance. Beginning in the fourteenth century, artists began to depict the human form realistically, which contrasted with the stylized, unrealistic, pre-Renaissance depictions of the twelfth and thirteenth centuries. Artists also began to fill their canvases with objects. They used the recently discovered linear perspective to vary the objects' sizes, depending on where they fell on the canvas. In general, Renaissance art switched from religious concerns to secular concerns. Both art and culture emphasized human-ism, or the belief in the individual's potential for self-realization through reason and learning. In lines 282–306, Lippo Lippi explains that everything in the world is worthy of being painted since God made everything. He also claims that God made humans capable of appreciating the objects and forms they see represented in art. In this way, artists help people better appreciate the everyday stuff of their lives, and God uses artists to increase our sensibilities and powers of perception.

Browning used "Fra Lippo Lippi" to respond to the didacticism of much Victorian art. During the nineteenth century, many artists believed that art had to teach its viewers a moral lesson or give them a simple guide to conduct in a complex world. These views take shape in the figure of the Prior, who clashes with Lippo Lippi over the purpose of art. The Prior makes Lippo Lippi destroy his mural because it represents people too realistically. In the Prior's argu-ment, viewers will spend too much time concentrating on the realis-tic figures and not enough time learning a moral lesson. Lippo Lippi counters the Prior's argument by claiming that his realistic represen-tations will help viewers learn to better appreciate their lives. According to Lippo Lippi's view, his art is still teaching viewers, but it teaches them a secular, rather than religious, lesson. Both views hold that artists have the moral responsibility to teach their viewers.

ROBERT BROWNING

WALT WHITMAN

(1819–1892)

CONTEXT

Walt Whitman was born near Hempstead, Long Island, on May 31, 1819, just thirty years after George Washington was inaugurated as the first president of the United States. Whitman was born at a time when the young United States was still infused with the spirit of revolution. Whitman's father, Walter Whitman Sr., a carpenter and farmer, had known Thomas Paine, author of the revolutionary pamphlet *Common Sense*. He even named three of Whitman's four brothers after the heroes of the Revolutionary War and War of 1812: Andrew Jackson, George Washington, and Thomas Jefferson. Early America's patriotism and pride profoundly affected Whitman, and he expressed these sentiments in his poetry. He also chronicled every aspect of the young country, from its idyllic agricultural life to its bustling cities and industrial centers. In his most famous poems, Whitman detailed the great traumas of the Civil War and the death of Abraham Lincoln.

At around age four, Whitman moved with his family to Brooklyn. As a child, Whitman frequently took the ferry into Manhattan, which was then in the midst of a tremendous population explosion. In the early nineteenth century, the island had a population of only 60,000, and many families still raised cows and pigs on individual plots of land. By 1830, however, Manhattan was home to 200,000 people, and by 1850, half a million people lived there. Manhattan had become the industrial center of the United States, and it symbolized the promising future. Whitman attended newly founded public schools in Brooklyn, but he also spent a lot of time in libraries, in museums, and at lectures around New York City. He was largely self-taught and widely read, particularly in the works of Shakespeare, Homer, and Dante. At twelve, Whitman became an apprentice printer at a newspaper, the Long Island *Patriot*, and he published his first signed newspaper article in the New York *Mirror* in 1834, when he was only fifteen.

In 1833, Whitman's family moved back to Long Island while he remained on his own in Brooklyn. After fires destroyed much of Manhattan's business district in the mid-1830s, Whitman accepted a series of teaching positions in small towns throughout Long Island. Until 1841, Whitman taught large classes of mostly uneducated children, sometimes using his own poems, which were at that time very conventional, as reading assignments. Generally, he found teaching unsatisfying, and he tried, unsuccessfully, to start his own newspaper, the *Long Islander*, in 1838. After he stopped teaching at age nineteen, Whitman worked as a freelance journalist throughout New York City for the next eight years. Meanwhile, he also began writing short fiction and wrote a popular novel designed to aid the temperance movement, called *Franklin Evans; or, the Inebriate*. He became editor of the *Brooklyn Daily Eagle* in 1846. Just two years later, Whitman left New York for New Orleans, where he briefly became editor of a newspaper called the *Daily Crescent*. A few months later he returned to New York.

Whitman's exposure to the United States, especially its diverse landscapes and peoples, seemed to catalyze a political and poetic energy that had built up during his New York years. Throughout the 1830s and 1840s, Whitman had written unremarkable, extremely conventional poems that were occasionally published in local magazines. On July 4, 1855, however, Whitman published *Leaves of Grass*, his first book of poems, written in a unique style that he believed more suited to the vast, varied, energetic country he had seen. He paid for the publication himself, sending copies to writers he admired. Only one—Ralph Waldo Emerson—wrote back; Emerson wrote, "I greet you at the beginning of a great career." The book sold poorly, but Emerson correctly predicted Whitman's highly unusual success.

In its initial printing, *Leaves of Grass* contained only twelve poems, but throughout his life Whitman enlarged the book. By his death in 1892, *Leaves of Grass* contained hundreds of poems and had gone through countless editions. Each edition of *Leaves of Grass* was different, and Whitman revised and reorganized the poems each time, often adding new material that had previously been published elsewhere. Almost every edition opened with the autobiographical "Song of Myself," which Whitman also expanded and revised over the course of his life. Eventually that poem morphed into the 1,346 lines in 52 sections we read today. Having worked as a printer, Whitman paid close attention to the production of *Leaves of Grass*. The first edition was printed on extra-large paper to accommodate the long, rolling lines of his distinct poetic style, and Whitman published the book without printing his name for many years, preferring instead to write his name himself in each book that was sold. Today, almost every poem Whitman wrote and published is collected in the so-called deathbed edition of *Leaves of Grass*, the edition he approved before he died.

As the popularity of *Leaves of Grass* spread, Whitman became a celebrity poet, known for his enormous beard and crooked hat. In the 1860s, the Civil War provided him with what was probably his greatest subject, and his elegies for Abraham Lincoln, among them "O Captain! My Captain!" (1865) and "When Lilacs Last in the Dooryard Bloom'd" (1865), are some of poems that assured Whitman his place as a beloved, uniquely American poet. Whitman published his forty-three Civil War poems in a volume called *Drum-Taps* (1865), which he later incorporated into *Leaves of Grass* in 1871–1872. The darkness and heartbreak of the *Drum-Taps* poems stand in poignant contrast to the energetic and hopeful qualities of the verse Whitman wrote about America when it was not at war. For all of its energy and potential, Whitman's America was fragile, the collective work of many individual human beings, many of whom died on such battlefields such as Antietam and Gettysburg.

Around 1862, Whitman left New York to try to find his brother George, whom he feared was wounded or dead somewhere in Virginia as a result of the Civil War. He eventually found his brother, who had been only slightly injured, but the experience of seeing so many dying and dead soldiers profoundly affected him, and Whitman decided to stay with his brother's unit and work in the battlefield hospitals. He nursed young men, wrote and read their letters, and sometimes acted as an ambulance driver. Settling in Washington, D.C., Whitman eventually supplemented his nursing work by getting at job in the Indian Bureau in the federal Department of the Interior, only to be fired in 1865 after the new secretary found Whitman's poems to be of questionable morality. Whitman switched to another job in the attorney general's office, which he held until deteriorating health forced him to leave in 1874. He moved to Camden, New Jersey, where he would remain until his death in 1892.

Ultimately Whitman's contribution to American letters is two-fold. First, *Leaves of Grass* has become an American **epic**. For many readers, its poems capture the spirit, culture, and diversity of nineteenth-century life, which is exactly what Whitman set out to do. In fact, Whitman concluded in the preface to the 1855 edition of *Leaves of Grass* that "the United States themselves are essentially the greatest poem." Second, Whitman's poetic style has served as a beacon for experimentation in American poetry. His long, rhythmic, unrhymed lines; his inventive, unorthodox vocabulary; and the lengthy, leisurely, pulsating structure of the poems themselves have become touchstones for subsequent generations of poets. Much of the poetry produced in the United States before Whitman and Emily Dickinson simply echoed the poetry being published in England. Along with Dickinson, Whitman discovered a distinctly poetic voice that could reflect the American experience in all its beauty and portray all of its struggles.

Themes, Motifs & Symbols

Themes

Democracy As a Way of Life

Whitman envisioned democracy not just as a political system but as a way of experiencing the world. In the early nineteenth century, people still harbored many doubts about whether the United States could survive as a country and about whether democracy could thrive as a political system. To allay those fears and to praise democracy, Whitman tried to be democratic in both life and poetry. He imagined democracy as a way of interpersonal interaction and as a way for individuals to integrate their beliefs into their everyday lives. "Song of Myself" notes that democracy must include all individuals equally, or else it will fail.

In his poetry, Whitman widened the possibilities of **poetic diction** by including slang, colloquialisms, and regional dialects, rather than employing the stiff, erudite language so often found in nineteenth-century verse. Similarly, he broadened the possibilities of subject matter by describing myriad people and places. Like William Wordsworth, Whitman believed that everyday life and everyday people were fit subjects for poetry. Although much of Whitman's work does not explicitly discuss politics, most of it implicitly deals with democracy: it describes communities of people coming together, and it imagines many voices pouring into a unified whole. For Whitman, democracy was an idea that could and should permeate the world beyond politics, making itself felt in the ways we think, speak, work, fight, and even make art.

The Cycle of Growth and Death

Whitman's poetry reflects the vitality and growth of the early United States. During the nineteenth century, America expanded at a tremendous rate, and its growth and potential seemed limitless. But sectionalism and the violence of the Civil War threatened to break apart and destroy the boundless possibilities of the United States. As a way of dealing with both the population growth and the massive deaths during the Civil War, Whitman focused on the life cycles of individuals: people are born, they age and reproduce, and they die. Such poems as "When Lilacs Last in the Dooryard Bloom'd" imagine death as an integral part of life. The **speaker** of "When Lilacs Last in the Dooryard Bloom'd" realizes that flowers die in the winter, but they rebloom in the springtime, and he vows to mourn his fallen friends every year just as new buds are appearing. Describing the life cycle of nature helped Whitman contextualize the severe injuries and trauma he witnessed during the Civil War—linking death to life helped give the deaths of so many soldiers meaning.

THE BEAUTY OF THE INDIVIDUAL

Throughout his poetry, Whitman praised the individual. He imagined a democratic nation as a unified whole composed of unique but equal individuals. "Song of Myself" opens in a triumphant paean to the individual: "I celebrate myself, and sing myself" (1). Elsewhere the speaker of that exuberant poem identifies himself as Walt Whitman and claims that, through him, the voices of many will speak. In this way, many individuals make up the individual democracy, a single entity composed of myriad parts. Every voice and every part will carry the same weight within the single democracy—and thus every voice and every individual is equally beautiful. Despite this pluralist view, Whitman still singled out specific individuals for praise in his poetry, particularly Abraham Lincoln. In 1865, Lincoln was assassinated, and Whitman began composing several **elegies**, including "O Captain! My Captain!" Although all individuals were beautiful and worthy of praise, some individuals merited their own poems because of their contributions to society and democracy.

MOTIFS

LISTS

Whitman filled his poetry with long lists. Often a sentence will be broken into many clauses, separated by commas, and each clause will describe some scene, person, or object. These lists create a sense of expansiveness in the poem, as they mirror the growth of the United States. Also, these lists layer images atop one another to reflect the diversity of American landscapes and people. In "Song of Myself," for example, the speaker lists several adjectives to describe Walt Whitman in section 24. The speaker uses multiple adjectives to demonstrate the complexity of the individual: true individuals cannot be described using just one or two words. Later in this section, the speaker also lists the different types of voices who speak through Whitman. Lists are another way of demonstrating democracy in action: in lists, all items possess equal weight, and no item is more important than another item in the list. In a democracy, all individuals possess equal weight, and no individual is more important than another.

THE HUMAN BODY

Whitman's poetry revels in its depictions of the human body and the body's capacity for physical contact. The speaker of "Song of Myself" claims that "copulation is no more rank to me than death is" (521) to demonstrate the naturalness of taking pleasure in the body's physical possibilities. With physical contact comes spiritual communion: two touching bodies form one individual unit of togetherness. Several poems praise the bodies of both women and men, describing them at work, at play, and interacting. The speaker of "I Sing the Body Electric" (1855) boldly praises the perfection of the human form and worships the body because the body houses the soul. This free expression of sexuality horrified some of Whitman's early readers, and Whitman was fired from his job at the Indian Bureau in 1865 because the secretary of the interior found *Leaves of Grass* offensive. Whitman's unabashed praise of the male form has led many critics to argue that he was homosexual or bisexual, but the repressive culture of the nineteenth century prevented him from truly expressing those feelings in his work.

RHYTHM AND INCANTATION

Many of Whitman's poems rely on **rhythm** and repetition to create a captivating, spellbinding quality of incantation. Often, Whitman begins several lines in a row with the same word or phrase, a literary device called **anaphora**. For example, the first four lines of "When I Heard the Learn'd Astronomer" (1865) each begin with the word *when*. The long lines of such poems as "Song of Myself" and "When Lilacs Last in the Dooryard Bloom'd" force readers to inhale several bits of text without pausing for breath, and this breathlessness contributes to the incantatory quality of the poems. Generally, the anaphora and the rhythm transform the poems into celebratory chants, and the joyous form and structure reflect the joyousness of the poetic content. Elsewhere, however, the repetition and rhythm contribute to an elegiac tone, as in "O Captain! My Captain!" This poem uses short lines and words, such as *heart* and *father*, to mournfully incant an elegy for the assassinated Abraham Lincoln.

SYMBOLS

PLANTS

Throughout Whitman's poetry, plant life symbolizes both growth and multiplicity. Rapid, regular plant growth also stands in for the rapid, regular expansion of the population of the United States. In "When Lilacs Last in the Dooryard Bloom'd," Whitman uses flowers, bushes, wheat, trees, and other plant life to signify the possibilities of regeneration and re-growth after death. As the speaker mourns the loss of Lincoln, he drops a lilac spray onto the coffin; the act of laying a flower on the coffin not only honors the person who has died but lends death a measure of dignity and respect. The title *Leaves of Grass* highlights another of Whitman's themes: the beauty of the individual. Each leaf or blade of grass possesses its own distinct beauty, and together the blades form a beautiful unified whole, an idea Whitman explores in the sixth section of "Song of Myself." Multiple leaves of grass thus symbolize democracy, another instance of a beautiful whole composed of individual parts. In 1860, Whitman published an edition of *Leaves of Grass* that included a number of poems celebrating love between men. He titled this section "The Calamus Poems," after the phallic calamus plant.

THE SELF

Whitman's interest in the self ties into his praise of the individual. Whitman links the self to the conception of poetry throughout his work, envisioning the self as the birthplace of poetry. Most of his poems are spoken from the first person, using the pronoun *I*. The speaker of Whitman's most famous poem, "Song of Myself," even assumes the name Walt Whitman, but nevertheless the speaker remains a fictional creation employed by the poet Whitman. Although Whitman borrows from his own autobiography for some of the speaker's experiences, he also borrows many experiences from popular works of art, music, and literature. Repeatedly the speaker of this poem exclaims that he contains everything and everyone, which is a way for Whitman to reimagine the boundary between the self and the world. By imaging a person capable of carrying the entire world within him, Whitman can create an elaborate analogy about the ideal democracy, which would, like the self, be capable of containing the whole world.

SUMMARY & ANALYSIS

"SONG OF MYSELF"

EXCERPT FROM "SONG OF MYSELF"

I celebrate myself, and sing myself,
And what I assume you shall assume,
For every atom belonging to me as good belongs to you.

I loafe and invite my soul,
I lean and loafe at my ease observing a spear of summer grass.

My tongue, every atom of my blood, form'd from this soil, this
* air,*
Born here of parents born here from parents the same, and their
* parents the same,*
I, now thirty-seven years old in perfect health begin,
Hoping to cease not till death.

Creeds and schools in abeyance,
Retiring back a while sufficed at what they are, but never
* forgotten,*
I harbor for good or bad, I permit to speak at every hazard,
Nature without check with original energy.

       .   .   .   .   .

A child said What is the grass? *fetching it to me with full hands;*
How could I answer the child? I do not know what it is any more
* than he.*

SUMMARY

"Song of Myself" ranges from biography to philosophical meditations to metaphoric discussions of democracy to descriptions of
nature to abstract exultations of joy. Our summary focuses on section 1, section 6, and section 24 because these sections represent the
tenor, tone, and form of the long poem. In section 1, the speaker
declares a celebration and begins his song. He links himself to his
readers, telling them that his experiences and sensations will be their

experiences and sensations. Everything he celebrates about himself must also be celebrated by readers about themselves. Watching a single blade of grass, he invites his soul to become known to him. The speaker describes himself as "thirty-seven years old in perfect health" (8). Putting all ideologies and philosophies aside, the speaker claims that he will now speak naturally and without restraint.

In section 6, a child asks the speaker, "What is grass?" The speaker then spends much of the section defining grass: it is the human personality or character, God's creation, a child, a way of communicating, hair growing on a corpse. Next, the speaker addresses the grass itself, imaging that the grass grows from familial and friendly relationships between people. The grass grows from people, young and old, who have died. Even though they have died, they remain alive in the grass and in nature's life cycle. Section 24 begins with the speaker's announcement of his name and background in the first line: "Walt Whitman, a kosmos, of Manhattan the son" (497). Like other people, the speaker has sinned—and this behavior makes him equal to everyone else.

Transforming himself into an everyman, the speaker claims that all wounds and injuries committed upon others hurt him. He can speak and write and feel because the divine current of inspiration blows through him. Many voices speak through him, and he "gives the sign of democracy" (506). These voices represent the old, the sick, and the diseased, as well as the healthy and the living. The speaker does not censor himself but rather lets the voices speak, even when they talk about bad or immoral behavior. He believes that the body is sacred, so whatever comes out of the body or whatever the body does is also sacred. The speaker claims that he will worship his body. He might not know how his body works, but he knows that he loves his own body and that his body, particularly its hidden workings, makes him very happy. The speaker stops on some steps to watch the sunrise and feels immensely connected to the physical, natural world.

ANALYSIS

Whitman first published "Song of Myself" in the first edition of *Leaves of Grass* in 1855. Originally named "Poem of Walt Whitman, An American," the poem went through several revisions before it achieved its present title, "Song of Myself," and present form, 52 sections and 1,346 lines, in 1881. As a whole, the poem operates under the assumption that the speaker and his readers share values, beliefs, and assumptions, and therefore the speaker can speak for all Americans. In this way, the poem is something of an American epic: a long narrative poem that details the heroic deeds of one person. The one person of Whitman's poem is an American everyman-poet named Walt Whitman, who longs to "sound [his] barbaric yawp over the roofs of the world" (1333). As the poem moves from vignette to vignette, Whitman defines democracy and describes the vast people, landscapes, and experiences that make up the United States in the nineteenth century.

The poem's first section acts as a manifesto and announces some of the poem's major **themes**, styles, and **tones**. From the very beginning of the poem, the speaker expresses great joy: "I celebrate myself, and sing myself" (1). He will speak and exult in a relaxed manner, taking his cue from the blades of grass he lies watching. By observing the outside world, we will learn something about the inner world we carry within us. In section 51, the speaker famously claims, "I am large, I contain multitudes" (1326). The speaker will stand in for everyone: what he feels, we will feel, and what he thinks, we will think. Poetry becomes the vehicle with which to portray joy, and this joy encompasses all the people of America. The speaker has special powers of perception: the speaker feels the hurts, pains, sorrows, and joys of everyone, so that what is done to someone else is also done to him. He speaks for us because he knows us intimately.

Sections 6 and 24 demonstrate the methods used to joyously portray the American experience. In section 6, Whitman uses grass as a metaphor for democracy: democracy links people across generations and across great distances, democracy grows or continues even after its cultivators have died, and democracy is a feeling that must be intuited, rather than explained outright. After the Civil War, this **metaphor** takes on a special significance since thousands of people died in the name of democracy. Their deaths allowed democracy to continue. Both sections rely on lists. Section 24 lists the voices that articulate their experience through the speaker, who will not judge them. As in a true democracy, the speaker allows everyone a say: from the immoral to the aged to the enslaved to the depressed, everyone has a right to speak and participate. Another section, 15, uses lists to present many types of Americans, including singers, carpenters, sailors, hunters, clergymen, gentlemen, and connoisseurs.

Throughout the poem, Whitman struggles to find the language capable of describing democracy and America. Several times, the speaker admits to being unable to find the right words: in section 6, the speaker says, "I wish I could translate the hints about the dead young men and women" (121). He finds it almost impossible to adequately portray the internecine warfare. In the final section of the poem, the speaker worries that readers haven't understood him and won't know, he says, "what I mean" (1341). He and his poem are "too . . . untranslatable" (1332). Elsewhere, Whitman links the act of articulating with the act of seeing, as in section 25. The speaker of the poem sees; therefore he must speak. But he also hears and touches, and these sensations must also be articulated as part of the catalog of experiences and emotions the poem seeks to create. That the poem includes a myriad of feelings and visions becomes more important than how these feelings and visions are verbalized or explained.

"Song of Myself" describes every type of person performing myriad activities in order to uncover the organicist scheme underlying the world. According to organicism, every part of the world affects every other part, and the world itself exists as a whole, organically connected system. But finding the words to describe every part of the world proves difficult, particularly when the speaker longs to uncover the ineffable human soul. Democracy and America consist of individuals, each of whom is made unique by the presence of a soul. In this way, effectively describing the soul and its experiences, sensations, and feelings becomes necessary to the poetic project of describing a political system and the way it engenders a country.

"CROSSING BROOKLYN FERRY"

EXCERPT FROM "CROSSING BROOKLYN FERRY"

Flood-tide below me! I watch you face to face!
Clouds of the west—sun there half an hour high—I see you also
face to face.

Crowds of men and women attired in the usual costumes, how
curious you are to me!
On the ferry-boats, the hundreds and hundreds that cross,
returning home, are more curious to me than you suppose,
And you that shall cross from shore to shore years hence, are
more to me, and more in my meditations, than you might
suppose.

.   .   .   .   .

Just as you feel when you look on the river and sky, so I felt,
Just as any of you is one of a living crowd, I was one of a crowd,
Just as you are refresh'd by the gladness of the river and the bright
  flow, I was refresh'd,
Just as you stand and lean on the rail, yet hurry with the swift
  current, I stood, yet was Hurried,
Just as you look on the numberless masts of ships, and the thick-
  stem'd pipes of steamboats, I look'd.

  .   .   .   .   .

I loved well those cities, loved well the stately and rapid river;
The men and women I saw were all near to me,
Others the same—others who look back on me, because I look'd
  forward to them,
(The time will come, though I stop here to-day and to-night.)

SUMMARY

Standing on the ferry as it moves from Brooklyn to Manhattan, the speaker looks down at the water below, then up at the sun rising in the sky above. He watches the men and women on the boat with great interest, thinking about the many people who have taken this journey and the many people who will take it in the future. In the second section, the speaker watches the river move and begins discoursing on the abstract "scheme" (7) of life. This scheme includes everyone who has ever lived and who will ever live, as well as all possible sensations and the past, the present, and the future. Other people will take the ferry, other people will notice the river's currents, others will look out on the industries of Brooklyn and Manhattan, and others will notice the scheme. For decades and centuries, other people will continue to make the same ferry journey as the speaker is making right now—and they too will watch the sunset and the movements of the tide.

In the third section, the speaker imagines himself as part of every generation, including those from the past and those in the future. Like those people who preceded him, he has looked out at the sky and the water and been moved. Like those others, he has been part of a group, watched the water, stood against the railing, and admired other vessels. The movement of the river has made him happy, much as it made others happy. He has crossed the river many times, and he describes some of the sights he has seen: seagulls in

December, the sun on the water, the view of distant hills, other ships, sailors, flags, houses with smoking chimneys, sunsets, and the varied movement of light on the water in different seasons and times. In section 4, the speaker expresses a feeling of love and closeness for all of humanity, past and future.

Section 5 continues the speaker's abstract musings as he imagines addressing someone from the past. Neither space nor time affects the relationship between this hypothetical person and the speaker. Like this hypothetical person, the speaker has walked around Brooklyn and Manhattan. Like him, the speaker has thought deeply about himself and his experiences, and he has discovered his identity. He continues addressing this person in section 6, explaining that he too has felt despair and experienced human evil. He has sinned, but he has also loved. He has assumed a mask and acted his role in life, which, like anyone, he can make wonderful or horrible. In section 7, the speaker addresses a lover in the second person, again noting their powerful connection that transcends time.

The speaker shifts his attention to describing Manhattan in section 8. He praises the island and describes the birds, sunlight, and waves that dance around it. This vista produces feelings of connection and ecstasy in him. In the final section, the speaker addresses the river and tells it to continue moving along. He enthusiastically praises the waves, clouds, people on the ferries, Manhattan, and Brooklyn. In his enthusiasm, he commands people to keep singing, living, playing, and enjoying their lives. The speaker finds fellowship and joy everywhere as he simultaneously acknowledges the interconnectedness of humanity.

ANALYSIS

Written in 1856, "Crossing Brooklyn Ferry" uses the experience of riding the commuter ferry between Brooklyn and Manhattan to meditate on time, humanity, and brotherhood. Each of the poem's nine sections consists of loosely self-contained meditations that link to the poem's larger themes through repeated words, phrases, and images. As a whole, the poem explores the continuity and connectivity of humanity across time, space, and place. The speaker both discusses this continuity, which he terms a "scheme" in section 2, and embodies this continuity because he claims to have intimate knowledge of the minds and hearts of people who lived long before him. Riding the ferry—which itself connects two places—the speaker believes that a common set of experiences and feelings connect all people: many people before him have witnessed the movement of the water, the play of light, and beautiful sights while on the water, and these sights fill their viewers with great joy. The sights occurred in the past, the speaker notices the sights in the present, and he believes the sights and their attendant emotions will occur in the future.

Whitman links the poem's meditations using several poetic features. The poem moves logically through a series of lists, as in section 2. Here the speaker recognizes the scheme of life and begins listing the scheme's features, which include the river's current and the industry of New York City. Everything belongs in the scheme. Like the scheme, everything belongs in the poem: from descriptions of people on the boat (section 2) to descriptions of what can be seen from the boat as it moves across the river (section 3) to abstract musings about life and love (section 5) to confessions of past sins (section 6). Several words appear repeatedly throughout the poem, including *you*, *I*, *look'd*, and *saw*, and images also repeat, including the descriptions of currents and sunlight. Whitman repeats words and images from section to section in order to remind readers that sensations and perceptions repeat themselves from generation to generation.

"Crossing Brooklyn Ferry" urges readers to find pleasure in quotidian, everyday activities. Instead of feeling frustrated by the ferry ride or instead of giving into the feelings of boredom sometimes bred by repetition, the speaker exults in his daily commute. He leans against the railing; he watches the water beneath the ferry. Rather than feel irritated by the crowds, the speaker feels invigorated by them and speculates on the unique character behind each face. Indeed, he uses his daily commute across the East River to speculate on human connectedness. Subtly, Whitman shows us how we could enjoy our lives more: we should concentrate on the joy to be found everywhere, at all times. He does not didactically preach to us but instead uses exclamation points and incantatory anaphora to demonstrate the ecstasy to be gained from adopting this attitude. Whitman lets the speaker's happiness speak for itself.

"When Lilacs Last in the Dooryard Bloom'd"

Excerpt from "When Lilacs Last in the Dooryard Bloom'd"

When lilacs last in the door-yard bloom'd,
And the great star early droop'd in the western sky in the night,
I mourn'd—and yet shall mourn with ever-returning spring.
O ever-returning spring! trinity sure to me you bring;
Lilac blooming perennial, and drooping star in the west,
And thought of him I love.

O powerful, western, fallen star!
O shades of night! O moody, tearful night!
O great star disappear'd! O the black murk that hides the star!
O cruel hands that hold me powerless! O helpless soul of me!
O harsh surrounding cloud, that will not free my soul!

.   .   .   .   .

In the swamp in secluded recesses,
A shy and hidden bird is warbling a song.
Solitary, the thrush, The hermit, withdrawn to himself, avoiding
the settlements,
Sings by himself a song.
Song of the bleeding throat!
Death's outlet song of life—(for well, dear brother, I know,
If thou wast not gifted to sing, thou would'st surely die.)

.   .   .   .   .

(Nor for you, for one, alone;
Blossoms and branches green to coffins all I bring:
For fresh as the morning—thus would I carol a song for you, O
sane and sacred death.
All over bouquets of roses,
O death! I cover you over with roses and early lilies;
But mostly and now the lilac that blooms the first,
Copious, I break, I break the sprigs from the bushes;
With loaded arms I come, pouring for you,
For you, and the coffins all of you, O death.)

WALT WHITMAN

SUMMARY

The speaker begins the poem by recalling the last time lilacs bloomed and Venus set in the night sky. Then, as now, he was in mourning—and every year around this time he will continue to mourn. As he mourns, he will remember the deceased, whom he loved dearly. In section 2, the speaker addresses Venus, which he calls a star, as a cloud begins to obscure the star's light. He compares the cloud to his mourning soul. The speaker describes the lilac bush in section 3, and he calls "every leaf a miracle" (15). He breaks off a lilac blossom. Section 4 describes a bird singing in a nearby swamp. If the bird stopped singing, the bird would die. Meanwhile, in section 5, a coffin winds its way through the countryside, passing shrouded mourners and torch-lit churches.

The coffin travels all day and all night, through country and city. Crowds of people mourn. As the coffin passes him, the speaker presents it with his lilac blossom in section 6. Next the speaker explains that he always brings lilac to funerals to show his respect for death and the dead. One night, as he goes on an insomniac walk, the speaker sees Venus in the sky and imagines that Venus has appeared to herald bad news. In section 9, the speaker tells the swamp bird to keep singing, even as the speaker must remain looking at the star. In section 10, the speaker wonders how he will mourn and which songs he should sing to his departed friend. In section 11, the speaker wonders how he should decorate the friend's grave. He decides to decorate it with pictures of the urban and rural landscape. Section 12 continues describing the beauty of the vast United States.

In section 13, the speaker again tells the bird to keep singing. The speaker goes to the swamp in section 14 to find the bird and feel consoled by its mournful song. He has now known death, along with everyone else across the country. The speaker then adds lyrics to the bird's song, which respectfully discusses the power of death to affect us all. Section 15 describes the speaker sitting near the bird and listening to its song. He closes his eyes and has visions of war, violence, and death. While the dead rest peacefully, their remaining fellow soldiers and families grieve. As the night ends, the speaker walks away from the swamp, leaving behind his lilac blossom and taking with him the memories of the departed and the night of mourning. The speaker will return next spring, but the bird, the flower, and the star will always remain in his soul.

ANALYSIS

Whitman wrote "When Lilacs Last in the Dooryard Bloom'd" in the weeks after the assassination of Abraham Lincoln on April 14, 1865. The poem memorializes Lincoln and treats mourning as a necessary, cathartic experience. Lincoln and Whitman shared several characteristics: both were born in the early nineteenth century, both were self-taught iconoclasts, both believed in the sacredness of democracy. "O Captain! My Captain!," "Hush'd Be the Camps Today" (1865), and "This Dust Was Once the Man" (1871) also eulogize Lincoln. As president, Lincoln worked to bring about democracy institutionally, through the law and military force before and during the Civil War. As a poet, Whitman worked to bring democracy about personally, by showing individual Americans how to see the world in a democratic way and how to incorporate democratic ideals into their everyday lives. In his elegy, Whitman removes Lincoln from the political world and brings him into the emotional, subjective world of poetry.

The poem closely examines the mourning process and its relationship to democracy. At first, the speaker feels solitary and alone in his grief: he stands alone in the first section of the poem and breaks off a single lilac blossom in the third section. Likewise, the singing bird is also isolated and alone in the swamp. Eventually, however, the speaker gathers strength by connecting to other mourners, who gather to watch the coffin pass by their houses. He realizes that a "silent sea of faces" (48) mourn the fallen president. Lincoln's death affects the entire United States, not just solitary individuals. In section 14, the speaker links hands with other mourners, and together they face the long night of wailing and weeping. Communal grieving serves two purposes: it lessens the collective grief of individuals, and it strengthens the ties binding those individuals together into a community. Individuals feel united by their common grief. The feeling of being an individual yet simultaneously united and tied to a community is an important tenet of democracy—and this tenet was severely tested during the period of secession and Civil War.

"When Lilacs Last in the Dooryard Bloom'd" eulogizes both Lincoln and the United States. The Civil War began in 1861, after eleven southern states seceded. Lincoln, elected in 1860 and re-elected in 1864, opposed slavery, which the southern economy relied on. American fought American in horrible battles on land and on sea, and more than 1.5 million soldiers were wounded or killed.

During the speaker's night of mourning, he has visions of the battle-field, including "battle-corpses, myriads of them, / And the white skeletons of young men" (178–179). At the time of Lincoln's assassination, General Robert E. Lee of the Confederate Army had just surrendered to General Ulysses S. Grant of the Union Army, and the Civil War was coming to an end. In mourning Lincoln, the speaker also mourns the other people who have fallen through American-on-American violence. Each year around springtime, the speaker will remember Lincoln. Whitman wants his readers to remember those people, including Lincoln, who fell so that democracy might live.

"O CAPTAIN! MY CAPTAIN!"

1

O Captain! my Captain! our fearful trip is done;
The ship has weather'd every rack, the prize we sought is won;
The port is near, the bells I hear, the people all exulting,
While follow eyes the steady keel, the vessel grim and daring:
But O heart! heart! heart!   5
O the bleeding drops of red,
Where on the deck my Captain lies,
Fallen cold and dead.

2

O Captain! my Captain! rise up and hear the bells;
Rise up—for you the flag is flung—for you the bugle trills;   10
For you bouquets and ribbon'd wreaths—for you the shores a-
crowding;
For you they call, the swaying mass, their eager faces turning;
Here Captain! dear father!
This arm beneath your head;
It is some dream that on the deck,   15
You've fallen cold and dead.

3

My Captain does not answer, his lips are pale and still;
My father does not feel my arm, he has no pulse nor will;
The ship is anchor'd safe and sound, its voyage closed and done;
From fearful trip, the victor ship, comes in with object won;   20
Exult, O shores, and ring, O bells!

> But I, *with mournful tread,*
>   *Walk the deck my Captain lies,*
>   *Fallen cold and dead.*

SUMMARY

The speaker addresses his captain as their ship approaches the harbor. They have survived terrible weather to arrive home amid cheering crowds. But the speaker notices blood on the deck because the captain has died. In the second stanza, the speaker urges the dead captain to wake up and hear the cheering crowds and ringing bells. People, eager to see the captain, have come to the harbor and brought flowers. The captain remains dead, looking as if he were alive. In the third stanza, the speaker realizes that the dead captain no longer sees, breathes, or senses. The trip has ended, the ship has safely docked, but the speaker walks with a "mournful tread" (22), for his captain is no longer alive.

ANALYSIS

Like "When Lilacs Last in the Dooryard Bloom'd," "O Captain! My Captain!" eulogizes Lincoln after his assassination in April 1865. Unlike most of Whitman's verse, this poem has a regular rhythm and rhyme scheme, and it also tells a straightforward story: a ship arrives into harbor as crowds cheer, but the sailors on board mourn their dead captain. Metaphorically, the ship symbolizes the United States, and the captain stands for Lincoln. Onshore crowds enthuse for the captain, unaware that he has died. Even though Lincoln has died, the country, like the ship, must continue on. The ship has "weather'd every rack" (2), much like the country weathered the fierce, bloody battles of the Civil War. Finally, the crowds represent the people of the United States, who elected Lincoln as president in 1860 and 1864 and who mourned his death. These crowds cheer for the end of the war, which was imminent after the Confederate surrender at Appomattox Court House in April 1865, just five days before Lincoln's death.

Whitman uses the poem to personalize the president's death and the deaths of American soldiers. From the poem's title, the speaker expresses his deep kinship to the fallen captain: the speaker calls him "my captain." The speaker then repeats this phrase five times throughout the poem. In stanza 2, the speaker deepens the intimacy of his relationship by calling the captain "dear father" (13). In stanza 3, the speaker cradles the dead captain in his arms, a gesture that physically conveys the sentiments of the previous stanzas. As the speaker explains, the "object" has been "won" (20) since the Union Army has won the war, but the cost of this win was much bloodshed and destruction on both sides. Lincoln's death gives mourners a chance to grieve for the nation as well as for the dead president. The grief felt for a single individual represents the grief felt for an almost inconceivable number of individuals and for the intangible effects of the war. Mourning the loss of Lincoln allows readers the opportunity to mourn the countless unknown men and women who died during the war—and to find the strength to carry on.

EMILY
DICKINSON

(1830–1886)

CONTEXT

Born in 1830 in the same house in which she died in 1886, Emily Dickinson led a relatively untroubled life in Amherst, Massachusetts, an isolated, bucolic New England town that did without most of the technological amenities afforded to the cities of that time, including running water and rail lines. She took very few extended trips, preferring to remain in Amherst, where she received a first-rate local education. Though the popular myth portrays Dickinson as reclusive and nunlike in her social behavior, Dickinson enjoyed an active social life within Amherst, joyously taking part in leisurely communal activities, such as sleigh rides, pleasure trips through the countryside, and parties. She also had several boyfriends in her youth, although neither she nor her sister, Lavinia, married.

Due to a lifelong illness, Dickinson developed a solitary nature. Throughout her life, Dickinson endured an eye ailment that left her vision severely impaired for long stretches of time. Two of her approximately dozen trips outside Amherst were to Boston to treat this problem. This malady was a source of depression for Dickinson, who came to value her eyesight dearly and made it a constant subject of her poetry. During times of especially savage affliction, Dickinson withdrew from company, spending long periods alone in her room, forbidden to read for fear of exacerbating the condition. This behavior probably led to rumors of reclusion and definitely led to Dickinson's notoriously bad handwriting, which has consistently confounded her posthumous editors in their attempts to transcribe her poetry for publication. Interestingly, some good did come from the ailment. While it inspired some of Dickinson's best poetry, it also provided a means for scholars to place her poems in chronological order through handwriting analysis.

Dickinson's rejection of faith during the Great Trinitarian Revival of 1850 informed a great deal of her poetry. Only twenty years old and still in school at the time, Dickinson witnessed the majority of her hometown, including all of her family, swept up in a religious revival that urged Christians to reaffirm their faith in a God who was unconditionally loving and benevolent. Those who believed in this God were to give themselves over completely to the service of the Lord and "convert" so that they might lead meaningful lives. Dickinson was ardently possessed of the desire to lead a meaningful life, but for her this act of self-relinquishment was unconscionable. Furthermore, Dickinson saw too much evidence of a difficult God who wounds and brings death in both the Bible and the world around her. Ultimately, she could not assent to the revivalists' insistence on an unquestioning acceptance of Christ's promises and their optimistic interpretation of God's nature. Instead, she elected the path of *Non serviam* ("I will not serve," in Latin), ready and willing to forsake a God who she thought was very capable of being unjust and altogether absent. Her poems are replete with depictions of this God, her **speakers** striving against his cruel omnipotence.

Perhaps Dickinson's greatest achievement as a poet was the development of her unique poetic voice. She was acutely aware that as a woman and a sufferer of a crippling eye ailment, she could not play the role of literary celebrity that her contemporary Walt Whitman had popularized by leading an extraordinary life. Dickinson nevertheless saw the necessity of having a representative voice, one that speaks to all of humanity, regardless of time, place, or situation. Her strategy for accomplishing this voice was the opposite of Whitman's: rather than imbibe her epoch's social and political movements—the Civil War, the Lincoln assassination, the turmoil of Reconstruction, the awesome power of industrialism—Dickinson turned away from them, toward the milieu of the mind. Social and historical events enter her poems obliquely, but the ultimate context of her poetry is the self. Although both Dickinson and the poetic voice she created changed over the years, the fundamental premise that informed her poetry remained constant: the panorama of the personal, the universe made up of the individual. Thus, even from her bedroom in Amherst, in a New England that had diminished in national importance since the American Revolution, Dickinson felt as if she could look into eternity and speak for all humankind in all times.

Dickinson published just eleven poems in her lifetime, although she wrote 1,775 poems between 1850 and 1883. In April of 1862, at the age of thirty-one, Dickinson enclosed four poems to her most encouraging friend of literary importance, Thomas Wentworth Higginson, one of which was the second version of "Safe in Their Alabaster Chambers." By this time, Dickinson had written roughly 300 poems and published a mere four. Higginson's response was subdued, politely advising Dickinson to delay attempts at publication. Dickinson took this cool response as a sign that the literary world likely would not be ready to receive her during her lifetime and that she must continue to write from Amherst in relative anonymity. Several hundred of these poems appeared in Dickinson's letters to friends and family, though the bulk of her poetry remained private, kept in her chambers in her Amherst home.

Of the eleven poems Dickinson published in her lifetime, six appeared in the Springfield *Daily Republican*, a literary journal once edited by Dickinson's father, Edward. At the time of their publication, Samuel Bowles was chief editor and had transformed the magazine into one of America's most prominent journals. Although the *Republican* was famous for printing the work of several "women-poets," as they were then called, Bowles did not have great esteem for Dickinson's work because it often did not conform to the standards of poetry written by women. Dickinson's five other publications appeared in 1864 in journals situated in the New York metropolitan area. It is likely that these poems found their way into print as a result of the efforts of several of Dickinson's friends and acquaintances who had contacts at the journals. Scholars suggest that these friends probably extracted the poems from letters Dickinson had written to them. In any case, one Dickinson scholar maintains that these poems were received favorably and that the journals likely would have continued to accept Dickinson's poems had she sent more. Dickinson actually had one more publication late in life, though technically she did not receive credit for it since it was published anonymously. In 1878, Dickinson's friend Helen Hunt Jackson, one of America's most popular female writers at that time, begged Dickinson to permit her to submit a poem to a collection of verse called *A Masque of Poets*. Interestingly, the poem Dickinson printed was one of the first she wrote, "Success is counted sweetest."

After Dickinson's death, her sister, Lavinia, discovered several poems carefully sewn and bound into notebooks among her personal effects and, determined to publish the contents, enlisted the help of friends to transcribe and edit them. The result—115 poems bound in a collection called *Poems of Emily Dickinson*—was an immediate success. A larger volume of 166 poems, titled *Poems, Second Series*, appeared in 1891, and *Poems, Third Series*, a volume of 168 poems, appeared in 1896. By this point, Dickinson was internationally famous. Readers were infatuated with the woman behind these curiously quiet poems and inquired about her of the citizens of Amherst, who told several conflicting stories about Dickinson, only adding to the sense of mystery that surrounded her life.

In 1914, Dickinson's niece and literary heir, Martha Dickinson Bianchi, put forth *The Single Hound*, then published *Further Poems* in 1929 and *Unpublished Poems* in 1935. By the 1945 publication of *Bolts of Melody*, nearly all of Dickinson's work saw publication. The final important publication of Dickinson's poetry came in 1955, when Thomas H. Johnson edited all 1,775 poems and assigned them numbers, based on handwriting analysis of Dickinson and the dates of letters that contained poems, which indicate chronological order. According to Johnson's ordering, poem 67 ("Success is counted sweetest") was the sixty-seventh that Dickinson wrote. While ordering, Johnson also undertook a significant editing of Dickinson's work: previous editors had systematized spelling, lowercased words she had capitalized, deleted dashes, altered punctuation, and generally cleaned up her **lyrics** and lines, and Johnson published Dickinson's poems exactly as she had transcribed them. Today, scholars refer to her poems by Johnson's number, by the poem's first line, or by a combination of those two systems (the third naming system is followed throughout this chapter). Through her poetry, Dickinson has come to define the very era that seemed to have such an imperceptible impact on her poetry. Along with Walt Whitman, Dickinson is considered to be the most important poetic voice of the nineteenth century.

EMILY DICKINSON

THEMES, MOTIFS & SYMBOLS

THEMES

THE INDIVIDUAL'S STRUGGLE WITH GOD

Dickinson devoted a great amount of her work to exploring the relationship between an individual and a Judeo-Christian God. Many poems describe a protracted rebellion against the God whom she deemed scornful and indifferent to human suffering, a divine being perpetually committed to subjugating human identity. In a sense, she was a religious poet. Unlike other religious poets, who inevitably saw themselves as subordinate to God, Dickinson rejected this premise in her poetry. She was dissatisfied with the notion that the poet can engage with God only insofar as God ordains the poet as his instrument, and she challenged God's dominion throughout her life, refusing to submit to his divine will at the cost of her self. Perhaps her most fiery challenge comes in "Mine by the Right of the White Election!" (528), in which the speaker roars in revolt against God, claiming the earth and heavens for herself or himself.

Elsewhere, Dickinson's poetry criticizes God not by speaking out directly against him, but by detailing the suffering he causes and his various affronts to an individual's sense of self. Though the speaker of "Tell all the Truth but tell it slant" (1129) never mentions God, the poem refers obliquely to his suppression of the apostle Paul in the last two lines. Here, the speaker describes how unmitigated truth (in the form of light) causes blindness. In the Bible (Acts 9:4), God decides to enlighten Paul by making him blind and then healing him on the condition that thenceforth Paul becomes "a chosen vessel" of God, performing his will. The speaker recoils from this instance of God's juggernaut-like domination of Paul in this poem but follows the poem's advice and tells the truth "slant," or indirectly, rather than censuring God directly. In another instance of implicit criticism, Dickinson portrays God as a murderous hunter of man in "My Life had stood—a Loaded Gun" (754), in which Death goes about gleefully executing people for his divine master. These poems are among the hundreds of verses in which Dickinson portrays God as aloof, cruel, invasive, insensitive, or vindictive.

THE ASSERTION OF THE SELF

In her work, Dickinson asserts the importance of the self, a **theme** closely related to Dickinson's censure of God. As Dickinson understood it, the mere act of speaking or writing is an affirmation of the will, and the call of the poet, in particular, is the call to explore and express the self to others. For Dickinson, the "self" entails an understanding of identity according to the way it systematizes its perceptions of the world, forms its goals and values, and comes to judgments regarding what it perceives.

Nearly all Dickinson's speakers behave according to the primacy of the self, despite the efforts of others to intrude on them. Indeed, the self is never more apparent in Dickinson's poetry than when the speaker brandishes it against some potentially violating force. In "They shut me up in Prose—" (613), the speaker taunts her captives, who have imprisoned her body but not her mind, which remains free and roaming. Because God most often plays the role of culprit as an omnipotent being, he can and does impose compromising conditions upon individuals according to his whim in Dickinson's work. Against this power, the self is essentially defined. The individual is subject to any amount of suffering, but so long as he or she remains a sovereign self, he or she still has that which separates him or her from other animate and inanimate beings.

THE POWER OF WORDS AND POETRY

Though Dickinson sequestered herself in Amherst for most of her life, she was quite attuned to the modern trends of thought that circulated throughout Europe and North America. Perhaps the most important of these was Charles Darwin's theory of evolution, published in 1859. Besides the tidal wave it unleashed in the scientific community, evolution throttled the notion of a world created by God's grand design. For Dickinson, who renounced obedience to God through the steps of her own mental evolution, this development only reinforced the opposition to the belief in a transcendent and divine design in an increasingly secularized world.

Dickinson began to see language and the word, which were formerly part of God's domain, as the province of the poet. The duty of the poet was to re-create, through words, a sense of the world as a place in which objects have an essential and almost mythic relationship to each other. Dickinson's poems often link abstract entities to

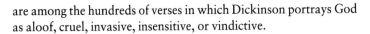

EMILY DICKINSON

physical things in an attempt to embrace or create an integral design in the world. This act is most apparent in her poems of definition, such as "'Hope' is the thing with feathers—" (254) or "Hope is a subtle Glutton" (1547). In these poems, Dickinson employs **metaphors** that assign physical qualities to the abstract feeling of "hope" in order to flesh out the nature of the word and what it means to human consciousness.

Nature as a "Haunted House"

In a letter to a friend, Dickinson once wrote: 'Nature is a Haunted House—but Art—a House that tries to be haunted." The first part of the sentence implies that the natural world is replete with mystery and false signs, which deceive humankind as to the purpose of things in nature as well as to God's purpose in the creation of nature. The sentence's second part reveals the poet's role. The poet does not exist merely to render aspects of nature, but rather to ascertain the character of God's power in the world.

For Dickinson, however, the characterizing of God's power proved to be complicated since she often abstained from using the established religious **symbols** for things in nature. This abstention is most evident in Dickinson's poem about a snake, "A narrow Fellow in the Grass" (986), in which Dickinson refrains from the easy reference to Satan in Eden. Indeed, in many of her nature poems, such as "A Bird came down the Walk" (328), Dickinson ultimately insists on depicting nature as unapologetically incomprehensible, and thus haunted.

Motifs

The Speaker's Unique Poetic Voice

Dickinson's speakers are numerous and varied, but each exhibits a similar voice, or distinctive **tone** and style. Poets create speakers to literally speak their poems; while these speakers might share traits with their creators or might be based on real historical figures, ultimately they are fictional entities distinct from their writers. Frequently, Dickinson employs the first person, which lends her poems the immediacy of a dialogue between two people, the speaker and the reader. She sometimes aligns multiple speakers in one poem with the use of the plural personal pronoun *we*. The first-person singular and plural allow Dickinson to write about specific experiences in the world: her speakers convey distinct, subjective emotions and individual thoughts rather than objective, concrete truths. Readers are thus invited to compare their experiences, emotions, and thoughts with those expressed in Dickinson's lyrics. By emphasizing the subjectivity, or individuality, of experience, Dickinson rails against those educational and religious institutions that attempt to limit individual knowledge and experience.

THE CONNECTION BETWEEN SIGHT AND SELF

For Dickinson, seeing is a form of individual power. Sight requires that the seer have the authority to associate with the world around her or him in meaningful ways and the sovereignty to act based on what she or he believes exists as opposed to what another entity dictates. In this sense, sight becomes an important expression of the self, and consequently the speakers in Dickinson's poems value it highly. The horror that the speaker of "I heard a Fly buzz—when I died—" (465) experiences is attributable to her loss of eyesight in the moments leading up to her death. The final utterance, "I could not see to see" (16), points to the fact that the last gasp of life, and thus of selfhood, is concentrated on the desire to "see" more than anything else. In this poem, sight and self are so synonymous that the end of one (blindness) translates into the end of the other (death).

In other poems, sight and self seem literally fused, a connection that Dickinson toys with by playing on the sonic similarity of the words *I* and *eye*. This wordplay abounds in Dickinson's body of work. It is used especially effectively in the third **stanza** of "The Soul selects her own Society—" (303), in which the speaker declares that she knows the soul, or the self. She commands the soul to choose one person from a great number of people and then "close the lids" of attention. In this poem, the "I" that is the soul has eyelike properties: closing the lids, an act that would prevent seeing, is tantamount to cutting off the "I" from the rest of society.

SYMBOLS

FEET

Feet enter Dickinson's poems self-referentially, since the words *foot* and *feet* denote poetic terms as well as body parts. In poetry, "feet" are the groups of syllables in a line that form a metrical unit. Dickinson's mention of feet in her poems generally serves the dual task of describing functioning body parts and commenting on poetry itself. Thus, when the speaker of "A narrow Fellow in the Grass" (986)

EMILY DICKINSON

remembers himself a "Barefoot" boy (11), he indirectly alludes to a time when his sense of poetry was not fully formed. Likewise, when the speaker of "After great pain, a formal feeling comes" (341) notes that feet are going around in his head while he is going mad, he points to the fact that his ability to make poetry is compromised.

STONE

In Dickinson's poems, stones represent immutability and finality: unlike flowers or the light of day, stones remain essentially unchanged. The speaker in "Safe in their Alabaster Chambers" (216) imagines the dead lying unaffected by the breezes of nature—and of life. After the speaker chooses her soul in "The Soul selects her own Society—" (303), she shuts her eyes "Like Stone—" (12), firmly closing herself off from sensory perception or society. A stone becomes an object of envy in "How happy is the little Stone" (1510), a poem in which the speaker longs for the rootless independence of a stone bumping along, free from human cares.

BIRDS

Dickinson uses the symbol of birds rather flexibly. In "A Bird came down the Walk" (328), the bird becomes an emblem of the unyielding mystery of nature, while in "'Hope' is the thing with feathers" (254), the bird becomes a **personification** of hope. Elsewhere, Dickinson links birds to poets, whose job is to sing whether or not people hear. In "Split—the Lark—and you'll find the Music" (861), Dickinson compares the sounds of birds to the lyrical sounds of poetry; the poem concludes by asking rhetorically whether its listeners now understand the truths produced by both birds and poetry. Like nature, symbolized by the bird, art produces soothing, truthful sounds.

Summary & Analysis

"Wild Nights—Wild Nights!" (249)

Wild Nights—Wild Nights!
Were I with thee,
Wild nights should be
Our luxury!

Futile—the Winds—   5
To a Heart in port—
Done with the Compass—
Done with the Chart!

Rowing in Eden—
Ah, the Sea!   10
Might I but moor—Tonight—
In Thee!

Summary

Twice crying out, "Wild Nights," the speaker addresses an absent lover, avowing that if they were together they would luxuriate in "Wild Nights" in the first stanza. In the second stanza, the speaker compares his or her heart to a seacraft, unaffected by sea breezes. There, safe in port, the speaker claims that the boat no longer needs the tools of navigation. In the final stanza, the speaker imagines Eden, which becomes linked to the ocean. Lines 11–12 ostensibly refer to this ocean, but they might also refer to the absent lover.

Analysis

Notable for its eroticism and rebelliousness, this poem is more straightforwardly sexual than much of Dickinson's other work. The speaker's initial exclamations make clear that she or he is fantasizing about rowdy and tempestuous sex. During the mid-nineteenth century, the word *luxury*, which appears in line 4, conveyed a meaning more lascivious than it does now. In Dickinson's New England, allegiance to social mores would have suppressed any outward expression of lust. Exhibiting any rebellious behavior would have guaranteed that the person be ostracized by his or her community, a situation portrayed in Nathaniel Hawthorne's *The Scarlet Letter* (1850). Like the novel, Dickinson's poem imagines the consequences of rebelling against the status quo, but, unlike the novel, the speaker imagines that his or her rebellion would lead to happiness in the form of sexual pleasure.

Throughout her life, Dickinson believed that individuals were capable of having relationships with God that did not involve authoritative religious figures or intermediaries. "Wild Nights" compares sexual ecstasy to Judeo-Christian paradise in the third stanza. The introduction of religious **imagery** removes any taint of sin from the sexual act and focuses instead on its sheer joy. Indeed, the word *eden* originally comes from the Greek *hedonia*, or pleasure. While the first "thee" (2) of the poem is lowercased, the second "thee" (12) is capitalized. This change in capitalization might signify a change in address, from the human lover in the first stanza to a divine in the third, thus linking the pleasure derived from religious worship to that derived from sexual activity. However, the poem expresses a fantasy, not reality, as evidenced by the speaker's use of the conditional tense. As the poem ends, the speaker remains within the community, worshiping and behaving conventionally but wishing that he or she could worship and behave freely and ecstatically, away from conventionalities.

"I HEARD A FLY BUZZ—WHEN I DIED" (465)

I heard a Fly buzz—when I died—
The Stillness in the Room
Was like the Stillness in the Air—
Between the Heaves of Storm—

The Eyes around—had wrung them dry—   5
And Breaths were gathering firm
For that last Onset—when the King
Be witnessed— in the Room—

I willed my Keepsakes—Signed away
What portion of me be   10

Assignable—and then it was
There interposed a Fly—

With Blue—uncertain, stumbling Buzz—
Between the light—and me—
And then the Windows failed—and then   *15*
I could not see to see—

SUMMARY

The speaker begins by stating that she heard a fly as she passed away. The subsequent lines and stanzas re-create the scene of death: the air is motionless, the mourners have ceased crying and are prepared for the speaker's passing, and the speaker feels God's presence. In the third stanza, the speaker gives away her worldly possessions as she hears the fly moving. She fixates on the buzzing sound as the light begins to dim and she begins to lose her sight.

ANALYSIS

The most distinctive feature of this poem is the lucid and quiet voice of the speaker during her last moments of life. Whereas some poets might have chosen to portray the final moments before death as hysterical, Dickinson chooses instead to portray them as peaceful and soft. Though the speaker hovers between existence (life) and nonexistence (death), her voice remains calm and unwavering. In this way, the poem acts as a soothing **hymn**, meant to comfort readers about the fate that awaits us all. Here, Dickinson uses the so-called common hymn **meter**: alternating lines of four beats (**iambic tetrameter**) and three beats (**iambic trimeter**). Employing a religious meter for nonreligious ends allows Dickinson to subvert organized religion and subtly reassert the importance of the self.

As in many of Dickinson's poems, an obsession with death constitutes the main subject matter. Here, death functions as the great divider: it separates the speaker from the company around her; it separates sight from sound, as the speaker expires in darkness, able only to hear the fly; and most important, it separates the body from the soul or spirit. God arrives to take the spirit of the dying speaker in lines 7–8. Much as the mourners witness the speaker's willing of possessions, they also witness the will of God being done as the speaker expires. While the soul goes with God, the body stays on earth, and the fly acts as a reminder of bodily decay. God and the fly come together at the moment of death, both poised to take from the speaker once she dies.

The primary action of the poem comes from the speaker's struggle to maintain an identity as she dies. God watches her death, waiting for her soul. Nature, in the form of the fly, also watches the speaker's death, waiting for her body. In between these opposing forces, the speaker monitors her own sensory experiences: hearing the fly, noticing the mourners, feeling God, giving away her objects, straining to see the light. The poem posits a strong connection between identity and perception—even personifying the mourners as "Eyes" (5)—and the speaker's final statement concerns her inability to see the window as the fly closes in. Although Dickinson employed the em dash throughout her poems, the concluding em dash of this poem implies that the speaker was literally cut off from speaking, that perhaps she had more left to say before she lost her sight and died.

"BECAUSE I COULD NOT STOP FOR DEATH—" (712)

Because I could not stop for Death—
He kindly stopped for me—
The Carriage held but just Ourselves—
And Immortality.

We slowly drove—He knew no haste 5
And I had put away
My labor and my leisure too,
For his Civility—
We passed the School, where Children strove
At recess—in the Ring— 10
We passed the Fields of Gazing Grain—
We passed the Setting Sun—

Or rather—He passed Us—
The Dews grew quivering and chill—
For only Gossamer, my Gown— 15
My Tippet—only Tulle—

We paused before a House that seemed
A Swelling of the Ground;
The Roof was scarcely visible,
The Cornice—in the Ground—   20

Since then—'tis Centuries—and yet
Feels shorter than the Day
I first surmised the Horses' Heads
Were toward Eternity—

SUMMARY

The speaker begins by imaging Death as a person riding in a wagon that picks her up. Death, the speaker, and "immortality" (4) leisurely ride together in the wagon. For the pleasure of Death's company, the speaker has given up her interests, her activities, and her work. In the third stanza, the wagon rides by schoolchildren at play in front of a school, as well as fields full of crops, as the sun sets. The speaker corrects herself, noting that the sun moves beyond the group and leaves behind a dampness that seeps through her clothes. Next, the wagon stops in front of a house that appears to be swallowed up by earth. She can barely see its top, which is almost buried. Since stopping at the house, notes the speaker, hundreds of years have passed. Despite the movement of time, the speaker still recalls the day on which she met Death and he took her "toward Eternity" (24).

ANALYSIS

"Because I could not stop for Death—" depicts the process of dying, as the speaker transitions from life to death to everlasting life (immortality). The first three stanzas describe the moment of death, and the final three stanzas describe what happens after death. Personified as a man, Death and his wagon go to victims according to his schedule, regardless of whether people might be ready to die. With the exception of those who kill themselves, people cannot choose when to die, as the speaker explains in the first stanza when she portrays death coming to her. His kindness, though, helps the speaker leave behind her life, and she willingly gets into his wagon. In stanza 3, the speaker, dying, transitions from real time, symbolized by the children playing, to immortality, symbolized by the sun's movement. The speaker's life ebbs away as the ride continues, echoed by the repetition of "We passed" in lines 9, 11, and 12. Stanza 4 begins the transition from a discussion of death to a discussion of life after death, or immortality. Whereas the first three stanzas alternate tetrameter (four-beat lines) with trimeter (three-beat lines), the final three stanzas alternate trimeter with tetrameter. Although she's dead, the speaker still has the ability to feel chilled, a reference to the cold earth of the grave. Similarly, the submerged house symbolizes a mausoleum (a large tomb). By the sixth stanza, the speaker has lost this ability to feel and can only remember the day she died.

The poem obviously describes death, but Dickinson also wryly uses the death imagery to comment on marriage. Death, personified as a man, drives a horse-and-buggy contraption, a vehicle commonly driven by male suitors in nineteenth-century New England. He finds a woman wearing a flimsy dress and shawl, which evokes a wedding dress, and he slowly takes her away from the life she knew to an unfamiliar place. In stanza 5, the couple stops before a house, much as a man would have brought his bride to a new home on their wedding day. Traditional Judeo-Christian wedding vows note that a couple marries "till death do them part," or for all of eternity. Nineteenth-century married women had virtually no rights: they couldn't vote, seek a divorce, inherit or own property, or, in some cases, work outside of the home. Married women were, in effect, the property of their spouses, and society, with support from evolutionists, such as Charles Darwin, largely considered women to be innately inferior to men. Within this sociohistorical context, marriage became a kind of death for a woman as an individual because her identity was subsumed beneath that of her husband.

"My Life had stood—a Loaded Gun—" (754)

My Life had stood—a Loaded Gun—
In Corners—till a Day
The Owner passed—identified—
And carried Me away—

And now We roam in Sovereign Woods—   5
And now We hunt the Doe—
And every time I speak for Him—
The Mountains straight reply—

And do I smile, such cordial light
Upon the Valley glow—
It is as a Vesuvian face   10
Had let its pleasure through—

And when at Night—Our good Day done—
I guard My Master's Head—
'Tis better than the Eider-Duck's   15
Deep Pillow—to have shared—

To foe of His—I'm deadly foe—
None stir the second time—
On whom I lay a Yellow Eye—
Or an emphatic Thumb—   20

Though I than He—may longer live
He longer must—than I—
For I have but the power to kill,
Without—the power to die—

EMILY DICKINSON

Summary

The speaker imagines himself or herself as a cocked firearm, waiting for its owner to pick it up and put it to use. In the second stanza, the speaker continues to imagine the self as a weapon, now being carried by the owner through forests as he hunts deer. Each time the owner fires the gun, the echo reverberates off nearby mountains. The third stanza also describes the gun firing, focusing on the blaze of light emitted by the barrel and comparing it to an erupting volcano. During the night, the gun protects its owner, and the speaker/gun says that this protection is better than a down-filled pillow. By the fifth stanza, the speaker/gun states that its owner's enemies become its enemies and boasts that it has the power to kill these enemies. In the last stanza, the speaker/gun explains that while it may live longer than its owner, actually its owner will live longer through Christian rebirth. The speaker/gun concludes by stating that although it can kill, it cannot die (subtly implying that as an inanimate object, it cannot be reborn through religion).

ANALYSIS

Scholars group Dickinson's poems into several categories, including hymns, allegories, complaints, and riddles. "My Life had stood—a Loaded Gun" falls into the latter category: not only does the poem itself resembles a mystery begging to be solved, but its final stanza presents a specific riddle. The poem forces readers to guess the identity of the speaker, who compares herself or himself to a dangerous weapon capable of killing animals and people. The final stanza probably refers to the Bible, specifically 1 Corinthians, in which St. Paul discusses the power of Christ to subdue his enemies, including death. Read this way, the poem implies that death is the gun, being mastered by its owner, Christ as God. Since Christ, as the human embodiment of God, is subject to death, death may outlive Christ. But with Christ's resurrection, Christ ultimately outlives death—and makes it possible for others to do the same.

Dickinson obliquely refers to current political and social events in her work, and this poem subtly comments on pressing nineteenth-century issues, including the subjugation of women and slavery. In the poem, a "Master" (14) literally moves the speaker, metaphorically transformed into a gun, from place to place. This speaker/gun kills at the master's behest, protects him while he sleeps, and defends him from enemies. A related but alternative reading of the poem imagines the speaker as a woman, subjugated to her "owner" (3), or husband. Neither slaves nor women had much power in Dickinson's day since both groups of people were owned: masters literally owned slaves, whereas the lack of rights for women made them the de facto property of their husbands. In 1850, Congress passed the Fugitive Slave Act, which made it a crime to aid or abet runaway slaves. Also, the law sanctioned the arrests of suspected fugitive slaves without warrant, and suspects were not given either a trial or the opportunity to defend themselves. Essentially, the act legalized the harassment of African-American freedmen and freedwomen. Freedmen, freedwomen, and slaves were hunted down, like the deer in the poem, and captured. Seen from this perspective, the poem's tone becomes ironic, particularly when the speaker feels happiness in the second stanza at having accomplished a full day's work. The ability to comment indirectly but forcefully on contemporary issues stands as another hallmark of Dickinson's greatness.

"A narrow Fellow in the Grass" (986)

A narrow Fellow in the Grass
Occasionally rides—
You may have met Him—did you not
His notice sudden is—

The Grass divides as with a Comb—   5
A spotted shaft is seen—
And then it closes at your feet
And opens further on—

He likes a Boggy Acre
A Floor too cool for Corn—   10
Yet when a Boy, and Barefoot—
I more than once at Noon
Have passed, I thought, a Whip lash
Unbraiding in the Sun
When stooping to secure it,   15
It wrinkled, and was gone—

Several of Nature's People
I know, and they know me—
I feel for them a transport
Of cordiality—   20

But never met this Fellow,
Attended, or alone,
Without a tighter breathing,
And Zero at the Bone—

Summary

The speaker describes a slithering snake that he suddenly sees moving through the grass. He addresses the reader, telling us that we might have met this snake at some point as well. In the second stanza, the speaker imagines the way the grass parts as the snake slithers through it. Stanza 3 details both the snake, which generally prefers wet and cold areas, and the speaker, who as a child sometimes spied a coiled snake sunning itself in the afternoon. In the fourth stanza, the speaker explains that he has great knowledge of many animals in the animal kingdom and feels a particular kinship with most animals, except for the snake. In fact, as he explains in the final stanza, whenever he sees a snake, his breathing becomes strained and he gets a chill.

ANALYSIS

"A narrow Fellow in the Grass" was originally published and much admired in Dickinson's lifetime under the title "The Snake." Many critics classify this work as one of her nature poems. Like "A Bird came down the Walk" (328), another nature poem that imagines a brief interaction between a human and an animal, "A narrow Fellow" describes the observations and experiences of its speaker as he confronts a snake. The speaker's dislike of slithery creatures affects every aspect of the poem—from its imagery to its **similes** to its alliterative sounds. Indeed, "s" sounds dominate the poem: "sudden" (4), "spotted shaft is seen" (6), "stooping to secure it" (15). As we read the poem, the consonance, or the repetition of identical consonant sounds, causes us to sound or hiss like snakes. Here Dickinson closely links the form and content of her poem for dramatic effect: we read about snakes as we perform like snakes during the act of reading.

Throughout her work, Dickinson uses metaphors to convey multiple meanings, usually one obvious meaning and at least another subtle, more interesting meaning. In this poem, the speaker obviously fears snakes, which he refers to as "narrow Fellow[s]" (1). Thus, "fellow," a slangy, rather stilted term for "friend," stands in for the word *snake*. In addition to this meaning, some critics have read the opening line as a reference to the male phallus. Other words used to refer to the snake have a sexual connotation, including "shaft" (6) and "Whip" (13), and line 4 can be interpreted as a reference to an erection. Seen this way, the poem becomes a highly metaphoric discussion of the heterosexual act, like the poem "Wild Nights—Wild Nights." Unlike the speaker of that poem, the speaker of this poem fears the sexual act, as evidenced by the final stanza, in which he describes the tightening and chill in his chest felt when he sees snakes. In stanza 4, he explains that he has found other ways of relating to people and enjoying interpersonal relationships. By expressing distaste for sex, the speaker criticizes nineteenth-century gender roles, which made women subservient to and bestowed all the power onto men: this speaker does not want to participate in acts, including sex, that envision or establish women as less than equal to men.

The poem bounces between two distinct time periods, the civilized present and the wild past, as a way of commenting on the taming of the New England frontier. Writers frequently imagined the wilderness as a dangerous place, full of scary beings and unknown horrors. This American literary tradition began with the Puritans, who had to tame the land in order to establish settlements, and extended through the nineteenth century and beyond (M. Night Shyamalan's 2004 movie, *The Village*, graphically portrays the dangers of the dark forest). Dickinson, though, slyly makes fun of the speaker's fear: despite his trappings of urbanity, the adult speaker remains afraid of a harmless snake. In his youth, however, he would playfully mistake snakes for "whips" and try to grab at them, although their slimy quickness always eluded his grasp. Growing into an adult caused the speaker to lose this playfulness and curiosity about the world, much as a snake sheds its skin, and his aversion to snakes perhaps stems from the knowledge that he has lost a significant part of himself as he entered adulthood. Similarly, Dickinson implies that we have lost a significant part of ourselves by taming the wilderness.

GERARD MANLEY HOPKINS

(1844–1889)

CONTEXT

Gerard Manley Hopkins was born on July 28, 1844, to a family of comfortable means in Stratford, Essex. Like much of England during the nineteenth century, Essex was in the process of becoming industrialized, as human labor transitioned from farm work to factory work and increasing numbers moved to cities to find jobs. Hopkins's father supported Hopkins's artistic pursuits: the elder Hopkins occasionally wrote verse and, later, two other sons became artists. In 1854, Hopkins began attending the Highgate School, where he was a brilliant student and where he won prizes for two poems. Both poems were noted for their musicality and sensuality, characteristics, in part, inspired by Hopkins's love of the poetry of John Keats. In 1863, Hopkins entered Balliol College at Oxford University to study classics.

In 1866, Hopkins converted from Anglicanism to Roman Catholicism, a conversion that would have significant personal and poetical repercussions. As a child, Hopkins had attended the Anglican Church, also called the Church of England, with his family. Anglicanism began in 1534, when King Henry VIII broke England's religious ties to the Roman Catholic Church after the pope refused to annul the king's marriage to Katharine of Aragon. Although Anglicanism shares several beliefs with Catholicism, Anglicans, unlike Catholics, believe that the English king is the earthly head of the church—not the pope. While at Oxford, Hopkins met John Henry Newman, who spearheaded the movement to bring the Anglican Church more in line with the rituals of the Catholic Church. Hopkins's conversion and subsequent decision to become a Jesuit priest eroded his relationship with his family. As part of his Jesuit training, Hopkins withdrew from the pleasures of life, including writing poetry, subscribing instead to the core Jesuit values of poverty, chastity, and obedience. He traveled to various colleges across England to perfect his religious practice and burned all of his early poems.

Encouraged by church leaders, Hopkins began writing poetry again in 1876, and his work reflected his strong religious beliefs. After hearing that five nuns had drowned, Hopkins wrote the long **ode** *The Wreck of the Deutschland* (1876). Although Hopkins submitted it to a Jesuit magazine, the editors refused to publish it, due to its startling uniqueness. Hopkins continued writing for the remainder of his life, but he never again tried to publish: he felt both that seeking fame as a poet contrasted with his life as a priest and that his verse was unique and too difficult to find readers. In his poetry, Hopkins tried to describe his worship of God, as well as the bounties and beauties of the earthly world, which he felt were threatened by the effects of Industrial Revolution. Electricity and railroads changed the way goods were manufactured and transported throughout Europe during the nineteenth century. People began leaving the rural areas to find work in the cities, which suffered from overpopulation, poverty, and disease. The novels of Charles Dickens, George Eliot, and Thomas Hardy explore the effects of the Industrial Revolution on English cities and country towns.

After his ordination as a Jesuit priest in 1877, Hopkins traveled across England, doing parish work, and he saw the dismal environment created by urbanization and industrialization. The bleak reality of cities, such as Liverpool, stood in stark contrast to the natural world, which Hopkins believed was symbolic of God's wonders. Hopkins wrote several devotional **sonnets** connecting nature and religion, including "Hurrahing in Harvest," "The Starlight Night," "Pied Beauty," and "The Windhover," in 1877 to celebrate his ordination. He was appointed professor of Greek and Latin at University College in Dublin in 1884, following a fellowship in classics at the Royal University of Ireland. During this period in Ireland, Hopkins composed a series of sonnets later termed the "terrible sonnets," poems without any sense of hope that depict Hopkins's emotional weariness and sense of isolation. Shortly after this bleak artistic period, Hopkins suffered a series of physical setbacks. He died of typhoid at age forty-five, in 1889.

Hopkins developed an original, complex theory of poetry: poems should strive to express the "inscape" and "instress" of all things in the universe. The term *inscape* connotes the constantly shifting pattern, design, set of characteristics, or self of an object or thing that makes that object or thing unique. When we intellectually or emotionally grasp the inscape of an object or thing, we can understand why God created that object or thing. Hopkins called this act of recognition *instress*. In the performance of instress—that is, in the detection of the imprint of God on an object—humans are brought closer to Christ. For Hopkins, poetry became a way to enact inscape and instress, to both identify the distinctiveness of an object and to demonstrate that distinctiveness to readers as celebration of God and Christ.

GERARD M. HOPKINS

To convey inscape and instress, Hopkins created a **meter** called **sprung rhythm**. He also gave each poem a unique design on the page. The most common meter in English poetry is **iambic pentameter**, a line of five **feet** alternating one unstressed and one stressed syllable per foot. Sprung rhythm counts only stressed syllables, creating a flexible metrical structure that allows for much variation in word choice and for a variable number of syllables per foot. Every line of sprung rhythm contains an initial stressed syllable followed by one to three unstressed syllables. Hopkins believed that sprung rhythm was closer to natural speech, as opposed to the "da-dum, da-dum" regularity of iambic pentameter. Sometimes Hopkins used diacritical marks to indicate where the stress should fall on a word, as in the first two lines from "Spring and Fall" (1880): "Márgarét, áre you gríeving / Over Goldengrove unleaving?" The first line of "Pied Beauty" (1877) scans as follows: "Glóry | bé to | Gód for | dáppled | thíngs—," where the acute accent indicates stress and the vertical line separates feet.

Upon his death in 1889, Hopkins appointed his good friend and longtime correspondent Robert Bridges, former poet laureate of England, as literary executor. Bridges waited until 1918 to bring out Hopkins's first book. For many years, critics classified Hopkins along with the modernist poets of the early twentieth century, including T. S. Eliot, W. B. Yeats, and Ezra Pound. Indeed, the originality of Hopkins's syntax and rejection of traditional meter has more in common with the free verse of Eliot and Pound than with his Victorian contemporaries Alfred, Lord Tennyson and John Keats. Now, however, anthologies group Hopkins with other nineteenth-century poets to emphasize their shared **themes**, including worries about the effects of industrialization, praise for the beauty of the natural world, distaste for urban environments, and attention to human consciousness and perceptions.

THEMES, MOTIFS & SYMBOLS

THEMES

THE MANIFESTATION OF GOD IN NATURE

Hopkins used poetry to express his religious devotion, drawing his images from the natural world. He found nature inspiring and developed his theories of inscape and instress to explore the manifestation of God in every living thing. According to these theories, the recognition of an object's unique identity, which was bestowed upon that object by God, brings us closer to Christ. Similarly, the beauty of the natural world—and our appreciation of that beauty—helps us worship God. Many poems, including "Hurrahing in Harvest" and "The Windhover," begin with the speaker praising an aspect of nature, which then leads the speaker into a consideration of an aspect of God or Christ. For instance, in "The Starlight Night," the speaker urges readers to notice the marvels of the night sky and compares the sky to a structure, which houses Christ, his mother, and the saints. The stars' link to Christianity makes them more beautiful.

THE REGENERATIVE POWER OF NATURE

Hopkins's early poetry praises nature, particularly nature's unique ability to regenerate and rejuvenate. Throughout his travels in England and Ireland, Hopkins witnessed the detrimental effects of industrialization on the environment, including pollution, urbanization, and diminished rural landscapes. While he lamented these effects, he also believed in nature's power of regeneration, which comes from God. In "God's Grandeur," the speaker notes the wellspring that runs through nature and through humans. While Hopkins never doubted the presence of God in nature, he became increasingly depressed by late nineteenth-century life and began to doubt nature's ability to withstand human destruction. His later poems, the so-called terrible sonnets, focus on images of death, including the harvest and vultures picking at prey. Rather than depict the glory of nature's rebirth, these poems depict the deaths that must occur in order for the cycle of nature to continue. "Thou

Art Indeed Just, Lord" (1889) uses parched roots as a metaphor for despair: the speaker begs Christ to help him because Christ's love will rejuvenate him, just as water helps rejuvenate dying foliage.

MOTIFS

COLORS

According to Hopkins's theory of inscape, all living things have a constantly shifting design or pattern that gives each object a unique identity. Hopkins frequently uses color to describe these inscapes. "Pied Beauty" praises God for giving every object a distinct visual pattern, from sunlight as multicolored as a cow to the beauty of birds' wings and freshly plowed fields. Indeed, the word *pied* means "having splotches of two or more colors." In "Hurrahing in Harvest," the speaker describes "azorous hung hills" (9) that are "very-violet-sweet" (10). Elsewhere, the use of color to describe nature becomes more complicated, as in "Spring." Rather than just call the birds' eggs "blue," the speaker describes them as resembling pieces of the sky and thus demonstrates the interlocking order of objects in the natural world. In "The Windhover," the speaker yokes adjectives to convey the peculiar, precise beauty of the bird in flight—and to convey the idea that nature's colors are so magnificent that they require new combinations of words in order to be imagined.

ECSTATIC, TRANSCENDENT MOMENTS

Many of Hopkins's poems feature an ecstatic outcry, a moment at which the speaker expresses his transcendence of the real world into the spiritual world. The words *ah*, *o*, and *oh* usually signal the point at which the poem moves from a description of nature's beauty to an overt expression of religious sentiment. "Binsey Poplars" (1879), a poem about the destruction of a forest, begins with a description of the downed trees but switches dramatically to a lamentation about the human role in the devastation; Hopkins signals the switch by not only beginning a new stanza but also by beginning the line with "O" (9). Hopkins also uses exclamation points and appositives to articulate ecstasy: in "Carrion Comfort," the speaker concludes with two cries to Christ, one enclosed in parentheses and punctuated with an exclamation point and the other punctuated with a period. The words and the punctuation alert the reader to the instant at which the poem shifts from secular concerns to religious feeling.

Bold Musicality

To express inscape and instress, Hopkins experimented with rhythm and sound to create sprung rhythm, a distinct musicality that resembles the patterns of natural speech in English. The flexible meter allowed Hopkins to convey the fast, swooping falcon in "The Windhover" and the slow movement of heavy clouds in "Hurrahing in Harvest." To indicate how his lines should be read aloud, Hopkins often marked words with acute accents, as in "As Kingfishers Catch Fire" and "Spring and Fall." **Alliteration**, or the juxtaposition of similar sounds, links form with content, as in this line from "God's Grandeur": "And all is seared with trade; bleared, smeared with toil" (6). In the act of repeating "red," our mouths make a long, low sound that resembles the languid movements of humans made tired from factory labor. Elsewhere, the alliterative lines become another way of worshiping the divine because the sounds roll and bump together in pleasure. "Spring" begins, "Nothing is so beautiful as Spring— / When weeds, in wheels, shoot long and lovely and lush" (1–2).

Symbols

Birds

Birds appear throughout Hopkins's poetry, frequently as stand-ins for God and Christ. In "The Windhover," a poem dedicated to Christ, the speaker watches a falcon flying through the sky and finds traces of Christ in its flight path. The beauty of the bird causes the speaker to reflect on the beauty of Christ because the speaker sees a divine imprint on all living things. Similarly, "As Kingfishers Catch Fire" meditates on the innate behaviors and patterns of beings in the universe: the inscape of birds manifests in their flights, much as the inscape of stone manifests in the sound of flowing water. Christ appears everywhere in these inscape manifestations. In Christian iconography, birds serve as reminders that there is life away from earth, in heaven—and the Holy Ghost is often represented as a dove. "God's Grandeur" portrays the Holy Ghost literally, as a bird big enough to brood over the entire world, protecting all its inhabitants.

Fire

Hopkins uses images of fire to symbolize the passion behind religious feeling, as well as to symbolize God and Christ. In "God's Grandeur," Hopkins compares the glory of God and the beautiful bounty of his world to fire, a miraculous presence that warms and beguiles those nearby. He links fire and Christ in "The Windhover," as the speaker sees a flame burst at the exact moment in which he realizes that the falcon contains Christ. Likewise, "As Kingfishers Catch Fire" uses the phrase "catch fire" as a metaphor for the birds' manifestation of the divine imprint, or inscape, in their natural behavior. In that poem too, the dragonflies "draw flame" (1), or create light, to show their distinct identities as living things. Nature's fire—lightning—appears in other poems as a way of demonstrating the innate signs of God and Christ in the natural world: God and Christ appear throughout nature, regardless of whether humans are there to witness their appearances.

TREES
Trees appear in Hopkins's poems to dramatize the earthly effects of time and to show the detrimental effects of humans on nature. In "Spring and Fall," the changing seasons become a metaphor for maturation, aging, and the life cycle, as the speaker explains death to a young girl: all mortal things die, just as all deciduous trees lose their leaves. In "Binsey Poplars," the speaker mourns the loss of a forest from human destruction, then urges readers to be mindful of damaging the natural world. Cutting down a tree becomes a metaphor for the larger destruction being enacted by nineteenth-century urbanization and industrialization. Trees help make an area more beautiful, but they do not manifest God or Christ in the same way as animate objects, such as animals or humans.

SUMMARY & ANALYSIS

"PIED BEAUTY"

> Glory be to God for dappled things—
>   For skies of couple-colour as a brinded cow;
>   For rose-moles all in stipple upon trout that swim;
> Fresh-firecoal chestnut-falls; finches' wings;
>   Landscape plotted and pieced—fold, fallow, and plough;   5
>   And áll trádes, their gear and tackle and trim.
>
> All things counter, original, spare, strange;
>   Whatever is fickle, freckled (who knows how?)
>   With swift, slow; sweet, sour; adazzle, dim;
> He fathers-forth whose beauty is past change: 10
>   Praise him.

SUMMARY

The speaker begins by praising God for the endless color and variety visible in the world, embodied in "dappled things" (1). He describes a series of vivid images in the first stanza, including the multicolored heavens, fish, birds, freshly plowed land, and the equipment used by humans to farm. In the second stanza, the speaker lists several adjectives that describe all living things, which were created by God. Unlike the beauty of nature, the beauty of God is steadfast and unchanging. A simple command to pray concludes the poem.

ANALYSIS

This poem, written shortly after Hopkins's Jesuit ordination, celebrates God by listing the myriad beautiful things found in nature. The poem demonstrates Hopkins's theories of inscape and instress: the speaker recognizes and lists the special characteristics that make each object unique. In the first stanza, the speaker precisely identifies the unique characteristic color of several objects, but the second stanza lumps together all living beings, calling them all "counter, original, spare, strange" (7). God created these multihued objects, including tools used by humans, and it is to him that we should give thanks, according to the poem. In our recognition of the objects' beauty, we honor God. Hopkins makes this meaning clear in the final line, in which the speaker extols readers to "Praise him." Simply reading the poem is not enough, however, so the speaker must tell us to actively worship God. This abrupt finish, coupled with the white space that precedes the phrase, gives us space to worship God in our own way. Rather than didactically tell us how to worship, the speaker merely extols us to do so.

Throughout the poem, Hopkins plays with words, punctuation, and syntax, cramming sounds together to create a dappled lyrical effect. The first stanza juxtaposes both singular adjectives and objects, whereas the second stanza lists adjectives that describe all living things. Like God, who creates all this beauty, the poet's powers of perception and creation range from the specifics of the first stanza to the generalities of the second. He relies on alliteration, including "l" and "p" sounds in line 5, and "s" and "d" sounds in line 9. Rather than use prepositional phrases, Hopkins links colors to their objects, as in "rose-mole" (3), and links descriptive adjectives to one another, as in "couple-colour" (2). Dashes help control the poem's pace, eradicating the need for a **caesura** or pause for breath. The poem, with its contrasting sounds and varying pacing, becomes as musically textured as the visions it describes.

"GOD'S GRANDEUR"

> The World is charged with the grandeur of God.
>   It will flame out, like shining from shook foil;
>   It gathers to a greatness, like the ooze of oil
> Crushed. Why do men then now not reck his rod?
> Generations have trod, have trod, have trod;   5
>   And all is seared with trade; bleared, smeared with toil;
>   And wears man's smudge and shares man's smell: the soil
> Is bare now, nor can foot feel, being shod.
>
> And for all this, nature is never spent;
>   There lives the dearest freshness deep down things;   10
> And though the last lights off the black West went
>   Oh, morning, at the brown brink eastward, springs—
> Because the Holy Ghost over the bent
>   World broods with warm breast and with ah! bright wings.

SUMMARY

This sonnet begins with the claim that the world is filled with the glory of God. The first four lines of the poem compare God's glory to a flash of light, then to a gathering pool of oil (as in olive oil, not as in petroleum). Next the speaker wonders rhetorically why humans choose to disregard the wrath of God. The final lines of the stanza bemoan the menial toil and factory labor of modern society, which deadens its workers through boredom, ruins the environment, and separates humans from the natural world. In the second stanza, the speaker explains that despite this destruction, nature endures, constantly refreshed by a wellspring that lurks deep below the surface of all things. The speaker describes the dawn's sunlight rising from the east to illuminate the darkness of the west, a process driven by the Holy Ghost, who covers the world with its brilliant, cozy wings.

ANALYSIS

Hopkins's sonnet expresses love for God, the Holy Ghost, and nature. Like a traditional sonnet, this poem idolizes a beloved and praises the beloved's qualities and capabilities. Unlike a traditional sonnet, however, Hopkins's work praises otherworldly religious figures—God and the Holy Ghost—rather than an earthly lady. In this poem, Christian deities receive the speaker's passion, love, and devotion. As is typical of **Petrarchan (Italian) sonnets**, the poem has an interlocking *abbaabba cdcdcd* rhyme scheme, the first stanza explains a theme, and the second stanza elaborates and twists that theme: here, the first stanza both praises the manifestation of God in nature and describes the human destruction of the natural world. The second stanza explains that the Holy Ghost gently cups the earth, allowing nature to both withstand its human destruction and manifest the divine.

From its first line, the poem displays a fascination with nineteenth-century technology, even as it laments the modern condition of humans separated from the soil by industrialization. The speaker compares God's glory to an electrical current that surges through the world: like electricity, this current is not always seen, but it always exists, and it can be both marvelous, as demonstrated by nature's beauty, and destructive, as demonstrated by the "rod" in line 4. This rod implies both a weapon of punishment and a lightning rod, which harnesses nature's own electricity. In Hopkins's day, scientists experimented with gold-leaf foil, and they also discovered the power of electricity, which many attributed to divine forces. Instead of ignoring or demeaning the discoveries of modern science, Hopkins incorporates them into his poem of worship, and he takes these discoveries as further evidence of God's wonder and magnificence.

Throughout the poem, the speaker laments the separation of humans from nature, but the reasons for this separation prove historically and socially complex. Humans can no longer feel the earth beneath their feet, nor do they fear the wrath of a God who feels ignored and disrespected by their indifference. Rather than simply attribute the separation to present-day industrialization, however, the speaker indicts past "generations," who "have trod, have trod" (5). Humans have imprinted their labor and work, as well as their smell, into the earth. Neglect of God leads to neglect of the environment and vice versa, but the problem began long before the nineteenth century. The poem proposes close attention as a solution to the separation: evidence of God and the Holy Ghost surround us, if only we care to notice, the poem implies. While the man-made lights of the West flicker on and off, the light of God—that is, the dawn's light—ceaselessly appears day after day, a reminder of God's power.

"THE WINDHOVER"
TO CHRIST OUR LORD

I caught this morning morning's minion, king-
   dom of daylight's dauphin, dapple-dawn-drawn Falcon, in
      his riding
   Of the rolling level underneath him steady air, and striding
High there, how he rung upon the rein of a wimpling wing
In his ecstasy! then off, off forth on swing,   5
   As a skate's heel sweeps smooth on a bow-bend: the hurl and
      gliding
   Rebuffed the big wind. My heart in hiding
Stirred for a bird,—the achieve of; the mastery of the thing!

Brute beauty and valour and act, oh, air, pride, plume, here
   Buckle! and the fire that breaks from thee then, a billion   10
Times told lovelier, more dangerous, O my chevalier!

   No wonder of it: shéer plód makes plough down sillion
Shine, and blue-bleak embers, ah my dear,
   Fall, gall themselves, and gash gold-vermillion.

SUMMARY

Hopkins dedicates this sonnet to Jesus Christ. In the first stanza, the speaker glimpses a falcon, and he describes the falcon's flight in highly alliterative language for the next several lines. Watching the bird's powerful presence and impressive swooping lifts the speaker's spirits, but the speaker also feels humbled by the experience. In the second stanza, the speaker labels the bird with royal names and continues to describe its flight. As the bird flies, the surrounding air moves, shifts, and bursts into a flame more fantastic than the bird itself. In the final stanza, the speaker claims to not be surprised to have experienced such a vision because, as he metaphorically explains, his faith has prepared him for such wondrous spiritual apparitions. He compares his faith to a freshly plowed field, as well as to a fire, in which blue embers and gold flashes sparkle and shine.

ANALYSIS

This sonnet asks its readers to make an imaginative leap similar to that made by its speaker: like the speaker, we must imagine a bird taking on the figurative shape of Christ. After the dedication, at no point does the poem mention Christ, yet the poem is filled with implicit religious symbolism. Each image contains a religious undertone, a literary technique that mirrors Hopkins's belief in instress, or the manifestation of the religious spirit that underlies all living things and provides them with unique identities. In the falcon's fells and swoops, the speaker commits an act of inscape by recognizing Christ in the falcon's instress. This recognition prompts him to name the falcon "dauphin" (2) and "chevalier" (11), French terms for royalty that suggest valor, heroism, and sacrifice, characteristics of Christ's martyrdom. The speaker also claims that the air around the bird breaks into flames, a fantastical symbol of purification and martyrdom. Finally, the speaker recalls falling embers that "gall themselves, and gash gold-vermillion" (14), a reference to Christ's wound from a soldier's spear during the crucifixion. Gold-vermillion, the color of his regal blood, flowed to purify the world' sins. Hopkins's use of figurative language and **allusions** evokes Christ without describing him outright.

The pattern of this poem is typical of so many of Hopkins's other sonnets in that a sensuous experience or description leads to a set of moral and religious reflections. Hopkins shifts the poem's focus from a depiction of the bird to the response of the speaker's heart to an expression of the speaker's faith. When the mind perceives the glory of God by witnessing some element of nature, its physical body responds by quickening the pace of heartbeats, as portrayed in lines 7–8. The verb *buckle* acts as the poem's hinge: the word describes the fastening together of the physical and the mental, of the natural and the spiritual, and of the external vision and internal passion. But the word also describes the act of acquiescence or crumpling, as in the phrase *my knees buckled*. In this second sense, the word describes the kneeling prayer position or an act performed by a body overcome with religious fervor. The poem concludes by reminding readers of the quotidian nature of faith: like a newly farmed field or crackling fire, religious visions are open to anyone who deigns to pay attention to the natural world.

"SPRING AND FALL"
TO A YOUNG CHILD

GERARD M. HOPKINS

> Márgarét, áre you gríeving
> Over Goldengrove unleaving?
> Leáves, líke the things of man, you
> With your fresh thoughts care for, can you?
> Áh! ás the heart grows older   5
> It will come to such sights colder
> By and by, nor spare a sigh
> Though worlds of wanwood leafmeal lie;
> And yet you wíll weep and know why.
> Now no matter, child, the name: 10
> Sórrow's spríngs áre the same.
> Nor mouth had, no nor mind, expressed
> What heart heard of, ghost guessed:
> It ís the blight man was born for,
> It is Margaret you mourn for.   15

SUMMARY

The speaker asks Margaret if she is crying over the sight of the trees in Goldengrove, which have lost their leaves in anticipation of winter. He consoles her by explaining that as she grows older, she will be less affected by and, in fact, will become numb to such sights as bare forests. But, he explains, she will still cry, albeit for a different reason. Eventually, she will understand that she cries for herself, for the human condition that promises death to all who live. She will learn that a mourning for mortality lies beneath all tears, even when it appears that the tears have another, more immediate cause. The heart, unlike the mind, understands the common source of sorrow and conjures a devastation that speaks to our emotional unconscious. Margaret is really crying for Margaret, a being who will someday die, a victim of the same cycle of nature that causes trees to shed their leaves.

ANALYSIS

This poem comes from Hopkins's so-called terrible sonnets, a group of poems that share overtones of despair, helplessness, and a preoccupation with human sorrow. In these poems, Hopkins grappled with physical and spiritual isolation and asked questions of an angry, wrathful God. Like his earlier sonnets, "Spring and Fall" relies on an ecstatic moment of transformation to shift the poem's content from a specific instance of observation or interaction to a universal truth. Here, the "ah" (5) transforms the poem from a fictional encounter between an older, wiser adult and a young child into a lyrical **exegesis** on grief, mortality, and hopelessness. Unlike the earlier sonnets, there is no hope, beauty, or redemption: the bare trees symbolize our eventual death, or "blight" (14). We have no choice but to acknowledge the poem's truth: we too shall die.

The very structure of the poem echoes its transition from child-like concerns to mournful lamentations. In the first four lines, the poem has a singsong, nursery-rhyme meter. "Goldengrove," the name of the forest, implies an Eden filled with lush trees and fairies, and the young Margaret perhaps cries for the loss of her play area. By line 5, however, the poem's syntax becomes increasingly fractured and disconnected, as verbs are separated from their subjects and modifiers. Rather than employ images, figurative language, or other poetic techniques, the speaker attempts to use reason to explain sadness to Margaret. But the speaker—and the poem—conclude with the realization that death and its attendant collective human sorrow can only be understood with the heart and the spirit or soul, not with the mind. While the speaker laments the human condition, he also subtly implies that the real tragedy lies in the inability of humans to articulate deep grief or sadness. The poem itself mourns the inability of poetry to adequately express matters of the heart or soul.

GERARD M. HOPKINS

WILLIAM BUTLER YEATS

(1865–1939)

CONTEXT

William Butler Yeats was born near Dublin, Ireland, in 1865. His father was a lawyer turned portrait painter. His mother came from a successful landed-merchant family in County Sligo, Ireland. Yeats spent much of his childhood in this area—a rustic, misty region that became a major influence on his imagination. The family divided their time between Dublin and London, until they finally settled in Dublin when Yeats was a teenager. After an unremarkable performance in secondary school, Yeats began studying at the Metropolitan School of Art in Dublin. He developed a fervent interest in poetry and was known to spend hours in his father's studio reciting verse.

Throughout his life, Yeats remained interested in Irish culture, myths, and folklore. In 1888, he helped edit *Fairy and Folk Tales of the Irish Peasantry*, which recounted Irish myths and legends. A year later, he published *The Wanderings of Oisin*, a book of poetry also filled with Irish **themes** and characters, including St. Patrick. Yeats's early fascination with the magical landscape of County Sligo led to his involvement in the Celtic Revival, a literary movement begun in the 1880s that wanted to unearth a distinctly Irish history and literature. The Celtic Revival, also known as the Irish Renaissance, was, in turn, linked to the larger political issue of Irish home rule. After the great potato famine of the 1840s, various nationalist revolutionary groups began agitating for the dissolution of British rule and the return of Irish sovereignty. These groups believed that the British government had no vested interest in Irish affairs and therefore thought that the Irish should govern themselves.

As he achieved some measure of literary success, Yeats also began to develop a lifelong interest in the occult, a belief system that figured prominently in his poetry. He joined the Dublin Hermetic Society, where he studied Theosophy, a set of spiritual teachings based on a belief in the transmission of the soul through various stages of reincarnation. Theosophy—with its roots in Western mystic and occult traditions, as well as in various strains of Eastern thought and religion—was wildly popular in the upper classes of Victorian England, which were similarly fascinated by reincarnation, séances, divination, and secret societies. In 1890, Yeats joined an elite secret society called the Hermetic Order of the Golden Dawn in London, where he was living at the time, and took the

WILLIAM BUTLER YEATS

name Demon est Desus Inversus. He would remain closely involved with the order and its rituals for the next thirty years, even after he moved back to Ireland in 1896.

Around this time, Yeats met two women who would have a major influence on his life and literary career: Maud Gonne and Lady Isabella Augusta Gregory. Maud Gonne was an actress, political activist, and fervent Irish nationalist. Yeats instantly fell in love with the striking beauty when they met in 1889, and while the two would maintain a close, complex relationship for the rest of their lives, she never reciprocated his romantic interest. Even though Gonne married Irish revolutionary John MacBride in 1903, Yeats's fascination with her never waned. She starred in many of his plays and frequently appeared as a figure in his poetry. Yeats met his other great love, Lady Augusta Gregory, in 1896. Together, the pair founded the Irish Literary Theatre, a nationalist playhouse devoted to producing Irish works, in 1897. Modeled after Yeats's successful Irish Literary Society, it moved to its permanent—and present—home at the Abbey Theatre in Dublin in 1904. The theater housed performances of plays by Irish playwrights, many of them culled from Irish history and mythology. The most famous performances include Yeats's *Cathleen ni Houlihan* (1902), which starred Maude Gonne in the title role, and John Synge's *The Playboy of the Western World* (1907), which caused audience riots when it was first performed. Yeats maintained close involvement with the theater for years, serving not only as a playwright-in-residence for the theater but also as manager and director.

After meeting Ezra Pound in 1912, Yeats's poetry changed dramatically through his association with the young poet. Pound was instrumental in developing **modernism**, a literary movement intent on breaking with past models and discovering new means of artistic and philosophical expression, In the first ten years of the twentieth century, Yeats began to turn away from the mythic **romanticism** that dominated his earlier works in favor of a harder-edged, more political poetry. His newer writings were heavily influenced by social and political conditions in Ireland and Europe, as well as by his own developing spiritual and philosophical belief system and the literary innovations of the modernist poets, such as Pound and T. S. Eliot, with whom he came into contact.

The modernist influence on Yeats's poetry became especially marked as a result of several crucial events that occurred between 1910 and 1920. The outbreak of World War I had a profound influence on the members of the European artistic community, causing many of them to question dominant cultural ideals and explore alternative methods of creative expression. At home in Ireland, the political climate was tense. The resistance led by the Irish Republican Brotherhood exploded into violence during the Easter Rebellion of 1916. The brotherhood took over major landmarks in Dublin, and although their coalition was small, they hoped the Irish people would rise up with them in revolt. The British declared martial law and quickly squashed the rebellion, leading the rebels to prison in shame. Many of them were executed, including Maud Gonne's husband, John MacBride. Despite an initial backlash from the population of Dublin, within days the rebels were held up as heroes, leading to a shift in Irish mentality about the possibility for home rule. In the midst of these events, and after failed proposals to Maud Gonne and her daughter, Iseult, Yeats married Georgiana Hydes-Lees, a mystic who introduced Yeats to automatic writing, and purchased Thoor Ballyle, a rundown Norman stone tower. He restored the structure and turned it into his summer residence.

Yeats continued writing and remained closely involved in Irish political affairs until the end of his life. He became a senator of the Irish Free State in 1922, and although he avoided tense political confrontation, he fulfilled an important role as a cultural emissary in the political sphere. He was awarded the Nobel Prize in 1923. At the time, he was heavily involved with writing and revising *A Vision*, which put forth his highly developed spiritual philosophy about the passage of the soul through the universe. Despite facing a variety of health problems in the 1930s, Yeats founded the Irish Academy of Letters, developed his interest in Hinduism by traveling to India, completed and published his autobiography, and had a brief (albeit controversial) involvement with the Fascist Blue Shirt group in Dublin. He died in January 1939 in Menton, France, and his body was interred at the Drumcliff Cemetery in County Sligo.

Themes, Motifs & Symbols

Themes

The Relationship Between Art and Politics

Yeats believed that art and politics were intrinsically linked and used his writing to express his attitudes toward Irish politics, as well as to educate his readers about Irish cultural history. From an early age, Yeats felt a deep connection to Ireland and his national identity, and he thought that British rule negatively impacted Irish politics and social life. His early compilation of folklore sought to teach a literary history that had been suppressed by British rule, and his early poems were **odes** to the beauty and mystery of the Irish countryside. This work frequently integrated references to myths and mythic figures, including Oisin and Cuchulain. As Yeats became more involved in Irish politics—through his relationships with the Irish National Theatre, the Irish Literary Society, the Irish Republican Brotherhood, and Maud Gonne—his poems increasingly resembled political manifestos. Yeats wrote numerous poems about Ireland's involvement in World War I ("An Irish Airman Foresees His Death" [1919], "A Meditation in Time of War" [1921]), Irish nationalists and political activists ("On a Political Prisoner" [1921], "In Memory of Eva Gore Booth and Con Markiewicz" [1933]), and the Easter Rebellion ("Easter 1916" [1916]). Yeats believed that art could serve a political function: poems could both critique and comment on political events, as well as educate and inform a population.

The Impact of Fate and the Divine on History

Yeats's devotion to mysticism led to the development of a unique spiritual and philosophical system that emphasized the role of fate and historical determinism, or the belief that events have been preordained. Yeats had rejected Christianity early in his life, but his lifelong study of mythology, Theosophy, spiritualism, philosophy, and the occult demonstrate his profound interest in the divine and how it interacts with humanity. Over the course of his life, he created a complex system of spirituality, using the image of interlocking gyres (similar to spiral cones) to map out the development and reincarnation of the soul. Yeats believed that history was determined by fate and that fate revealed its plan in moments when the human and divine interact. A **tone** of historically determined inevitability permeates his poems, particularly in descriptions of situations of human and divine interaction. The divine takes on many forms in Yeats's poetry, sometimes literally ("Leda and the Swan" [1923]), sometimes abstractly ("The Second Coming" [1919]). In other poems, the divine is only gestured to (as in the sense of the divine in the Byzantine mosaics in "Sailing to Byzantium" [1926]). No matter what shape it takes, the divine signals the role of fate in determining the course of history.

THE TRANSITION FROM ROMANTICISM TO MODERNISM

Yeats started his long literary career as a romantic poet and gradually evolved into a modernist poet. When he began publishing poetry in the 1880s, his poems had a lyrical, romantic style, and they focused on love, longing and loss, and Irish myths. His early writing follows the conventions of romantic verse, utilizing familiar rhyme schemes, metric patterns, and poetic structures. Although it is lighter than his later writings, his early poetry is still sophisticated and accomplished. Several factors contributed to his poetic evolution: his interest in mysticism and the occult led him to explore spiritually and philosophically complex subjects. Yeats's frustrated romantic relationship with Maud Gonne caused the starry-eyed romantic idealism of his early work to become more knowing and cynical. Additionally, his concern with Irish subjects evolved as he became more closely connected to nationalist political causes. As a result, Yeats shifted his focus from myth and folklore to contemporary politics, often linking the two to make potent statements that reflected political agitation and turbulence in Ireland and abroad. Finally, and most significantly, Yeats's connection with the changing face of literary culture in the early twentieth century led him to pick up some of the styles and conventions of the modernist poets. The modernists experimented with verse forms, aggressively engaged with contemporary politics, challenged poetic conventions and the literary tradition at large, and rejected the notion that poetry should simply be lyrical and beautiful. These influences caused his poetry to become darker, edgier, and more concise. Although he never abandoned the verse forms that provided the sounds and rhythms of his earlier poetry, there is still a noticeable shift in style and tone over the course of his career.

MOTIFS

IRISH NATIONALISM AND POLITICS

Throughout his literary career, Yeats incorporated distinctly Irish themes and issues into his work. He used his writing as a tool to comment on Irish politics and the home rule movement and to educate and inform people about Irish history and culture. Yeats also used the backdrop of the Irish countryside to retell stories and legends from Irish folklore. As he became increasingly involved in nationalist politics, his poems took on a patriotic tone. Yeats addressed Irish politics in a variety of ways: sometimes his statements are explicit political commentary, as in "An Irish Airman Foresees His Death," in which he addresses the hypocrisy of the British use of Irish soldiers in World War I. Such poems as "Easter 1916" and "In Memory of Eva Gore Booth and Con Markiewicz" address individuals and events connected to Irish nationalist politics, while "The Second Coming" and "Leda and the Swan" subtly include the idea of Irish nationalism. In these poems, a sense of cultural crisis and conflict seeps through, even though the poems are not explicitly about Ireland. By using images of chaos, disorder, and war, Yeats engaged in an understated commentary on the political situations in Ireland and abroad. Yeats's active participation in Irish politics informed his poetry, and he used his work to further comment on the nationalist issues of his day.

MYSTICISM AND THE OCCULT

Yeats had a deep fascination with mysticism and the occult, and his poetry is infused with a sense of the otherworldly, the spiritual, and the unknown. His interest in the occult began with his study of Theosophy as a young man and expanded and developed through his participation in the Hermetic Order of the Golden Dawn, a mystical secret society. Mysticism figures prominently in Yeats's discussion of the reincarnation of the soul, as well as in his philosophical model of the conical gyres used to explain the journey of the soul, the passage of time, and the guiding hand of fate. Mysticism and the occult occur again and again in Yeats's poetry, most explicitly in "The Second Coming" but also in poems such as "Sailing to Byzantium" and "The Magi" (1916). The rejection of Christian principles in favor of a more supernatural approach to spirituality creates a unique flavor in Yeats's poetry that impacts his discussion of history, politics, and love.

IRISH MYTH AND FOLKLORE

Yeats's participation in the Irish political system had origins in his interest in Irish myth and folklore. Irish myth and folklore had been suppressed by church doctrine and British control of the school system. Yeats used his poetry as a tool for re-educating the Irish population about their heritage and as a strategy for developing Irish nationalism. He retold entire folktales in **epic** poems and plays, such as *The Wanderings of Oisin* (1889) and *The Death of Cuchulain* (1939), and used fragments of stories in shorter poems, such as "The Stolen Child" (1886), which retells a parable of fairies luring a child away from his home, and "Cuchulain's Fight with the Sea" (1925), which recounts part of an epic where the Irish folk hero Cuchulain battles his long-lost son by at the edge of the sea. Other poems deal with subjects, images, and themes culled from folklore. In "Who Goes with Fergus?" (1893) Yeats imagines a meeting with the exiled wandering king of Irish legend, while "The Song of Wandering Aengus" (1899) captures the experiences of the lovelorn god Aengus as he searches for the beautiful maiden seen in his dreams. Most important, Yeats infused his poetry with a rich sense of Irish culture. Even poems that do not deal explicitly with subjects from myth retain powerful tinges of indigenous Irish culture. Yeats often borrowed word selection, verse form, and patterns of **imagery** directly from traditional Irish myth and folklore.

SYMBOLS

THE GYRE

The gyre, a circular or conical shape, appears frequently in Yeats's poems and was developed as part of the philosophical system outlined in his book *A Vision*. At first, Yeats used the phases of the moon to articulate his belief that history was structured in terms of ages, but he later settled upon the gyre as a more useful model. He chose the image of interlocking gyres—visually represented as two intersecting conical spirals—to symbolize his philosophical belief that all things could be described in terms of cycles and patterns. The soul (or the civilization, the age, and so on) would move from the smallest point of the spiral to the largest before moving along to the other gyre. Although this is a difficult concept to grasp abstractly, the image makes sense when applied to the waxing and waning of a particular historical age or the evolution of a human life from youth to adulthood to old age. The symbol of the interlocking gyres reveals Yeats's belief in fate and historical determinism as well as his spiritual attitudes toward the development of the soul, since creatures and events must evolve according to the conical shape. With the image of the gyre, Yeats created a shorthand reference in his poetry that stood for his entire philosophy of history and spirituality.

THE SWAN

Swans are a common **symbol** in poetry, often used to depict idealized nature. Yeats employs this convention in "The Wild Swans at Coole" (1919), in which the regal birds represent an unchanging, flawless ideal. In "Leda and the Swan," Yeats rewrites the Greek myth of Zeus and Leda to comment on fate and historical inevitability: Zeus disguises himself as a swan to rape the unsuspecting Leda. In this poem, the bird is fearsome and destructive, and it possesses a divine power that violates Leda and initiates the dire consequences of war and devastation depicted in the final lines. Even though Yeats clearly states that the swan is the god Zeus, he also emphasizes the physicality of the swan: the beating wings, the dark webbed feet, the long neck and beak. Through this description of its physical characteristics, the swan becomes a violent divine force. By rendering a well-known poetic symbol as violent and terrifying rather than idealized and beautiful, Yeats manipulates poetic conventions, an act of literary modernism, and adds to the power of the poem.

THE GREAT BEAST

Yeats employs the figure of a great beast—a horrific, violent animal—to embody difficult abstract concepts. The great beast as a symbol comes from Christian iconography, in which it represents evil and darkness. In "The Second Coming," the great beast emerges from the Spiritus Mundi, or soul of the universe, to function as the primary image of destruction in the poem. Yeats describes the onset of apocalyptic events in which the "blood-dimmed tide is loosed" and the "ceremony of innocence is drowned" as the world enters a new age and falls apart as a result of the widening of the historical gyres. The speaker predicts the arrival of the Second Coming, and this prediction summons a "vast image" of a frightening monster pulled from the collective consciousness of the world. Yeats modifies the well-known image of the sphinx to embody the poem's vision of the climactic coming. By rendering the terrifying prospect of disruption and change into an easily imagined horrifying monster, Yeats makes an abstract fear become tangible and real. The great beast slouches toward Bethlehem to be born, where it will evolve into a second Christ (or anti-Christ) figure for the dark new age. In this way, Yeats uses distinct, concrete imagery to symbolize complex ideas about the state of the modern world.

WILLIAM BUTLER YEATS

Summary & Analysis

"The Lake Isle of Innisfree"

I will arise and go now, and go to Innisfree,
And a small cabin build there, of clay and wattles made:
Nine bean-rows will I have there, a hive for the honey-bee;
And live alone in the bee-loud glade.

And I shall have some peace there, for peace comes dropping
slow,   5
Dropping from the veils of the morning to where the cricket
sings;
There midnight's all a glimmer, and noon a purple glow,
And evening full of the linnet's wings.

I will arise and go now, for always night and day
I hear lake water lapping with low sounds by the shore;   10
While I stand on the roadway, or on the pavements grey,
I hear it in the deep heart's core.

Summary

The speaker begins by declaring that he will rise up and go to Innisfree, a small island in the middle of Lough (Lake) Gill, located in the Irish countryside. There, the speaker will construct a cabin of mud and poles intertwined with twigs, reeds, and branches. In a life of quiet solitude, the speaker will keep busy with his garden of beans and a beehive. In the second stanza, the speaker reiterates that he will find calm in the easy pace of dripping dew and singing crickets in the morning light, and this calm will continue throughout the shimmering of midnight, the colored light of the afternoon, and the beating of finches' wings in the evening. In the final stanza, the speaker explains that he will always hear the intermingling sounds of the lake and noises on the shore as he goes about his daily business. Even though the speaker lives in an urban area, he will hear the sounds of tranquil nature on the byways and sidewalks because they will resonate in the deepest part of the speaker's being.

ANALYSIS

Typical of Yeats's early poetry, "The Lake Isle of Innisfree" (1890) expresses a romantic desire to escape from urban life to an idealized, pastoral retreat. Like his earlier work, the poem focuses on specific landmarks in the Irish countryside near where he grew up (Innisfree, Lough Gill) and emphasizes the experiences and sensations of being in rural Ireland. The isle has a magical, otherworldly quality. The glade is filled with sounds throughout the day, and the sky seems to glow from morning to glimmering midnight.

The poem extols the idyllic tranquility available to those who live a rural life, and the poem concludes by contrasting the tranquility with the bustle of modern city living. The speaker longs to escape the city for the comforts of the Irish countryside. At Innisfree, the speaker can focus on life-sustaining labor on the land (growing beans and raising bees). Throughout the poem, the speaker expresses his desire to rise up and go, but from where he intends to depart is unclear until the end. This outdoor work will give him the peace he has been longing for. He hears the sound of lake water echoing in his heart, and in the final lines it is revealed that he currently lives in an urban environment. Thus, he hears the sounds of the lake as he stands on the sidewalk or along the road—a sound that vibrates "in the deep heart's core" (12). Yeats uses a gentle *abab* rhyme scheme and a hexameter meter to echo the peaceful sounds of the lake. In this way, readers, like the speaker, can feel calmed by nature as they read the poem, regardless of where they might be standing as they read.

"The Lake Isle of Innisfree" reflects Yeats's method of incorporating fantastical, pastoral **imagery** to praise rural life, to evoke a unique spirituality, and to encourage the development of a distinctly Irish identity. The spiritual undertones of the poem are emphasized in the final lines, in which the speaker talks about hearing the sounds of the lake in the soulful center of his being. The profound sense of spiritual connection to the landscape, and to the *spirit* of the landscape, is a recurring theme in Yeats's poetry. Additionally, Yeats abstractly gestures to the idea that the Irish might escape the trappings of the political life of the city by discovering the culture, history, and lifestyle of the countryside. By discussing one person's desire to leave the city in search of connection and communion with the "true" Ireland, Yeats makes a larger statement about the necessity for all Irish people to reconnect with the culture, history, and lifestyle associated with the land.

WILLIAM BUTLER YEATS

"THE SECOND COMING"

Turning and turning in the widening gyre
The falcon cannot hear the falconer;
Things fall apart; the centre cannot hold;
Mere anarchy is loosed upon the world,
The blood-dimmed tide is loosed, and everywhere
The ceremony of innocence is drowned;
The best lack all conviction, while the worst
Are full of passionate intensity.

Surely some revelation is at hand;
Surely the Second Coming is at hand.
The Second Coming! Hardly are those words out
When a vast image out of Spiritus Mundi
Troubles my sight: somewhere in sands of the desert
A shape with lion body and the head of a man,
A gaze blank and pitiless as the sun,
Is moving its slow thighs, while all about it
Reel shadows of the indignant desert birds.
The darkness drops again; but now I know
That twenty centuries of stony sleep
Were vexed to nightmare by a rocking cradle,
And what rough beast, its hour come round at last,
Slouches towards Bethlehem to be born?

SUMMARY

The speaker begins by imagining a falcon, unable to hear its keeper, flying outward in a spiral that becomes wider. Then the speaker declares that "things fall apart" (3) and that unity and order cannot be maintained. As a result, chaos runs rampant, a bloody deluge is unleashed, and innocence—and all pretenses relating to innocence—are lost. Those that are considered the greatest are unable to act, while those considered to be the worst are full of drive and power.

In the second stanza, the speaker claims that this state of affairs must indicate that some major change is looming, possibly the second coming of Christ. With this articulation, the speaker sees a huge beast emerge in the distance from the spirit world. He visualizes a sphinx with the body of a lion and the head of a man somewhere out in the desert. This distorted sphinx has an empty, merciless stare, and it moves its hulking form among the shadows birds flying above it in a circle. Again, darkness falls. The speaker then states that he now knows the beast has been in a deep sleep for 2,000 years, since the last great revelation—that is, the birth of Christ—an event represented by an image of a gently swaying crib. Now that the time of the horrific animal is here, the speaker wonders about the nature and meaning of the beast heading toward Bethlehem to be born.

Analysis

One of Yeats's best-known poems, "The Second Coming" describes an apocalyptic vision that encapsulates many of his philosophies about history, spirituality, and the development of the soul. Considered by some to be one of the definitive statements of modern poetry—and thus of the modern age—"The Second Coming" hearkens the arrival of a new period in history marked by fragmentation, chaos, and disillusionment. The poem also shows the vivid distinction between the innocent, romantic tone of Yeats's earlier poems and the dark, prophetic style of his later poetry.

The central image of the poem is the falcon flying in the widening gyre, an image that emerged in Yeats's writing in the early twentieth century but that was only fully realized in his philosophical treatise *A Vision*. There, Yeats developed a philosophy that rejected Christian moral principles in favor of a spiritual system organized around ancient mysticism. He originally framed his philosophical approach around the lunar phases, in which the soul moved from the dark (objectivity) to the full moon (subjectivity) and back again. This image could be used to account not only for one person's life but also for the cycles of history or the growth and collapse of a civilization. After some thought, he rejected this model in favor of the image of the gyre. He described his philosophical approach in terms of two interlocking cones, through which the soul passed around in an ascending and descending spiral from birth to adulthood to death. Yeats's guiding principles about spirituality were dictated by this image, in which the slow movement along the spiral gyres imitated the progression of the soul, the passage of time, and the cycles of history.

The cone and gyre are introduced in this poem through the flight of the falcon, whose movements spiral away from the falconer. Like the cone and gyre, the falcon and falconer are pulled apart, and as a result the center that held them together collapses, leading to anarchy and chaos. Yeats believed that the early twentieth century was the dawning of a new age and that a 2,000-year cycle of the gyres was complete. Just as Christ was born 2,000 years before, heralding the arrival of the Christian age, the arrival of the deformed sphinx creature signals a second coming. This beast emerges from the Spiritus Mundi, the collective unconscious of the age. He describes its monstrous form, then imagines it "slouching" toward Bethlehem to be born, thus marking the dawn of a new era.

In contrast to the first coming of Christ—which, for Christians, was a joyous event—the second coming portrayed in this poem brings not optimism or hope, but pessimism and despair. A frightening, sinister occasion, the second coming heralds an age of anarchy and chaos, in which the power of the worst of humanity overtakes the ideals of the best, who are unable to act. Instead of the Christ child, the figure that signals the arrival of the new age is a horrifying monster that has emerged from the spirit of the world. The creature resembles the sphinx of Greek mythology. Although it has a man's head, the being is decidedly inhuman, and its lurching through the desert is ominous. The poem ends by simultaneously acknowledging the beast's arrival and questioning its true nature, thereby presenting a tone of frightened anticipation.

Critics have multiple interpretations of "The Second Coming." Many see it as a general description of the post–World War I world. The ideals of reason and order developed during the **Enlightenment** seemed to fall away as Europe was torn apart by war, and Yeats was one of many artists whose increasingly cynical view of humanity manifested in literary work. Some scholars think that Yeats was speaking of a more specific situation and that the beast he describes is Aleister Crowley, a former associate of Yeats's from the Hermetic Order of the Golden Dawn who corrupted many of the ideals of the institution. Others believe Yeats is describing the events surrounding the Russian Revolution or the Irish troubles, both of which led to dramatic political upheaval around the time the poem was composed. In its dark tone and apocalyptic images, the poem lends itself to a variety of interpretations and can easily refer to the numerous instances of political and social transformation that occurred between 1910 and 1920. Ultimately, Yeats's poem echoes his philosophy about history and the passage of time, darkly heralding the arrival of a new age.

"Sailing to Byzantium"[1]

I

That is no country for old men. The young
In one another's arms, birds in the trees
—Those dying generations—at their song,
The salmon-falls, the mackerel-crowded seas,
Fish, flesh, or fowl, commend all summer long 5
Whatever is begotten, born, and dies.
Caught in that sensual music all neglect
Monuments of unageing intellect.

II

An aged man is but a paltry thing,
A tattered coat upon a stick, unless 10
Soul clap its hands and sing, and louder sing
For every tatter in its mortal dress,
Nor is there singing school but studying
Monuments of its own magnificence;
And therefore I have sailed the seas and come 15
To the holy city of Byzantium.

III

O sages standing in God's holy fire
As in the gold mosaic of a wall,
Come from the holy fire, perne in a gyre,
And be the singing-masters of my soul. 20
Consume my heart away; sick with desire
And fastened to a dying animal
It knows not what it is; and gather me
Into the artifice of eternity.

IV

Once out of nature I shall never take 25
My bodily form from any natural thing,
But such a form as Grecian goldsmiths make

1. Reprinted with the permission of Scribner, an imprint of Simon & Schuster Adult Publishing Group, from *The Collected Works of W.B. Yeats, Volume I: The Poems, Revised*, edited by Richard J. Finneran. Copyright © 1928 by The Macmillan Company; copyright renewed © 1956 by Georgie Yeats.

WILLIAM BUTLER YEATS

Of hammered gold and gold enamelling
To keep a drowsy Emperor awake;
Or set upon a golden bough to sing   30
To lords and ladies of Byzantium
Of what is past, or passing, or to come.

SUMMARY

The speaker begins by denying that an area is fit for the aged. He describes this area as filled with lovers and singing birds. Nearby, fish fill the sea and animals roam the land in a luscious atmosphere. But the speaker also mentions death, explaining that all the beings born in this area—who are too caught up in their sensuality to take note of permanent monuments to intellect and human achievement—will eventually die. In the second stanza, the speaker muses on the sad state of an older man, likening him to a neglected coat left on a bare branch. The human form is fragile, but the soul can somehow rise above bodily suffering by examining paeans to the awesomeness of the human soul. The speaker then states that he has sailed across the seas and come to the holy city of Byzantium to pay homage to the awesomeness of the human soul.

In the third stanza, the speaker looks at Byzantine mosaics depicting Christian martyrs burning in holy fire, and he bids them to come to him and command his soul. He wants them to devour his heart, which he thinks is sick with want and too tied to a decaying thing, so that he might live forever. In the final stanza, the speaker explains that once he's been removed from the world, he will relinquish his corporeal frame and become a permanent object, akin to the artifacts constructed by Greek goldsmiths to amuse a bored ruler. Put on top of a golden branch, he will sing to the lords and ladies of Byzantium of what has happened, what is happening, or what will happen.

ANALYSIS

"Sailing to Byzantium" is Yeats's comment on the brevity of human life and the permanence of art. Byzantium was a politically and culturally advanced dynasty, which began in the fourth century in Constantinople (now Istanbul) as an offshoot of the Holy Roman Empire. Yeats had viewed Byzantine mosaics in churches in Ravenna and Sicily when he made a trip to Italy in 1924, and he was inspired by what he saw there. He viewed Byzantium as a center of civilization and spiritual life, and the idea of a "journey to Byzantium" symbolizes a search for sacred fulfillment and artistic permanence.

The first two stanzas of the poem express the desire to transcend the aging body by departing Ireland for the artistic treasures of Byzantium. The first stanza identifies Ireland as "no country for old men" (1) listing a series of images that demonstrate how youth—and nature itself—reject the idea of permanence in favor of perpetually existing in a sensual present. Although they are caught up in the moment, Yeats terms this group "dying generations" (3). Their time on earth will be short, and they completely neglect those "moments of unageing intellect" (8) captured in the Byzantine mosaics. The second stanza focuses on the decrepitude of the aging body. Here, the withery form of an old man metaphorically becomes a stick dressed in a tattered coat. Only by moving and shouting can the soul overcome the frailty of the human body and thus defy aging. Studying "monuments" (14), according to the poem, can help the soul move and shout. To accomplish this, the speaker flees the country of old men for the holy city of Byzantium.

The third and fourth stanzas concentrate on the ways the soul gains permanence through art. The third stanza begins with a plea to the images viewed in the Byzantine mosaics. The gold mosaics depict Christian martyrs burning in God's holy fire. The martyrs move as if in a gyre, an image Yeats pulls from his book of mystical spirituality, *A Vision*, to describe the progression of history and humanity. The speaker wants the martyrs to inhabit his body, thereby allowing him to maintain artistic permanence despite his mortality. While his very being longs for immortality, he is stuck with a decaying body, which he calls a "dying animal" (22) divorced from the spiritual perfection of the soul.

The final stanza voices an unexpected desire: the wish to depart life for a permanent existence as an object of art. The speaker longs to escape the sensual trappings of nature described in the first stanza and to never again exist in a natural state. Yeats's study of mysticism led to an interest in reincarnation. For Yeats, the highest state of spiritual perfection is the self's transformation into a piece of art. The speaker wants to exist as a golden bird, created by the hands of Grecian goldsmiths, who were known for their sophisticated craftsmanship. Even though he might be constructed solely to provide passing amusement to a bored emperor, the speaker believes he might also sit upon a similarly constructed golden bough and sing to the lords and ladies of Byzantium about what has past, what is happening in the moment, and what is to come.

WILLIAM BUTLER YEATS

"Sailing to Byzantium" articulates a human fear of aging, dying, and being forgotten, and it proposes art as an antidote to those fears. For Yeats, Byzantium represents a cultural ideal in which religious, aesthetic, and spiritual life are unified. This idealized culture greatly contrasts with what he perceived to be the sensual obsession with the present afflicting the youth of his native land. In nature, what is born dies. In art, however, what is created remains, long after the death of the creator. Through art—and through poetry—an artist can escape the constraints of mortality and the natural world and can perpetually exist in an artificial form that will still allow him to carry out his poetic project. By entering the world of artifice, the speaker can become immortal, just as the images on the Byzantine mosaics are immortal. By becoming the golden bird, Yeats could ensure the permanence of his poetry. Ultimately, the poem reveals an ambivalence about the lasting effects of poetry and the potential of art to speak through the ages.

"LEDA AND THE SWAN"[1]

> A sudden blow: the great wings beating still
> Above the staggering girl, her thighs caressed
> By the dark webs, her nape caught in his bill,
> He holds her helpless breast upon his breast.
>
> How can those terrified vague fingers push   5
> The feathered glory from her loosening thighs?
> And how can body, laid in that white rush,
> But feel the strange heart beating where it lies?
>
> A shudder in the loins engenders there
> The broken wall, the burning roof and tower   10
> And Agamemnon dead.
>   Being so caught up,
>
> So mastered by the brute blood of the air
> Did she put on his knowledge with his power
> Before the indifferent beak could let her drop?

1. Reprinted with the permission of Scribner, an imprint of Simon & Schuster Adult Publishing Group, from *The Collected Works of W.B. Yeats, Volume I: The Poems, Revised*, edited by Richard J. Finneran. Copyright © 1928 by The Macmillan Company; copyright renewed © 1956 by Georgie Yeats.

SUMMARY

"Leda and the Swan" recounts the Greek myth of the rape of Leda, the queen of Sparta, by Zeus, the king of the gods. The poem begins with an unexpected force—the fierce attack of the swan on the unsuspecting Leda. As the swan strikes her with his wings, he also uses his webbed feet to caress her thighs and catches the nape of her neck in his beak. He holds her helpless, crushing her chest against his chest.

The second stanza consists of two rhetorical questions: first, how can Leda's frightened human hands push away the god's body? Second, how can she, trapped in the rush of wings and feathers, feel the god's beating heart in his chest? The third stanza jumps into the future, foreseeing the result of the coupling: the destruction of Troy, the subsequent war, and the death of Agamemnon. The poem ends by wondering whether Leda, swept up in the moment of attack, was able to assume Zeus's insight into the future and thus see the long-term consequences of the rape before the swan let her go.

ANALYSIS

"Leda and the Swan" is a prophetic, apocalyptic poem typical of Yeats's later writing, in which he articulates his philosophy of history and myth. The poem retells the Greek myth of Leda and the swan: according to the story, Leda was a queen of Sparta who coupled with Zeus, king of the gods, while he was in the form of a swan. Their union brought forth four offspring, including Helen of Sparta and Clytemnestra. These two women are hugely influential in classical myth. The capture of Helen of Sparta, considered to be the most beautiful woman in the world, led to the Trojan War, in which the city of Troy fell to the Greeks, as told by Homer. The fall of the city, in turn, supposedly led to the birth of Rome, as told by Virgil in the *Aeneid*. In the plays of Aeschylus, Clytemnestra kills her husband, King Agamemnon, after his return from Troy. She is later killed by her son, Orestes. Yeats collapses these mythical events into a single moment, in which these fictional world-changing events are set into motion by the rape of a girl by a god.

In "Leda and the Swan," Yeats applies the conventions of a Christian narrative to a secular series of events and thus creates an **annunciation poem** (or a poem that announces or retells a specific biblical, Christian narrative). In the New Testament Gospels, the annunciation story recounts the visit to the Virgin Mary by the angel Gabriel. During this visit, he tells her that she will bear the son of God. This story is important in Christianity because this single moment anticipates the birth, life, and death of Christ, thereby symbolically standing in for the central tenets of the faith. In this poem, the annunciation is drastically different. The situation is wholly secular, representative of not only the events surrounding the rape of Leda, the Trojan War, and its aftermath, but also the literary and cultural history that emerged from these events. Yeats's collapse of Western political, social, and literary history to one crucial event thus presents a secular alternative to the Christian annunciation. The poem also comments on the lasting consequences resulting from the interaction between the human and the divine.

The structure of the poem mirrors its content. The poem is a sonnet, a fourteen-line poetic form conventionally used in love poetry. It is structured so that the first eight lines of the poem (the **octet**) present one idea, while the final six lines (the **sestet**) present a twist on the idea put forth in the octave. Here, the rape of Leda is described in the octet, a story that many of Yeats's readers would know. The moment seems to retell a familiar story. The sestet's twist links the rape to its long-term consequences, showing the far-reaching repercussions of one small event. The rhetorical question at the end of stanza 2 illustrates Yeats's recurring interest in the acquisition of knowledge: it reminds us that Leda, despite being trapped and almost smothered by the swan's wings, can still feel his heart beating. The beating of the bird's heart reminds Leda of Zeus's humanity, even as his violent, brute physicality overwhelms her. In his poems, Yeats frequently explores the notion of fate and tries to uncover the ways individuals are connected not only to their own fates, but also to larger historical patterns. Yeats continually probes how individual experiences play into larger political, social, and cultural trends.

Although "Leda and the Swan" is a retelling of a classical myth, a well-worn convention of Western poetry, Yeats provides his own unique spin on the tale by exploring the ideas of destiny, inevitability, and the interaction between the human and the divine. Written in 1924, this poem resembles the dark, prophetic poetry Yeats wrote later in his life, poetry largely influenced by political turmoil in Ireland, the larger conflict of World War I and the sociopolitical state of Europe, and Yeats's own developing ideas of spirituality and individual destiny.

WILLIAM BUTLER YEATS

ROBERT FROST

(1874–1963)

CONTEXT

Robert Frost was born in 1874 in San Francisco, California, and lived there until 1885, when his alcoholic father died penniless and his mother was forced to move the family back to New Hampshire. There Frost's mother found work as a teacher, and Frost enjoyed the New England countryside, which would have a profound effect on his creative output in later years. Soon after Frost turned thirteen, his mother relocated the family to Lawrence, Massachusetts, where he began high school and eventually started writing poetry. Prior to his schooling in Lawrence, Frost had had no formal education, and he didn't read comfortably on his own until he was fourteen. At school in Lawrence, he met Elinor Miriam White, who would later become his wife. The two were well matched intellectually—and they shared valedictory honors at graduation. After high school, Frost enrolled in Dartmouth College, but he was bored by life in Durham, New Hampshire, and felt stifled by the academic atmosphere. He returned to Massachusetts after one semester and worked odd jobs around Lawrence as he continued to hone his poetry. Frost's persistence as a writer paid off with the publication of "My Butterfly: An Elegy" in the prestigious literary journal the *New York Independent* in 1894.

Although Frost made several attempts to convince Elinor to marry him, she waited to graduate from college before consenting to wed in December of 1895. The pair made their living teaching at various schools in Massachusetts and had their first child, Elliott, in 1896. Frost decided to try college again, this time at Harvard, but his stay in Cambridge was short-lived, and family obligations forced him to return home. Shortly after his homecoming, Frost's infant son, Elliott, died of cholera, and then his mother passed away. Devastated by these losses, Frost sank into a deep depression. Elinor called on Frost's paternal grandfather and acquired from him a loan in 1900 to purchase a farm in Derry, New Hampshire, so that her family could recuperate. Frost was revitalized by his time at Derry, and over the course of his ten years there he wrote the poems that would later make up the bulk of his first two collections.

A failure as a farmer and unable to find an American publisher, Frost sold the Derry farm and moved his wife and their four children to England in 1912. He developed close ties with influential literary figures there. Ezra Pound, a controversial experimental poet, took a particular interest in Frost and guided him through the avant-garde literary and artistic circles in London. In 1913, Frost submitted his first collection of poetry, *A Boy's Will*, to a small English publishing house. Printed later that year, the volume gained Frost favorable reviews on both sides of the Atlantic. Organized around the theme of a young boy traveling out into the wilderness, the poems reflect on youth, travel, and self-discovery. A year later, he matched the achievement of his first volume with his second collection, *North of Boston* (1915). This collection features numerous dramatic narrative poems set in rural New England. Drawing on gothic images and cultivating the superstitious atmosphere present in the American wilderness at the turn of the century, many of the poems reveal a simultaneous love for and fear of nature. Despite his success as a published poet, Frost felt the financial pressures of supporting his family abroad, as well as the tensions produced by England's entry into World War I. The Frost family returned to the United States in 1915.

Settling into a farm in Franconia, New Hampshire, Frost enjoyed building critical and popular support for his poetry. By this time, an American publisher, Henry Holt, had released *North of Boston* to great acclaim. Holt released Frost's third volume of poetry, *Mountain Interval*, in 1916. Frost began giving a series of lectures across the United States, at which he would read his poems aloud and offer significant comments, and he accepted various university teaching positions, including a long engagement as a professor at Amherst College. In the 1920s, his popularity soared, and he was flooded with recognition, including a series of Pulitzer Prizes (awarded in 1924, 1931, 1937, and 1943). Readers responded to the direct language and lyrical **imagery** of his poems in volumes, such as *New Hampshire* (1923) and *A Further Range* (1936), which stimulated nostalgia for a specific time and place in American history. At a time of tremendous political and social turbulence resulting from World War I and World War II, Frost's poetry provided comfort and reassurance to a culture undergoing massive change.

Despite popular success, Frost faced a series of dramatic personal tragedies, set off by the slow, painful death of his daughter, Marjorie, with whom he was very close, in 1934. Still reeling from this, Frost was dealt another blow when his wife died unexpectedly in 1938. Over the next few years, Frost continued to suffer losses. His son, Carol, committed suicide in 1940, and his daughter, Irma, was institutionalized soon thereafter. These tragedies had a profound impact on Frost's poetry. The pessimistic undertones of his earlier poems bubbled up to the surface, and his poetic voice lost its gentle touch and became increasingly dry and heavy-handed. Nevertheless, Frost himself felt that some of the poems in *A Witness Tree* (1942) ranked among his best work. Through the 1940s and beyond, Frost wrote poetry sporadically, rather than intensely, as he had earlier in his career.

Later in life, Frost cemented his celebrity status through his active involvement with American politics. He recited a poem at John F. Kennedy's inauguration in 1961 and formed close ties to the Kennedy administration, later becoming a goodwill ambassador to the Soviet Union. Frost met with Premier Nikita Khrushchev in an attempt to smooth tensions between the United States and the Soviet Union in 1962, a remarkable responsibility for even a distinguished man of letters. At the peak of his acclaim, Frost fell ill and was hospitalized in December of 1962. Several weeks later, he died from complications related to a pulmonary embolism on January 29, 1963, in Boston. His death sparked an outpouring of tributes. The definitive American poet, as he was then considered, had accumulated forty-four honorary degrees, four Pulitzer Prizes, and myriad governmental honors, including a Congressional Medal of Honor and the position of the consultant to the Library of Congress (now known as poet laureate). Although deeply loved by his massive following, his image was tarnished with the publication of Lawrence Thompson's biography *Robert Frost: The Years of Triumph, 1915–1938* (1970). Frost's biographer portrayed his former mentor as an egotistical monster, a stigma that clung to his name for years afterward. Today, Frost has been returned to his former status as the most beloved of all American poets.

THEMES, MOTIFS & SYMBOLS

THEMES

YOUTH AND THE LOSS OF INNOCENCE

Youth appears prominently in Frost's poetry, particularly in connection with innocence and its loss. *A Boy's Will* deals with this **theme** explicitly, tracing the development of a solitary youth as he explores and questions the world around him. Frost's later work depicts youth as an idealized, edenic state full of possibility and opportunity. But as his poetic **tone** became increasingly jaded and didactic, he imagines youth as a time of unchecked freedom that is taken for granted and then lost. The theme of lost innocence becomes particularly poignant for Frost after the horrors of World War I and World War II, in which he witnessed the physical and psychic wounding of entire generations of young people. Later poems, including "Birches" (1916), "Acquainted with the Night" (1928), and "Desert Places" (1936), explore the realities of aging and loss, contrasting adult experiences with the carefree pleasures of youth.

SELF-KNOWLEDGE THROUGH NATURE

Nature figures prominently in Frost's poetry, and his poems usually include a moment of interaction or encounter between a human **speaker** and a natural subject or phenomenon. These encounters culminate in profound realizations or revelations, which have significant consequences for the speakers. Actively engaging with nature—whether through manual labor or exploration—has a variety of results, including self-knowledge, deeper understanding of the human condition, and increased insight into the metaphysical world. Frost's earlier work focuses on the act of discovery and demonstrates how being engaged with nature leads to growth and knowledge. For instance, a day of harvesting fruit leads to a new understanding of life's final sleep, or death, in "After Apple-Picking" (1915). Mid-career, however, Frost used encounters in nature to comment on the human condition. In his later works, experiencing nature provided access to the universal, the supernatural, and the divine, even as the poems themselves became increasingly focused on aging and mortality.

Throughout Frost's work, speakers learn about themselves by exploring nature, but nature always stays indifferent to the human world. In other words, people learn from nature because nature allows people to gain knowledge about themselves and because nature requires people to reach for new insights, but nature itself does not provide answers. Frost believed in the capacity of humans to achieve feats of understanding in natural settings, but he also believed that nature was unconcerned with either human achievement or human misery. Indeed, in Frost's work, nature could be both generous and malicious. The speaker of "Design" (1936), for example, wonders about the "design of darkness" (13) that has led a spider to kill a moth over the course of a night. While humans might learn about themselves through nature, nature and its ways remain mysterious.

COMMUNITY VS. ISOLATION

Frost marveled at the contrast between the human capacity to connect with one another and to experience feelings of profound isolation. In several Frost poems, solitary individuals wander through a natural setting and encounter another individual, an object, or an animal. These encounters stimulate moments of revelation in which the speaker realizes her or his connection to others or, conversely, the ways that she or he feels isolated from the community. Earlier poems feature speakers who actively choose solitude and isolation in order to learn more about themselves, but these speakers ultimately discover a firm connection to the world around them, as in "The Tufts of Flowers" (1915) and "Mending Wall" (1915). Longer dramatic poems explore how people isolate themselves even within social contexts. Later poems return the focus to solitude, exploring how encounters and community only heighten loneliness and isolation. This deeply pessimistic, almost misanthropic perspective sneaks into the most cheerful of late Frost poems, including "Acquainted with the Night" and "Desert Places."

MOTIFS

MANUAL LABOR

Labor functions as a tool for self-analysis and discovery in Frost's poetry. Work allows his speakers to understand themselves and the world around them. Traditionally, pastoral and romantic poets emphasized a passive relationship with nature, wherein people would achieve understanding and knowledge by observing and meditating, not by directly interacting with the natural world. In contrast, Frost's speakers work, labor, and act—mending fences, as in "Mending Wall"; harvesting fruit, as in "After Apple-Picking"; or cutting hay, as in "Mowing" (1915). Even children work, although the hard labor of the little boy in "Out, Out—" (1920) leads to his death. The boy's death implies that while work was necessary for adults, children should be exempted from difficult labor until they have attained the required maturity with which to handle both the physical and the mental stress that goes along with rural life. Frost implies that a connection with the earth and with one's self can only be achieved by actively communing with the natural world through work.

NEW ENGLAND

Long considered the quintessential regional poet, Frost uses New England as a recurring setting throughout his work. Although he spent his early life in California, Frost moved to the East Coast in his early teens and spent the majority of his adult life in Massachusetts and New Hampshire. The region's landscape, history, culture, and attitudes fill his poetry, and he emphasizes local color and natural elements of the forests, orchards, fields, and small towns. His speakers wander through dense woods and snowstorms, pick apples, and climb mountains. *North of Boston*, the title of Frost's second collection of poetry, firmly established him as the chronicler of small-town, rural life in New England. Frost found inspiration in his day-to-day experiences, basing "Mending Wall," for instance, on a fence near his farm in Derry, New Hampshire, and "The Oven Bird" (1920) on birds indigenous to the nearby woods.

THE SOUND OF SENSE

Frost coined the phrase the *sound of sense* to emphasize the **poetic diction**, or word choice, used throughout his work. According to letters he wrote in 1913 and 1914, the sound of sense should be positive, as well as proactive, and should resemble everyday speech. To achieve the sound of sense, Frost chose words for tone and sound, in addition to considering each word's meaning. Many poems replicate content through rhyme, **meter**, and **alliteration**. For instance, "Mowing" captures the back-and-forth sound of a scythe swinging, while "Out, Out—" imitates the jerky, noisy roar of a buzz saw. Believing that poetry should be recited, rather than read, Frost not only paid attention to the sound of his poems but also went on speaking tours throughout the United States, where he would read, comment, and discuss his work. Storytelling has a long history in the United States, particularly in New England, and Frost wanted to tap into this history to emphasize poetry as an oral art.

SYMBOLS

TREES

Trees delineate borders in Frost's poetry. They not only mark boundaries on earth, such as that between a pasture and a forest, but also boundaries between earth and heaven. In some poems, such as "After Apple-Picking" and "Birches," trees are the link between earth, or humanity, and the sky, or the divine. Trees function as boundary spaces, where moments of connection or revelation become possible. Humans can observe and think critically about humanity and the divine under the shade of these trees or standing nearby, inside the trees' boundary space. Forests and edges of forests function similarly as boundary spaces, as in "Into My Own" (1915) or "Desert Places." Finally, trees acts as boundaries or borders between different areas or types of experiences. When Frost's speakers and subjects are near the edge of a forest, wandering in a forest, or climbing a tree, they exist in liminal spaces, halfway between the earth and the sky, which allow the speakers to engage with nature and experience moments of revelation.

BIRDS AND BIRDSONG

In Frost's poetry, birds represent nature, and their songs represent nature's attitudes toward humanity. Birds provide a voice for the natural world to communicate with humans. But their songs communicate only nature's indifference toward the human world, as in "The Need of Being Versed in Country Things" (1923) and "Never Again Would Birds' Song Be the Same" (1942). Their beautiful melodies belie an absence of feeling for humanity and our situations. Nevertheless, as a part of nature, birds have a right to their song, even if it annoys or distresses human listeners. In "A Minor Bird" (1928), the speaker eventually realizes that all songs must continue to exist, whether those songs are found in nature, as with birds, or in culture, as with poems. Frost also uses birds and birdsong to symbolize poetry, and birds become a medium through which to comment on the efficacy of poetry as a tool of emotional expression, as in "The Oven Bird" (1920).

SOLITARY TRAVELERS

Solitary travelers appear frequently in Frost's poems, and their attitudes toward their journeys and their surroundings highlight poetic and historical themes, including the figure of the wanderer and the changing social landscape of New England in the twentieth century. As in **romanticism**, a literary movement active in England from roughly 1750 to 1830, Frost's poetry demonstrates great respect for the social outcast, or wanderer, who exists on the fringes of a community. Like the romanticized notion of the solitary traveler, the poet was also separated from the community, which allowed him to view social interactions, as well as the natural world, with a sense of wonder, fear, and admiration. Able to engage with his surroundings using fresh eyes, the solitary traveler simultaneously exists as a part of the landscape and as an observer of the landscape. Found in "Stopping By Woods on a Snowy Evening" (1923), "Into My Own," "Acquainted with the Night," and "The Road Not Taken" (1920), among other poems, the solitary traveler demonstrates the historical and regional context of Frost's poetry. In the early twentieth century, the development of transportation and industry created the social type of the wandering "tramp," who lived a transient lifestyle, looking for work in a rapidly developing industrial society. Like Frost's speakers and subjects, these people lived on the outskirts of the community, largely away from the warmth and complexity of human interaction.

ROBERT FROST

Summary & Analysis

"Mending Wall"

Something there is that doesn't love a wall,
That sends the frozen-ground-swell under it,
And spills the upper boulders in the sun;
And makes gaps even two can pass abreast.
The work of hunters is another thing: 5
I have come after them and made repair
Where they have left not one stone on a stone,
But they would have the rabbit out of hiding,
To please the yelping dogs. The gaps I mean,
No one has seen them made or heard them made,   10
But at spring mending-time we find them there.
I let my neighbor know beyond the hill;
And on a day we meet to walk the line
And set the wall between us once again.
We keep the wall between us as we go.   15
To each the boulders that have fallen to each.
And some are loaves and some so nearly balls
We have to use a spell to make them balance:
"Stay where you are until our backs are turned!"
We wear our fingers rough with handling them.   20
Oh, just another kind of outdoor game,
One on a side. It comes to little more:
There where it is we do not need the wall:
He is all pine and I am apple orchard.
My apple trees will never get across   25
And eat the cones under his pines, I tell him.
He only says, "Good fences make good neighbors."
Spring is the mischief in me, and I wonder
If I could put a notion in his head:
"Why do they make good neighbors? Isn't it   30
Where there are cows? But here there are no cows.
Before I built a wall I'd ask to know
What I was walling in or walling out,
And to whom I was like to give offence.

ROBERT FROST

Something there is that doesn't love a wall,   35
That wants it down." I could say "Elves" to him,
But it's not elves exactly, and I'd rather
He said it for himself. I see him there
Bringing a stone grasped firmly by the top
In each hand, like an old-stone savage armed.   40
He moves in darkness as it seems to me,
Not of woods only and the shade of trees.
He will not go behind his father's saying,
And he likes having thought of it so well
He says again, "Good fences make good neighbors."   45

Summary

The speaker declares that there is something "that doesn't love a wall" (1). Each year, this thing damages the wall by causing the earth beneath the wall to freeze and shift, which displaces the wall's topmost rocks into the sunlight and creates holes big enough for two people to walk through. Hunters also damage the wall: they tear holes in it to let their dogs get at rabbits hiding between the rocks. Elsewhere, holes just seem to appear since no one sees or hears them being made, but the speaker and his neighbor discover them in the spring, during "mending-time" (11).

One day, the speaker tells his neighbor that the time has come to repair the wall, and they meet to fix it. As they walk, they keep the wall between them, passing the boulders that have fallen off the wall back and forth. The wall's stones balance precariously, and, as the speaker and his neighbor turn to grab the next stone, they tell the stones not to move. Their hands get sore and rubbed raw. But the speaker likens wall mending to playing, even as he explains that the wall itself is unnecessary. They do not need the wall since the speaker's apple trees will never cross over the property line to munch on his neighbor's pine tress. When the speaker makes this observation to his neighbor, though, his neighbor replies, "Good fences make good neighbors" (27). Spring makes the speaker feel playful, so he presses his neighbor to explain that comment. He considers the possibility that walls are built to fence in cows, but neither he nor his neighbor raises cows. This leads him to wonder who or what the wall keeps in and who or what the wall keeps out and who or what might be offended by the wall. The speaker then repeats the poem's first line, which explains that "something" wants to tear the wall down.

ROBERT FROST

In his mind, the speaker wonders whimsically if elves might be responsible for the wall's damage, but he'd rather that the neighbor offer a suggestion. He begins describing his neighbor, who stands holding stones in each hand, and he likens his neighbor to an ancient man carrying a weapon. But the neighbor will not entertain an option for the wall's existence other than the one he learned from his father. He likes this saying so much and feels so proud of his interpretation of this saying that he repeats it.

ANALYSIS

"Mending Wall" describes the boundaries, both physical and metaphorical, erected between people. Yet despite these self-imposed divisions, people are somehow able to connect with one another. Indeed, the two neighbors connect and interact through the mending of the wall, which proves the adage that good fences do make good neighbors. Inspired by the stone walls that snake through the New England countryside, the poem wonders why people insist on constructing boundaries. As the speaker points out, walls fence in livestock, but he and his neighbor are only containing trees within their walls. The wall simply divides property, a way for both the speaker and the neighbor to establish ownership of the land. Thus, the wall becomes a **symbol** for the tendency of individuals and society to section off, to cordon, and to exclude.

A sense of the unexplained haunts the poem. The speaker refers to a mysterious "something" that creates gaps and causes stones to tumble down. With the exception of the hunters, no human force acts to destroy the wall, yet every year the wall must be rebuilt. Whatever it may be, this strange force hates the wall. But the mysterious thing isn't to be feared, and the speaker thinks of the wall mending as "just another kind of outdoor game" (21). At one point, the speaker teasingly suggests that elves are responsible for the wall's damage. The speaker sympathizes with nature, whose force destroys the wall each year, and he agrees that the wall seems arbitrary and unnecessary. In fact, the speaker links the two men directly to nature when he says, "He is all pine and I am apple orchard" (24). Rather than own the land, the speaker and his neighbor are a part of the land, and they have become as natural as the trees that grow there. Nature—in all its mysterious glory—rejects man-made divisions and actively seeks to destroy the wall. The speaker spends much of the poem trying to convince his neighbor to understand the natural, anti-wall point of view.

Frost's simple subject matter often masks astute political commentary, and "Mending Wall" uses the annual wall rebuilding to show the complexity of social divisions. In the poem, two men meet, chat amicably, and learn about each other, all in the name of fixing the wall that divides their properties. The wall has no real purpose but to divide the properties—and to separate the men from each other. Watching his neighbor lifting stones, the speaker describes him as "an old-stone savage" (40), a comparison that highlights the history of wall building. Early ancestors built walls throughout the world in order to create the first societies: walls allowed early humans to domesticate animals, as well as to protect food supplies. Skeptically, the speaker listens to his neighbor's appeal to tradition as justification for wall building: his father believed that walls helped make "good neighbors," and now the neighbor believes that as well. But by mending the wall, the speaker and the neighbor have become "good neighbors." At the time of the poem's first publication, World War I had just begun. Among the complex reasons for war was a desire to erases boundaries and unify Serbia, and the war engulfed all of Europe partly because of ancient treaties that mandated automatic participation when an ally was attacked or at war. "Mending Walls" simultaneously demonstrates the arbitrary nature of human boundaries and the necessity of those boundaries.

"THE ROAD NOT TAKEN"

Two roads diverged in a yellow wood,
And sorry I could not travel both
And be one traveler, long I stood
And looked down one as far as I could
To where it bent in the undergrowth;   5

Then took the other, as just as fair,
And having perhaps the better claim,
Because it was grassy and wanted wear;
Though as for that the passing there
Had worn them really about the same,   10

And both that morning equally lay
In leaves no step had trodden black.
Oh, I kept the first for another day!

ROBERT FROST

> Yet knowing how way leads on to way,
> I doubted if I should ever come back.   15
>
> I shall be telling this with a sigh
> Somewhere ages and ages hence:
> Two roads diverged in a wood, and I—
> I took the one less traveled by,
> And that has made all the difference.   20

SUMMARY

The speaker—a traveler—describes the thought process that occurred one day as he came to a fork in the road and had to choose which road to continue walking along. He regretted not being able to travel down both as he stood and stared down the two roads, one at a time, until he could no longer see where each led. Ultimately he decided to take the second road since it looked less used, as if fewer people had traveled there. Upon further consideration, though, the speaker realized that both roads were about the same. Both were covered with leaves, and both looked as if they had rarely seen many travelers. The speaker hopes that someday he might return to travel the first road, but he knows that paths connect to other paths and still more paths. He realizes that he'll probably never return. When he tells the story someday in the future, the speaker will say that he took the road "less traveled" (19). Although he knows the roads were essentially the same, he shall say that his choice has made "all the difference" (20).

ANALYSIS

A very popular poem, "The Road Not Taken" is also a very misunderstood poem. Many readers see the poem as extolling its listeners to make unexpected choices rather than as a poem reminding them of the justifications used to make sense of past decisions. In our eagerness to understand the present in terms of the past, we sometimes forget the arbitrary nature of decision-making. As the speaker points out, the two roads from which the speaker must choose are "really about the same" (10), with no discernable difference in the leaves or tracks. Life rarely presents us with two equal choices, and decisions are rarely as simple as choosing a road. We also fictionalize, or tell stories about, our past to make it more interesting, a tendency the speaker points out in the final stanza. There he explains that he will jazz up his choice to take the second road, even though he knows how random the actual events were. But in the retelling, his choice will assume a great but entirely undeserved significance. Like the speaker, we also frequently comb over the past for clues to the present, ascribing weight and meaning to some events while forgetting about or ignoring others.

Frost buried the poem's **irony** and humor beneath its simple rhyme scheme and form. In quintets, or five-line **stanzas**, Frost employs an *abaab* rhyme scheme and **iambic tetrameter** meter. The first road, or the road not taken, looks more traveled, according to the speaker. But in stanza 3, the speaker acknowledges that neither road looks particularly traveled—one of the poem's central ironies. Similarly, the poem's title refers to the road that has not made all the difference—that is, the title refers to the first road, the road the speaker did not choose. Frost wrote the poem for his friend Edward Thomas, who was notorious for agonizing over decisions and then sighing constantly about them once he had committed to a choice. To capture this angst, Frost punctuates line 18 with an em dash; this dash demonstrates a hesitancy, as if the speaker still wondered whether he had taken the "right" road. On their walks together, Thomas would lament paths not chosen and feel great distress over what might have been had the pair veered elsewhere. Although some decisions require much thought, Frost implies that choosing a road down which to stroll is not one of them. The greatest irony, of course, is the way in which a humorous poem poking fun at Frost's friend has been elevated to the status of sage advice about life.

"BIRCHES"

> When I see birches bend to left and right
> Across the lines of straighter darker trees,
> I like to think some boy's been swinging them.
> But swinging doesn't bend them down to stay.
> Ice-storms do that. Often you must have seen them   5
> Loaded with ice a sunny winter morning
> After a rain. They click upon themselves
> As the breeze rises, and turn many-coloured
> As the stir cracks and crazes their enamel.
> Soon the sun's warmth makes them shed crystal shells   10
> Shattering and avalanching on the snow-crust
> Such heaps of broken glass to sweep away
> You'd think the inner dome of heaven had fallen.

They are dragged to the withered bracken by the load,
And they seem not to break; though once they are bowed   15
So low for long, they never right themselves:
You may see their trunks arching in the woods
Years afterwards, trailing their leaves on the ground,
Like girls on hands and knees that throw their hair
Before them over their heads to dry in the sun.   20
But I was going to say when Truth broke in
With all her matter-of-fact about the ice-storm,
I should prefer to have some boy bend them
As he went out and in to fetch the cows—
Some boy too far from town to learn baseball,   25
Whose only play was what he found himself,
Summer or winter, and could play alone.
One by one he subdued his father's trees
By riding them down over and over again
Until he took the stiffness out of them,   30
And not one but hung limp, not one was left
For him to conquer. He learned all there was
To learn about not launching out too soon
And so not carrying the tree away
Clear to the ground. He always kept his poise   35
To the top branches, climbing carefully
With the same pains you use to fill a cup
Up to the brim, and even above the brim.
Then he flung outward, feet first, with a swish,
Kicking his way down through the air to the ground.   40
So was I once myself a swinger of birches.
And so I dream of going back to be.
It's when I'm weary of considerations,
And life is too much like a pathless wood
Where your face burns and tickles with the cobwebs   45
Broken across it, and one eye is weeping
From a twig's having lashed across it open.
I'd like to get away from earth awhile
And then come back to it and begin over.
May no fate willfully misunderstand me   50
And half grant what I wish and snatch me away
Not to return. Earth's the right place for love:
I don't know where it's likely to go better.
I'd like to go by climbing a birch tree

> And climb black branches up a snow-white trunk   55
> Toward *heaven, till the tree could bear no more,*
> *But dipped its top and set me down again.*
> *That would be good both going and coming back.*
> *One could do worse than be a swinger of birches.*

SUMMARY

When the speaker sees lilting or curving birch trees, he likes to imagine that a playful boy caused the damage by swinging on the trees. However, the speaker acknowledges that the trees are permanently damaged from ice storms—not from a boy's play. Musing on the beauty of the trees when they are encased in ice, he compares the ice shards that fall to the ground to pieces of glass, as if the roof of heaven itself had been shattered. Once the trees are bent, they stay that way, never again growing upright or straight. The bent trees resemble girls who have contorted themselves in the sunlight after washing their hair.

The speaker explains that he would have continued to attribute the bent trees to the play of a young boy had not "Truth broke in" (21) to give the real reason for the misshapen trees—that is, the ice storm. After this interjection, the speaker returns to the image of one boy frolicking in the woods, having been sent to collect his family's livestock. Since the boy lives outside of town, the speaker explains, he must invent activities for himself rather than playing organized games with other young people. Instead of focusing on this invented boy, the speaker begins describing the boy's actions in the past tense. He describes how the boy repeatedly swung on the trees until every tree was bent and floppy. Next the speaker describes how the boy would swing: after much practice, he learned to scramble up the tree with care, with "the same pains you use to fill a cup" (37). At the top of the tree, the boy would fling himself forward, writhing until he reached the earth.

In the final few lines of the poem, the speaker reveals that he was once like this boy, a scamp and climber of trees. When he gets sick of adulthood, the speaker imagines that he can return to being a carefree youth. He has grown tired of making decisions and compares his life to a tangled forest with no direction. Now he wishes he could start life over. Qualifying this statement, the speaker explains that he does not want to be misunderstood: he does not want to die and not come back. Rather, he says, he would like to leave the earth for a while by going up a birch tree. When he has scampered to the top, the tree will begin to bend under his weight and return him to the ground. This would be a good way to leave and to return to the earth, and he concludes, "One could do worse than be a swinger of birches" (59).

ANALYSIS

Published in 1916, "Birches" marks a stylistic shift in Frost's poetry. The poem merges the bucolic natural imagery of his earlier work with the dark, pessimistic metaphysical style of his later work. Images of the countryside appears throughout "Birches," particularly in the meticulous care with which Frost describes the iced-over trees. The earlier Frost also appears in the willful, mischievous attribution of bent trees to boys, rather than to ice storms, and in the playful image of the boy swinging through the trees. The later Frost appears in the voice of "Truth," who gives her "matter-of-fact" (22) opinion about the real reason for the bent birches and in the speaker's wish to abandon adulthood for the carefree innocence of childhood. Indeed, the speaker seems to weigh death and reincarnation against continuing on, even as his worries enervate him. Although the speaker values the love to be found in the earthly world, by the end of the poem, he seems ready to trade his day-to-day reality for his birch-swinging fantasy.

"Birches" comments directly on the poetry-writing process and provides insight into Frost's specific process. Two contrasting voices appear in the poem. The first is that of the speaker, whose musings on birch trees generate the poem, and the second is that of Truth, who retrieves the speaker from reverie and returns him to reality. These two voices clash, much the same as nonfiction and fiction sometimes present competing views of the same situation—the idea of what really happened versus what we wished had happened. In the poem, the fictional explanation for the bent trees competes with the real explanation: the image of boys playing on trees is far more appealing than the image of ice storms, even though Frost compares the ice shards to pieces of glass. The poem describes the progression of the poet's imagination: sparked by the natural landscape, the speaker imagines an alternative explanation for an aspect of the landscape and uses this natural aspect to launch a lyrical meditation on some facet of the human condition. His poem reenacts this process, as it opens with the speaker looking at some bent birch trees, imagining that boys had done the damage rather than ice storms, and closes with an extended meditation on aging, adulthood, and lost innocence. Poetry functions like the birches, allowing the poet and his readers to escape from worldly cares temporarily.

Frost uses "Birches" to idealize youth and to contrast the experiences of youth to the experiences of aging. To formulate this contrast between youth and adulthood, the speaker's verb tense switches from the present, used in lines 1–27, to the past, used in lines 28–59. A similar switch in perspective occurs when the speaker confesses to himself having once swung from trees, in line 41. Rather than imagining a fictional boy, the speaker begins to recall his own experiences, which leads him to use the past tense. He mournfully compares the worries of his adulthood with the carefree attitudes of his childhood. Now that the speaker has grown up, he has become jaded. For him, nature has become menacing and fills him with pain. As an adult, when the speaker sees ice shards, he imagines that "the inner dome of heaven had fallen" (13), an indication of his lost illusions. The speaker also agonizes over situations, including whether fate might misconstrue his lamentations, causing him to die but without returning him to an idyllic childhood. Even as the speaker longs to return to the breezy life of youth, he also qualifies his earlier statements by explaining that he simply wants a quick release from his troubles, not death and not reincarnation. He wants to swing along the branches, away from earthly concerns, but he still wants to return to the earth eventually.

"Stopping by Woods on a Snowy Evening" [1]

Whose woods these are I think I know.
His house is in the village, though;
He will not see me stopping here
To watch his woods fill up with snow.

My little horse must think it queer   5
To stop without a farmhouse near
Between the woods and frozen lake
The darkest evening of the year.

1. "Stopping by Woods on a Snowy Evening" from *The Poetry of Robert Frost* edited by Edward Connery Lathem. Copyright 1923, 1969 by Henry Holt and Company. Copyright 1951 by Robert Frost. Reprinted by permission of Henry Holt and Company, LLC.

ROBERT FROST

> *He gives his harness bells a shake*
> *To ask if there is some mistake.*   10
> *The only other sound's the sweep*
> *Of easy wind and downy flake.*
>
> *The woods are lovely, dark and deep,*
> *But I have promises to keep,*
> *And miles to go before I sleep,*   15
> *And miles to go before I sleep.*

SUMMARY

A lone traveler pauses during the course of his journey to watch snow fall in the woods at night. The forest looks familiar, and the speaker thinks he knows the owner, who keeps his home in the village and will not know that the traveler has stopped on his property. As the speaker takes a moment to watch the snow fall and to enjoy the beauty of the scene, his horse indicates some confusion about why they have stopped. Normally, the horse and the speaker stop only to turn in for the night, but now they are completely alone, far away from any houses, stopped in the middle of a dark forest. At the sound of the horse's bells, the speaker awakes from his reverie, for the forest is silent except for the whisper of wind and snow falling. Although the beauty of the scene almost hypnotizes the speaker, he realizes that he must continue traveling. He has many obligations to fulfill, and he has far to go before he can stop to rest.

ANALYSIS

Perhaps Frost's most famous poem, "Stopping by Woods on a Snowy Evening" captivates readers with its singsong meter and its mostly interlocking *aaba bbcb* rhyme scheme while simultaneously seducing readers with its images of great beauty. Nevertheless, the poem actually portrays a dark, scary scene of great ambiguity, in which the traveler falls into a trance as he watches the snow fall. Alone in the woods, the traveler will freeze to death should he fall asleep during a nighttime winter storm in New England. Had the horse not made some noise, the traveler might have continued to stay and watch. A scene of much beauty, therefore, is actually fraught with danger. Like the traveler fascinated by the snow, readers become hypnotized by the poem's iambic tetrameter and the repetition of the poem's final lines. And like the traveler, readers might subsequently neglect to notice its dark undertones. As in so many Frost poems, "Stopping by Woods on a Snowy Evening" contains veins of pessimism running beneath seemingly simple cadence and diction.

The central conflict of the poem lies in the tension between society and nature. Stopping to admire the snow, the traveler takes a momentary break from his long journey. But his horse urges the traveler on and reminds the traveler of his obligations to society. He must continue traveling, even as he longs to admire nature's beauty and to rest among the "lovely, dark, and deep" woods (13). The last stanza emphasizes this tension: although the first line of the quatrain describes the soporific effect of the trees, the remaining three lines remind the traveler—and the reader—that civilization beckons. Three lines tip the balance, and the traveler leaves. Another manifestation of the tension between society and nature appears in the forest itself. Although the woods are domesticated and legally possessed, the owner lives in town, thereby allowing the woods to be wild and uninhabited. Thus, both society and nature inhabit the woods, making the forest simultaneously civilized and uncivilized, as well as making the forest an ideal border space in which to mediate on the pull between community and country.

"Stopping by Woods on a Snowy Evening" contemplates death to ultimately comment on poetry. Metaphorically, the woods and sleep represent death, and the journey represents life. The enchantment the speaker feels in looking at the woods perhaps indicates a weariness with life, much the same as the speaker in "Birches" longed to be rid of his adult worries and return to the carefree attitude of childhood. The final stanza, the only stanza in which all four lines rhyme with one another, demonstrates the speaker's weariness by repeating the word *sleep* and the phrase "miles to go." In assessing whether to fulfill his obligations and continue the journey, the speaker resembles a poet weary from writing and worried about the efficacy of poetry. Constantly ruminating over nature and then articulating these ruminations in verse produces a mental strain. Also, writing poetry isolates the writer from the community because the poet must always be an observer, paying attention for material rather than participating. However, like the speaker of "Stopping by Woods on a Snowy Evening," true poets feel obligations to their readers and their craft, and they ultimately choose to keep writing.

ROBERT FROST

T. S. ELIOT

(1888–1965)

CONTEXT

Thomas Stearns Eliot was born in St. Louis, Missouri, on September 26, 1888, into a wealthy, successful family. His grandfather, Walter Eliot, had left Boston society to found a Unitarian church in St. Louis. Once there, he established himself in the community, eventually serving as one of the founders of Washington University. Eliot's father was a successful businessman in the brick trade, and his mother, Charlotte Stearns, was a teacher, volunteer, and poet.

As a child, Eliot lived in St. Louis and vacationed at the family summer home in Gloucester, Massachusetts. He attended Smith Academy in St. Louis, then left to attend Milton Academy in Massachusetts and entered Harvard in 1906. Within four years, he had earned a bachelor's degree in comparative literature and a master's degree in English literature. At Harvard, Eliot began distinguishing himself as a poet. A book he discovered in 1908, Arthur Symond's *The Symbolist Movement in Literature* (1899), introduced him to a group of French poets noted for their unique use of **symbols** and **imagery**. After graduating from Harvard in 1910, Eliot spent a year at the Sorbonne, studying French writers and participating in the cultural and intellectual life of Paris. Within a year, he returned to Harvard to pursue further graduate work in philosophy, studying both Western and non-Western traditions with William James, Bertrand Russell, and other well-known minds of the day. He left Harvard again for the University of Marburg in Germany in 1914, then went to complete his studies at Oxford University in England. Eliot never returned to Harvard to defend his doctoral thesis, preferring to settle in England on completion of his studies, where he took up work as a schoolteacher.

Eliot quickly became a part of the London literary community, in which he received some praise for his poetry. With an introduction from poet Conrad Aiken, Eliot met Ezra Pound, the renowned critic and imagist poet. Under Pound's tutelage, the poems that Eliot had composed at Harvard took shape and were published in various literary magazines. Eventually, these poems were published as Eliot's first full collection, titled *Prufrock and Other Observations*, in 1917. Around this time, Eliot was also introduced to Vivien Haigh-Wood. Charmed by the dancer's directness and poise, Eliot married her, despite objections from his family, who worried about her history of emotional problems and mental illness. With his marriage to an Englishwoman, Eliot cemented his expatriate status.

The Eliots socialized with Pound's expatriate crowd and the Bloomsbury group, a loose cadre of intellectuals and artists, including the publisher Leonard Woolf, the writer Virginia Woolf, the artist and critic Roger Fry, and the economist John Maynard Keyes. In 1917, Eliot stopped teaching and began working at Lloyd's Bank. When not at work, he wrote vigorously, garnering a strong reputation as a critic and lecturer. After suffering a minor breakdown, Eliot spent a few months on a rest cure in Switzerland. There he started work on what would become his poetic opus and arguably the most important poem of the twentieth century, *The Waste Land* (1922). Initial reviews of the poem were somewhat mixed, and many expressed bewilderment and frustration at the dauntingly ambitious poem, but the overwhelming reaction was one of acclaim for Eliot's masterpiece, and Eliot was heralded as a master poet.

Despite his career success, Eliot faced many challenges in his personal life. Eliot began editing the literary journal *Criterion* and joined Faber and Gwyer, a well-known London publishing house that later became Faber and Faber. He continued writing, publishing few poems but many pieces of criticism and some plays, and he gave the influential Norton Lectures at Harvard in 1932–1933. Meanwhile, his wife, Vivien, grew increasingly unstable, and Eliot played at least some role in having her committed to Northumberland House, a mental hospital, in 1938. She died there in 1947. (Their marriage and emotional life was fictionalized in the 1994 movie *Tom & Viv*.) By far the most dramatic changes in Eliot's life were his conversion to Anglicanism and his taking of British citizenship in 1927. Eliot's newfound zeal for the church resulted in a major change in his poetry, which took on a spiritual bent and focused on Christian subjects. "The Hollow Men" (1925), *Ash Wednesday* (1930), and *Murder in the Cathedral* (1935) are some notable Eliot works that grapple with religion, spirituality, and philosophy in an increasingly violent, modern world.

Four Quartets, Eliot's last major poetic work, appeared in 1943. World War II destroyed much of the London literary world, both figuratively and literally. During the Blitz, Eliot worked as an air raid warden, but he spent much of the war in rural Guildford. After the war, Eliot received several significant honors and awards, including the Order of Merit and the Nobel Prize in Literature, both

T. S. ELIOT

in 1948. He married Valerie Fletcher in 1957 and continued to lecture, write, and publish up until his death in London in January 1965. Eliot's criticism, particularly the 1920 volume of prose, *The Sacred Wood*, was extremely influential: the New Critics of the 1950s used Eliot's theories to develop a rigid commitment to reading poems as self-contained works. New Criticism emphasized so-called close readings of poetry's formal structures. In his prose, Eliot argued for a return to classical themes, the importance of scholarship and knowledge, and the acknowledgment and acceptance of authority. He favored order over chaos and valued difficulty and density in writing. According to his views, good poetry should contain an "objective correlative," in which precise language should be used to correspond to specific emotional experiences of the reader.

Some scholars argue that both Eliot and Pound wrote *The Waste Land*. For many years, Eliot kept silent about the composition history of his poem, although he occasionally acknowledged that he had received some editing help from his friend Pound and even from his wife Vivien. In 1971, Eliot's second wife, Valerie, published a facsimile edition of *The Waste Land*, which allowed readers to see firsthand the extent of Pound's help. The facsimile edition reprints handwritten notes from Pound, in which he made extensive suggestions for cutting and revision. Eliot's original draft of the poem is dramatically different from the poem we now read as *The Waste Land*: the original was much longer, contained more explanations, and had a different structure than the difficult, dense work that was ultimately published. The extent of the revision has led some scholars to argue that the names of both Eliot and Pound should appear on the title page as the authors. Other critics argue that Pound simply helped Eliot achieve the poem Eliot had in mind but couldn't quite get out on paper, much as editors help writers shape their work without actually rewriting their words. Today, *The Waste Land* stands as not only a crucial modernist poem but also as an important example of the collaborative process that occurs between all writers and editors.

As a poet, Eliot was strongly influenced by the imagist and symbolist movements of the early twentieth century. The imagist poets, including Pound and H. D. (Hilda Doolittle), rejected the sentimental mannerism of romantic poetry. Instead, they used images, vivid sensory description, and common language to create concentrated free verse that spoke directly to emotions and experience. In turn, the imagists cross-pollinated with the symbolists, who drew on the use of private symbols within the romantic poetry of William Blake,

John Keats, William Wordsworth, and others. French poets, such as Stéphane Mallarmé, Arthur Rimbaud, and Paul Verlaine, created systems of **symbols** of rich suggestiveness in their poems, which drew subtle analogies between language, emotion, and spirituality. The joint influences of imagism and symbolism led, in part, to the development of literary **modernism**. In Eliot, modernism developed an allusive **irony** that blended elements from high and low culture.

Many critics consider *The Waste Land* to be the definitive poetic statement of modernist poetry. The term *modernism*, when applied to literary study, refers to a trend that began around World War I. This trend rejected traditional models of social organization, morality, religion, and art. The war transformed the moral structure of civilization, causing artists to question the validity of a stable social order. Modernist poems challenged readers to draw connections among complex jumbles of symbols and **imagery** and dealt with heady subject matter, such as political disillusion, sexual alienation, and cultural disenfranchisement. *The Waste Land* became the model of the modernist long poem, drawing upon the traditions of the Western **epic** poem, the short symbolist poem, and the romantic **ode**, among others. Modernism, and Eliot himself, rejuvenated literature, influencing the ways that poetry and novels were written and read, and changed the face of Western literary culture.

T. S. ELIOT

THEMES, MOTIFS & SYMBOLS

THEMES

THE DAMAGED PSYCHE OF HUMANITY

Like many modernist writers, Eliot wanted his poetry to express the fragile psychological state of humanity in the twentieth century. The passing of Victorian ideals and the trauma of World War I challenged cultural notions of masculine identity, causing artists to question the romantic literary ideal of a visionary-poet capable of changing the world through verse. Modernist writers wanted to capture their transformed world, which they perceived as fractured, alienated, and denigrated. Europe lost an entire generation of young men to the horrors of the so-called Great War, causing a general crisis of masculinity as survivors struggled to find their place in a radically altered society. As for England, the aftershocks of World War I directly contributed to the dissolution of the British Empire. Eliot saw society as paralyzed and wounded, and he imagined that culture was crumbling and dissolving. "The Love Song of J. Alfred Prufrock" (1917) demonstrates this sense of indecisive paralysis as the titular **speaker** wonders whether he should eat a piece of fruit, make a radical change, or if he has the fortitude to keep living. Humanity's collectively damaged psyche prevented people from communicating with one another, an idea that Eliot explored in many works, including "A Game of Chess" (the second part of *The Waste Land*) and "The Hollow Men."

THE POWER OF LITERARY HISTORY

Eliot maintained great reverence for myth and the Western literary **canon**, and he packed his work full of **allusions**, quotations, footnotes, and scholarly **exegeses**. In "The Tradition and the Individual Talent," an essay first published in 1919, Eliot praises the literary tradition and states that the best writers are those who write with a sense of continuity with those writers who came before, as if all of literature constituted a stream in which each new writer must enter and swim. Only the very best new work will subtly shift the stream's current and thus improve the literary tradition. Eliot also argued that the literary past must be integrated into contemporary poetry. But the poet must guard against excessive academic knowledge and distill only the most essential bits of the past into a poem, thereby enlightening readers. *The Waste Land* juxtaposes fragments of various elements of literary and mythic traditions with scenes and sounds from modern life. The effect of this poetic collage is both a reinterpretation of canonical texts and a historical context for his examination of society and humanity.

THE CHANGING NATURE OF GENDER ROLES

Over the course of Eliot's life, gender roles and sexuality became increasingly flexible, and Eliot reflected those changes in his work. In the repressive **Victorian era** of the nineteenth century, women were confined to the domestic sphere, sexuality was not discussed or publicly explored, and a puritanical atmosphere dictated most social interactions. Queen Victoria's death in 1887 helped usher in a new era of excess and forthrightness, now called the Edwardian Age, from 1901 to 1910. World War I, from 1914 to 1918, further transformed society, as people felt both increasingly alienated from one another and empowered to break social mores. English women began agitating in earnest for the right to vote in 1918, and the flappers of the Jazz Age began smoking and drinking alcohol in public. Women were allowed to attend school, and women who could afford it continued their education at those universities that began accepting women in the early twentieth century. Modernist writers created gay and lesbian characters and re-imagined masculinity and femininity as characteristics people could assume or shrug off rather than as absolute identities dictated by society.

Eliot simultaneously lauded the end of the Victorian era and expressed concern about the freedoms inherent in the modern age. "The Love Song of J. Alfred Prufrock" reflects the feelings of emasculation experienced by many men as they returned home from World War I to find women empowered by their new role as wage earners. Prufrock, unable to make a decision, watches women wander in and out of a room, "talking of Michelangelo" (14), and elsewhere admires their downy, bare arms. A disdain for unchecked sexuality appears in both "Sweeney Among the Nightingales" (1918) and *The Waste Land*. The latter portrays rape, prostitution, a conversation about abortion, and other incidences of nonreproductive sexuality. Nevertheless, the poem's central character, Tiresias, is a hermaphrodite—and his powers of prophesy and transformation are, in some sense, due to his male and female genitalia. With Tiresias, Eliot creates a character that embodies wholeness, represented by the two genders coming together in one body.

MOTIFS

FRAGMENTATION

Eliot used fragmentation in his poetry both to demonstrate the chaotic state of modern existence and to juxtapose literary texts against one another. In Eliot's view, humanity's psyche had been shattered by World War I and by the collapse of the British Empire. Collaging bits and pieces of dialogue, images, scholarly ideas, foreign words, formal styles, and **tones** within one poetic work was a way for Eliot to represent humanity's damaged psyche and the modern world, with its barrage of sensory perceptions. Critics read the following line from *The Waste Land* as a statement of Eliot's poetic project: "These fragments I have shored against my ruins" (431). Practically every line in *The Waste Land* echoes an academic work or canonical literary text, and many lines also have long footnotes written by Eliot as an attempt to explain his references and to encourage his readers to educate themselves by delving deeper into his sources. These echoes and references are fragments themselves, since Eliot includes only parts, rather than whole texts from the **canon**. Using these fragments, Eliot tries to highlight recurrent themes and images in the literary tradition, as well as to place his ideas about the contemporary state of humanity along the spectrum of history.

MYTHIC AND RELIGIOUS RITUAL

Eliot's tremendous knowledge of myth, religious ritual, academic works, and key books in the literary tradition informs every aspect of his poetry. He filled his poems with references to both the obscure and the well known, thereby teaching his readers as he writes. In his notes to *The Waste Land*, Eliot explains the crucial role played by religious symbols and myths. He drew heavily from ancient fertility rituals, in which the fertility of the land was linked to the health of the Fisher King, a wounded figure who could be healed through the sacrifice of an effigy. The Fisher King is, in turn, linked to the Holy Grail legends, in which a knight quests to find the grail, the only object capable of healing the land. Ultimately, ritual fails as the tool for healing the wasteland, even as Eliot presents alternative religious possibilities, including Hindu chants, Buddhist speeches, and pagan ceremonies. Later poems take their images almost exclusively from Christianity, such as the echoes of the Lord's Prayer in "The Hollow Men" and the retelling of the story of the wise men in "Journey of the Magi" (1927).

INFERTILITY

Eliot envisioned the modern world as a wasteland, in which neither the land nor the people could conceive. In *The Waste Land*, various characters are sexually frustrated or dysfunctional, unable to cope with either reproductive or nonreproductive sexuality: the Fisher King represents damaged sexuality (according to myth, his impotence causes the land to wither and dry up), Tiresias represents confused or ambiguous sexuality, and the women chattering in "A Game of Chess" represent an out-of-control sexuality. World War I not only eradicated an entire generation of young men in Europe but also ruined the land. Trench warfare and chemical weapons, the two primary methods by which the war was fought, decimated plant life, leaving behind detritus and carnage. In "The Hollow Men," the speaker discusses the dead land, now filled with stone and cacti. Corpses salute the stars with their upraised hands, stiffened from rigor mortis. Trying to process the destruction has caused the speaker's mind to become infertile: his head has been filled with straw, and he is now unable to think properly, to perceive accurately, or to conceive of images or thoughts.

SYMBOLS

WATER

In Eliot's poetry, water symbolizes both life and death. Eliot's characters wait for water to quench their thirst, watch rivers overflow their banks, cry for rain to quench the dry earth, and pass by fetid pools of standing water. Although water has the regenerative possibility of restoring life and fertility, it can also lead to drowning and death, as in the case of Phlebas the sailor from *The Waste Land*. Traditionally, water can imply baptism, Christianity, and the figure of Jesus Christ, and Eliot draws upon these traditional meanings: water cleanses, water provides solace, and water brings relief elsewhere in *The Waste Land* and in "Little Gidding," the fourth part of *Four Quartets*. Prufrock hears the seductive calls of mermaids as he walks along the shore in "The Love Song of J. Alfred Prufrock," but, like Odysseus in Homer's *Odyssey* (ca. 800 B.C.E.), he realizes that a malicious intent lies behind the sweet voices: the poem concludes "we drown" (131). Eliot thus cautions us to beware of simple solutions or cures, for what looks innocuous might turn out to be very dangerous.

THE FISHER KING

The Fisher King is the central character in *The Waste Land*. While writing his long poem, Eliot drew on *From Ritual to Romance*, a 1920 book about the legend of the Holy Grail by Miss Jessie L. Weston, for many of his symbols and images. Weston's book examined the connections between ancient fertility rites and Christianity, including following the evolution of the Fisher King into early representations of Jesus Christ as a fish. Traditionally, the impotence or death of the Fisher King brought unhappiness and famine. Eliot saw the Fisher King as symbolic of humanity, robbed of its sexual potency in the modern world and connected to the meaninglessness of urban existence. But the Fisher King also stands in for Christ and other religious figures associated with divine resurrection and rebirth. The speaker of "What the Thunder Said" fishes from the banks of the Thames toward the end of the poem as the thunder sounds Hindu chants into the air. Eliot's scene echoes the scene in the Bible in which Christ performs one of his miracles: Christ manages to feed his multitude of followers by the Sea of Galilee with just a small amount of fish.

MUSIC AND SINGING

Like most modernist writers, Eliot was interested in the divide between high and low culture, which he symbolized using music. He believed that high culture, including art, opera, and drama, was in decline while popular culture was on the rise. In *The Waste Land*, Eliot blended high culture with low culture by juxtaposing lyrics from an opera by Richard Wagner with songs from pubs, American ragtime, and Australian troops. Eliot splices nursery rhymes with phrases from the Lord's Prayer in "The Hollow Men," and "The Love Song of J. Alfred Prufrock" is, as the title, implies a song, with various lines repeated as refrains. That poem ends with the song of mermaids luring humans to their deaths by drowning—a scene that echoes Odysseus's interactions with the Sirens in the *Odyssey*. Music thus becomes another way in which Eliot collages and references books from past literary traditions. Elsewhere Eliot uses lyrics as a kind of chorus, seconding and echoing the action of the poem, much as the chorus functions in Greek tragedies.

Summary & Analysis

"The Love Song of J. Alfred Prufrock"

S'io credesse che mia risposta fosse
A persona che mai tornasse al mondo,
Questa fiamma staria senza piu scosse.
Ma perciocche giammai di questo fondo
Non torno vivo alcun, s'i'odo il vero,
Senza tema d'infamia ti rispondo.

Let us go then, you and I,
When the evening is spread out against the sky
Like a patient etherised upon a table;
Let us go, through certain half-deserted streets,
The muttering retreats   5
Of restless nights in one-night cheap hotels
And sawdust restaurants with oyster-shells:
Streets that follow like a tedious argument
Of insidious intent
To lead you to an overwhelming question ...   10
Oh, do not ask, "What is it?"
Let us go and make our visit.

In the room the women come and go
Talking of Michelangelo.

The yellow fog that rubs its back upon the window-panes, 15
The yellow smoke that rubs its muzzle on the window-panes
Licked its tongue into the corners of the evening,
Lingered upon the pools that stand in drains,
Let fall upon its back the soot that falls from chimneys,
Slipped by the terrace, made a sudden leap,   20
And seeing that it was a soft October night,
Curled once about the house, and fell asleep.

And indeed there will be time
For the yellow smoke that slides along the street,
Rubbing its back upon the window-panes;   25
There will be time, there will be time
To prepare a face to meet the faces that you meet;
There will be time to murder and create,
And time for all the works and days of hands
That lift and drop a question on your plate;   30
Time for you and time for me,
And time yet for a hundred indecisions,
And for a hundred visions and revisions,
Before the taking of a toast and tea.

In the room the women come and go   35
Talking of Michelangelo.

And indeed there will be time
To wonder, "Do I dare?" and, "Do I dare?"
Time to turn back and descend the stair,
With a bald spot in the middle of my hair—   40
(They will say: "How his hair is growing thin!")
My morning coat, my collar mounting firmly to the chin,
My necktie rich and modest, but asserted by a simple pin—
(They will say: "But how his arms and legs are thin!")
Do I dare   45
Disturb the universe?
In a minute there is time
For decisions and revisions which a minute will reverse.

For I have known them all already, known them all—
Have known the evenings, mornings, afternoons,   50
I have measured out my life with coffee spoons;
I know the voices dying with a dying fall
Beneath the music from a farther room.
    So how should I presume?

And I have known the eyes already, known them all—   55
The eyes that fix you in a formulated phrase,
And when I am formulated, sprawling on a pin,
When I am pinned and wriggling on the wall,
Then how should I begin

To spit out all the butt-ends of my days and ways?   60
    And how should I presume?

And I have known the arms already, known them all—
Arms that are braceleted and white and bare
(But in the lamplight, downed with light brown hair!)
Is it perfume from a dress   65
That makes me so digress?
Arms that lie along a table, or wrap about a shawl.
    And should I then presume?
    And how should I begin?

        .   .   .   .   .

Shall I say, I have gone at dusk through narrow streets   70
And watched the smoke that rises from the pipes
Of lonely men in shirt-sleeves, leaning out of windows? . . .
I should have been a pair of ragged claws
Scuttling across the floors of silent seas.

        .   .   .   .   .

And the afternoon, the evening, sleeps so peacefully!   75
Smoothed by long fingers,
Asleep . . . tired . . . or it malingers,
Stretched on the floor, here beside you and me.
Should I, after tea and cakes and ices,
Have the strength to force the moment to its crisis?   80
But though I have wept and fasted, wept and prayed,
Though I have seen my head (grown slightly bald) brought in
    upon a platter,
I am no prophet—and here's no great matter;
I have seen the moment of my greatness flicker,
And I have seen the eternal Footman hold my coat, and snicker, 85
And in short, I was afraid.

And would it have been worth it, after all,
After the cups, the marmalade, the tea,
Among the porcelain, among some talk of you and me,
Would it have been worth while,   90
To have bitten off the matter with a smile,
To have squeezed the universe into a ball
To roll it toward some overwhelming question,

T. S. ELIOT

To say: "I am Lazarus, come from the dead,
Come back to tell you all, I shall tell you all" —   95
If one, settling a pillow by her head,
   Should say: "That is not what I meant at all.
   That is not it, at all."

And would it have been worth it, after all,
Would it have been worth while,   100
After the sunsets and the dooryards and the sprinkled streets,
After the novels, after the teacups, after the skirts that trail
   along the floor—
And this, and so much more?—
It is impossible to say just what I mean!
But as if a magic lantern threw the nerves in patterns on
   a screen: 105
Would it have been worth while
If one, settling a pillow or throwing off a shawl,
And turning toward the window, should say:
   "That is not it at all,
   That is not what I meant, at all."   110

   .   .   .   .

No! I am not Prince Hamlet, nor was meant to be;
Am an attendant lord, one that will do
To swell a progress, start a scene or two,
Advise the prince; no doubt, an easy tool,
Deferential, glad to be of use,   115
Politic, cautious, and meticulous;
Full of high sentence, but a bit obtuse;
At times, indeed, almost ridiculous—
Almost, at times, the Fool.

I grow old . . . I grow old . . .   120
I shall wear the bottoms of my trousers rolled.
Shall I part my hair behind? Do I dare to eat a peach?
I shall wear white flannel trousers, and walk upon the beach.
I have heard the mermaids singing, each to each.

I do not think that they will sing to me.   125
I have seen them riding seaward on the waves
Combing the white hair of the waves blown back
When the wind blows the water white and black.

T. S. ELIOT

We have lingered in the chambers of the sea
By sea-girls wreathed with seaweed red and brown   *130*
Till human voices wake us, and we drown.

SUMMARY

"The Love Song of J. Alfred Prufrock" is a **dramatic monologue** and character study that does not follow a single plot. The poem begins as an invitation from the speaker to walk into the foggy evening, through almost-empty byways, and go call on some people. Neither the listener nor the people are named. Inside a room, women enter and leave, talking about Michelangelo; these lines become a refrain in the first half of the poem. The speaker describes a dismal mist that covers everything on that October night. Facing a world covered in this mist, the speaker thinks that there will be enough time for him to take action, but he is paralyzed by indecision, wondering, "Do I dare?" (38). The speaker describes his bald spot and his suit and wonders if people will think him too thin. He hesitates, questioning whether his actions might "disturb the universe" (46). The speaker notes the passage of time, as well as the passing of his own life. All his waiting has caused him to feel trapped, like an insect pinned to the wall.

Prufrock repeats himself in **stanzas** 7 through 9, explaining what he has had knowledge of, including women. He asks whether he should mention his strolls at evening, walking past men hanging out of windows, then concludes that he should have been born a crab. The speaker describes the way afternoons bleed into evenings, his attempts at prayer, and his fear. Next he wonders if it would have been useful for him to take action by transforming himself into Lazarus, who revived himself from the dead. The speaker expresses his frustration at not being able to adequately verbalize his thoughts. He knows he is not a great man, like Prince Hamlet, but wishes that he had at least played a role in the drama of his (or anyone's) life, acting as a counselor or valet who could have moved the action along, even if he was not in its center. He mourns the passing of his life and rhetorically wonders if he should change his hairstyle or eat a piece of fruit. Overanalyzing even the smallest of decisions, Prufrock concludes his love song by losing himself in a reverie of romantic love, which involves walks along the beach and singing mermaids.

T. S. ELIOT

ANALYSIS

Upon reading Eliot's poem in 1914, Ezra Pound declared "The Love Song of J. Alfred Prufrock" to be the most important work to have been written by an American thus far. Indeed, Eliot's dramatic monologue heralded a new age of poetry, one in which free verse replaced rhymed **meter**, in which **irony** replaced earnest sentiment, and in which writers juxtaposed stark images of the modern world with traditional or clichéd symbols. Eliot began the poem while still at Harvard in 1910–1911 and published it in *Poetry* magazine in 1915; he also included it in his first published collection, *Prufrock and Other Observations*, in 1917. The dramatic monologue, spoken by a middle-aged, balding man, portrays someone paralyzed by inaction, for whom even the smallest of decisions have a ridiculous, outsized significance. Eliot named his **persona** for a wholesale furniture emporium in St. Louis, close to where Eliot grew up—a fitting moniker for an individual whose middling attitude toward the world fits in with a middle-class, bourgeois state of mind. Rather than delve deeply into Prufrock's consciousness, his love song presents loosely sketched scenes and preoccupations.

As a character, Prufrock stands in direct contrast to the poet-heroes of nineteenth-century romantic writers. Poets, such as Percy Bysshe Shelley and William Blake, peopled their verses with visionary personae who could change their societies through poetry, and Shelley wrote in his *Defense of Poetry* (1821) that poets were the "unacknowledged legislators of the world." In Prufrock, Eliot deliberately created the opposite of the romantic poet-hero: Prufrock is paralyzed by indecision, unable to act and incapable of becoming a leader or of transforming readers through passionate expression. Instead, his days run into each other with a certain sameness as he tries to navigate a world of displacement and anomie, symbolized by the pervasive mist. Eliot attributed Prufrock's character deficiencies and erotic obsessions to the modern world, which rendered thinking, intelligent beings into alienated, fractured, powerless psyches. In Eliot's view, romantic poetry expressed a soft subjectivity not capable of portraying the twentieth century, which was turning all of humanity into Prufrock-like, anesthetized patients.

Although Prufrock's particular form of indecision stems directly from his place in the twentieth century, the ideas about the passage of time and the individual's battle against being forgotten by history have many precedents. Eliot illustrates these precedents through

T. S. ELIOT

allusions to the Bible, Shakespeare, and Andrew Marvell. Even though Prufrock desires to be great, he lacks the tools to take any action, including a firm resolve. He overanalyzes every part of his life and eventually becomes convinced that his every decision will affect the world's harmony. Meanwhile, his life slips by, "measured out . . . with coffee spoons" (51), rather than by accomplishments or dreams. Like Prufrock, Shakespeare's Hamlet famously weighs his decisions, including whether to kill himself. Other lines obliquely reference Marvell's "To His Coy Mistress," a carpe diem poem written in the seventeenth century. There, the speaker tries to convince his beloved to take advantage of their youth by making love rather than saving her virginity. Marvell's speaker, like Eliot's, is hyperaware of the passage of time. Prufrock eventually decides that he'd rather play the part of a valet, counselor, or jester: this decision to become the blundering Fool, who'd rather make people laugh than lead them, is arguably the only action he undertakes in the poem.

"The Love Song of J. Alfred Prufrock" is, as the title suggests, a love song: from Prufrock to an unnamed listener and from Eliot to his readers—Eliot's ironic attempt to serenade us with a portrait of the modern world. Prufrock's song expresses his sexual longing to someone he addresses as "you": he claims to have been with many women but becomes lost in a romantic fantasy of mermaids at the end of the poem. Emasculated by his experiences, Prufrock can only watch as women wander in and out of his life, unable to communicate with them or to articulate his desire. Ultimately, he shuns real women and the possibility of actual sexual relations for "sea-girls wreathed with seaweed" (130). Eliot lulls us by repeating various lines throughout the poem, creating a soft, sensual tone that matches the desensitizing ether portrayed in stanzas 3 and 4: lost in the beauty of the language, we might initially overlook the harshness of some of the images, including mostly empty streets, someone stretched out on an operating table, and fetid pools of water. The fictional voices of poetry soothe us, much as the mermaids soothe Prufrock, until our senses have been smothered and our capacity to react destroyed.

T. S. ELIOT

THE WASTE LAND

EXCERPT FROM "THE BURIAL OF THE DEAD," PART I

April is the cruellest month, breeding
Lilacs out of the dead land, mixing
Memory and desire, stirring
Dull roots with spring rain.
Winter kept us warm, covering
Earth in forgetful snow, feeding
A little life with dried tubers.
Summer surprised us, coming over the Starnbergersee
With a shower of rain; we stopped in the colonnade,
And went on in sunlight, into the Hofgarten,
And drank coffee, and talked for an hour.
Bin gar keine Russin, stamm' aus Litauen, echt deutsch.
And when we were children, staying at the archduke's,
My cousin's, he took me out on a sled,
And I was frightened. He said, Marie,
Marie, hold on tight. And down we went.
In the mountains, there you feel free.

EXCERPT FROM "WHAT THE THUNDER SAID," PART V

Da
Dayadhvam: *I have heard the key*

Turn in the door once and turn once only
We think of the key, each in his prison
Thinking of the key, each confirms a prison
Only at nightfall, aetherial rumours
Revive for a moment a broken Coriolanus
Da
Damyata: *The boat responded*
Gaily, to the hand expert with sail and oar
The sea was calm, your heart would have responded
Gaily, when invited, beating obedient
To controlling hands

                              I sat upon the shore
Fishing, with the arid plain behind me

Shall I at least set my lands in order?
London Bridge is falling down falling down falling down
Poi s'ascose nel foco che gli affina
Quando fiam uti chelidon—*O swallow swallow*
Le Prince d'Aquitaine à la tour abolie
These fragments I have shored against my ruins
Why then Ile fit you. Hieronymo's mad againe.
Datta. Dayadhvam. Damyata.
                    Shantih shantih shantih

PART I: "THE BURIAL OF THE DEAD"

SUMMARY

The Waste Land opens with a quotation in Greek about the Cumaen Sibyl, a siren or prophetess, and a dedication to Ezra Pound. "The Burial of the Dead" consists of a few vignettes cobbled together. First, the speaker announces the arrival of spring, which will cause a painful but necessary rebirth of the dry earth after a long winter. Next, the voice switches to describe memories of Marie, a German aristocrat and cousin of Archduke Ferdinand. Marie remembers sledding with her cousin and declares that she spends her nights reading and travels south during the winter. In the second stanza, a stern, prophetic voice interrupts Marie's reverie to describe a barren desert. He invokes biblical passages about stones and shadows, and he threatens his listeners. Lines in German interrupt the voice's mysterious invitation, after which another speaker recalls a conversation with a girl in a lush garden of blooming flowers.

Madame Sosostris, a fortune-teller, appears even though she is sick. She uses her deck of tarot cards to predict the future, envisioning a series of personages, including a dead sailor and Belladonna. She casually inquires after her friend Mrs. Equitone but not before warning her listeners to "fear death by water" (55). The final stanza describes a dreamlike city filled with spectral people walking back and forth over London Bridge and wandering through the streets of the city. The speaker sees his friend Stetson and calls out to him. He asks if the dead person Stetson had buried in his garden had begun to bloom or if it had been disrupted by frost or digging animals. His question remains unanswered as he cries out a line from *"Au Lecteur"* (1857), a poem by Charles Baudelaire, a symbolist French poet, which calls the reader a "brother."

ANALYSIS

The Waste Land immediately confounds readers with its density: it begins with an excerpt from Greek myth, continues with a dedication to Ezra Pound in Italian, and includes lines in German from an opera by Richard Wagner. Conscious of these difficulties, Eliot provides footnotes throughout his poem, but sometimes these footnotes are just as confusing as the text they mean to elucidate. Some footnotes include translations, and others cite the original sources, implying that interested readers should seek out these sources. Like most modernist writers, Eliot believed in challenging his readers and in forcing them to work at deriving meaning from his poem. In his essay "Tradition and the Individual Talent," Eliot explains his poetic philosophy, noting that contemporary poets must honor their relationships with those who have come before, as well as the natural order that develops to organize writers and artists from the past. The use of allusions, foreign languages, and footnotes are Eliot's way of asserting his right to participate in the literary tradition.

Eliot derives many of his symbols and images from two influential works of cultural anthropology, Miss Jessie L. Weston's *From Ritual to Romance* and Sir James George Frazier's *The Golden Bough*. Weston and Frazier describe the Holy Grail legend and its connections to ancient fertility rituals. The myth of the grail knight's quest to heal the land occurs throughout the Western literary tradition. According to Weston, the grail was not the cup of Christ, as it was conventionally imagined, but a fertility symbol. This symbol is linked to the myth of the Fisher King, a wounded figure who must be healed to restore fertility to the land. In order to heal the Fisher King, cults made sacrifices, usually involving a ritual act of drowning an effigy. Eliot draws from these myths to highlight themes of fertility and infertility, barrenness and regeneration, and sexual dysfunction, all of which were endemic to the modern wasteland.

"The Burial of the Dead" establishes the setting of the wasteland. Spring has arrived, but spring is cruel rather than gentle and barren rather than fertile. Eliot uses his opening to echo *The General Prologue* from Geoffrey Chaucer's *The Canterbury Tales* (1386–1400), which describes feelings of anticipation and hope for a pilgrimage to a holy site. For Eliot, April is not a time of promised healing, but a malicious month that stirs the earth and disrupts slumber. As the speaker morphs from a discourse on spring to the reminiscences of a noblewoman named Marie, we move in time and location into mod-

T. S. ELIOT

ern Europe. Marie discusses her cousin, Archduke Ferdinand, whose murder served as the catalyst for World War I. The entire poem shifts in time and place, constantly combing the memories of the various speakers with contemporary conversations and images of both a parched desert and a dreamlike city filled with ghosts.

Although the symbols, fragments, and multiple voices interrupt the narrative, preventing readers from constructing a story from the poem, they also provide cohesion within the work by presenting some common themes. Stanza 2 further develops the image of the wasteland as a barren desert in need of water. Lines from *Tristan und Isolde*, an opera by Richard Wagner about doomed lovers, interrupt this image, and a speaker cuts in to describe herself in a flower garden. Eliot collages images of infertility, the dry desert, with images of fertility, the young girl surrounded by blooming flowers. The water sorely needed by the barren land appears later to separate the lovers in the opera: Tristan lays dying as he waits for Isolde to sail to him. Water thus becomes both a sustaining and malignant force. Madame Sosostris sees characters who appear later: the Phoenician Sailor whom she sees in the cards appears as Phlebas in Part IV, and the Merchant appears again as Mr. Eugenides in "The Fire Sermon." But Madame Sosostris cannot locate the Hanged Man, whom Eliot links to the Hanged God described by Frazier and who may know how to heal the hurt Fisher King.

In the final stanza, Eliot introduces the "Unreal City" (60), leading many critics to conceive of the poem as an anti-urban tirade. The dreamlike city contrasts with the desert: Eliot compares contemporary London to the biblical desert lands described in stanza 2. He uses images of the city drawn from French symbolist Charles Baudelaire, Charles Dickens, and Dante. Here dead souls shuffle over London Bridge to work in the City, London's financial district, and then shuffle home at the end of the day. Like Prufrock, these people are bland, corpselike, and emasculated. The speaker, observing these crowds, calls out to a friend, Stetson, about a corpse buried in his garden. With these lines, Eliot directly references World War I: those lucky enough to survive the war returned home completely traumatized by their experiences of violent modern warfare. Millions of decomposing bodies were left behind during the war, inadvertently fertilizing the fields of Europe.

PART II: "A GAME OF CHESS"

SUMMARY

The title "A Game of Chess" comes from a seventeenth-century play by Thomas Middleton, in which the moves in a chess game represent stages in a seduction. In Eliot's poem, a wealthy woman sits in a lavishly decorated room, and the speaker compares her to tragic queens from literature, such as Cleopatra and Dido. In the second stanza, the woman begins commanding someone to sit with her, as she is feeling shaky. She asks her companion what he is thinking, then gets angry at his lack of response. An ominous voice interrupts her harangue to describe an empty alley filled with rats. The woman's thoughts are a jumble as she hums snatches of ragtime music and the ominous voice intones about a corpse. Frantic, she demands to know what she should do but calms herself by thinking of her routine: a hot bath, a drive, and a game of chess.

In the next section, the location shifts to a bar at closing time as a group of lower-class women gossip about their friend Lil and her husband, Albert, who is returning home from war. The women have advised Lil to fix herself up and look nice for him since he once gave her money to buy a new set of teeth. They know that Albert will come back home desiring some fun after a difficult four years at war. If she doesn't look good for him, he will take another lover. They chastise her for looking so old at the age of thirty-one, but Lil blames her appearance on some pills she had taken to induce an abortion. The women do not understand why Lil got married if she doesn't want children. As the bartender calls for everyone to clear out, the women call their good-byes to one another, echoing lines spoken by Ophelia in Shakespeare's *Hamlet*.

ANALYSIS

"A Game of Chess" transfers images of the wasteland onto two modern settings and contrasts two women confronting sexual anxieties. It begins by luxuriously describing the furniture and bedchamber of a wealthy older woman, echoing Alexander Pope's *The Rape of the Lock* (1712). These descriptions link the woman to Shakespeare's Cleopatra and Virgil's Dido, two decadent queens whose sexual desire for conquerors led to them to suicide. Above the mantel appears the story of Philomel from Ovid's *Metamorphoses* (ca. C.E. 10). In that story, King Tereus rapes his sister-in-law, Philomel, then cuts out her

T. S. ELIOT

tongue to prevent her from telling anyone. Somehow she manages to tell her sister, and the two enact their revenge by murdering the king and feeding him to Tereus. The two sisters are then transformed into birds, Philomel into a nightingale. Eliot's use of the story underscores themes of sexual dysfunction and sexual violence toward women.

The two women in this part exhibit different types of sexual failure. Although the first woman's surroundings give her an aura of lazy sensuality, her neurotic behavior toward the end of the first stanza reveals her failure to connect with other human beings—and thus her words demonstrate her sexual failure. Instead of dying tragically as a result of an epic love like the queens with whom she is compared, she has ended up nervous and alone. She is surrounded by images of fertility, but her world is one of anticlimax. The wealthy woman becomes a socially isolated figure emblematic of the sexual confusion and problems of the wasteland. Lil's story reveals the shortcomings of childbearing and the effects of class structures on female sexual identity. Like the wasteland itself, Lil is the model of failed fertility: she's had five children, at least once almost dying from childbirth. Her status as a mother has debased rather than elevated her and destroyed the qualities that once made her sexually appealing.

Eliot highlights the sense of despair surrounding romantic relationships, as well as the failure of sexual intimacy and child rearing to become sources of fulfillment and meaning. Just as the wasteland hinders the land's ability to reproduce and bear fruit, it similarly destroys humanity's capacity to reproduce and bear fruit, afflicting individuals of all social sets and classes with the same problem. In the final lines, Eliot references Ophelia, Hamlet's lover who goes mad and drowns herself. Like Ophelia, the two women have been driven to extremes because of their relationships. The wasteland causes sexual dysfunction and damages women's reproductive capabilities.

PART III: "THE FIRE SERMON"

SUMMARY

"The Fire Sermon" begins with the speaker, probably the Fisher King, standing on the banks of the River Thames in London. The nymphs who once imbued the river with life have now vanished, and the riverbanks are empty, bereft of the trash left over from people spending warm summer nights at the river's edge. In the second

T. S. ELIOT

stanza, the speaker, now Ferdinand, a character from Shakespeare's *The Tempest*, watches a rat crawling through the grassy banks. As he fishes, Ferdinand remembers his brother's shipwreck and his father's death, invoking battlefield images of broken bodies. He hears the sounds of cars, which remind him of a bawdy **ballad** he once knew. From the ballad, the speaker moves into a quotation from a poem by French symbolist Paul Verlaine. In Verlaine's poem, the hero's feet are washed in water poured from the grail. The next stanza morphs into the song of Philomel, who cries out as Tereus rapes her.

Stanza 4 switches to the dreamlike city, where Mr. Eugenides, the merchant mentioned by Madame Sosostris in Part I, asks the speaker in colloquial French to have lunch at the Cannon Street Hotel, a busy business hub and well-known site of homosexual encounters. At dusk, the speaker declares himself to be Tiresias, a seer from classical myth who exhibited traits of both genders, in stanza 5. He looks into the apartment of a young female typist, who sits at home in her shabby apartment. When her lover, a clerk, arrives home, he attempts to seduce her, but she is uninterested in sex. He forces himself on her and then stumbles down the dark apartment stairs as she stares out the window, barely aware of what has happened. She wanders around the room and puts on a record.

Next, a new speaker explains that sometimes he hears music along the Strand as he stands near the Thames, and this music mixes with the sounds of human chatter. The remaining lines of this juxtapose speech with snatches of song sung by the Thames maidens. They hum and sing about ships moving down the river and Queen Elizabeth and her lover, the earl of Leicester. As the songs end, another voice begins quoting fragments that recall St. Augustine's confessions and Buddha's fire sermon against human lust.

ANALYSIS

"The Fire Sermon" opens with a depiction of the devastated wasteland: the river nymphs, symbols of natural fruitfulness, have departed. There are no humans, nor are there any signs of the trash left by people as they come to the river on summer nights. Now the banks of the Thames resemble a battlefield, crawling with rats and littered with bodies and bones. A cacophony of conflicting voices emerges, but the voices blend into one another and the speaker cannot understand them. Car sounds blend with a raunchy song about Sweeney and Mrs. Porter; a line from Paul Verlaine's "Parsifal"

(1886), a poem about the grail quest of Parsifal; and the cries of Philomel as the nightingale. Eliot has brought the wasteland into focus: a place in which there is no life and no joy, in which every sound seems to resemble some older song or lyric, but without any context or meaning.

Throughout this section of the poem, Eliot employs several speakers to emphasize the disjunctive nature of the wasteland. Like the speaker in the first stanza who cannot understand the sounds he hears, readers must work to figure out who is speaking which part of the poem—and why. Three important figures from Western literature appear: first, the Fisher King, the wounded figure who must be healed in order to restore fertility to the land; second, Ferdinand, the shipwrecked prince who believes he is doomed until he falls in love with Miranda, daughter of the sorcerer Prospero, from Shakespeare's *The Tempest*; and third, Tiresias, the blind prophet from classical myth. In addition, three Thames maidens sing their songs, which echo lines from Dante's *Purgatorio* (1314), a prophetlike voice intones lines from religious tracts, and a seemingly ordinary human voice mentions a proposal for a sexual tryst he received from Mr. Eugenides. Speakers interrupt one another, producing a layering effect that resembles the auditory experience of contemporary urban life.

Eliot takes the title of this part from a speech given by Buddha against lust, and this part of the poem explores the consequences of regenerative failure and presents new examples of sexual dysfunction. Images of sexual confusion abound: Mr. Eugenides, the merchant from Madame Sosostris's tarot deck, propositions the speaker. Tiresias, a being with breasts and male genitalia, describes a modern scene of sexual trouble. A clerk returns home to his lover, a typist who lives in a dingy apartment. She meets his attempts at seduction with chilly boredom, but he forces himself on her. Watching the rape, Tiresias internalizes the hopelessness and violation of the victim. However, for the participants, this sexual violation is not traumatic, but routine and mundane. The clerk gets what he wants and scuttles off, while the typist nonchalantly gets up and puts on a record. Here, sexuality does not have the potential for reproduction or regeneration because it is homosexual (Mr. Eugenides), sexually ambiguous (Tiresias), or stripped of pleasure (the typist and the clerk). Just as the wasteland cannot regenerate itself, its people are unable to engage in fruitful reproduction.

T. S. ELIOT

Formally, "The Fire Sermon" proposes a cure for the damaged wasteland. A speaker cries, "I can connect / Nothing with nothing" (301–302), parodying religious messages of harmony and emphasizing Eliot's poetic method of juxtaposing images without any sort of connection or transition. While the barrage of images without connection represents the wasteland, a mixture of the past and present is the only way to mend the land. Disconnect thus becomes the only way to connect. In the last several lines, Eliot blends lines from St. Augustine's *Confessions* (C.E. 397), in which he describes his arrival in Carthage and feels shocked by the city's licentiousness, with lines from a sermon given by Buddha against lust. Eliot indicates in a footnote that the combination of Western and Eastern philosophies provides a possible solution to the problem of sexual confusion and infertility: sexual interactions should be meaningful and productive. If figures like the bored typist, the impotent Fisher King, and polysexual Tiresias listen to the two messages of St. Augustine and Buddha, they may be able to end sexual confusion in themselves and begin to heal the damaged land.

PART IV: "DEATH BY WATER"

SUMMARY

The shortest part of *The Waste Land*, "Death by Water," tells the story of Phlebas the Phoenician, first mentioned by Madame Sosostris in "The Burial of the Dead." Phlebas has been dead for two weeks, having drowned in swift current. As his body is tossed about by the ebb and flow, he reenters the various stages of his young life. It ends with a warning to sailors (and readers): Phlebas, despite being young and strong, met his end on the water.

ANALYSIS

Ezra Pound, in his pruning, cut this part down from a long meditation on sea travel to a short, moralizing fragment about regenerative possibility. Phlebas's death mirrors the fertility ritual in which ancient cults threw effigies into water to try to heal the Fisher King. But here the ritual has failed, and Phlebas is simply dead. His story serves as a warning to sailors in particular, but also to readers who discovered a glimmer of hope at the end of "The Fire Sermon." Young, strong people have a difficult time imagining death, but, as the poem warns, death can strike at any time. There is no moment of healing, nor is there any suggestion for resolution or regeneration.

The possible solution has failed; the wasteland remains damaged. "Death by Water" acts as a cautionary transition: as the poem simultaneously explores regenerative failure and rejuvenation in "The Fire Sermon" and "What the Thunder Said," this section warns us to beware of easy answers and solutions.

PART V: "WHAT THE THUNDER SAID"

SUMMARY

"What the Thunder Said" concludes *The Waste Land*. Its opening evokes a journey through a hellish landscape and upset crowds. The speaker arrives at parched desert. Although he hears thunder reverberating in the mountains, there is no rain, nor any signs of rain to come. Longing for water, the speaker parodies the sound of rain falling and water dripping. The speaker addresses his walking companion, asking this unnamed person about another, possibly imaginary person, who is walking nearby. Eerie cries fill the air, and the speaker catches sight of a city in the mountains. He does not recognize it— the falling towers of the dreamlike city could be those of Jerusalem, Athens, Alexandria, Vienna, or even London. The city breaks and crumbles before his eyes.

Cradled in the mountains is a chapel, a reference to the Chapel Perilous, the site of the final test of the grail knight, who must witness absolute solitude and decay before claiming the grail. A rooster breaks the silence, announcing the arrival of morning. The rains arrive in a gust of wind. The speaker, now along the banks of the Ganges in India, sees dark clouds gathering over the Himalayas, and he begins understanding the language of thunder. Using language taken from the Upanishads, poetic texts inspired by Hindu scriptures, the thunder intones the three Hindu words for "give," "sympathize," and "control." Between the booming thunder's commands and cries are poetic fragments about fear, suffering, and death that coalesce and overlap.

In the final stanza, the Fisher King sits on the banks of the Thames, wondering if he should prepare for death. An old nursery rhyme about London Bridge bleeds into Italian lines taken from Dante's *Purgatorio*, a phrase from Philomel's song, and a line from a French sonnet. The speaker then utters perhaps the most famous line of the poem, "These fragments I have shored against my ruins" (431), followed by a line from a sixteenth-century play, the three

Hindu words spoken by the thunder, and concluding with the traditional ending of an Upanishad, which loosely translates as "the peace that passeth understanding."

ANALYSIS

"What the Thunder Said" provides an apocalyptic conclusion to and serves as the dramatic climax of *The Waste Land*. It anticipates the possibility of healing and resurrection but does not actually provide either the means for such a healing or a vision of healed lands. In its hellish setting, the first stanza recalls Golgotha, the site of Christ's crucifixion. Death is all around, but resurrection is anticipated. Eliot continues to employ desert imagery throughout the section as he has throughout the poem, and he imagines the Unreal City crumbling from decay and disgust. Eventually, rain falls and a purifying fire ravages the land. The Fisher King prepares for his own renewal in the final stanza, but the poem ends before we can see him resurrected or see the effects of the newly fertile land. Instead, we are left only with the word *shantih*, the traditional conclusion of an Upanishad.

A hallucinatory tone emphasizes the power of the poem's apocalyptic vision. The speaker, desperate for water, imagines he hears water dripping and thunder speaking. He questions his companion about a mysterious figure he believes is walking near them, an echo of a hymn written by St. Patrick: "Christ be with me, Christ within me, / Christ behind me, Christ before me." A city, like a mirage, rises up in the mountains, but the speaker cannot identify it beyond the label "unreal" (377). Like the past seats of great civilizations he names, this mysterious city begins to crumble as well. Surreal images of a woman playing with her hair and bats with the faces of infants heighten the nightmarelike atmosphere. Readers cannot know if the contemplation of the wasteland has driven the speakers insane, a likely possibility, or if Eliot merely wants to portray the final stages of decay. Like "Death by Water," this section also serves as a warning for the total emptiness that must come before regeneration can begin.

Eliot symbolizes the potential for regeneration and renewal throughout "What the Thunder Said." Initially, the speaker yearns for water, which has the potential to sustain life. As he journeys through the desert and his hallucinations, he arrives at an empty chapel, which invokes the last stop on the quest for the holy grail. According to the legend, the Chapel Perilous contains the key to restoring the land, but first the knight must overcome the false impression of nothingness to find the sacred object. Nearby, a rooster cries, and dawn arrives, signaling the potential for rebirth, and the so-longed-for rains finally come, an echo of the poem's first lines. The scene shifts to the river Ganges in India, the site of the fertile crescent and the birthplace of civilization, as the thunder brings the message of healing. Quoting from sacred Hindu texts, the thunder shows how the acts of giving, sympathizing, and controlling lead to the path of revelation for gods, humans, and devils. But the messages are cryptic, and readers probably require Eliot's footnotes in order to understand. As in the conclusion of "The Fire Sermon," here Eliot shows an alternative path to knowledge by combining various literary, religious, and mythic traditions.

The Waste Land frustrates readers seeking a coherent meaning, message, or conclusion to a difficult and troubling poem. Eliot perceived a culture in crisis and realized that there were no easy solutions or answers, only more questions. In the final part of the poem, Eliot, like the speaker, gathers together his poetic fragments by revisiting characters from other parts, including the Fisher King and Philomel: piling the fragments on top of one another thus becomes one method of stopping the creeping decay of the modern world. Combinations of literary texts and mythologies present possible fixes, but they are frustrated by the realities of war, social behavior, class, sexuality, and power emerging in the early twentieth century. Rather than foreshadow doom and despair, Eliot proposes combing the world's religions for healing methods that, when combined, might provide relief. While contemporary society crumbles into decay, clouds gather on the horizon, demonstrating the potential for blessed relief and rejuvenation.

T. S. ELIOT

GLOSSARY

POETIC TERMS

allegory The use of *symbols* and extended *metaphors* to implicitly tell a story or reference a phenomenon, person, or event.

alliteration The repetition of similar sounds, usually consonants, at the beginning of words. For example, Robert Frost's poem "Out, out—" contains the alliterative phrase "sweet-scented stuff."

allusion An implicit reference within a literary work to a historical or literary person, place, or event. Authors use allusion to add symbolic weight because it makes subtle or implicit connections with other works.

anxiety of influence A theory that the critic Harold Bloom put forth in *The Anxiety of Influence: A Theory of Poetry* (1973). Bloom uses Freud's idea of the Oedipus complex to suggest that poets, plagued by anxiety that they have nothing new to say, struggle against the influence of earlier generations of poets. Bloom suggests that poets find their distinctive voices in an act of misprision, or misreading, of earlier influences, thus refiguring the poetic tradition. Although Bloom presents his thesis as a theory of poetry, it can be applied to other arts as well.

aposiopesis A breaking off of speech, usually because of rising emotion or excitement.

apostrophe A direct address to an absent or dead person or to an object, quality, or idea. Walt Whitman's poem "O Captain! My Captain!" written upon the death of Abraham Lincoln, is an example of apostrophe.

archetype A *theme*, *motif*, *symbol*, or stock character that holds a familiar and fixed place in a culture's consciousness.

GLOSSARY

assonance The repetition of similar vowel sounds in a sequence of nearby words. For example, Alfred, Lord Tennyson creates assonance with the "o" sound in this line from "The Lotos-Eaters": "All day the wind breathes low with mellower tone."

bathos A sudden and unexpected drop from the lofty to the trivial or excessively sentimental. Bathos sometimes is used intentionally, to create humor, but just as often is derided as miscalculation or poor judgment on a writer's part. An example from Alexander Pope: "Ye Gods! Annihilate but Space and Time / And make two lovers happy."

cacophony The clash of discordant or harsh sounds within a sentence or phrase. Cacophony is a familiar feature of tongue twisters but can also be used to poetic effect, as in the phrase "anfractuous rocks" from T. S. Eliot's "Sweeney Erect."

canon A group of literary works commonly regarded as central or authoritative to the literary tradition. The Western canon—the central literary works of Western civilization—includes the writings of Homer, Shakespeare, and Tolstoy. A canon is an evolving entity, as works are added or subtracted as their perceived value shifts over time. In recent decades, the idea of an authoritative canon has come under attack, especially from feminist and postcolonial critics, who see the canon as a tyranny of dead white males that marginalizes less mainstream voices.

caricature A description or characterization that exaggerates or distorts a character's prominent features, usually to elicit mockery.

chiasmus Two phrases in which the syntax is the same but the placement of words is reversed, as in these lines from the Bible (Genesis 9.6): "Whoever sheds the blood of man by man shall his blood be shed."

cliché An expression, such as "turn over a new leaf," that has been used so frequently it has lost its expressive power.

GLOSSARY

colloquialism An informal expression or slang, especially in the context of formal writing, as in Philip Larkin's "Send No Money": "All the other lads there / Were itching to have a bash."

conceit An elaborate, intellectual parallel *simile* or *metaphor* between two seemingly dissimilar objects or ideas. The metaphysical poets are especially known for their conceits, as in John Donne's "The Flea" and "A Valediction: Forbidding Mourning."

cosmic irony The perception of fate or the universe as malicious or indifferent to human suffering, which creates a painful contrast between our purposeful activity and its ultimate meaninglessness.

dramatic irony A technique in which the author lets the audience in on a character's situation while the character remains in the dark. With dramatic irony, the character's words or actions carry a significance that the character is not aware of. When used in tragedy, dramatic irony is called *tragic irony*.

emblem A concrete object that represents something abstract. For example, the Star of David is an emblem of Judaism. An emblem differs from a *symbol* in that an emblem's meaning is fixed: the Star of David always represents Judaism, regardless of context.

epiphany A sudden, powerful, and often spiritual or life-changing realization that a character reaches in an otherwise ordinary or everyday moment.

euphemism The use of decorous language to express vulgar or unpleasant ideas, events, or actions. For example, "passed away" instead of "died."

euphony A pleasing arrangement of sounds. Many consider "cellar door" one of the most euphonious phrases in English.

exegesis An explanation of a text that clarifies difficult passages and analyzes its contemporary relevance or application.

explication   A close reading of a text that identifies and explains the figurative language and forms within the work.

figure of speech   An expression that stretches words beyond their literal meanings. By connecting or juxtaposing different sounds and thoughts, figures of speech increase the breadth and subtlety of expression.

hermeneutics   The study of textual interpretation and of the way in which a text communicates meaning.

hyperbole   An excessive overstatement or conscious exaggeration of fact.

idiom   A common expression that has acquired a meaning that differs from its literal meaning, such as "it's raining cats and dogs" or "a bolt from the blue."

imagery   Language that brings to mind sense impressions, especially via *figures of speech*. Sometimes, certain imagery is characteristic of a particular writer or work. For example, many of Shakespeare's plays contain nautical imagery.

in medias res   Latin for "in the middle of things." The phrase refers to the technique of starting a narrative in the middle of the action. For example, John Milton's *Paradise Lost,* which concerns the war among the angels in heaven, opens after the fallen angels already are in hell and only later examines the events that led to their expulsion from heaven.

interior monologue   A record of a character's thoughts, unmediated by a narrator. Interior monologue sometimes takes the form of stream-of-consciousness narration but often is more structured and logical than stream of consciousness.

intertextuality   The various relationships a text may have with other texts, through *allusions*, borrowing of formal or thematic elements, or simply by reference to traditional literary forms. The term is important to structuralist and poststructuralist critics, who argue that texts relate primarily to one another and not to an external reality.

invocation A prayer for inspiration to a god or muse, usually placed at the beginning of an epic. Homer's *Iliad* and *Odyssey* both open with invocations.

irony A wide-ranging technique of detachment that draws awareness to the discrepancy between words and their meanings, between expectation and fulfillment, or, most generally, between what is and what seems to be. See also *cosmic irony*, *dramatic irony*, *situational irony*, and *verbal irony*.

litotes A form of understatement in which a statement is affirmed by negating its opposite: "He is not unfriendly."

meiosis Intentional understatement, as, for example, in Shakespeare's *Romeo and Juliet*, when Mercutio is mortally wounded and says it is only "a scratch." Meiosis is the opposite of *hyperbole* and often employs *litotes* to ironic effect.

melodrama The use of sentimentality, gushing emotion, or sensational action or plot twists to provoke audience or reader response. Melodrama was popular in Victorian England, but critics now deride it as manipulative and hokey.

metaphor The comparison of one thing to another that does not use the terms *like* or *as*. Shakespeare is famous for his metaphors, as in *Macbeth*: "Life is but a walking shadow, a poor player / That struts and frets his hour upon the stage."

metonymy The substitution of one term for another that generally is associated with it. For example, "suits" instead of "businesspeople."

motif A recurring structure, contrast, or other device that develops or informs a work's major themes. A motif may relate to concrete objects, or it may be a recurrent idea, phrase, or emotion.

onomatopoeia The use of words, such as *pop*, *hiss*, and *zip*, that sound like the thing they refer to.

oxymoron The association of two contrary terms, as in the expressions "same difference" or "wise fool."

paradox A statement that seems absurd or even contradictory on its face but often expresses a deeper truth.

paralipsis Also known as *praeteritio*, the technique of drawing attention to something by claiming not to mention it.

parallelism The use of similar grammatical structures or word order in two sentences, phrases, or lines to suggest a comparison or contrast between them. In Shakespeare's Sonnet 129: "Before, a joy proposed; behind, a dream."

pathetic fallacy The attribution of human feeling or motivation to a nonhuman object, especially an object found in nature. For example, John Keats's "Ode to Melancholy" describes a "weeping" cloud.

pathos From the Greek word for "feeling," the quality in a work of literature that evokes high emotion, most commonly sorrow, pity, or compassion.

periphrasis An elaborate and roundabout manner of speech that uses more words than necessary. Saying, "I appear to be entirely without financial resources," rather than, "I'm broke," is an example. *Euphemisms* often employ periphrasis.

persona A fictional mask or assumed identity created by the poet to literally speak a poem. Although the persona might (or might not) share traits with the poet, as in *confessional poetry*, the persona is a fictional *speaker* created by the poet. In other words, the persona is never the poet.

personification The use of human characteristics to describe animals, things, or ideas. Carl Sandburg's poem "Chicago" describes the city as "Stormy, husky, brawling, / City of the Big Shoulders."

poetic diction The use of specific types of words, phrases, *figures of speech*, or literary structures that are not common in contemporary speech or prose.

GLOSSARY

poetic license   The liberty that authors sometimes take with ordinary rules of syntax and grammar, employing unusual vocabulary, metrical devices, or *figures of speech* or committing factual errors in order to strengthen a passage of writing. For example, the modernist poet e. e. cummings takes poetic license in violating rules of capitalization in his works.

pun   A play on words that exploits the similarity in sound between two words with distinctly different meanings.

rhetorical question   A question that is asked not to elicit a response but to make an impact or call attention to something.

romantic irony   An author's persistent reminding of his or her presence in the work. By drawing attention to the artifice of the work, the author ensures that the reader will maintain critical detachment and not simply accept the writing at face value.

sarcasm   A simple form of verbal irony in which it is obvious from context and tone that the speaker means the opposite of what he or she says. Sarcasm usually, but not always, expresses scorn. Saying, "That was graceful," when someone trips and falls is an example.

simile   A comparison of two things through the use of *like* or *as*.

situational irony   A technique in which one understanding of a situation stands in sharp contrast to another, usually more prevalent understanding of the same situation.

speaker   The character created by a poet to speak the poem. Although the speaker might (or might not) share traits with the poet, as in *confessional poetry*, the speaker is a fictional *persona* created by the poet. In other words, the speaker is never the poet.

stanza   A grouping of lines, equivalent to a paragraph in prose.

symbol   An object, character, figure, or color that is used to represent an abstract idea or concept. Unlike an *emblem*, a symbol may have different meanings in different contexts.

synesthesia   The use of one kind of sensory experience to describe another.

synecdoche   A form of *metonymy* in which a part of an entity is used to refer to the whole. For example, using "my wheels" for "my car."

theme   A fundamental and universal idea explored in a literary work.

tone   The general atmosphere created in a story or a poem.

trope   A category of *figures of speech* that extend the literal meanings of words by inviting a comparison to other words, things, or ideas. *Metaphor*, *metonymy*, and *simile* are three common tropes.

verbal irony   The use of a statement that, by its context, implies its opposite. *Sarcasm* is a particularly blunt form of verbal irony.

wit   A form of wordplay that displays cleverness or ingenuity with language. Often, but not always, wit displays humor.

zeugma   The use of one word in a sentence to modify two other words in the sentence, typically in two different ways.

RHYTHM, METER, AND RHYME

accentual (strong-stress) meter The number of stressed syllables in a line is fixed, but the number of total syllables is not. This kind of meter is common in Anglo-Saxon poetry, such as *Beowulf*. Gerard Manley Hopkins developed a form of accentual meter called *sprung rhythm*, which had considerable influence on twentieth-century poetry.

accentual-syllabic meter Both the number of stressed syllables and the number of total syllables is fixed. Accentual-syllabic meter has been the most common kind of meter in English poetry since Geoffrey Chaucer in the late Middle Ages. Accentual-syllabic meter is determined by the number and type of feet in a line of verse.

blank verse Unrhymed *iambic pentameter*. Blank verse bears a close resemblance to the rhythms of ordinary speech, giving poetry a natural feel. Shakespeare's plays are written primarily in blank verse.

cadence The rise and fall of spoken language.

caesura An especially pronounced pause between *feet*.

couplet Two successive rhymed lines that are equal in length. A *heroic couplet* is a pair of rhyming lines in *iambic pentameter*.

end rhyme A rhyme that comes at the end of a line of verse. Most rhyming poetry uses end rhymes.

end-stopped A break at the end of a line denoted by a comma, period, semicolon, or other punctuation mark.

enjambment A sentence or clause runs onto the next line without a break. Enjambment creates a sense of suspense or excitement and gives added emphasis to the word at the end of the line.

feminine rhyme   A rhyme consisting of a stressed syllable followed by an unstressed syllable, as in the rhyme between "mother" and "brother."

foot (feet)   The basic rhythmic unit into which a line of verse can be divided. When verse is recited, there usually is a slight pause between feet. These are the most common types of feet in English poetry:

- **iamb**: an unstressed syllable followed by a stressed syllable: "to**day**"
- **trochee**: a stressed syllable followed by an unstressed syllable: "**car**ry"
- **dactyl**: a stressed syllable followed by two unstressed syllables: "**dif**ficult"
- **anapest**: two unstressed syllables followed by a stressed syllable: "it is **time**"
- **spondee**: two successive syllables with strong stresses: "**stop, thief**"
- **pyrrhic**: two successive syllables with light stresses: "up to"

Most English poetry has four or five feet in a line, but it is not uncommon to see as few as one or as many as eight.

- **monometer**: one foot
- **dimeter**: two feet
- **trimeter**: three feet
- **tetrameter**: four feet
- **pentameter**: five feet
- **hexameter**: six feet
- **heptameter**: seven feet
- **octameter**: eight feet

free verse   Verse that does not conform to any fixed meter or rhyme scheme. Free verse is not, however, loose or unrestricted: its rules of composition are as strict and difficult as traditional verse, for they rely on less evident rhythmic patterns to give the poem shape. Walt Whitman's *Leaves of Grass* is a seminal work of free verse.

GLOSSARY

iambic pentameter   Each line of verse has five feet (*pentameter*), each of which consists of an unstressed syllable followed by a stressed syllable (*iamb*). *Iambic pentameter* is one of the most popular metrical schemes in English poetry.

internal rhyme   A rhyme between two or more words within a single line of verse.

masculine rhyme   A rhyme consisting of a single stressed syllable, as in the rhyme between "car" and "far."

meter   The rhythmic pattern created in a line of verse. There are four basic types of meter: *accentual meter*, *accentual-syllabic meter*, *quantitative meter*, and *syllabic meter*.

octet (octave)   A grouping of eight lines.

perfect rhyme   An exact match of sounds in a rhyme.

quantitative meter   The duration of sound of each syllable, rather than its stress, determines the meter. Quantitative meter is common in Greek, Latin, Sanskrit, and Arabic but not in English.

quatrain   A four-line stanza. The most common form of English verse, the quatrain has many variants. One of the most important is the heroic quatrain, written in iambic pentameter with an *abab* rhyme scheme.

refrain   A phrase or group of lines that is repeated at significant moments within a poem, usually at the end of a *stanza*.

repetition   Words, sounds, phrases, lines, or elements of syntax may repeat within a poem. Sometimes, repetition can enhance an element of meaning, but at other times it can dilute or dissipate meaning.

rhythm   The pattern of sound created by the varying length and emphasis given to different syllables.

GLOSSARY

scansion The process of analyzing the number and type of *feet* in a line.

sestet A grouping of six lines.

slant rhyme An imperfect rhyme, also called oblique rhyme or off rhyme, in which the sounds are similar but not exactly the same, as between "port" and "heart." Modern poets often use slant rhyme as a subtler alternative to perfect rhyme.

sprung rhythm A unique rhyme scheme developed by Gerard Manley Hopkins that uses *alliteration* and counts the number of stressed syllables. This rhythm combines *accentual meter* with *free verse*.

syllabic meter The number of total syllables in a line is fixed, but the number of stressed syllables is not. This kind of meter is relatively rare in English poetry.

tercet A grouping of three lines, often bearing a single rhyme.

terza rima A system of interlaced *tercets* linked by common rhymes: *aba bcb cdc*, etc. Dante pioneered terza rima in *The Divine Comedy*. The form is hard to maintain in English, although there are some notable exceptions, such as Percy Bysshe Shelley's "Ode to the West Wind."

Poetic Forms

ballad Alternating *tetrameter* and *trimeter*, usually *iambic* and rhyming. Ballad form, which is common in traditional folk poetry and song, enjoyed a revival in the romantic period with such poems as Samuel Taylor Coleridge's "The Rime of the Ancient Mariner."

burlesque A humorous imitation of a serious work of literature. The humor often arises from the incongruity between the imitation and the work being imitated. For example, Alexander Pope's *The Rape of the Lock* uses the high diction of *epic* poetry to talk about a domestic matter.

didactic literature Literature intended to instruct or educate.

dirge A short poetic expression of grief. A dirge differs from an *elegy* in that it often is embedded within a larger work, is less highly structured, and is meant to be sung.

dramatic monologue A poem that contains words that a fictional or historical character speaks to a particular audience. Alfred, Lord Tennyson's "Ulysses" is a famous example.

eclogue A short *pastoral* poem in the form of a *soliloquy* or dialogue between two shepherds.

elegy A formal poem that laments the death of a friend or public figure or, occasionally, a meditation on death itself. In Greek and Latin poetry, the term applies to a specific type of meter (alternating *hexameters* and *pentameters*) regardless of content, but only some elegies in English obey that meter. Percy Bysshe Shelley's poem *Adonais*, which mourns the death of John Keats, is an example of an elegy.

epic A lengthy narrative that describes the deeds of a heroic figure, often of national or cultural importance, in elevated language. Strictly, the term applies only to verse narratives such as *Beowulf* or Virgil's *Aeneid,* but it is used to describe prose, drama, or film works of similar scope.

epigram A succinct, witty statement, often in verse. For example, William Wordsworth's observation "The child is the father of the man."

essay A form of nonfictional discussion or argument that Michel de Montaigne pioneered in the 1500s. Essays are flexible in form: although they usually are short prose works, there are also examples of book-length essays (by John Locke) and verse essays (by Alexander Pope).

fable A short prose or verse narrative, such as those by Aesop, that illustrates a moral, which often is stated explicitly at the end. Frequently, the characters in a fable are animals that embody different human character traits.

haiku A compact form of Japanese poetry written in three lines of five, seven, and five syllables, respectively.

hymn A *lyric* poem or song in praise of a god, divine being, or lofty subject.

limerick A fanciful five-line poem with an *aabba* rhyme scheme in which the first, second, and fifth lines have three *feet* and the third and fourth have two feet.

lyric A short poetic composition that describes the thoughts of a single *speaker*. Most modern poetry is lyrical (as opposed to *dramatic monologue* or narrative), employing such common forms as the *ode* and *sonnet*.

ode A serious *lyric* poem, often of significant length, that usually conforms to an elaborate metrical structure. An example is William Wordsworth's "Ode: Intimations of Immortality."

ottava rima In English, an eight-line stanza with *iambic pentameter* and the rhyme scheme *abababcc*. This form is difficult to use in English, where it is hard to find two rhyming triplets that do not sound childish. Its effect is majestic yet simple. William Butler Yeats's poem "Among School Children" uses ottava rima.

pastiche A work that imitates the style of a previous author, work, or literary genre. Alternatively, the term may refer to a work that contains a hodgepodge of elements or fragments from different sources or influences. Pastiche differs from *parody* in that its imitation is not meant as a form of mockery.

pastoral A celebration of the simple, rustic life of shepherds and shepherdesses, usually written by a sophisticated, urban writer. Christopher Marlowe's poem "The Passionate Shepherd to His Love" epitomizes pastoral themes.

Petrarchan (Italian) sonnet Developed by the Italian poet Petrarch, this sonnet is divided into an *octet* with the rhyme scheme *abbaabba* or *abbacddc* and a *sestet* with the rhyme scheme *cdecde* or *cdccdc*.

prose poem A poetic work that features the strong rhythms of *free verse* but is presented on the page in the form of prose, without line breaks. Arthur Rimbaud's *Illuminations* is an example of a prose poem.

sestina Six six-line *stanzas* followed by a three-line stanza. The same six words are repeated at the end of lines throughout the poem in a predetermined pattern. The last word in the last line of one stanza becomes the last word of the first line in the next. All six end words appear in the final three-line stanza. Sir Philip Sidney's *Arcadia* contains examples of the sestina.

Shakespearean sonnet Also called the *English sonnet* or *Elizabethan sonnet*, this poetic form, which Shakespeare made famous, contains three *quatrains* and a final *couplet*. The rhyme scheme is *abab cdcd efef gg*.

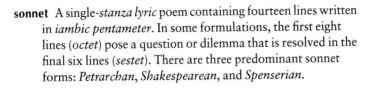

sonnet   A single-*stanza lyric* poem containing fourteen lines written in *iambic pentameter*. In some formulations, the first eight lines (*octet*) pose a question or dilemma that is resolved in the final six lines (*sestet*). There are three predominant sonnet forms: *Petrarchan*, *Shakespearean*, and *Spenserian*.

Spenserian sonnet   A variant that the poet Edmund Spenser developed from the Shakespearean sonnet. The Spenserian sonnet has the rhyme scheme *abab bcbc cdcd ee*.

verse novel   A full-length fictional work that is novelistic in nature but written in verse rather than prose. Examples include Aleksandr Pushkin's *Eugene Onegin* and Vikram Seth's *The Golden Gate*.

villanelle   A nineteen-line poem made up of five *tercets* and a final *quatrain* in which all nineteen lines carry one of only two rhymes. There are two *refrains*, alternating between the ends of each tercet and then forming the last two lines of the quatrain. Dylan Thomas's "Do Not Go Gentle Into That Good Night" is a famous example.

LITERARY MOVEMENTS

absurd, literature of the (ca. 1930–1970) A movement, primarily in the theater, that responded to the seeming illogicality and purposelessness of human life in works marked by a lack of clear narrative, understandable psychological motives, or emotional catharsis. Samuel Beckett's *Waiting for Godot* is one of the most celebrated works in the theater of the absurd.

aestheticism (ca. 1835–1910) A late nineteenth-century movement that believed in art as an end in itself. Aesthetes, such as Oscar Wilde and Walter Pater, rejected the view that art had to posses a higher moral or political value and believed instead in "art for art's sake."

Beat generation (1950s–1960s) A group of American writers in the 1950s and 1960s who sought release and illumination though a bohemian counterculture of sex, drugs, and Zen Buddhism. Beat writers, such as Jack Kerouac (*On the Road*) and Allen Ginsberg (*Howl*), gained fame by giving readings in coffeehouses, often accompanied by jazz music.

Bloomsbury group (ca. 1906–1930s) An informal group of friends and lovers, including Clive Bell, E. M. Forster, Roger Fry, Lytton Strachey, Virginia Woolf, and John Maynard Keynes, who lived in the Bloomsbury section of London in the early twentieth century and who had a considerable liberalizing influence on British culture.

confessional poetry An autobiographical poetic genre in which the poet discusses intensely personal subject matter with unusual frankness. The genre was popular from the late 1950s to the late 1960s, due in part to Robert Lowell's *Life Studies* (1959).

dadaism (1916–1922) An avant-garde movement that began in response to the devastation of World War I. Based in Paris and led by the poet Tristan Tzara, the dadaists produced nihilistic and antilogical prose, poetry, and art, and they rejected the traditions, rules, and ideals of prewar Europe.

Enlightenment (ca. 1660–1790)   An intellectual movement in France and other parts of Europe that emphasized the importance of reason, progress, and liberty. The Enlightenment, sometimes called the Age of Reason, is primarily associated with nonfiction writing, such as essays and philosophical treatises. Major Enlightenment writers include Thomas Hobbes, John Locke, Jean-Jacques Rousseau, and René Descartes.

Elizabethan era (ca. 1558–1603)   A flourishing period in English literature, particularly drama, that coincided with the reign of Queen Elizabeth I and included such writers as Francis Bacon, Ben Jonson, Christopher Marlowe, William Shakespeare, Sir Philip Sidney, and Edmund Spenser.

Gothic fiction (ca. 1764–1820)   A genre of late eighteenth-century literature that featured brooding, mysterious settings and plots. What we now call "horror stories" are descended from works in this genre. Horace Walpole's *Castle of Otranto,* set inside a medieval castle, was the first major Gothic novel. Later, the term "Gothic" grew to include any work that attempted to create an atmosphere of terror or the unknown, such as Edgar Allan Poe's short stories.

Harlem Renaissance (ca. 1918–1930)   A flowering of African-American literature, art, and music during the 1920s in New York City. W. E. B. DuBois's *The Souls of Black Folk* anticipated the movement, which included Alain Locke's anthology *The New Negro,* Zora Neale Hurston's novel *Their Eyes Were Watching God,* and the poetry of Langston Hughes and Countee Cullen.

high modernism (1920s)   Generally considered the golden age of modernist literature, this period saw the publication of James Joyce's *Ulysses,* T. S. Eliot's *The Waste Land,* Virginia Woolf's *Mrs. Dalloway,* and Marcel Proust's *Remembrance of Things Past.*

language poets (ca. 1971–present)   A loosely connected group of postmodern poets interested in the way language conveys assumptions and messages. Notable language poets, including Susan Howe and Charles Bernstein, often stress the process of

GLOSSARY

writing over the product of writing, and they use their work to explore politics and social constraints relating to the uses of language.

Lost Generation (ca. 1918–1930s)   A term used to describe the generation of writers, many of them soldiers, that came to maturity during World War I. Notable members of this group include F. Scott Fitzgerald, John Dos Passos, and Ernest Hemingway, whose novel *The Sun Also Rises* embodies the Lost Generation's sense of disillusionment.

magic realism (ca. 1935–present)   A style of writing, popularized by Jorge Luis Borges, Gabriel García Márquez, Günter Grass, and others, that combines realism with moments of dreamlike fantasy within a single prose narrative.

metaphysical poets (ca. 1633–1680)   A group of seventeenth-century poets who combined direct language with ingenious images, paradoxes, and conceits. John Donne and Andrew Marvell are the best-known poets of this school.

Middle English (ca. 1066–1500)   The transitional period between Anglo-Saxon and modern English. The cultural upheaval that followed the Norman Conquest of England, in 1066, saw a flowering of secular literature, including *ballads*, chivalric romances, allegorical poems, and a variety of religious plays. Geoffrey Chaucer's *The Canterbury Tales* is the most celebrated work of this period.

modernism (1890s–1940s)   A literary and artistic movement that provided a radical break with traditional modes of Western art, thought, religion, social conventions, and morality. Major themes of this period include the attack on notions of hierarchy; experimentation in new forms of narrative, such as stream of consciousness; doubt about the existence of knowable, objective reality; attention to alternative viewpoints and modes of thinking; and self-referentiality as a means of drawing attention to the relationships between artist and audience, and form and content.

neoclassicism (ca. 1660–1798) A literary movement, inspired by the rediscovery of classical works of ancient Greece and Rome, that emphasized balance, restraint, and order. Neoclassicism roughly coincided with the Enlightenment, which espoused reason over passion. Notable neoclassical writers include John Dryden, Samuel Johnson, Alexander Pope, and Jonathan Swift.

postcolonial literature (ca. 1950s–present) Literature by and about people from former European colonies, primarily in Africa, Asia, South America, and the Caribbean. This literature aims both to expand the traditional *canon* of Western literature and to challenge Eurocentric assumptions about literature, especially through examination of questions of otherness, identity, and race. Prominent postcolonial works include the poems of Derek Walcott and Agha Shahid Ali. Edward Said's *Orientalism* (1978) provided an important theoretical basis for understanding postcolonial literature.

postmodernism (ca. 1945–present) A notoriously ambiguous term, especially as it refers to literature, postmodernism can be seen as a response to the elitism of high modernism, as well as to the horrors of World War II. Postmodern literature is characterized by a disjointed, fragmented pastiche of high and low culture that reflects the absence of tradition and structure in a world driven by technology and consumerism. Louis Zukofsky, A. R. Ammons, and W. S. Merwin are well-known postmodern poets.

Pre-Raphaelites (ca. 1848–1870) The literary arm of an artistic movement that drew inspiration from Italian artists working before Raphael (1483–1520). The Pre-Raphaelites combined sensuousness and religiosity through archaic poetic forms and medieval settings. William Morris, Christina Rossetti, Dante Gabriel Rossetti, and Charles Swinburne were leading poets in the movement.

realism (ca. 1830–1900) A loose term that can refer to any work that aims at honest portrayal over sensationalism, exaggeration, or *melodrama*. Technically, realism refers to a late nineteenth-century literary movement—primarily French, English, and American—that aimed at accurate, detailed portrayals of ordinary, contemporary life.

romanticism (ca. 1798–1832) A literary and artistic movement that reacted against the restraint and universalism of the Enlightenment. The romantics celebrated spontaneity, imagination, subjectivity, and the purity of nature. Notable English romantic writers include William Blake, Lord Byron, Samuel Taylor Coleridge, John Keats, Percy Bysshe Shelley, and William Wordsworth.

surrealism (1920s–1930s) An avant-garde movement, based primarily in France, that sought to break down the boundaries between rational and irrational, conscious and unconscious, through a variety of literary and artistic experiments. The surrealist poets, such as André Breton and Paul Eluard, were not as successful as their artist counterparts, who included Salvador Dalí, Joan Miró, and René Magritte.

symbolists (1870s–1890s) A group of French poets who reacted against *realism* with a poetry of suggestion based on private symbols and experimented with new poetic forms, such as free verse and the *prose poem*. The symbolists—Stéphane Mallarmé, Arthur Rimbaud, and Paul Verlaine are the most well known—were influenced by Charles Baudelaire. In turn, they had a seminal influence on the modernist poetry of the early twentieth century.

transcendentalism (ca. 1835–1860) An American philosophical and spiritual movement, based in New England, that focused on the primacy of the individual conscience and rejected materialism in favor of closer communion with nature. Ralph Waldo Emerson's "Self-Reliance" and Henry David Thoreau's *Walden* are famous transcendentalist works.

Victorian era (ca. 1832–1901) The period of English history between the passage of the first Reform Bill (1832) and the death of Queen Victoria (r. 1837–1901). Though remembered for strict social, political, and sexual conservatism and frequent clashes between religion and science, the period also saw prolific literary activity and significant social reform and criticism. Notable Victorian poets include Matthew Arnold, Robert Browning, Elizabeth Barrett Browning, Gerard Manley Hopkins, and Alfred, Lord Tennyson.